ROBERT LACEY is a renowned British historian, the author of numerous international bestsellers, and the historical consultant on the award-winning Netflix series *The Crown*. He wrote *The Crown: The Official Companion*, Volumes 1–2. For more than forty years, Lacey has been writing about Queen Elizabeth II and her extraordinary life, making him an expert on her long reign and the royal family. *Majesty*, his pioneering biography of the Queen, is a landmark study of British monarchy – a subject on which Lacey lectures around the world, appearing regularly on television.

www.robertlacey.com

Battle
of
Brothers

The *Sunday Times* and *New York Times* bestseller

'The royal book of the year ... You've read *their* side of the story, now read the real story'   *Daily Mail*

'Poignant ... The credible modern perspective of two unhappy boys whose parents didn't love each other and who fought excruciatingly in~~timate battles in public~~ ... [Yet also] hil~~ari~~ous ... We can thank ⸻⸻⸻⸻⸻⸻⸻⸻⸻⸻ *The Times*

'A portrayal of the royal heir and the spare that rebalances our perceptions of both … It may also convince some readers that Harry made the right decision' *Sunday Times*

'It picks apart – in uncompromising detail – the feud between Prince William and Prince Harry … Paints a devastating picture' *Daily Mail*

'Tells the story of the recent schism separating Prince Harry and Meghan Markle from the rest of the royal family from the very beginning: when Prince Charles and Princess Diana first met … Lacey takes a closer look at the way the press itself shaped the lives of the people they were writing about … Brings a new eye to some of the biggest tabloid controversies and mysteries of the last quarter century … Fascinating' *Vanity Fair*

'An inside look … Boasting not just excellent knowledge of the inner workings of court, but also impeccable sources close to the royals … It also includes details from a high-level insider who has never spoken before about the confrontation between Prince Harry and the Palace following the Sussexes' announcement that they were leaving the Royal Family. You've read *Finding Freedom* – now discover the whole story' *Tatler*

'[A] bombshell book … Explosive … It charts the deepening rift between the royal brothers' *Mirror*

Aristocrats

Princess

The Kingdom: Arabia and the House of Sa'ud

Majesty: Elizabeth II and the House of Windsor

Sir Walter Ralegh

The Queens of the North Atlantic

The Life and Times of Henry VIII

Robert, Earl of Essex: An Elizabethan Icarus

Battle
of
Brothers

William, Harry and the
Inside Story of a
Family in Tumult

ROBERT LACEY

WILLIAM
COLLINS

William Collins
An imprint of HarperCollins*Publishers*
1 London Bridge Street
London SE1 9GF

WilliamCollinsBooks.com

HarperCollins*Publishers*
1st Floor, Watermarque Building, Ringsend Road
Dublin 4, Ireland

First published in Great Britain in 2020 by William Collins
This William Collins paperback edition published in 2021

1

A catalogue record for this book is
available from the British Library

ISBN 978-0-00-840854-1

Typeset in Adobe Garamond Pro
Printed and bound in Great Britain by
CPI Group (UK) Ltd, Croydon

MIX
Paper from
responsible sources
FSC™ C007454

This book is produced from independently certified FSC™ paper
to ensure responsible forest management.

For more information visit: www.harpercollins.co.uk/green

This paperback edition of *Battle of Brothers*
contains twelve fresh chapters
and extensive other updatings
which make it, in some respects, a new book.

I dedicate this edition, as before, to my own brother Graham,
to my daughter Scarlett
who contributed so many new ideas –
and, above all, to my darling wife Jane
who inspired me every day,
and also contributed the best joke of all in the book.

CONTENTS

ILLUSTRATIONS

1st section

Prince and Princess of Wales at Highgrove with William and Harry, 1986 (*Tim Graham Photo Library/Getty Images*)

Prince Charles with Princess Anne, 1954 (*Camera Press*)

Prince of Wales's wedding, 1981 (*Lichfield Archive/Getty Images*)

Lady Diana Spencer and Camilla Parker Bowles, 1980 (*Express Newspapers/Archive Photos/Getty Images*)

Prince Harry and Prince William, 1985 (*Tim Graham Photo Library/Getty Images*)

Princess Diana with Princes William and Harry, 1997 (*John Swannell/Camera Press*)

Prince Harry at Trooping the Colour, 1989 (*Anwar Hussein/Getty Images*)

Diana in Angola minefield, 1997 (*Tim Graham Photo Library/Getty Images*)

Princess Diana presenting polo trophy to James Hewitt, 1989 (*Iain Burns/Camera Press*)

Princess Diana in car with Dodi Fayed, 1997 (*Sipa Press/Shutterstock*)

Funeral service of Princess of Wales, 1997 (*Jeff J. Mitchell/AFP/ Getty Images*)

Funeral of Princess of Wales with flowers, 1997 (*Wayne Starr/ Camera Press*)

2nd section

Prince William at Eton, 2000 (*Anwar Hussein/WireImage/Getty Images*)

Prince William and Kate Middleton at St Andrews University, 2005 (*Royal/Alamy Stock Photo*)

Kate Middleton on catwalk, 2002 (*Malcolm Clarke/Daily Mail/ Shutterstock*)

Wedding of Prince William, 2011 (*George Pimentel/Getty Images*)

Wedding of Prince of Wales, 2005 (*Hugo Burnand/Getty Images*)

Duke and Duchess of Cambridge at Lindo Wing with Prince George, 2013 (*Alan Chapman/Film Magic/Getty Images*)

The 'Fab Four'. Harry, Meghan, Kate and William – Making a Difference Together, 2018 (*Goff Photos.com*)

David Cholmondeley and Rose Hanbury greet Prince William and Kate (*PA Images/Alamy Stock Photo*)

Rose Hanbury (*David M. Benett/Dave Benett/Getty Images for Chris Levine*)

Kate and Meghan at Wimbledon, 2019 (*Karwai Tang/Getty Images*)

Queen at Christmas, 2019 (*Steve Parsons/Getty Images*)

Prince William, Kate Middleton and their children at Trooping the Colour, 2019 (*JS/Dana Press Photos/PA Images*)

3rd section

Cartoons

1

Brothers at War

*'There are disagreements, obviously,
as all families have, and when there are,
they are big disagreements.'*

(Prince William, *BBC News*,
19 November 2004)

Talk to each other, for God's sake! That was the way Diana had raised her boys – to get their feelings fully out in the open in a direct fashion, not stumbling and mumbling into their emotional cups of tea like so many other members of the Windsor clan. 'Never complain, never explain!' – what kind of philosophy for life was that?

Thanks to their mother, William and Harry had grown up to be two expressive straight-talkers – and ambitious world-changers too. Their straight-talking – along with their attempts at changing – make up the substance of this book. And we jump into our story in May 2019 with the birth of Prince Harry's first child and the chance that this happy event offered the two battling brothers to reconcile – to embrace and to make up. Would they take it?

There had been tiffs and troubles before, of course, in the run-up to the wedding – you know, that little wedding at Windsor Castle between the Anglo-Saxon prince and the American, mixed-race, divorcee TV star in the spring of 2018 that attracted some 1.9 billion viewers around the world. What family wedding would be complete without a few family hiccups: a disputed brides-maid's outfit here, a missing tiara there – and oh yes, an absentee father of the bride?

But twelve months later, almost to the day (19 May 2018 to 6 May 2019), here was the fruit of the blessed union about to arrive, a springtime baby to thrill its parents and to bring all the family back together again – especially those two Windsor broth-ers and their allegedly warring wives.

Royal births, like royal weddings, are the human happenings that cement the affections of a modern people to its monarchy. Constitutional historians like to explain the theory – the paradox of how a modern democracy can actually be strengthened by the elitist and undemocratic traditions of an ancient crown. But there's nothing like the practical appeal of a newborn baby in its swaddled slumber – the fresh arrival of new life that encourages life for all.

Just as with coronations and royal weddings, a set of popular ceremonies has developed around royal births in the age of mass communications – the jostling crowd outside the hospital, the smiling parents with their baby on the steps, the shouted compli-

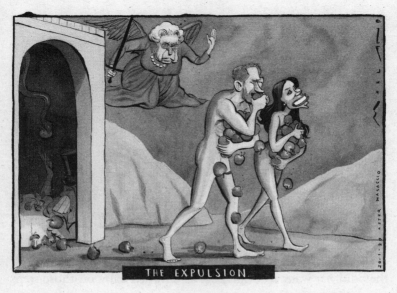

Exiting Eden. Morten Morland, *The Times*, 20 January 2020

ments, the flashguns exploding. Then later, the quieter, more formal christening photograph and the announcement of all the godparents' names.

That's how Charles and Diana set the modern style in 1982. Their son William, on 21 June that year, was the first ever heir to the British throne to be born in a regular hospital – St Mary's in west London, right beside Paddington railway station and smelling not a little of the trains. Charles's sister, Princess Anne, had discovered the attractions of St Mary's private maternity wing – named after the philanthropic Portuguese-Jewish Lindo family – for the births of her children Peter (b.1977) and Zara (b.1981). Harry followed two years after William on 15 September 1984 to make up a royal quartet of Lindo births.

When William himself became a father, he and Kate adopted the same tradition, choosing Lindo for their children, George (b.2013), Charlotte (b.2015) and Louis (b.2018). By this last date the footmarks of proud royal parents displaying their newborn to the world had almost worn grooves into those stone steps at Paddington. There was an anthropological thesis to be written on the success of populist monarchies who chose to display their offspring outside railway stations at birth: Austria's archdukes snootily kept their child production away from the public eye, and who now cared about the archdukes – in Austria or anywhere else in the world?

In May 2019, however, Harry and Meghan had decided that they did *not* want to display *their* newborn baby on those steps outside the Lindo Wing. They wanted to be royal in a new style – and maybe not royal at all. And to understand why this mattered so much, we have to go back in royal history – to the legend of the warming pan.

The warming pan was the electric blanket or rubber hot water bottle of its day, a couple of centuries back. Before his lordship retired for the night, his chambermaid would heat up his sheets by smoothing them energetically with the warming pan – a large, flat, circular brass container on the end of a long wooden handle, with a high curved lid that meant it could hold a generous quantity of red-hot coals from the fireplace. Or a newborn baby …

Such a warming pan, it was alleged, had been used in 1688 to smuggle a healthy substitute baby into the birthing bed of Mary of Modena, wife of the hated Catholic King James II, replacing the legitimate heir who was said to have been born sickly. Until

1688 the unpopular monarch had been tolerated because his successor was going to be his Protestant elder daughter Mary and her still more Protestant Dutch husband, William of Orange. Loyal anti-Catholic Brits had hoped that the generally popular and non-popish couple would succeed the childless and far-too-popish James as joint monarchs, William-and-Mary, thus preserving what passed for democracy in those days – as well as the Church of England.

The unexpected appearance of the living and healthy 'warming pan' baby, James Francis Edward Stuart, however, threatened this scheme – and 1688 turned into a landmark year in the history of Britain's monarchy. William of Orange sailed his invasion fleet into Torbay that November, bloodlessly persuading James II to flee London with his warming pan son.

The 'Glorious Revolution' was history's memorable moniker for the stirring events of 1688 and its resulting settlement that became the model for our modern system of enhanced and democratic powers for Parliament and reduced powers for an increasingly symbolic 'constitutional' monarchy. Alongside the theoretical changes came the very practical provision that all royal births must, in future, be personally attended by the home secretary of the day, whose job it would be to make sure that the new royal arrival had been delivered properly, and not in a warming pan.

So, well into modern times, attendance beside the royal birthing bed became the duty of every British home secretary. Queen Victoria gave birth to all nine of her children with her home secretary in the room, along with assorted privy councillors – and this intrusive custom lasted long into the twentieth century. Sir William Joynson-Hicks was present at the birth of the future Queen Elizabeth II at her parents' London townhouse in April 1926, and, four years later, his Labour successor, John Robert Clynes, had to travel up to Glamis Castle in Scotland to be at the birth of her sister Margaret – he found himself stranded there with a single, operator-controlled telephone line for two whole weeks because the princess arrived late.

In November 1948 Prince Charles became the first post-1688 heir to the British throne to be born without the ritualised scrutiny of his arrival on behalf of the people. Clement Attlee's postwar Labour government had wasted no time in sweeping away the outdated practice. But Charles revived its spirit in 1982 and 1984 with the births of William and Harry, when he and Diana proudly – and dutifully – brought their sons out onto the steps of the Lindo Wing for public inspection and approval, within hours of their births.

Prince William continued the tradition unquestioningly – though by 2013 the performance had turned into a menacing and undignified scrum among the ever-growing mass of paparazzi, in a most alarming free-for-all. But William still did his duty sturdily, with Kate beside him, immaculate and smiling despite the traumas of delivery. As an heir to the throne who had done his homework, Prince William knew about warming pans and the importance of making the people feel that you were at one with them.

But as the 'spare', his younger brother had received no such special instruction in the ancient legend, let alone its sociological importance – and if he had, Harry could not have cared less. The heir could choose to suffer the ordeal of inspection on the Paddington steps if he wished. The spare had other ideas, and his wife totally agreed. Harry and Meghan were resolute that their newborn baby's first sight of the world should not be the same insane and lethal camera-flashings that had attended – had actually brought about – the death of Diana.

A cursory glance at the photograph of baby Harry in his mother's arms outside the Lindo Wing in September 1984 also suggested that Diana must have spent a good hour or more washing and blow-drying her hair before she emerged onto the steps for her 'spontaneous' greeting of the people. Cautious Kate might put up with all that primping and prepping for the sake of 'the Firm', but mercurial Meghan would not.

So Harry and Meghan, the Duke and Duchess of Sussex, had agreed that their new child should be delivered at home in the peace and seclusion of Frogmore 'Cottage' – not so much a cottage, in fact, as a *collection* of cottages in Windsor Great Park that had recently been renovated and amalgamated into a long, twenty-three-room dwelling at a cost of some £2.4 million in public funds. Here was another mildly difficult issue. If the royal parents were not going to display their baby to the public for the sake of warming pans, what about all those pots and pans and cooker(s) in their lovely new kitchen? Perhaps some public gesture would be appreciated to say thank you for all that taxpayers' money?

As events turned out, the question would be academic. Baby Sussex took his time a'coming, and when his expected arrival became two weeks late Meghan's doctor advised a hospital-assisted delivery. Frimley Park was a perfectly good National Health Service hospital a dozen miles down the road near Farnborough, but the couple set off instead with Meghan's mother Doria on the longer journey to London and Britain's most expensive delivery facility, the US-owned Portland Hospital, famous for its celebrity births. Victoria Beckham, Liz Hurley, Kate Winslet – all these glamorous mothers had delivered their babies in the luxury of the Portland, where a basic birth package started at £6,100, with four poster cots for the babies. And not a nasty, smelly railway station in sight.

Here was another issue with Harry and Meghan – the deluxe, five-star instincts to which these reach-out-and-touch-me tribunes of the common people so regularly surrendered, from their fondness for private jets and Hollywood friends to their need to 'hide away' in expensively renovated twenty-three-room 'cottages' or, when they first moved to California in 2020, an $18 million, twelve-bathroom Tuscan-style mansion occupying twenty-two acres in Los Angeles' exclusive Beverly Ridge Estates.

'It's a matter of security,' their handlers would explain. 'And they *DO* need their privacy.'

But the Portland Hospital did its job efficiently and confidentially through the night of 5 May 2019. On the morning of 6 May, Meghan was duly delivered of her delayed but healthy son, weighing in at 7lbs 3oz. Baby Archie had arrived with the dawn at 5.26 a.m., allowing grandmother Doria and the happy couple to return to Windsor with their precious cargo undetected. Their stratagem was bolstered by Buckingham Palace's putting out a strangely misleading statement at 2 p.m. that day saying that the Duchess of Sussex was just going into labour – when she had, in fact, been delivered of her new son eight hours earlier.

Harry and Meghan had played fast and loose with both royal tradition and the truth, but for once they had successfully outwitted the hated press.

2
Family Matters

*'He is the one person on this earth that
I can actually talk to about anything and
we understand each other.'*

(Prince Harry, January 2006)

The helpful 'friends' who brief the media from time to time about the inner thoughts of royal folk have let it be known that elder brother William did not think too highly of Harry and Meghan's 'prima donna' manoeuvres to conceal the birth of their son in May 2019 – and this impression was confirmed by the failure of William and Kate to visit the new arrival for a full eight days. By contrast, the Queen, Prince Philip, Charles and Camilla all turned up within hours to coo over the baby – and it seemed strange that, when the Cambridges did finally pitch up more than a week later, they didn't bring along little George, Charlotte and Louis to welcome their new cousin.

But Harry won the next round. On 8 May he had appeared with Meghan cradling the two-day-old Archie Harrison

Mountbatten-Windsor in the soaring and magnificent surroundings of St George's Hall, Windsor, with the press pack excluded. There was just a single photographer of their choice and a small group of TV cameras with whom they spoke of their joy.

'It's magic, it's pretty amazing,' declared Meghan. 'I have the two best guys in the world, so I'm really happy.'

'He has the sweetest temperament,' disclosed Harry. 'He's really calm. I don't know who he gets that from!'

The name 'Archie' was said by Sandhurst mates to have been inspired by a mentor of Harry's in the army – Major Tom Archer-Burton – while the baby's mother offered a more learned clarification. '*Arche*', the Duchess of Sussex explained, was a term from ancient Greek meaning 'origin' or 'source of action' – Meghan had picked up more classical learning at school in Los Angeles than ever Harry had at Eton – and the couple would later bestow the same name on their charitable foundation. As for Harrison, well, that was sort of a joke – 'Harry's son' – leading some commentators to wonder if the name had anything to do with the mystic and meditational aura of George Harrison, Meghan's particular idol in the Beatles.

Swaddled in a white blanket and wearing a delicate white knitted hat, little Archie appeared to sleep peacefully throughout his first official photo call – which was, of course, exactly as his father and mother had planned it.

'Thank you, everybody,' said Meghan, 'for all the well wishes and kindness. It just means so much.'

The entire private-public occasion was just pitch-perfect – with the splendid lofted windows of St George's Hall providing the ideal backdrop – a touch of history along with modernity: it was Harry the father who, fifty-fifty parenting style, was cradling the baby, not the mother, unlike every previous photograph on those wretched Paddington steps.

And then came an even warmer family occasion when the proud parents were shown presenting Archie to the Queen, Prince Philip and Doria. The picture made the front page of every British newspaper – and a good many others around the world – with the two grandmothers, black and white, smiling down on the British monarchy's first mixed-race baby.

'How any woman does what they do is beyond comprehension,' remarked Harry in one of his post-birth interviews. 'It's been the most amazing experience I could ever have possibly imagined.'

But here came the real crunch: the godparents. An essential component of any Church of England christening process, these adult mentors who will guide the new baby spiritually, morally and often materially through life are considered even more important for members of the royal family. Technically, they carry the title of 'sponsor'.

Numbers six and seven in the order of succession may not seem particularly close to inheriting the crown, but who knows what can happen in an age of mass terrorist attack and global pandemics. Six and seven could well get promoted to three and four – or even higher. And, more profoundly, anyone in the single figures – Harry stands at six at the time of writing, Archie at seven – is certainly 'royal' whether they like it or not, since they have been sanctified by the public's emotional commitment to them, as well as by taxpayers' largesse.

It is well understood at Buckingham Palace that not all godparents can make it to a hastily arranged christening service. So in July 2019, Elizabeth II's Holyrood Week duties in Scotland meant that she and Prince Philip could not attend the ceremony for Archie on 6 July. And this date had already been the result of some shuffling of schedules to accommodate the busy summer diaries of Charles, Camilla, William and Kate – not to mention the Archbishop of Canterbury who was to preside over the rite.

Yet it *is* still expected by monarch, palace and just about anyone with a stake in the game that the world should be told who the new royal baby's 'sponsors' *are*. How can you judge the suitability of a sponsor who remains unknown? 'Secret sponsor' has a dodgy sound to it. And it is an ingredient of Britain's representative monarchy that Brits should have the right to know who is giving moral guidance to their possible future king or queen. Here again, however, precedent, protocol and practice all collided headlong with Harry and Meghan's firm insistence on their privacy – and that of their new baby.

'Archie Harrison Mountbatten-Windsor will be christened in a small private ceremony by the Archbishop of Canterbury in the Private Chapel at Windsor Castle on Saturday 6th July,' announced Buckingham Palace in a statement on 3 July. 'The Duke and Duchess of Sussex look forward to sharing some images taken on the day by photographer Chris Allerton. The [names of the] godparents, in keeping with their wishes, will remain private.'

Confirming the palace announcement, the Sussex Royal office made clear that the whole 'sponsor' issue was non-negotiable. The godparents' names would not be revealed.

'I've covered five or six christenings in my royal career,' commented *Majesty* magazine's editor-in-chief Ingrid Seward on the *Today* programme. 'And I've never come across such secrecy.'

Was brother William outraged? Just angry? Or merely perplexed?

'Friends' tried to keep the temperature down by suggesting the last – that the future king, only five places clear of Archie in the order of succession, could not comprehend how such a basic matter of constitutional principle had been misunderstood. How could any new Windsor royal be christened in a meaningful sense without the newcomer's sponsors being known, if not present?

William was smiling after a fashion on the morning of Saturday, 6 July, when he turned up for his nephew Archie's christening in the Queen's Private Chapel at Windsor, and the family photograph that would follow in the formality of the Green Drawing Room. But it was a wry and curious smile, and commentators had a field day interpreting what the prince's face and posture – and those of his wife – might portend. Kate was thoughtfully wearing a pair of her late mother-in-law's pearl drop earrings – the very pair that Diana was said to have worn to Harry's christening in 1984. Yet Kate was sitting rather 'awkwardly upright', thought body language expert Judi James. The duchess was leaning forward in a 'ready to flee' posture.

This was nothing, however, when compared to Ms James's verdict on William, standing to attention behind his wife with a 'fig leaf hand clasp' shielding his trouser crotch, in her opinion, and a 'raised chin pose that a policeman might adopt before collaring a suspect'.

A few Internet commentators agreed. 'William looks like he would rather be elsewhere,' tweeted one, with another 'royal fan' responding, 'William should have a much bigger smile on his face.'

Oh, the lot of a future king! Was this the captious and carping destiny for which Prince William, second in line to the throne, had been working for over twenty years since his visits to Windsor Castle for lunch with his grandmother the Queen in the late 1990s? Aged thirteen in the autumn of 1995, the prince had just started school at Eton College, the exclusive all-male academy (founded 1440) across the Thames from Windsor.

It was then three years after his parents' separation – just two years before Diana's death – and the Queen was worried about her grandson's state of mind. Was Charles too wrapped up in his own concerns to be a proper father, with *that* Camilla Parker Bowles and everything else in the picture? While Diana, of course, with her motley succession of largely foreign boyfriends, was deliberately acting as a subversive anti-royal 'flake'. The Queen actually feared that the boy might be heading for some sort of breakdown, she confided to one of her advisors – just as the prince's mother herself had clearly cracked up mentally in several respects.

The Duke of Edinburgh intervened. Philip shared his wife's concerns and he suggested that she overcome her longstanding aversion to involvement in messy family matters by trying to get closer to this particular boy – who was not just her fragile grandson, but a future inheritor of her crown. Perhaps the lad could come up and join them both in the castle from time to time on a Sunday, when the Eton boys were allowed out into the town?

And so the lunches had begun. Every few Sundays – allowing for the weekends that William would spend with his separated mother or father – the teenager would walk along Eton High Street with his detective, and across the bridge up to Windsor, where he would join the Queen and the Duke of Edinburgh for a hearty and tasty meal.

Pudding ended, Philip would make a discreet exit, leaving his wife and grandson together in the panelled Oak Room with its six-arm chandelier hanging over the table in front of Queen Victoria's beautiful Gobelins tapestry of *The Hunt*. In this splendid and historic but also intimate setting, grandmother and grandson – monarch and future heir – would get down to brass tacks, talking and 'sharing' as only the pair of them could.

'There's a serenity about her,' William revealed ten years later, talking to the Queen's 2011 biographer Robert Hardman, and explaining how his grandmother had encouraged him to stay calm in the face of all that the world would throw at him one day. 'I think if you are of an age, you have a pretty old-fashioned faith, you do your best every day and say your prayers every night. Well, if you're criticised for it, you're not going to get much better whatever you do. What's the point of worrying?'

It was during these conversations in the Oak Room that Prince William learned from his grandmother how the institution of the crown was something to be upheld and respected, and how one might have to fight – he might have to become quite tough, in fact – in order to preserve it. It was *William's* birthright and legacy, after all, as much as his gran's. The prince was particularly impressed by the stories that his grandmother would tell him about her own early years on the throne – how she had had to step in to succeed her father King George VI in 1952, at the age of only twenty-five, to tackle a job that many men in those days believed they could do better.

'It must have been very daunting,' he said to Hardman. 'And I think how loads of twenty-five-year-olds – myself, my brother and lots of people included – didn't have anything like that. And we didn't have the extra pressure put on us at that age. It's amazing that she didn't crack. She just carried on and kept going. And that's the thing about her. You present a challenge in front of her and she'll climb it. And I think that to be doing that for sixty years – it's incredible.'

Talking to the BBC in 2005, as he neared the end of his studies at St Andrews University, William would again pay tribute to the personal support and advice that his grandmother gave him.

'She's just very helpful on any sort of difficulties or problems I might be having,' he said. 'She's been brilliant, she's a real role model.'

It was in the Oak Room conversations that William would have heard of warming pans and the Glorious Revolution, along with the role that the armed services would have to play in his future. Then there was the importance of the Church of England in his responsibilities as monarch – though none of this was presented to him in any formal, lecturing sort of way.

'I don't think she believes too heavily in instruction,' he said in 2016, expanding to the BBC on the subject of the Queen's personal style and input, which he described as 'more of a soft, influencing, modest kind of guidance'.

The Queen herself had received formal constitutional history lessons. In a curious mirror image of William, the young Princess Elizabeth used to walk over the Thames between Eton and Windsor twice a week in the months before the Second World War, when *she* was thirteen – but in the opposite direction. Accompanied by her nanny Marion Crawford ('Crawfie'), the princess had gone for history tutorials to the book-littered study of Sir Henry Marten, the Vice-Provost of Eton, an eccentric scholar whose habit, while ruminating, was to crunch on sugar lumps that he shared with his pet raven.

One of Sir Henry's particular enthusiasms had been the recent creation of the British Commonwealth of Nations, formalised by the Statute of Westminster of 1931, and the ingenious arrangement by which the Commonwealth contained at that date more than half a dozen monarchies – Canada and Australia, for example. There Elizabeth's father George VI did not reign as some remote imperial sovereign in London, but as Canada's or Australia's very *own* king and head of state.

Elizabeth II was particularly proud of having developed and built upon this decentralised system in the course of her reign – by the year 2000 there were no fewer than fourteen Commonwealth monarchies around the world – and she passed on to William the importance of maintaining Britain's Commonwealth links, especially in Africa, the Pacific, the Caribbean, the Indian subcontinent and other developing corners of the globe. And all this, of course, came on top of the challenge to the young man of having to prove himself one day as a dignified and respected – but not too snooty and remote – truly 'representative' monarch of the United Kingdom at home to the satisfaction of the fractious Brits.

As William absorbed his grandmother's principles, there was a sense, he later described, in which he became as one with her, establishing a warm personal closeness – a strong and quite extraordinary partnership across the generations that he defined as a 'shared understanding of what's needed'.

The prince's conversations in the Oak Room helped to turn the fragile schoolboy heading for a breakdown into quite a tough young man who would one day be compared to a 'nightclub bouncer' protecting the standards of and entry to his highly exclusive royal club. The prince was not prepared to allow anyone – and certainly not his brother and his American celebrity wife – to threaten the precious legacy that had been entrusted to him by his gran.

'She cares not for celebrity, that's for sure,' William declared in 2011. 'That's not what monarchy's about. It's about setting examples. It's about doing one's duty, as she would say. It's about using your position for the good. It's about serving the country – and that's really the crux of it.'

Brother Harry might be heading for La-La Land, but brother William was heading to be king.

'I've put my arm round his shoulder all our lives together,' said the prince in October 2019, explaining why Harry and Meghan's behaviour and the succession of erratic decisions surrounding Archie's birth and christening – followed by the confrontation we will be describing in Chapter 26 – had led to the rupture between the brothers that Harry had memorably described as the pursuit of 'different paths'.

'I can't do it any more,' said William.

The identity of those 'secret' godparents, of course, did not stay secret for very long. Secrets will out, and the names of Archie's three British sponsors became public within months of his christening.

Tiggy Pettifer, née Legge-Bourke, had been the beloved nanny of both William and Harry. Mark Dyer had played a similarly formative role in the lives of the young princes – 'a former equerry to the Prince of Wales', as *The Times* described him, 'who became a mentor and close friend to Charles' sons'. Then there was Charlie van Straubenzee, one of Harry's closest childhood friends and Ludgrove schoolmates. Meghan and Harry had attended his wedding in August 2018.

A combination of newspaper digging and high society contacts got these three British names on the record by the end of 2019, and, once out there, the names were not denied by Buckingham Palace, the Sussex Royal office, nor the godparents themselves. The question was – who were the others? The three British names clearly represented Harry's choices of sponsor. So the focus turned upon whom Meghan might have chosen.

If there were three British sponsors, logic suggested there must be one, two or three American sponsors. And the three US names on whom speculation, informed or otherwise, centred were tennis star Serena Williams, film star George Clooney and one or other of the political star couple, ex-President Barack and Michelle Obama. All four were friends of Meghan, who had gone to watch Serena at Wimbledon in the summer of 2019, while George Clooney had already cheerily dismissed the rumours in a cleverly crafted non-denial denial.

'You don't want me to be a godparent of anybody,' Clooney said at the time of Archie's birth. 'I'm barely a parent at this point. It's frightening.'

When it came to the Obamas, the husband and wife team were close to both Meghan and Harry. Barack Obama had joined the prince in Toronto in 2017 at the Invictus Games for injured ex-servicemen and women – Harry's own creation and one of his most dearly cherished causes – while Michelle had written an article for the UK issue of *Vogue* that Meghan had guest-edited in September 2019 – see Chapter 24 for more on *that*. Certain American commentators even wondered whether the Obamas were not encouraging the new duchess to pick up their liberal political legacy at some time in the future – on the way to Meghan achieving her teenage ambition to give the United States its first mixed-race female president, Kamala Harris permitting.

Such fanciful imaginings showed what can happen when you seek to divert the truth from its natural course – and the course of this book is to seek to reveal the truth. The pages that follow will narrate the story of two brave young men who have lived through extraordinary privilege and tragedy, each of them challenged from birth by their ultimately different destinies. For many years, the two brothers would work together, supporting each other in times of trouble. But as time and circumstance have changed, so William and Harry have, inevitably, grown in different directions.

In recent months – even as this book was being written – we saw the younger of the pair finding himself a new identity and seeking to follow, with his wife, a new way ahead. In Shakespearean terms, Prince Harry has decided to throw off his old and troubled past – the dissolute world of Falstaff and Prince Hal – to remake himself in the fresh and shining role of King Henry V, British history's heroic and exemplary monarch: 'Oh, happy band! Oh, band of brothers …'

The trouble is that brother William has claimed that job already.

3

Dynastic Marriage

*'Marriage is a much more important
business than falling in love ...'*

(Prince Charles, 1979)

So you are approaching the age of thirty. You are a single male of the species – reasonably attractive if rather shy, and not very sexy. You are heir to the throne of the United Kingdom of Great Britain and Northern Ireland – plus Canada, Australia, New Zealand and a dozen or so other Commonwealth monarchies – and you have your love life to organise.

No, sorry, you have a future queen to locate for this formidable array of thrones.

Is there a difference?

Well, yes, there is, actually – and that dilemma provides the basis of the story that is at the heart of this book. Princes William and Harry were the products of an arranged dynastic alliance, not a love match ...

* * *

As the future King Charles III responded to the nudgings of his family in the late 1970s to get on with the business of tracking down a lifetime companion, the Prince of Wales found himself on the horns of a dilemma – to which his great-uncle and 'honorary grandfather', Lord Mountbatten, had a solution that he would reiterate with relish:

'I believe, in a case like yours,' wrote Mountbatten to Charles on Valentine's Day, 1974, 'that a man should sow his wild oats and have as many affairs as he can before settling down. But for a wife he should choose a suitable, attractive, and sweet-charactered girl before she has met anyone else she might fall for.'

It was a measure of Charles's shyness that he did not tell his interfering 'Uncle Dickie' to stuff his cynical advice where the monkey puts his nuts, since his 'honorary grandfather' was not only peddling the values of a vanished age, he was also pushing the candidacy of his own granddaughter, Amanda Knatchbull, just sixteen, as the 'suitable, attractive, and sweet-charactered girl' whom Charles should eventually select as his future queen – thus bringing even more Mountbatten blood into the dynasty of Windsor.

Nine years his junior, Amanda knew the prince well, and in time she would come genuinely to love Charles, in her grandfather's opinion. But as a teenager she was clearly too young to commit to marriage – so the old man's worldly counsel was offered in the hope that his great-nephew would 'keep' himself for Amanda.

'I am sure,' Charles responded a few weeks later, 'that she must know that I am very fond of her …'

In the event, Charles's and Mountbatten's imaginative ambitions for Amanda Knatchbull – discussed in her total absence and ignorance – came to naught. Over the years the two cousins did grow close, developing a mutual respect and friendship that has lasted to the present day. But when the prince finally made his proposal in the summer of 1979 – shortly before Lord Mountbatten's assassination by the IRA – the independent-minded Amanda politely turned him down.

'The surrender of self to a system,' she explained, was so absolute when joining the royal family, it involved a loss of independence 'far greater than matrimony usually invites'.

These powerful if formal words come to us via the memory of Prince Charles, as he recounted the details of his rejection to his biographer Jonathan Dimbleby. The prince could recall every reason Amanda had given him for her refusal – and especially 'the exposure to publicity, an intrusion more pervasive than attends any other public figure except at the zenith of a chosen career'.

'Her response,' concluded Dimbleby, 'served only to confirm his own belief that to marry into the House of Windsor was a sacrifice that no-one should be expected to make.'

The future king would clearly have to find himself another suitable and sweet-charactered girl. But in the meantime, Charles had enjoyed several years of success pursuing Uncle Dickie's alternative line of advice on the sowing of wild oats, since he had made the acquaintance of a certain Camilla Parker Bowles (née Shand), a characterful lady noted for her sheer brass nerve. Long before her royal future was assured, Mrs Parker Bowles had taken her young children, Laura and Tom, shopping to Sainsbury's in the Wiltshire market town of Chippenham.

'Most of the parking spaces were filled,' recalled Laura, 'but Mummy saw an empty one right outside the front door and nipped in there. The parking space was "Reserved for the Mayor of Chippenham".'

When the family came out with their shopping bags, a man stopped Camilla and asked her what she was doing in the mayor's parking place.

'Mummy smiled and said, "I'm so sorry, I'm the Mayor's wife …" and hurried me into the car. The man followed us and said, "What a joy to meet you for the first time – I'm the Mayor!"'

The story gives credence to the scarcely believable tale of how Camilla is often said to have first introduced herself to Charles, sometime in the early 1970s. It was a pouring wet afternoon and the prince, aged twenty-two, was just stroking one of his ponies after a polo match on Smith's Lawn in Windsor Great Park, when Camilla Shand, then twenty-four, approached for a chat – without any introduction.

'That's a fine animal, sir,' she said. 'I'm Camilla Shand.'

'I'm so pleased to meet you,' replied Charles politely – only for Camilla to dive straight in with a reference to her ancestor, the notorious Alice Keppel, mistress of King Edward VII.

'You know, sir, my great-grandmother was the mistress of your great-great-grandfather – so how about it?'

This extraordinary tale puts the mayor of Chippenham to shame, and many of the prince's biographers have questioned its reliability. Charles himself, via his semi-official biographer

Dimbleby, is quite clear that although he did meet Camilla at the polo from time to time, he *first* met her properly in London, through his former girlfriend Lucia Santa Cruz, the Chilean research assistant of Lord Butler, who was the master of Trinity, Charles's college at Cambridge.

Before he became master of Cambridge's largest and grandest college, Richard Austen Butler, universally known after his initials as 'Rab', was a Tory grandee who had occupied numerous Cabinet ranks. But for all his record of public achievement, Rab's fondest private boast was how he had used the Trinity Master's Lodge to facilitate the liaison by which a 'young South American had instructed an innocent Prince in the consummation of physical love'. In 1978 Butler indiscreetly told the author Anthony Holden, who was writing a semi-authorised biography of Prince Charles, that he had 'slipped' Lucia Santa Cruz a key to the Master's Lodge, after Charles had asked if the young lady could stay there with him 'for privacy'.

When Holden's book was published in 1979, Buckingham Palace indignantly denied Rab's suggestion that Lucia had initiated Charles into the delights of the sexual dimension.

'Most of what Rab Butler says is preposterous,' complained the prince himself, fiercely denying that Butler was any sort of 'mentor', 'guru' or '*éminence grise*' to him.

But Butler's wife Mollie stood by her husband's claim in quite explicit terms. Lucia, she wrote in her own 1992 memoir, was a 'happy example of someone on whom [Charles] could safely cut his teeth, if I may put it thus'.

* * *

Sometime in the spring of 1972, Santa Cruz, who had remained friendly with Charles after Trinity, invited him round for a drink at her Cundy Street flat in Victoria, at the back of Buckingham Palace, saying that she had found 'just the girl' for the prince. Camilla lived in the same block and Gyles Brandreth, a friend of Charles and a chronicler of the couple's love affair, favours this version.

By contrast, however, another chronicler, Caroline Graham, sets the meeting on the polo field, quoting an onlooker as saying that Camilla 'saw the Prince standing alone on the other side of the field. Cool as you like, she walked across and started talking to him.'

So which account is true? We should probably accept the less exciting Santa Cruz-Cundy Street version as the *historical* truth of the couple's first meeting, since that is how the prince himself remembers it.

But when it comes to the tale of the polo field and the 'mistress of your great-great-grandfather' introduction, that surely expresses the more important *emotional* truth – that Camilla Shand embodied all the emotional freedom and sense of fun for which the dutiful Prince Charles had been yearning. With the benefit of hindsight, we can certainly cite those personal qualities as the reason why, nearly fifty years later, Charles and Camilla are living their lives together solidly as man and wife.

The fact that such a marriage between a future king and a non-royal divorcee is accepted today, but would have seemed outlandish thirty years ago – not to say improper and impossible – is another example of the social prejudices that confronted

Prince Charles as he faced up to the challenge of choosing his partner for life in the mid-1970s.

The newspapers of the time were perfectly candid as they discussed the requirements for his future queen – and they were also perfectly candid that, as tribunes of the people, *they* had the right to lay down the rules. The candidate should preferably be royal (which meant foreign, exotic and newsworthy) or, failing that, noble – and she should definitely be a virgin, the v-word being deployed unashamedly in the age of free love as if during the reign of the first Elizabeth.

Camilla was none of these things. She had cast off her virginity long before, and she was neither royal nor noble, though she unquestionably came from respectable upper-middle-class 'county' stock. Her father, Major Bruce Shand, was a master of foxhounds who was a friend of the Queen Mother. Her mother Rosalind – the money in the family – descended from the Cubitts who had built Belgravia and the smartest swathes of central London. Camilla was not that young – she was two years older than Charles – and, to go back to the v-word, she was quite well known in society circles for being 'a bit of a goer'.

But Ms Shand herself had the sharpness to see all these drawbacks, and she had the enticing honesty to go for the next best thing. She liked the prospect of some fun with Prince Charles for his own sake. She did *not* want to collar him just so that she could marry a future king – and that is fundamentally why, of course, she has ended up married to him.

The Goons played a big part in all this. Early in their friendship Charles and Camilla discovered that they shared a fondness for the silly accents and daft looks of *The Goon Show* – BBC radio's classic comedy of the absurd, the Home Service predecessor to and, indeed, the original inspiration for *Monty Python's Flying Circus*. The couple rapidly registered their mutual affection by bestowing Goon nicknames upon each other, 'Fred' and 'Gladys' – which, say friends, Charles and Camilla cheerfully call each other to this day.

'Your spirits rise whenever Camilla comes into a room,' recalled Charles's polo-playing companion, Lord Patrick Beresford. 'You can tell from her eyes and the smile on her face that you are going to have a bloody good laugh.'

'They have a terrific sense of humour,' says another friend, author Jilly Cooper. 'They laugh together a huge amount. And Camilla's ability to see the funny side of life has made an enormous difference over the years.'

Along with the shared silliness went a mutual delight in country pursuits. Charles and Camilla were both devotees of huntin', shootin' and fishin' – seldom happier than when decked out in their Barbours, tweeds and welly boots. Thanks to her father, Camilla could ride to hounds as well as the prince, and by the summer and autumn of 1972 the couple were wrapped up in a roaring romance.

'She was affectionate, she was unassuming,' wrote Jonathan Dimbleby, recording and reporting Charles's feelings for this new girlfriend, 'and – with all the intensity of first love – he lost his heart to her almost at once.'

Lord Mountbatten encouraged the relationship. He entertained the couple frequently at discreet weekends at Broadlands, his estate in Hampshire. In 1971–2 Charles was starting his naval career at Portsmouth, just half an hour to the south, and Camilla was precisely the companion Uncle Dickie had in mind to keep Charles busy until young Amanda came of age.

But by the late autumn of 1972 Charles was starting to appreciate Camilla Shand as rather more than Uncle Dickie's temporary 'wild oats'. The prince was coming to feel so at ease in Camilla's company that he dared to hope she could one day be his lifelong 'friend and companion to love and to cherish'. And 'to his delight' (Jonathan Dimbleby again) she was sending back the message that 'these feelings were reciprocated'.

Naval duties, however, stood in the way. Charles's frigate HMS *Minerva* was due to set sail for the Caribbean early in the new year – and was not going to return until the following autumn. On the weekend of 9–10 December, the prince took Camilla and Mountbatten down to Portsmouth for a guided tour of the vessel, then lunch, and the next weekend he was back at Broadlands with Camilla – 'the last time,' he wrote sadly to Mountbatten, 'I shall see her for eight months'.

Thirty-five years later the prince revealed that weekend in December 1972 as the moment when he first realised for sure that he wanted to marry Camilla – that she was his life's soulmate. But he did not have the courage to tell her properly or strongly enough.

'Charles declared his love,' wrote Gyles Brandreth in 2005, 'but not his hand. He whispered sweet nothings, but said nothing of substance. He made no commitment and he asked for none.'

Just twenty-four years old in November 1972, Charles felt too young to get involved in the whole complicated process of engagement and marriage as heir to the British throne. In the most banal sense, the prospect would have meant too many practical details to be fitted in before *Minerva* set sail – starting with an approach to his parents with whom he had not begun to broach his feelings. They would undoubtedly have raised some questions, since their views about Camilla's suitability were not that different from Uncle Dickie's. She was a nice horsey woman and excellent girlfriend material – but she was not an obvious future queen, especially since there was no need to hurry. So Charles did not hurry either.

'Sometimes,' as Gyles Brandreth shrewdly put it, 'the actions we do not take are indeed more significant than those we do.'

Camilla herself was not really surprised – nor greatly cast down. For half a dozen years she had been busily engaged in a colourful on-and-off relationship with Captain Andrew Parker Bowles, a handsome and eligible officer in the Household Cavalry, and a highly desirable catch in his own right, both in terms of his personal charm and his own royal connections. In 1953, aged thirteen, Andrew had been a pageboy, dressed in silk and satin, at the Queen's coronation, and his father Derek, High Sheriff of Berkshire, was a member of the Queen Mother's horse-racing and social circle.

The on-and-off aspect of their romance reflected Parker Bowles's foreign assignments – he had served in Germany, Cyprus and Ulster, as well as a spell in New Zealand. But the principal 'off' factor was his appalling infidelity. Major 'Poker' Bowles, as he was known in the regiment, was irresistible to other women, and he wasted little energy in denying their temptations.

From time to time, Camilla struck back – and this was one explanation of her direct approach to Charles in the spring of 1972. Andrew had been enjoying a fling with the still unmarried Princess Anne in the early months of that year – and it was soon after this that Camilla made her bid for Charles. Her approach to the prince was a lowly matter of tit for tat.

'She was determined to show [Andrew],' recalled one of the polo community, 'that she could do as well in the royal pulling stakes as he had done.'

By early 1973, however, both Andrew and Camilla had disentangled themselves from their royal relationships. They had been dating in their on-off way for nearly seven years, and Camilla's father was losing patience. The major had been amused by his daughter's relationship with Charles but, like Camilla herself, he did not believe it could possibly lead to a top-level royal marriage. So this was the moment, with the prince on the other side of the world. According to John Bowes-Lyon (Andrew's cousin), in March 1973 Camilla's family decided to force Andrew's hand by publishing an engagement notice in *The Times*.

Andrew Parker Bowles allowed himself to be trapped with good grace – the game was up. Aged thirty-three, it was a good time for him to settle down – and Camilla, coming up to twenty-six in July, had had enough of being always a bridesmaid. So on 4 July that year the Shand and Parker Bowles clans came together in the elegant surroundings of the Guards Chapel at Wellington

Barracks with dress uniforms and three senior members of the royal family – Princess Anne, Princess Margaret and the Queen Mother. It was the 'society wedding of the year', with eight hundred guests in attendance.

Though Charles had been invited, he sent his regrets on the grounds of 'duty', since he was representing his mother in Nassau, where the Bahamas were about to celebrate independence. But no one who knew the story believed him. The prince had locked himself in his cabin on *Minerva* on first hearing the news of the engagement, writing forlornly in a confidential letter, 'I suppose the feeling of emptiness will pass eventually.'

It took some time, but his sad feeling did pass – to some degree. By the mid-1970s the prince had begun dating again, enjoying the company of quite a number of eligible young women.

So had Andrew Parker Bowles. The galloping major had not waited that long after his 1973 wedding to resume his skirt-chasing ways, and his wife tolerated his philandering as she had done before their marriage. Enjoying domestic life in the country, Camilla concentrated on the raising of her two children, Tom (b.1974) and Laura (b.1978). She also maintained her friendly contact with Prince Charles, who had agreed to be the godfather of Tom.

Then, in August 1979, Lord Mountbatten was assassinated with members of his family by an IRA bomb on board his fishing boat off the coast of Mullaghmore, County Sligo. Charles was devastated and in his sorrow he turned to Camilla. He regarded her as his best friend – the person, above all, in whom he could totally confide. His former lover remained his 'touchstone' and 'sounding board', as he put it to Jonathan Dimbleby. From Camilla's point of view, her once-casual 'revenge bonk' over Andrew and Anne had become deeply serious.

Speaking mainly, and at length, on the telephone, Charles poured out his heart to Camilla, and she gave him the solace that only she could provide. In a matter of months their best friendship had turned again into love – certainly in the spiritual sense. There were some who believed that in 1979 and 1980 the pair secretly resumed a clandestine affair, and one or two members of the royal family were so concerned that they warned the prince directly of the damage his persistent 'illicit liaison' would do to the reputation of the monarchy. A feeling was growing that Charles, approaching the age of thirty-two, should be getting on with the job of finding himself a future queen – and that very summer of 1980 he was photographed at Balmoral in the company of Lady Diana Spencer.

Still only nineteen years old in September that year when she was caught in fishing mode with Prince Charles on the banks of the River Dee by a Fleet Street lens, Lady Diana Spencer had known the prince for some time already. Her elder sister Sarah had actually dated him for a spell in Silver Jubilee year (1977), while her maternal grandmother Ruth, Lady Fermoy, was a confidante of the Queen Mother and one of her ladies-in-waiting.

The Queen had invited Diana to Balmoral so that she and her husband could take a closer look at the young woman whom insiders were even then tipping as her future daughter-in-law. In the 1960s Diana had been one of the children who came to play with Andrew and Edward at Sandringham – happening to fall between the two younger brothers in age, and joining them to watch *Chitty Chitty Bang Bang* on the comfy sofas of the house's 'cinema'. Notably demure and polite in those days, how had the girl developed?

Diana passed the Balmoral test with flying colours.

'We went stalking together,' remembered fellow guest Patti Palmer-Tomkinson. 'We got hot, we got tired, she fell into a bog, she got covered in mud, laughed her head off, got puce in the face, her hair glued to her forehead because it was pouring with rain … She was a sort of wonderful English schoolgirl who was game for anything.'

Both the Queen and Prince Philip eyed Diana approvingly. Edward and Andrew competed to sit beside her at evening picnics, and the whole family liked her. Just a year after the death of his beloved honorary grandfather, Charles felt he had finally located 'the sweet-charactered girl' for whom Uncle Dickie had urged him to search – and the British press felt the same. Media around the entire world went so 'Di-crazy', in fact, that Charles's father became alarmed. As the press coverage intensified, Prince Philip told his son in a blunt intervention that Charles must either propose to the girl or walk away 'immediately' for the sake of her good name.

'Whichever choice he decided to make,' Charles later recalled his father counselling, 'he should not delay.'

That is how marriages get 'arranged' in the age of mass media scrutiny. Charles bowed to his father's 'advice' and proposed to

Diana at the beginning of February 1981. The couple announced their engagement at the end of the month, and Britain became even more hysterical in the weeks leading up to their spectacular union on 29 July. Over six hundred thousand people packed the pavements to cheer the couple to and from the wedding in St Paul's Cathedral, in front of an invited congregation of 3,500 and an estimated 750 million global viewers – then the largest TV audience in history.

The bride's intricate ivory taffeta gown was paired with a lace veil no less than 153 yards long, together with an eighteenth-century heirloom tiara, while her silk bridal slippers were embroidered with 542 sequins and 132 matching pearls – the heels kept deliberately low so as not to upstage the groom: at five foot ten, Diana was exactly the same height as Charles.

When it came to the couple's wedding vows, Diana was the first bride in royal history to promise to love, honour and cherish her husband but not necessarily to 'obey'.

4

Agape

'Put the needs of others above your own fears.'

(Meghan Markle, Graduation Speech at
Immaculate Heart School, 3 June 2020)

O n 4 August 1981, less than a week – just six days – after
the wedding of Charles and Diana in London, Rachel
Meghan Markle was born in Canoga Park, Los Angeles. Most of
the sixty thousand inhabitants of this leafy suburb in the San
Fernando Valley had access to a television that 'royal summer',
and those who were watching on 29 July would have had little
choice about their viewing. The Royal Wedding from London
was carried all day long by every US network.

If they had been among the millions watching the London
wedding in the week before their baby's birth, Meghan's parents
Tom and Doria Markle could hardly have failed to notice the
difference between the classical dome of St Paul's Cathedral and
the gold orb-topped turrets of the Self-Realization Fellowship

Temple on Sunset Boulevard where they had married eighteen months earlier. With its strikingly exotic Moorish entrance arch and plastic Buddhas, the Self-Realization Fellowship Temple stood out in the middle of LA's red-light district – it was just a stone's throw from where Hugh Grant would be caught in his car enjoying oral sex with prostitute Divine Brown in June 1995.

'A fresh new day … and it is ours,' read the opening line of the Markles' wedding invitation, with the promise of 'happy beginnings …'

Their ceremony of union had been presided over by Brother Bhaktananda, an ordained Buddhist priest in glowing orange robes who had been born Michael Krull in Pennsylvania. Founded in 1920 by Indian yogi Paramahansa Yogananda, the Fellowship Temple preached a gospel of 'spirituality and self-knowledge through meditation and Kriya yoga' and had been the choice of Doria, twenty-three years old at the time of her marriage to the thirty-five-year-old Thomas. According to her half-brother Joseph Johnson – Meghan's uncle – Doria 'was fascinated by alternative religions and yoga'.

Joseph would give Doria the credit for instilling in his niece Meghan her expansive self-confidence, along with the buoyant belief she developed early in her childhood that 'she could be anything and achieve anything'. Joseph traced this back to the profusion of striking female role models in the family – 'culturally our family did not have male figures around' – and especially to Doria's mother Jeanette, Meghan's grandmother, who was the daughter of a Cleveland bellhop and lift operator in a 'fancy whites-only hotel'.

Joseph recalled the searing experience of crossing America as a child with his half-sister in the days of segregation. Born in Cleveland, Ohio, in 1956, Doria had been just a baby when her mother packed her up to head west. Arriving one night in a small 'all white' town in the middle of Texas, they were cold and hungry, but no one would rent a room to them as non-whites.

'We wanted food and shelter, but we were turned away because of the colour of our skin.' It was the first time that Uncle Joseph, then seven years old, had experienced racism.

'I was young,' he recalls, 'but I remember one guy pointing off into the snow saying, "The highway is that way. Get going! You are not welcome here."'

Life got better in Los Angeles, where Doria was bussed with other black pupils under the recently passed desegregation laws to Fairfax High, a mostly white Jewish school.

'We were raised together,' Uncle Joseph recounted to the *Mail on Sunday*'s Caroline Graham. 'There was an age difference [seven years] with Doria. She was the youngest. But, like Meghan, she's whip-smart and always wanted more out of life.'

Priding herself on her hair, Doria grew 'a big beautiful Afro' and started work as a trainee make-up artist on the daytime TV show *General Hospital* – which was where, in her early twenties, she met Thomas Markle, twelve years her senior, recently divorced and working on the soap opera as the lighting director. The attraction was instant. On the highly successful long-running show nurses and doctors would engage in 'lusty' love affairs while performing heroic heart transplants. Tom and Doria couldn't match the medical heroics, but their love affair proved both powerful and immediate, and they wasted no time in getting married.

Thomas had arrived from the east coast where he had grown up in the small town of Newport, Pennsylvania, as the youngest of three sons in a talented Anglo-German family – known as 'Merckel' before they anglicised the name. One of his brothers joined the US air force and was later an international diplomat, while the other became a bishop in the small Eastern Orthodox Catholic Church in America – its motto 'God became human in order that human beings might become gods'.

Leaving school in his teens, the young and artistic Thomas had moved to the nearby Pocono Mountains, where he found back-stage work in playhouses catering to the tourist trade – before relocating to Chicago. In the Windy City he married for the first time, fathering two children, and became a lighting director.

The equivalent of the director of photography in movies or television, a lighting director inspired and set the 'mood' or look of any scene, and Tom Markle had a light touch. Although phys-ically heavy-set, he was creatively twinkle-toed, taking his inspi-ration from the Busby Berkeley movies he had loved to watch as a child with their extravagantly illuminated parades of elegantly clad dancers.

In later years, and certainly at the time of her marriage to Prince Harry, Thomas Markle would come to play the villain in Meghan's life, taking money for clunky press interviews in which he was outspoken in his criticism of his daughter. Eventually, and notoriously, he would fail to feature at her wedding to Harry. But as a young father by all accounts – including Meghan's own – Thomas's creativity and commitment were a parental inspiration.

'It's safe to say,' Meghan stated at the time of her engagement, 'I have always been a "Daddy's Girl".'

One Christmas Tom tackled the central question of his daughter's mixed-race identity by purchasing two sets of Barbie dolls – one black and one white. He took them apart and re-mixed them to create her own customised personal set – 'a black mom doll, a white dad doll and a child in each colour'. When Meghan went to school and found herself confronted by a tick-box form to complete about her ethnicity and realised that she did not fit in to just one category, 'my dad said words that will stay with me forever: "Draw your own box."'

Thanks to Tom Markle's earning power – swollen by a $750,000 win in the California State Lottery in 1990 – Meghan's upbringing was not as deprived as some have imagined. Canoga Park where she spent much of her childhood is a respectable blue-collar and middle-class suburb of Los Angeles – not fancy, perhaps, but cheerfully green and racially mixed.

When Meghan was six, Doria and Tom separated and divorced, and she went to live with Doria. But Tom remained a hands-on father. 'He taught me how to fish,' recalled Meghan, 'to appreciate Busby Berkeley films, write thank you notes and spend my weekends in Little Tokyo eating chicken teriyaki with vegetable tempura.'

It was her father's care and belief, she later said, that inspired her 'grand dream' of becoming an actress – and in a very practical sense. With Doria working – at jobs as a travel agent, a clothing designer and later a social worker – Tom would be the one to pick Meghan up from school and take her to work with him.

Her assurance and her familiarity with show business would come from nearly a decade of doing her homework on the sets of the sitcom *Married … with Children* and *General Hospital* – on which her father was the lighting supremo. In 1982, the year after Meghan's birth, Tom Markle had won a Daytime Emmy Award for his lighting direction of *General Hospital* and four years later he had been nominated for an award for his lighting work helping to stage the 58th Academy Awards – the Oscars.

Meghan was not obviously thrown off course by her parents' separation and divorce in 1987. If anything, it increased her self-reliance. Early in 1991, aged only nine, she was filmed by a local news channel holding up an anti-war protest sign in a demonstration against the first Gulf War that she herself had organised in the school playground. A boy in her class had burst into tears because his elder brother was heading out to fight against Iraq, and the boy thought he was going to die. So Meghan drew a sign saying 'Peace and Harmony for the World' and gathered her classmates into the protest.

'She was one of those children,' said her teacher Ilise Faye, 'that would stand up for the underdogs. She would stand up for what she believed in, and she was a leader among her friends, her peer group.'

A year or so later, Meghan went a stage further with her political and social campaigning. She was watching a TV show in school when a commercial came on for Ivory Clear dishwashing liquid, showing a sink full of dirty dishes, with the tagline 'Women all over America are fighting greasy pots and pans.' Two boys in the class piped up, 'Yeah, that's where women belong – in the kitchen!'

'I remember feeling shocked and angry,' Meghan said, 'and also just feeling so hurt … Something needed to be done. So I went home and told my dad what had happened, and he encouraged me to write letters. So I did – to the most powerful people I could think of.'

Starting at the top, the eleven-year-old wrote to the First Lady, Hillary Clinton; to Linda Ellerbee, the host of *Nick News*, her favourite kids' TV news programme; to the noted women's rights lawyer Gloria Allred; and to Ivory Clear's manufacturer, Procter & Gamble.

Procter & Gamble never replied. But Hillary Clinton and Gloria Allred did. Both sent letters of encouragement, and Linda Ellerbee sent a camera crew to interview the young campaigner. A month later Procter & Gamble changed its tagline. 'Women all over America' became 'People all over America', and its TV copy lines have tried to remain gender neutral ever since.

The Immaculate Heart School that Meghan attended from the age of eleven to seventeen might not have been ritzy, but it was an esteemed and fee-paying all-girls Catholic establishment that was known for producing hard-working, polite and civic-minded young women. About a third of its students were white, 20 per cent were Latina, 17 per cent were mixed-race like Meghan, 17 per cent were Asian and Pacific Islander, and 5 per cent or so were black. Former pupils included actresses Tyra Banks and Mary Tyler Moore, yet though the campus was sited below the hilltop lettering of the famous Hollywood sign, the religious – and even austere – academy was not celebrity-inclined.

Virtually all of Immaculate Heart's students went on to high-quality colleges, and many went to Harvard, Princeton or Stanford. But the teaching sisters were proudest of the number of pupils who volunteered for their out-of-school charity projects – among them a soup kitchen on Skid Row for which they equipped girls with the slogan, 'Put the needs of others above your own fears.'

Through these secondary school years Meghan stayed pretty much full-time at the home of her father, since Thomas lived within walking distance of Immaculate Heart. He would help with the lighting and stage sets of the school productions in which his daughter performed – including the musicals *Into the Woods* and *Annie*, in the latter of which Meghan sang her own solo number.

'I remember her being very excited and nervous about her song,' recalls Gigi Perreau, a former child actress who taught Meghan drama at Immaculate Heart for four years. 'She was very active in my drama department. We never had a moment's problem with her. She was spot on, learnt her lines when she had to – very dedicated, very focused.'

Immaculate Heart had a fondness for ancient Greek words with a religious connotation – '*kairos*', for example, meaning 'the time when God acts', was the title given to school spiritual sessions, in which Meghan participated as a group leader. Another was '*arche*', the term Aristotle coined to express the 'origin' of all things (as in the term 'archetype'); and then there was '*agape*', pronounced 'ah-gah-pay', or the highest form of unconditional love – 'the love of God for man and of man for God'.

According to Aristotle, there is regular love and then there is *agape*. During her summer vacations Meghan would take part in retreats organised by the Agape International Spiritual Center: 'We are on the planet,' ran Agape's manifesto, 'to be and express the Divine Love of God that is alive in every fiber of our being, waiting to be released through us onto our world. Living as love is a way of life that brings heaven on earth.'

Founded in 1986 in Los Angeles by Dr Michael Bernard Beckwith, Agape described itself as a 'trans-denominational' community that embraced Christianity without excluding other religions, teaching that Jesus, like Gandhi or Buddha, was not so much 'the great exception' as 'the great example'. Oprah Winfrey, Stevie Wonder and Van Morrison were among the celebrities to endorse Dr Beckwith's spiritual process that unlocked, as Oprah put it, 'everything that is unique, mighty and magnificent inside each of us'.

Agape's morning schedule at its summer camps started soon after dawn with meditation and teaching at 6.45, helping to set a pattern of early rising (and, later, early morning texting and emailing) that Meghan would maintain into her professional life. Aged thirteen, she enjoyed her first kiss at an Agape summer camp held at Santa Monica – with the future comedian Joshua Silverstein who, also thirteen that year, would recall it happening at the end of a drama workshop.

'We were kind of leaving and walking out,' Silverstein remembered in the spring of 2018 – he was by then a thirty-six-year-old married father of two, starring with James Corden on *The Late Late Show*. 'I noticed her making a beeline toward me with a lot of intention.'

The teenage couple had already met and bonded over their mixed-race heritage.

'She was charming and quirky,' said Silverstein. 'She wasn't a stereotypical thirteen-year-old girl … decked out in pink every day … flaunting make-up or anything. She was her own person, very authentic to who she was at the time … serious about her craft. I found out from our friends that she liked me and I liked her, and I just think that we decided it would be a good idea to become boyfriend and girlfriend.'

The pair had held hands previously and hugged, but now there was something different in Meghan's manner that caught Silverstein off guard.

'*She* kissed me. *She* made the move,' he recalled. 'And I think I was like, OK – we're at that phase of our relationship right now, we're kissing … But the kiss was definitely her – her initiative absolutely.'

Meghan confirmed Silverstein's memory in an interview she gave to talk show host Larry King: 'I was thirteen, it was a summer camp and I kissed him.'

According to Silverstein, he and Meghan continued their relationship for the rest of the Agape camp – with more kisses – then mutually decided to split up at the end of the summer. They discussed the matter dispassionately. Neither of them wanted to put a 'dampener' on what might happen when they got back to school – they wanted to be free to date other people – a couple of *extremely* mature thirteen-year-olds.

Agape has remained an important part of Meghan Markle's life. She would even become an Agape youth minister for a period and her mother Doria still attends Agape services on Sunset Boulevard. To the end of Meghan's school years and onwards through college at Northwestern University, Illinois, where she joined Kappa Kappa Gamma Sorority and participated in community and charity projects, she would rise early every day to meditate and repeat an Agape morning mantra – as she is thought to do to this day.

'God is on my side', runs one such mantra. 'God is coming into being through me. God wants me to be all I can be. God wants to come into its own through me' – the point of the word 'its' being that, for Agape, God is not so sexist as to be either male or female.

So here was the dedicated and definitely un-Windsor bombshell – the Agape kisser – who would be waiting for Prince Harry after all his trials and travails that we shall be reading about in the pages ahead.

5

'Whatever "in love" Means'

*'Jealousy, total jealousy … I felt I was
a lamb to the slaughter.'*

(Princess Diana, recording her thoughts for author
Andrew Morton in 1991)

When Elton John and his lyricist Bernie Taupin wanted to sum up the tragic legend of Diana, Princess of Wales, dead in August 1997 at the age of only thirty-six, they turned to the anthem they had composed twenty-four years earlier in tribute to another troubled heroine who had died at the very same age: Marilyn Monroe.

'Goodbye Norma Jean, Though I never knew you at all …'

Within hours of Diana's death, radio stations had started to play the original 'Candle in the Wind', catching the metaphor of the flickering, sensitive superstar destroyed by too much publicity and by her inability to find a partner who could sustain her difficult nature with solid emotional support and understanding – *'Never knowing who to cling to when the rain set in.'*

Quickly rewritten to be sung in Westminster Abbey just six days after her death, the Diana version of 'Candle' avoided those tricky targets in favour of safer praise:

> *You called out to our country and you whispered to those in*
> *   pain,*
> *Now you belong to heaven and the stars spell out your name.*

When Charles, Prince of Wales, aged thirty-two, made his momentous proposal of marriage to the still-teenage Diana, nineteen, on 3 February 1981, he had just come back from a skiing holiday.

'I've missed you so much,' he told her as they sat together in the nursery at Windsor – and then he simply dived in.

'Will you marry me?' he asked.

Diana laughed and later remembered thinking, This is a joke.

But the prince was deadly serious – 'You do realise,' he said sternly, 'that one day you will be Queen', reproving the teenager for her hilarity.

Diana got the point immediately.

You won't be Queen, she told herself, according to her subsequent account – but that was not what she said at the time to her future husband.

'I love you so much,' she declared, trying to shift the mood in a happier direction. 'I love you so much.'

Charles's response came back as a shrug of the shoulders and three historic words: 'Whatever "love" means.'

The prince was so pleased with his exercise in home-baked philosophy that he repeated it publicly three weeks later when the couple announced their engagement on 24 February. On this occasion the interviewer had served up a flaccid final question about how the couple were feeling: 'And, I suppose, in love?' To which Diana replied at once, 'Of course', leaving Charles to lift his eyebrows again: 'Whatever "in love" means.'

Friends pointed out later that he had been engaged in a serious exercise – taking issue with popular clichés about being 'in love'. But whatever Charles meant on television, that had not been the issue when Diana had first told him that she loved him 'so much'. Following her acceptance, the prince had gone straight upstairs to phone his mother with the crucial news the Queen had been waiting for.

'His choice of marrying Diana was really motivated by his parents pushing him to get the succession assured,' recalls a friend. 'He once actually said as much to me at a dinner with Elizabeth of Yugoslavia. He intimated that he was being pushed and pushed towards marriage.'

Prince Charles's proposal to Diana, in other words, had not been about his feelings or emotions, which were by then committed to another woman. It had been essentially a business proposition.

A few days into their honeymoon on the Royal Yacht *Britannia*, they opened their diaries to discuss their next engagements, when out of Charles's dropped not one, but *two* photos of Camilla.

Diana chose not to spoil the moment. She had already worked out the truth about Mrs Parker Bowles from a pre-wedding lunch à deux that Camilla herself had proposed to celebrate the engagement and to 'look at the ring' – an oddly proprietorial suggestion to make. Camilla had posed one strangely repeated question about whether Diana was planning to join her husband with the Beaufort Hunt – and Diana, no great horsewoman, deduced that hunting was an activity in which Mrs PB was hoping to keep the prince to herself.

'Whatever happens, I will always love you,' Diana overheard Charles proclaiming urgently one evening on his hand-held telephone in his bath. Then her husband told her he needed to find a country house that tied in with his work for the Duchy of Cornwall – and chose Highgrove House in Gloucestershire. Highgrove was over 190 miles from Cornwall, but less than half an hour's drive from Bolehyde Manor, the Parker Bowles's home near Chippenham – and it was smack in the middle of Beaufort Hunt country.

Getting ready while on honeymoon in Egypt for a white-tie dinner with President Anwar Sadat, Diana noticed that her husband's cufflinks were engraved with two intertwined letter Cs.

'Camilla gave you those, didn't she?'

'Yes,' replied Charles defensively. 'So what's wrong? They're a present from a friend.'

'Boy, did we have a row,' recalled Diana later, in words reported by the author Andrew Morton. 'Jealousy, total jealousy … I felt I was a lamb to the slaughter.'

Things got worse when the couple left *Britannia* to round off their honeymoon in Balmoral that September. Charles would take Diana for long walks around the Highlands, finding a hill-top where he could settle her down and read philosophy to her – Carl Gustav Jung, or the writings of his friend, the guru and conservationist Laurens van der Post. Two months into their marriage, she assumed that her husband was ringing up his mistress every five minutes the moment he got back to his room at the house, asking her advice on how to handle his difficult bride.

The emotional strain intensified Diana's bulimia nervosa, the eating disorder that had struck her, according to the princess, just a week after the couple had got engaged.

'A bit chubby here, aren't we?' Charles had said, putting his hand accusingly on his fiancée's waistline. 'And that triggered off something in me – and the Camilla thing. I was desperate, desperate.'

She remembered the first time she made herself sick. The vomiting released the tension she had been feeling, and she felt 'thrilled' – but it proved to be the beginning of a lethal pattern in which Diana would find herself vomiting every day. When first measured for her wedding dress in February 1981, Diana had been 29 inches around the waist; on her July wedding day, she was down to 23½ inches. On top of this, she had found herself dreaming about Camilla.

Charles invited Laurens van der Post himself up to Balmoral for some personal counselling to help his wife – with no success.

'Laurens didn't understand me,' Diana said. 'Everybody saw I was getting thinner and thinner and I was being sicker and sicker. Basically they thought I could adapt to being Princess of Wales

'Dear Roddy …' Elizabeth II writes to her sister's friend Roddy
Llewellyn. Mark Boxer, *Harper's Bazaar*, 1976

overnight. Anyway, a godsend – William was conceived in October. Marvellous news, occupied my mind.'

Diana's pregnancy with William scarcely prompted an improvement in her condition, however, for now the princess began suffering from both bulimia *and* morning sickness. Concerned about the health of the baby growing inside her, she refused to take her bulimia pills – with graphic consequences: 'Sick, sick, sick, sick, sick,' she related to Andrew Morton in the book that, ten years later when it was published, would blow the lid off the myth of the 'dream' royal marriage.

In 1981, the lid was already off so far as the royal family was concerned. They had witnessed Diana's weeping and fits – and their sympathies were all with Charles.

'So I was "a problem" and they registered Diana as "a problem",' the princess related to Morton. 'Poor Charles is having such a hard time.'

The Queen saw Diana's vomiting as a cause, not a symptom, of the marriage issues – but she did show sympathy when it came to her daughter-in-law's troubles with the press. Diana suffered something close to a nervous breakdown that December when she went out from Highgrove to buy some wine gums in the local village shop – only to find herself surrounded by the ever-developing pack of newspaper photographers and reporters. The princess broke down in tears.

For the first time in her reign, Elizabeth II summoned the editors of all Britain's national, daily and Sunday newspapers to Buckingham Palace, along with the principal news directors at the BBC and ITN. Never had there been a British media gathering like it. The Queen's press secretary Michael Shea received the Fleet Street grandees in the palace's magnificent white and gold 1844 Room, explaining how the princess was 'more than usually affected by morning sickness because of her age and build' and how the Queen was taking a personal interest in her privacy. Pleasantly suggesting that more restraint might be in order, Shea invited the editors for drinks next door in the still more magnificent Caernarvon Room decorated with paintings of Britain's triumphs against Napoleon.

Hardly had the editors taken their first sips of champagne,

when the Queen herself walked in escorted by her younger son Prince Andrew, who was just then approaching the height of his popularity as a naval helicopter pilot. The intrepid hacks were so overwhelmed by the royal presence that they simply exchanged humble banalities with their sovereign like any citizen would – until the editor of the *News of the World*, Barry Askew, also known as the Beast of Bouverie Street, finally dared to address the issue that had brought them all together.

'If Lady Di wants to buy some wine gums without being photographed,' he said, 'why doesn't she send a servant?'

'What an extremely pompous man you are!' replied Her Majesty with a gracious smile – and the hearty laughs around the room made clear who was considered the winner of *that* exchange. A month later Askew was sacked from the *News of the World* by his proprietor Rupert Murdoch – though it was not explained whether that was for making such a public fool of himself or because he had compromised his paper's independence by attending the meeting.

The palace gathering had identified the new dimension – and the new challenges – that Diana's glamour had brought to the royal family, and, sadly, it did not resolve them. Three months later, in February 1982, Charles and Diana flew to the Bahamas for a pre-baby holiday, staying at Windermere on the island of Eleuthera, the secluded home of Lord Mountbatten's daughter and son-in-law, Patricia and John Brabourne.

In this romantic setting, far from civilisation – and from Camilla – the royal couple sunbathed and swam together, splashing and kissing in the surf with their arms around one another. They grilled each other barbecue suppers – but they were not alone. Before dawn one morning, kitted out in full tropical gear, binoculars and a huge, long-distance telephoto lens, *Daily Star* reporter James Whitaker and his photographer accomplice Ken Lennox crawled through the darkness across a spit of land opposite the Brabourne beach. Lying patiently in wait as the sun rose, the spies were finally rewarded by the extraordinary sight of a bikini-clad Diana splashing into the sea with her five-month-pregnant belly clearly visible – and obviously imagining that she was quite alone. The revealing photos covered the front page of the *Star* next morning.

In vain did the Queen condemn the invasion of her daughter-in-law's privacy as 'tasteless behaviour' that was 'in breach of normally accepted British press standards'. The Press Council tut-tutted – and James Whitaker proudly claimed the coup as the high spot of his career.

'I've never done anything more brilliantly intrusive,' the reporter boasted. 'We'd crawled and waited for hours. It was one of the triumphs of my professional life.'

'Brilliantly' intrusive? A triumph? What profession? What life?

These are running themes to ponder as we leave Princess Diana for the moment, exposed on the front page with the unborn Prince William inside her. Before June 1982 when he enters our story, we have another character to meet, born five months ahead of William: Ms Catherine Middleton, and her family, who would, in due course, be joining the royal family.

6

Party Pieces

'Une nation de boutiquiers.' –
'A nation of shopkeepers.'

(Insult directed against the British,
attributed to Napoleon, 1822)

So that's enough for the moment from those wacky Windsors – not to mention the manic Markles on the other side of the Atlantic …

Let us turn our attention instead to those charmingly civilised, middle-of-the-road, middle-class, middle-England Middletons whose distaff side, the Goldsmiths, have risen so high, but also oh-so-modestly, from their salt-of-the-earth coal-mining origins, with no history of nasty plottings or family back-stabbings – no messy divorces, no scheming ambition …

Well, up to a point, Lord Copper …

Lord Copper was Evelyn Waugh's brilliantly fearsome amalgamation of the overbearing 1930s press lords Northcliffe and Beaverbrook, ruling imperiously over his imaginary tabloid rag

The Daily Beast[*] in *Scoop*, Waugh's 1938 novel of Fleet Street skulduggery. Lord Copper's editors were so scared of their boss that they never dared say no to his face, only disagreeing with him 'up to a point ...'

So let us not dare to doubt the perfection of the sainted Middletons – well, up to a point, dear reader – as they now enter our story with the birth of their daughter Catherine Elizabeth on 9 January 1982, five months before the birth of her future husband Prince William. It is interesting to note that the brides of both our royal heroes are older than their husbands – and how the histories of their royal recruitment present such instructive studies in social climbing. The Queen Catherines of England certainly form a society that is worth climbing into: Catherine of Valois (wife of Henry V and mother of Henry VI), Catherine of Aragon, Catherine Howard, Catherine Parr (all wives of Henry VIII, with Catherine of Aragon being the mother of Queen Mary I), Catherine of Braganza (childless wife of Charles II) – and Catherine Middleton ...

Let us start with the coal-mining. Kate Middleton's great-great-grandfather on her mother's side, John Harrison, came from Hetton-le-Hole in County Durham. Today Hetton is effectively a suburb of Sunderland, but it was a mining village in its own right in 1896, when John, aged twenty-two, married

---

* Anglo-American editor Tina Brown cannily took the *Daily Beast* as the title of the online news magazine that she created in 2008 with businessman Barry Diller.

domestic servant Jane Hill, by whom he would father nine children, including Kate's great-grandfather, Thomas. For some twenty years John went down the pit every working day, until he was trampled in a freak accident by a runaway pit pony. After being laid out flat on his back for months, Great-great-grandpa was compelled to take early retirement, and for the rest of his life he could walk only with the help of a stick.

Great-grandfather Thomas, known to the family as 'Tommy', was too canny to follow his father down the pit. He trained as a joiner and in the 1930s headed south to London with his wife Elizabeth, settling in the western railway depot suburb of Southall, where his carpentry earned them enough to buy a two-bedroomed terraced house facing the Grand Union Canal. There Tommy and Elizabeth raised Kate's grandmother Dorothy, who left school early to work on the high street as a shop assistant at a branch of the Dorothy Perkins fashion chain – and was known to family and friends as 'Lady Dorothy'.

Strong and aspirational women play an important role in the history of Kate Middleton's family – starting with her great-grand-mother Edith Goldsmith who smoked twenty Woodbines a day, brought up six children and, when widowed, went to work in the local jam factory. In 1953, just two months after Elizabeth II's coronation, Edith's twenty-two-year-old son Ron, a builder, who had left school at fourteen, married Lady Dorothy, then just eighteen.

Ron and Dorothy – Kate's grandparents – settled in a council flat in Southall, and 1955 saw the birth of their daughter Carole, Kate's mother. Delighted with her new baby, Lady Dorothy bought little Carole – in the words of one spiteful relative – 'the biggest Silver Cross pram you have ever seen'.

In 2021, a pink-topped Silver Cross Balmoral pram, complete with huge curved springs and wire-spoked wheels, will set you back £1,800 – and if that is a little too rich for your pocket, you can slum it with the lesser Kensington model at just £1,500. These prices come from John Lewis – to this day the Middletons' favourite store, motto: 'Never Knowingly Undersold'.

'We all thought Dorothy was a bit of a snob,' recalled Ron's niece, Ann Terry, who worked beside her in a jewellery store. 'She always wanted to better herself.'

Living upstairs in their cramped and unheated Southall flat that lay under the Heathrow flightpath, the Goldsmiths had to manhandle their Silver Cross perambulator up and down the staircase every time baby Carole needed some air.

'My grandmother used to grumble about Dorothy,' remembered another relative, 'because she thought she henpecked her Ronald. She thought Dorothy always wanted more and more money. She wanted to be the top brick in the chimney.'

After a dozen years of marriage, Dorothy and Ron were finally able to move out of the council flat to their first proper house – in Kingsbridge Road, Norwood Green, near Ealing, at the smarter end of Southall. By now Carole was about to enter her teens, but she only attended the local state school and then left when she was sixteen, since Ron could not afford to send her to teacher training college. Carole went straight out to work for 'the Pru' – the Prudential Insurance Company in Holborn.

* * *

The Pru and Carole Goldsmith did not get along. She had never seen herself working in an office, so she asked her father to stake her for two more years at school to get her A-levels – economics, English literature, geography and art. These helped her to win a place on the coveted retail trainee scheme of where else but John Lewis, learning her shopkeeping in the china and glass department at the Peter Jones branch on Sloane Square, Chelsea. Carole was loving the idea of a career in merchandising, until she was instructed to knuckle down for a full six months as a sales assistant on the shopfloor.

'Blow that!' she said in 2018 in an interview with the *Telegraph*. 'I'm not doing that for six months – it was really boring.'

No office and no shopfloor for Carole Goldsmith! Still aged only eighteen in 1973, she used her Pitman shorthand to get a job at BEA – British European Airways, just merging with British Overseas Airways Corporation to become the modern British Airways – and she also brushed up her schoolgirl French to secure a position with the ground staff. There she met the handsome and genial Michael Middleton, somewhat less forceful than her, but working in a quietly responsible job as a flight dispatcher, sharing with the pilot legal responsibility for passenger safety of the flights he supervised. The couple soon fell in love – and Lady Dorothy thoroughly approved.

Michael Middleton was exactly the sort of husband that Carole's mother had hoped her daughter would snag – charming, good-looking and rolling in class: a distant ancestor of Michael's had been Baroness Airedale who was present and photographed at the 1911 coronation of King George V.

We should note, therefore, that while the courtship and marriage of Kate Middleton to Prince William would give the Middleton family a reputation for social climbing – 'those ghastly Middletons!' would sneer Camilla and her kin – the Middletons had in fact already 'climbed'. The thrusting ambition came from the Goldsmith side of the family who were all too happy to link up with this genteel clan that could trace their descent back to Tudor times.

Middleton money derived from Yorkshire wool production during the Industrial Revolution. Shrewdly invested through a variety of trusts, the inheritance had cushioned the family for generations. Michael had been privately educated at Clifton College, Bristol's top public school, before moving to British Airways in hopes of becoming a pilot. Grounded by poor eyesight, he had switched to ground-crew work, where he met Carole.

When the couple married in 1980 it was Middleton money that bought their first home, a Victorian semi-detached cottage in a village near Bucklebury in Berkshire – whence they moved after three years with their baby daughters Catherine and Pippa to Amman in Jordan, where Michael had been transferred by British Airways.

As an expat mum there was not much for Carole to do in Amman except to stage and attend parties – and this may have helped to inspire what came next. On their return to the UK in 1987, Carole, by now thirty-two, was pregnant with their third child James.

Oooh, she recalled thinking. Bills to pay!

Within months of James's birth Carole Middleton had created her own trading company, Party Pieces.

It was a simple idea – a one-stop, mail-order destination from which you could order anything you needed for a children's party. Fancy dress, candles, going-home party bags, balloons, a dinosaur table piece – Carole could source it all. She went to the Spring Fair at Birmingham in 1987, hooked up with some suppliers of paper plates and cups, stuck up a self-designed flyer at Catherine's playgroup in Bucklebury – and began stuffing colourful party bags on her kitchen table.

You've got to hand it to Carole! From filling party bags, Mrs Middleton went on to create a thriving home-delivery enterprise – a British mini-Amazon – which did particularly good business when it came to crackers and tree decorations at Christmas.

There were lots of trips to the local post office in the months that followed, and business was slow to start with. These were pre-Internet days. But then Carole had the bright idea of advertising with a children's book club she had subscribed to. She paid to send out ten thousand flyers, then later a hundred thousand – and orders took off. She soon had to transfer from the kitchen table to the garden shed – and then to an office space in nearby Yattendon, where her husband built the packing benches. After a year or so Mike left his job at British Airways in order to help grow the business.

'We were pretty much the only ones doing this sort of thing when we started,' Carole told the *Telegraph* in a 2018 article celebrating thirty years of successful trading. 'It was really clear almost from the start that this was going to work ... Running a business is really very simple: you buy things and sell them for a profit.'

Moderate as always, the Middletons never took major risks. Happy to bide their time, they funded their growth from revenue – and they never allowed commerce to get in the way of their parenting.

'It was my business,' recalled Carole, 'so I could work around the holiday … Mike and I often talked about work in the evenings or on holiday, but we enjoyed it. I never really felt I was a working mother, although I was – and the children didn't either. They grew up with it.'

Catherine, Pippa and James were involved from the start, often modelling cutely for pictures in the increasingly elaborate brochures that their parents were sending out. Catherine/Kate was on the cover of one of the early Party Pieces catalogues, blowing out the candles – an image that will surely be much reproduced when she becomes Queen Catherine. As Kate grew older she styled images and helped to develop the business, showing a head for negotiation to match that of her mother.

'Catherine had all the makings of a fantastic trader,' says a business person who has dealt with Party Pieces and seen her operate at first hand. 'Everybody thinks of her now as a mother and future queen – whatever that means. But she's got a shrewd eye for profit and a very hard head on her shoulders. After university she worked with Party Pieces, and I am quite sure she would have taken the business into a new dimension if she had stayed – very much in her mother's style.'

Carole Middleton's haggling skills are legendary in the direct mail business. The family who developed today's successful Party

Pieces empire are not quite the gypsy pedlars depicted in Channel 4's satirical TV series *The Windsors*, but the clan are certainly neither noble nor royal. They are a tribe of Internet stallholders at the end of the day – with a keen nose for profit. In November 2020, for example, Carole's royal connections did not stop her posing for a marketing shot to promote the latest Party Pieces range of decorations designed for a COVID Christmas.

'Carole ran a very strong business and she ran it very well,' says one of her suppliers. 'But you did not want to get on the wrong side of her when it came to the pennies. Butter wouldn't melt in her mouth most of the time, but she was a ferocious negotiator – and if the haggling wasn't going her way, then the decibel level rose. I remember her almost screaming down the phone on one occasion when I refused to drop my price on something. People could hear her on the other side of the office – and that was in *my* office with her voice coming through the phone from Bucklebury, or wherever.'

Taxed on her negotiating style, Carole has ruefully acknowledged that her nickname with some is 'Hurricane' – but she undoubtedly got results. Within a few years Party Pieces was turning a handsome profit.

'No one seems to have picked up on the fact that both my sister and I were millionaires before we turned thirty,' said her younger brother, and only sibling, Gary, himself the developer of a successful UK IT recruitment enterprise. 'She with her Party Pieces business, and me with my company.'

In fact, Carole Middleton was already thirty-two when she founded Party Pieces, but she was clearly generating a healthy cash flow by her mid-thirties. Set up as a private partnership, with related family trusts, Party Pieces has never released figures, so it is impossible to say when the family attained the millionaire status that they enjoyed by the time Kate found herself at St Andrews University with Prince William in the early 2000s. Since Kate became royal in 2011, financial analysts have had a field day probing the family company's value – placing a £40 million estimate on the enterprise for 2020.

In August 2000 Carole Middleton née Goldsmith is said to have played a key role in the decision that transformed her daughter's destiny – and, indeed, the life of all the Middletons. On the seventeenth of the month, Kate's A-level results arrived in the post – two As and a B – precisely the grades that she needed to secure her place to study history of art at her first-choice university, Edinburgh. She and two of her best friends from Marlborough College, Alice and Emilia, had long hoped to study at this prestigious, Oxbridge-level university, and the three girls had already travelled up to Edinburgh together to set up their lodgings.

Out in Belize, where he was on military exercise with the Welsh Guards, Prince William received similarly welcome news – he had achieved the A, B and C grades that he needed to secure his place at the University of St Andrews to study history of art the following year, and the details of his results and university destination were made public.

It was the first time the world knew that the prince was planning to study at this pleasant Scottish seaside town between

Edinburgh and Dundee, starting at its highly rated university in 2001 – and Kate promptly changed her mind about her own degree arrangements. She told Alice and Emilia that she would not be joining them in Edinburgh after all. She had decided to switch to St Andrews to study history of art, like William – and she would also take a gap year so that, if she did get a place, she would go up at the same time, and join the very same course, as the prince.

'If' was the operative word. The moment the news of William's intentions became public, applications to St Andrews rocketed by 44 per cent – with many of the new applicants being female and from America. Conspiracy theorists might even wonder whether Kate had previously got wind of William's history of art and Scottish university plans through her Highgrove-connected friends, and now hastily adjusted her course towards the correct university.

Sometime at the end of August or the beginning of September 2000, Kate wrote formally to Edinburgh to turn down her place through the UCAS clearing system – Marlborough had insisted she write to the university to apologise – then made a new application to join the history of art course the following year at St Andrews, all with the help of her Marlborough advisors.

'After she left school,' recalled her housemistress, Ann Patching, 'Catherine made some different decisions. But why she made those decisions, I don't know.'

Kate presumably made this potentially dicey switch in full consultation with her mother and father. Throwing away a solid place at Edinburgh for the uncertainties of oversubscribed St

Andrews a year later was not a risk that many would-be students would have incurred in Britain at that time. But the Middletons must have discussed and supported the gamble their daughter was taking in full knowledge of the Prince William dimension.

What other rationale could there have been for this last-minute swerve? In *The Times* University Rankings for 1999, St Andrews had actually ranked two places below Edinburgh (10 to 8). The go-catch-a-royal strategy must have been a family decision – and the now-millionaire Middletons were comfortably able to underwrite their daughter's delay and ambitions financially.

A few years later the well-connected society journalist Matthew Bell presented his interpretation of Kate's life-changing switch, based on a 'reliable' inside source who, according to Bell, 'knew Kate very well'.

'Some insiders wonder,' wrote Bell for the *Spectator* on 6 August 2005, 'whether her university meeting with Prince William can really be ascribed to coincidence. Although, at the time of making her application to universities, it was unknown where the prince was intending to go, it has been suggested that her mother persuaded Kate to reject her first choice on hearing the news.'

So the spirit of Lady Dorothy and her Silver Cross rode again, possibly in Carole Middleton, and certainly in her purposeful daughter who was willing to throw away the security of a place at Edinburgh and take her chances elsewhere for the sake of what? The seaside air? Another good Scottish history of art course? Or, perhaps, the chance of meeting a prince and having a crack at becoming 'the top brick in the chimney'?

Kate Middleton's dramatic last-moment switch of university in August 2000 and her decision to delay her studies by twelve months would seem to display our future consort in a more go-getting and socially striving light than we have previously imagined …

Well, up to a point, Lord Copper. What is wrong with a bright and motivated young woman nursing the ambition to become England's sixth Queen Catherine? It must have been fun to be a fly on the wall in Bucklebury when the news of Kate Middleton's acceptance at St Andrews University did, in fact, come through.

7

An Heir and a 'Spare'

'I felt the whole country was in labour with me.'

(Diana, Princess of Wales, *Panorama*,
November 1995)

Diana, Princess of Wales was on Valium when she conceived her first son and sovereign-for-the-twenty-first-century, William, in the autumn of 1981 – 'high doses of Valium,' as she later recalled, 'and everything else'.

So her pregnancy was a reprieve – she could come off all the drugs. 'Thank heavens for William!'

But with the Valium-assisted future monarch came morning sickness. 'Couldn't sleep, didn't eat, whole world was collapsing around me,' she described to Andrew Morton. 'Very very difficult pregnancy indeed … All the analysts and psychiatrists came plodding in to try and sort me out.'

The experts' diagnosis was sympathetic, but they could hardly offer the princess a solution, since their verdict basically set out the dilemma in which this less-than-prepared twenty-year-old found herself trapped – 'One minute I was nobody. The next minute I was Princess of Wales, mother, media toy, member of this family, you name it …'

Matters came to a head that Christmas of 1981, when the family decamped to Sandringham for what was supposed to be a holiday.

'I threw myself down the stairs,' Diana related to Morton. 'Charles said I was crying wolf, and I said I felt so desperate and I was crying my eyes out and he said: "I'm not going to listen. You're always doing this to me. I'm going riding now." So I threw myself down the stairs. The Queen comes out, absolutely horrified, shaking – she was so frightened … Charles went out riding and when he came back, you know, it was just dismissal. Total dismissal. He just carried on out of the door.'

The Prince of Wales's behaviour reflected the advice of some of his trusted friends who had come to feel he should be tougher with what they interpreted as Diana's self-indulgence – they felt that the princess needed to 'pull herself together'. But Charles quickly abandoned that tactic. He could see that his young wife would not be in such misery if it were not for her extraordinary and scrutinised position bearing a future heir to the throne – 'the demands were too great, the pressures too daunting, the loss of freedom too stifling'.

As the delivery date grew closer he spent more and more time with his wife, eventually taking her to St Mary's, Paddington, with the dawn on 21 June 1982, and staying beside her throughout her long and painful labour which had lasted all day.

'The arrival of our small son has been an astonishing experience,' Charles wrote a few days later to his godmother, Patricia Brabourne, 'and one that has meant more to me than I could ever have imagined … I am *so* thankful I was beside Diana's bedside the whole time, because by the end of the day I really felt as though I'd shared deeply in the process of birth, and as a result was rewarded by seeing a small creature which belonged to *us*, even though he seemed to belong to everyone else as well!'

Charles was the first royal male known to be present at a birth – and it was the first time that an heir to the throne had been delivered in a hospital rather than in a royal home or palace. Tens of thousands of people had been milling outside St Mary's all day chanting 'We want Charlie!' and when the prince finally emerged sometime after 10 p.m., having smartened up and straightened his regimental striped tie, the cheers were deafening. One well-wisher planted a kiss on his cheek, leaving a smudge of lipstick.

'You're very kind,' the prince responded with a smile – and broke more fresh ground by lingering with the crowd informally for a chat. Asked if the baby looked like him, he replied, 'No, he's lucky enough not to.' And that was the line that the Queen followed when she came to visit her grandson the next day – 'Thank goodness he hasn't got ears like his father.'

William was ten months old when his parents embarked on their first major foreign tour together, to Australia and New Zealand in March 1983, taking their baby son with them, to be based with his nanny at the Woomargama sheep station in New South Wales. It made for an unusual tour structure, and Buckingham

Palace did not greatly approve of the couple's breaking off from their timetable at regular intervals to fly back to Woomargama. But it brought the young family together as never before.

'I still can't get over our luck in finding such an ideal place,' Charles wrote home to friends. 'We were extremely happy there whenever we were allowed to escape. The great joy was that we were totally alone together.'

This was the moment, on the other side of the world, when William chose to start moving.

'I must tell you that your godson couldn't be in better form,' wrote Charles to Lady Susan Hussey, the Queen's great friend and lady-in-waiting. 'Today he actually crawled for the first time. We laughed and laughed with sheer, hysterical pleasure and now we can't stop him crawling about everywhere. They pick up the idea very quickly don't they, when they've managed the first move?'

Within a week or so William was moving at 'high speed', reported his proud father, 'knocking everything off the tables and causing unbelievable destruction. He will be walking before long and is the greatest possible fun. You may have seen some photographs of him recently when he performed like a true professional in front of the cameras and did everything that could be expected of him. It is really encouraging to be able to provide people with some *nice* jolly news for a change!'

As the future King William V performed in public for the first time, Diana made her own debut on the international scene – and it could not have come at a better moment. The royal couple had brought William along at the suggestion of Malcolm Fraser, the Liberal prime minister of Australia who had proposed the tour. But in the meantime Fraser had lost an election by a land-slide to the anti-royal Labour leader Robert 'Bob' Hawke, who made no secret of his republican feelings – he wanted to see Australia jettison the entire outdated monarchical nonsense.

'I don't regard welcoming them as the most important thing I'm going to have to do in my first nine months in office,' said the new prime minister bluntly. 'I don't think we will be talking about kings of Australia forever more.'

Diana soon had Hawke hauling down his flag.

'I'd seen the crowds in Wales,' said the photographer Jayne Fincher, recalling the enthusiasm that had greeted Diana in the principality the previous year, 'but the crowds in Australia were incredible. We went to Sydney and wanted to photograph her with the Opera House, but just when we got there it was like the whole of Sydney had come out. It was just a sea of people … and all you could see was the top of this little pink hat bobbing along.'

In their forty flights shuttling between Australia's six states and two territories, Charles and Diana transformed the anti-crown dynamic that had greeted their arrival. By the end of the tour an opinion poll revealed that Australian monarchists had come to outnumber republicans two to one, and even Bob Hawke had fallen under Diana's spell. His wife, Hazel, actually found herself curtsying to the princess.

The success brought a certain uplift to the Waleses' previously depressed marriage. As they drove together through the vast crowds in their open car, Diana regularly reached for her husband's hand and squeezed it hard for comfort.

'Ron, isn't she absolutely beautiful?' asked Charles of the AP photographer Ron Bell, as the royal couple stepped out of the lift during a reception in Melbourne. 'I'm so proud of her.'

Crowds cheered when Diana got out of the car on their side of the street for any of the massively attended joint walkabouts – while those on the other side would groan in open disappointment at the prospect of having to put up with the prince.

'It's not fair, is it?' he would grin in a sporting attempt to shrug his shoulders. 'You'd better ask for your money back.'

It was not long, however, before the couple's press secretary, Vic Chapman, started receiving disgruntled late-night calls from Charles complaining about his scarce column inches when compared to the acres devoted to his wife. The prince retreated into the 'light' reading he had brought along – Turgenev's *First Love* and Jung's *Psychological Reflections*. They helped him, he wrote in a letter home, 'preserve my sanity and my faith when all is chaos, crowds, cameras, politicians, cynicism, sarcasm and intense scrutiny ...

'I do feel *desperate* for Diana,' he continued. 'There is no twitch she can make without these ghastly, and I'm quite convinced mindless, people photographing it ... What has got into them all? Can't they see further than the end of their noses and to what it is doing to her? How can anyone, let alone a 21-year-old, be expected to come out of all this obsessed and crazed attention unscathed?'

* * *

For the future head of Britain's most significant celebrity institution, Charles displayed a curious blindness to the realities of celebrity culture.

'Princess Superstar!' proclaimed the headlines. 'Without a doubt,' declared America's *Ladies' Home Journal*, 'she's the greatest media personality of the decade.' The princess, wrote one columnist, had scored 'a humdinger of a success' in a sceptical and potentially hostile atmosphere.

Almost single-handed, according to most commentators, Diana had saved Australia from becoming a republic – and if Charles did not get it, the young princess did. Finally she started to believe in herself.

'When we came back from our six-week tour,' she said later, 'I was a different person. I was more grown up, more mature … I learned to be royal, in inverted commas, in one week.'

Britain's left-wing *Daily Mirror*, not always an admirer of the monarchy, editorialised that Diana had done 'more for the Royalty she married into than other Princesses who were born into it'.

This was a less than subtle dig by the *Mirror* at Diana's sister-in-law Princess Anne, whose notorious frostiness seemed to grow a couple of degrees chillier whenever the subject of Diana came up. Aged thirty-one and a mother of two, Anne had been particularly unreceptive to the good news of William's arrival in June 1982, which had happened while she was in the American Southwest touring Indian reservations in New Mexico on behalf of Save the Children.

'I didn't know she had one,' the princess snapped when asked by one reporter about Diana's baby.

'Do you think everyone is making too much fuss of the baby?' asked another.

'Yes,' Anne replied shortly, moving on.

'Sweet as vinegar, cutting as a knife,' commented William Hickey in the *Daily Express*.

'Anne's behaviour,' said the *Mirror*, 'has confirmed for many Americans the stories that she is jealous of the adoration lavished on the Princess of Wales.'

There was a certain truth to this. In the early 1980s, the hard-working Anne was carrying out over two hundred engagements every year, compared to Diana's fifty or so – and an unimpressive ninety-plus for Charles.

'Anne works very hard,' explained one palace insider, 'and sees her sister-in-law picking up the glory. She's sick to the back teeth with it all.'

The conflict came into the open when it was time to choose the godparents for William. In 1977 Anne had invited Charles to be the godfather of her firstborn, Peter Phillips, but the prince did not return the compliment when it came to William – or, rather, according to rumour, he had very much wanted to invite his sister, only to be blocked by his wife. Diana had sensed the disdain of her no-nonsense sister-in-law, who was reported to find Diana 'gooey', and even to have labelled her 'the Dope'.

William's godparents were certainly not headline-catchers: the Queen's lady-in-waiting Susan Hussey, and cousin Alexandra of Kent; the Duchess of Westminster; Lord Romsey; the inevitable Laurens van der Post; and another of Charles's friends – Constantine II, the Hampstead-dwelling ex-king of Greece.

Prince Philip shrugged his shoulders at the roll call, assuming that the omission of Anne would be corrected next time round. But when Prince Harry appeared in the autumn of 1984, Anne would once again be omitted from the list – and the princess took it personally when she discovered that her younger brother Andrew had been selected from her siblings as a godparent for Harry, rather than herself. There was a former flatmate of Diana's, Carolyn Bartholomew; a wealthy polo-playing friend of Charles's, Gerald Ward; Princess Margaret's daughter, Lady Sarah Armstrong-Jones; a Gloucestershire neighbour, Celia Vestey; and the painter Bryan Organ, who had executed flattering portraits of both Diana and Charles – 'Yawns all round' was the press verdict on the list.

But Anne made her feelings obvious on the day. As the three-month-old Prince Henry Charles Albert David, third in line to the British throne, was being baptised at Windsor in the presence of the Queen, the Queen Mother, Philip and the rest of the royal family, there were two conspicuous absentees. His aunt Anne and her husband Captain Mark Phillips were out in the Gloucestershire countryside, eighty-five miles to the west, shooting rabbits. They had sent their children Peter, seven, and Zara, three, to the ceremony along with their apologies. But their shooting party, they explained, took precedence – it was a long-established date.

'Don't read a family row into it, for God's sake,' said Mark's mother Anne. 'The Princess and my son invited a party of 10 guns for a shoot three months ago. They decided it would be unfair to let these people down.'

* * *

Looking back three decades later from the twenty-first century, the 1984 row over Anne not being invited to become Harry's godmother seems neither here nor there. But just imagine if Anne *had* been serving as the prince's godmother in the years after the death of Diana in 1997. Would she not then have become the closest thing that Harry, twelve, had to a *real* mother?

In those tragic circumstances, Anne might well have operated alongside brother Charles as a more harmonious parental unit for Harry than anything the boy had previously known. The princess might be notorious for her prickly, shoulder-shrugging 'bolshie' mode, but this stemmed from an independence of mind that could see through the royal nonsense – harmonising with the reservations that Harry himself would come to feel about the values of royalty as he grew older.

Anne would certainly have been the one senior member of the royal family who was on the same wavelength as Harry as his disaffection with 'royalness' developed – and that disaffection was to grow so strong that he would take his own son across the Atlantic in order to escape the same fate. Would it have made any difference to this outcome if the prince had been under the godmotherly guidance of the 'Great Stroppy One' who successfully raised her own children, Peter and Zara, without titles and as non-royals?

Anne did manage to keep both of them living, for the most part, in Great Britain.

8

Bringing Up Babies

'She was our guardian, friend and protector . . .
Quite simply the best mother in the world.'

(Prince Harry, 31 August 2007)

'I think it's time we had one of *those* . . .'

Prince Charles was in London in the early 1980s on a 'walkabout', and as the prince said 'one of *those*', he was pointing down at the little daughter of the man in front of him. Charles had been delighted with Diana for producing a sturdy male heir within less than a year of marriage. Now he wanted a daughter to match, hoping to recreate the congenial brother–sister dynamic that he had always enjoyed with his own sister Anne.

Outside observers have tended to miss this – the closeness of Charles to his sister, deriving from her feisty companionship in a sometimes bleak childhood that was not over-supplied with fun. Anne's challenging tomboy-to-brother camaraderie contributed toughness to the havering-wavering Charles, rather as his father

Philip's decisive personality helped keep the cautious Queen on her toes.

When the prince had picked out Highgrove in Gloucestershire as his prospective family home before his marriage, people spotted that it was only fourteen miles from Camilla at Bolehyde Manor. But they failed to note that it was even closer to Anne's home at Gatcombe Park, which was just seven miles down the road. Charles and Anne were more of a team than people realised.

Diana respected this, and as her second pregnancy developed in the spring of 1984, she was by no means averse to the prospect of a daughter.

'She really didn't mind what she had,' recalls one of her girlfriends. 'And, yes, she did quite fancy having a little girl.'

But the hospital scans had told Diana otherwise. The photographs showed clearly that she was bearing another healthy son, and it was the measure of the princess's youth (twenty-three that July), her emotional inexperience and her distance from her much older husband (thirty-six that November) that she did not tell Charles straight away what the doctors had said.

These happened to be warm and rather close months in the Waleses' marriage – 'the closest,' the princess reported via Andrew Morton, 'we've ever, ever been' – and Diana was clearly scared of spoiling that. She did not want to disappoint her husband.

But the truth was the inescapable truth – and the baby's sex was not her fault in any way. What was the sense of not confiding in Charles and putting off his disappointment so that the problem would linger instead, lying in wait to surprise and sour what should have been the marvellous moment of birth? For surprise and sourness were certainly what happened inside the Lindo Wing on 15 September 1984 – in spades.

Diana later related her husband's horror at baby Harry's appearance.

'First comment was, "Oh God, it's a boy!"'

'Second comment, "And he's even got red hair!"'

By which the disappointed father presumably meant that the new arrival was not a nice, civilised Windsor, but an 'orrible sh*t-stirring Spencer along the lines of Diana's prickly (and red-haired) brother Charles.

'Diana told me that she just burst into tears,' recounts one of her confidantes. 'Instead of saying "What a sweet baby!" he did not praise her or thank her at all. He just sulked.'

In the photos of the couple leaving hospital with their new son, Charles does not even pretend to smile, and three months later at Harry's christening in December 1984, the frustrated father was still hanging on to his resentment, which he actually voiced to Frances, Diana's mother: 'I'm so disappointed,' complained the thwarted prince, 'I thought it would be a girl.'

The new baby's grandmother responded by snapping at her son-in-law's thoughtlessness. 'You should be thankful,' she retorted, 'that you had a child that was normal.'

'Ever since that day,' Diana said, 'the shutters have come down … That's what he does when he gets somebody answering back at him … It just went bang, our marriage – the whole thing went down the drain.'

By the end of 1984 Diana was also shutting him out. Someone had told her that Charles 'had gone back to his lady … Something inside me closed off.'

Despite the alarmingly premature erosion of their marriage, Charles and Diana worked very hard at being good parents. It was the one thing on which they totally agreed. Individually and as a couple, they wanted happiness for their sons.

Both father and mother had studied the childcare books. By the early 1980s Dr Benjamin Spock reigned supreme on both sides of the Atlantic with his emphasis on child-centred rearing.

'Every baby needs to be smiled at, talked to, played with, fondled, gently and lovingly – just as much as he needs vitamins and calories,' Spock had written in his bestselling *Common Sense Book of Baby and Child Care*. 'And the baby who doesn't get any loving will grow up cold and unresponsive.'

Prince Charles was a Spock-sceptic, disdaining what he regarded as 'these new-fangled ideas about parenthood'. But Diana felt quite the opposite. She even claimed some distant blood relationship with the famous educator, and St Mary's Lindo Wing boasted a few mini-Spocks of its own. The doctors went to some trouble to arrange with the royal couple how they would introduce the two-year-old William to his new baby brother in a positive and non-alienating fashion.

'It's important,' Diana told a nurse, 'that the first time William sees his brother, I'm holding him in my arms.'

Today the conventional wisdom is quite the contrary. Embracing the new baby is the very *worst* way to present a new child to a sibling, goes the modern orthodoxy, since it introduces the new arrival as a strange object that is physically blocking the older child from the maternal embrace that it craves. First hugging the older child is the twenty-first-century way, after which mother and child should turn together to look down on the newcomer in its crib – and, by happy chance, that is almost exactly what happened in the Lindo Wing in September 1984.

As soon as William arrived at the hospital and emerged from the lift with his father, he went scampering down the corridor, calling out for his mother. Startled, Diana's bodyguard knocked over the screen outside her door, which brought Diana jumping out of her bed to see what the commotion was – to look out of the door and see William running towards her.

The princess instantly and instinctively opened her arms to pick up her son with delight, kissing him and cuddling him – and it was therefore from the spontaneous embrace of his mother that William looked down to see his younger brother for the first time, swaddled in a white blanket. Jumping onto the floor, William rushed forward at once to plant a kiss on the baby's forehead, then sat on the bed and held the newborn warmly in his arms.

When the family went back to Kensington Palace, it was William who led the way in the presentation of the baby to the staff below stairs, smothering his little brother in kisses – though he did also attempt the odd headbutt on the new arrival. For years the world would be struck by the fondly possessive way in which young William liked to display his younger brother and show him off proudly – almost as his favourite toy. And it all started in the Lindo Wing from an episode of baby-and-child-care-gone-mildly-wrong. Don't knock the Spock.

The moment Diana had started producing children, Prince Charles felt quite sure that his wife needed a nanny to help her look after them, and he had no doubt who that nanny should be – Scottish-born Mabel Anderson who had looked after him as a child. Diana did not agree. She wanted to raise her children herself, and if she did turn to anyone for help, it would not be to Mrs Anderson who in 1982 was fifty-six years old, the same age as the Queen.

A compromise was reached, with Diana agreeing to the hiring of Barbara Barnes, the forty-two-year-old daughter of a Norfolk forestry worker. Ms Barnes did not wear a nanny's hat and uniform, but she had been recommended on the basis of fourteen years' loyal service to Princess Margaret's lady-in-waiting, Anne Glenconner, whose five children she had nursed with intelligence and care.

'I'm not a graduate of any sort of nannies' college,' said Barnes in her only brief contact with the press. 'I've accumulated my knowledge from many years of experience.' She might have added that as a grammar school graduate she had acquired mastery of Latin and Greek and could also speak very good French. She saw no special problems in bringing up a royal baby, she said – 'I treat all children as individuals … I'm here to help the princess, not take over.'

That turned out not to be the case, since Barnes rapidly discovered that she had to serve as nanny to her employer as much as to her offspring – though she had had some experience of this with Anne Glenconner's brilliantly crazed husband Colin, who was prone to dramatic outbursts and fits.

'Lord Glenconner,' Nanny Barnes would say firmly when she discovered him standing on the table stamping his feet and screaming at the top of his lungs. 'Will you get down and be quiet? You'll frighten the children.'

'And he did,' recalls Anne Glenconner. 'Just like that.'

The princess was by now suffering from bulimia and the accompanying self-harm that had reached the stage of her slashing her arms and wrists. Barnes soon found herself bandaging the princess's bloodied limbs – and she stepped in firmly to assert control.

'Barbara guarded the nursery floor like the Vatican,' one member of the Kensington Palace staff recounted to author Ingrid Seward. 'Trays would be grabbed and doors would be shut. It was her kingdom.'

Barnes was equally firm with the children, not allowing them comfort blankets and refusing them shoes until they had learned to walk properly. When they did get their first footwear, Nanny insisted on classic Start-Rites with button straps that were shaped to the boys' feet. Trainers were banned.

'She achieved the remarkable feat,' wrote Seward, 'of having both William and Harry sitting up straight before their first birthdays. They were made to say "Please" and "Thank you" almost as soon as they could talk.'

Within this social discipline, however, both William and, in due course, Harry were allowed extraordinary freedom. This was in accordance with Diana's liberal Spock-based ideas, which were shared by Barnes – whom William, and hence the whole family, called 'Baba'. With Charles proving to be an equally worshipping and indulgent parent, William became a law unto himself – loud and boisterous and earning the nickname 'His Royal Naughtiness' following his poor behaviour at his brother Harry's christening in December 1984. The little prince had wriggled continuously and rolled his eyes with real insolence towards his father when he was not allowed to cuddle his baby brother.

It was part of a pattern. William had developed the habit of sticking out his tongue at people as well as wielding his water pistol with gay abandon – squirting at least one guard at Highgrove who remained standing obediently at attention until he was soaked through. The prince also enjoyed a phase of pinching female backsides, starting with his mother who, in those less politically correct times, encouraged the practice with squeals of laughter, so that William moved on to maids at Kensington Palace and Highgrove who, like the helpless sentry, did not feel they could protest.

The Queen, however, was another matter. Her Majesty was not amused by her grandson's noisiness, which got worse as Harry became old enough to join in – with fighting, crying and boisterous running around whenever they came to stay at Windsor, Sandringham or Balmoral. It was poor behaviour that she did not expect of her grandchildren. Elizabeth II made some enquiries and was particularly horrified to learn that one of William's favourite lines ran: 'When *I* am king, I'm going to make a new rule that …'

'You really must do something, Charles,' the Queen said to her son. 'The boys need discipline. Perhaps a new nanny is in order.'

Barnes shrugged her shoulders when it reached her ears that the Queen herself felt William was getting 'a little bit out of control'.

'His behaviour was only natural for a boy in front of his grandmother,' she said to a fellow member of staff. 'What was she expecting, for God's sake, a mini Prince Charles?'

The dishevelled rock star and human rights activist Bob Geldof did not mince his words when confronted by the young prince's rudeness at Kensington Palace in the summer of 1985. Geldof had come to see Charles to discuss the preparations for his forthcoming Live Aid concert at Wembley, and William, barely three years old, was frustrated not to be receiving his father's full attention.

'Why do you have to talk to that man?' he asked Charles.

'Because we all have work to do,' replied the prince.

'He's all dirty,' said William.

'Shut up, you horrible little boy,' said Geldof.

'He's got scruffy hair and wet shoes,' continued William.

'Don't be rude,' said Charles in a vain fatherly attempt at discipline. 'Run along and play.'

'Your hair's scruffy too,' said Geldof in his own attempt at a final word.

'No, it's not,' responded William. 'My mummy brushed it.'

* * *

Harry just adored his elder brother. He looked up to 'Wills' – another of William's family nicknames – and he responded willingly to being treated as his brother's favourite toy. Both Charles and Diana were keen that their sons should mix with 'ordinary children' – those of friends both inside and outside the palace. But when playing with outsiders the two brothers usually still operated as a unit. They were encouraged by their parents to love each other and to express their love – and they did.

'William spends the entire time pouring an endless supply of hugs and kisses onto Harry,' reported Diana, 'and we are hardly allowed near.'

Nanny Barnes picked up and strengthened the family ethos of brotherliness. Both boys tended to wake with the dawn, so she would bring them into her bed most mornings to romp and play together, before giving them their breakfast and passing them on to their parents when they woke.

Diana would then take over if she did not have work to do, but with her pregnancies behind her and by then moving into her middle twenties, her time was more and more occupied by the charities and humanitarian causes for which she would become famous. She also had an increasingly active social life, meeting girlfriends (boyfriends would come later) to discuss the deteriorating state of her marriage, and she continued to accompany Charles on his major foreign tours. Diana, Princess of Wales was the British monarchy's number-one international selling point and the Prince of Wales was not going to miss out on the benefit of that when he travelled.

All this meant that Nanny Barnes spent more and more time with the boys, and she *did* become something of a surrogate mother, particularly to William who had been her solitary charge for two years before the appearance of Harry. She taught the boys to walk and talk and read. She comforted them when they woke crying in the night. She chose their clothes as well as their shoes.

In the absence of their parents, 'Baba' even took her charges away on their own 'family' holiday – to Scotland and the Scilly Isles, where she set the agenda every day as any mother would. As one observer admiringly put it, the two princes 'sailed from house to house under Nanny's calm captaincy'.

But less admiring observers felt that Barnes was getting too possessive with 'her' boys and the princess came to share that suspicion. 'It almost got to the stage where Diana felt she had to make an appointment to see her sons,' said deputy nanny Olga Powell, 'and she wasn't having any of that.'

Matters came to a head at the end of 1986, when Barnes took a holiday to attend the birthday party of her former employer, the ever-flamboyant Lord Glenconner, on his Caribbean island of Mustique. There the nanny was photographed alongside celebrities like Raquel Welch and Princess Margaret – to the intense irritation of Diana, who was a long-time addict of the gossip pages and did not expect to find her nanny sanctified in the hallowed columns of Nigel Dempster, the *Daily Mail*'s irrepressible diarist.

Baba had got above herself, Diana decided, and she made that clear when the nanny returned to work. During the Sandringham Christmas break of 1986–7, Barnes resumed her duties and daily routine with the boys as usual, but Diana cold-shouldered her to the point of frostiness, sharing scarcely a word until the family got back to Highgrove, where Diana brusquely informed her that it would be 'better', as she put it, if Barnes departed.

'One weekend she just wasn't there any more,' recalled Highgrove housekeeper Wendy Berry. Diana had given instructions that the nanny's bags should be packed ahead of time, and that all trace of her be removed. 'No one saw her again.'

It is not known how Baba's abrupt disappearance was explained to the boys by Diana – who had by this date quite a roster of dismissals to her credit, having successfully sacked several dozen members of staff, according to housekeeper Berry. Now Nanny had joined the club. Surrogate mother to Prince William for over four years and to Prince Harry for more than two, Baba Barnes had not been allowed to say the slightest word of farewell to her charges. She was forbidden even to send them a postcard. She just vanished into thin air.

Following the death of Diana in 1997, people remarked on how well the two princes William and Harry reacted to the unjust and unexpected removal of a mother figure from their lives – surprised, bewildered and tragically distraught though they were. Ten years earlier, they had had a little practice.

9

Entitlement

'To a certain respect, we will never be normal ...'

(Prince William, June 2007)

After the birth of Prince Harry in September 1984, Diana and Charles moved into separate bedrooms – and stayed there. The much-celebrated dynastic alliance of 1981, the future of the British monarchy, had lasted less than four years in the same marital bed. There were occasional happy flurries when the freeze thawed, particularly on working trips abroad when their hosts allocated them joint quarters. But this ended in February 1987 on the Waleses' tour of Portugal.

Diana had clapped her hands with delight in Lisbon's Queluz Palace when she was shown her bed, a romantic four-hundred-year-old four-poster that, as she later told one of her staff, was 'made to be shared' – until she realised that her husband had been shown to a separate room. It was the result, she was told, of a request that had come 'via' Buckingham Palace.

Diana would both bemoan and joke about the bedroom boycott with her girlfriends. Perhaps she should try to get Charles drunk one evening, she suggested, in the hope of encouraging a bit of princely 'leg-over'. Oh no, they would respond, you know what happens to the vital organ under the influence of too much alcohol – brewer's droop!

'How about turning down the lights and wearing a blonde wig?' asked one of them. 'That way he might mistake you for Camilla!'

Diana roared with laughter. After time and some rueful reflection, she had come to accept the reality of her husband's 'lady' in his life. Her coping strategy – in these early stages, at least – was to address the new vision that she was developing of her princessly role, and to concentrate on her sons and the responsibility she felt to care for them as a new kind of hands-on royal mother. As Diana's life went awry she created a new 'family' life around friends like psychotherapist Julia Samuel and Rosa Monckton, the wife of Dominic Lawson, editor of the *Spectator* and the *Sunday Telegraph* in these years, as well as Annabel Goldsmith, with whose children Zac, Ben and Jemima the two boys loved to play down at the Goldsmiths' Ormeley home in Richmond. William and Harry were the future – whatever mess she and Charles might make of the present.

Early in the 1990s Prince Charles commissioned an authorised version of his first forty years by the distinguished broadcaster and journalist Jonathan Dimbleby, who was granted special access to close friends and members of the family, including

Prince Philip. Dimbleby was given sight of Charles's personal letters, along with long hours of interviews with the prince himself. Published in the midst of raging controversy about the state of the Waleses' marriage, the object of the exercise was to rehabilitate Charles as both heir and husband.

In this latter respect the book sought to portray the prince as a man who had been totally 'loyal to his wife and faithful to his marriage vows'. Dimbleby claimed that Charles had had no improper contact with Camilla Parker Bowles during his first five years with Diana, turning to Camilla only when he 'reached the point of desperation' in the belief that his marriage had 'irretrievably broken down'. This was sometime late in 1986, noted Dimbleby. Until then, he wrote, Charles and Camilla 'had not talked to each other at all ... She had been wholly excluded from his life.'

Well, this was 'apart from the one occasion before the wedding, when he gave her the "farewell" bracelet,' wrote Dimbleby, and yes, admittedly, 'he had seen her fleetingly at occasional social gatherings'. Then there had been 'a few telephone conversations' during the engagement, and then 'one after his marriage (when he rang to report that the princess was pregnant with William) ...'

'Methinks,' as Shakespeare's Queen Gertrude remarked to Hamlet, the gentleman 'doth protest too much' – and most outside experts agree. Of the 'top twelve' distinguished writers or teams of writers who have examined the details of Charles and Diana's marriage in the early 1980s, only three unequivocally support Charles's claim of solid, five-year fidelity. And one of those is Dimbleby. So that leaves nine not believing that Camilla was 'wholly excluded from his life'.*

What did Prince Charles say at the time of his engagement to Diana? – '*Whatever* "in love" means'?

And what did Diana overhear her husband say to Camilla on the phone in his bath? '*Whatever* happens, I will always love you.'

Perhaps the truth can be found in the meaning and the message of those two very different 'whatevers' … Or in that conversation about the cufflinks with the intertwined Cs that Charles chose to wear on his honeymoon.

'Camilla gave you those, didn't she?' Diana asked.

'So what's wrong?' responded Charles. 'They're a present from a friend.'

This is where we go back to Jonathan Dimbleby for what is certainly the *emotional* truth. 'In Camilla Parker Bowles,' wrote Dimbleby, 'the Prince found the warmth, the understanding and the steadiness for which he had always longed *and had never been able to find with any other person*.' (Italics added.)

Charles did *not* love his wife, in other words, in the way that

---

* Dimbleby's supporters are Gyles Brandreth, and the writer–TV producer team of Tim Clayton and Phil Craig – see bibliography for details of their books, along with those of the authors who follow. The nine disbelievers, with the years from which they date Charles's infidelity, are: Christopher Andersen (1982), Anthony Holden (1982), Christopher Wilson (1982), Tina Brown (1982 or 1983 or 1986), Sally Bedell Smith (1982 or 1986), Sarah Bradford (1983), Andrew Morton (1984), James Whitaker (1984), Kitty Kelley (1985).

he truly loved his mistress. Maritally his mind and his heart had always been unfaithful.

And what about that 'wholly excluded' lady? According to Stuart Higgins, a royal correspondent in the 1980s and later editor of the *Sun*, Camilla Parker Bowles provided him with regular off-the-record briefings about the state of the royal marriage from 1982 to 1992.

'I talked to her once a week for ten years,' Higgins told Sally Bedell Smith in 1999. 'I talked to her about Diana and Charles. She guided me on things that were not true, or things that were off the beam. Everything was behind closed doors and I didn't write about her, although I spoke to her all the time during that period. I didn't sense that she and Charles were out of touch.'

So starting in 1982, the year following Charles and Diana's wedding, Charles's future wife dispensed royal nudges and whispers to one of Britain's top tabloid reporters in return for his keeping her name out of the papers.

The indefatigable James Whitaker and his binoculars bore witness to the state of the royal marriage in the summer of 1986, shortly after brother Andrew had married Sarah Ferguson – 'Fergie' – drawing popular and romantic attention away from the Waleses for some moments of relief. After the Andrew–Ferguson wedding Charles and Diana took the boys, then four and nearly two, on a bucket-and-spade holiday on the island of Majorca, staying with Spain's King Juan Carlos on board the *Fortuna*, his royal yacht.

'When we pulled into one of the tiny, idyllic bays,' wrote Whitaker, 'the royal party had no idea we were nearby. I stayed below deck out of sight and watched what was occurring on the *Fortuna* for the next five hours. It was illuminating ... Not once during the lengthy period did Charles or Diana sit anywhere near one another – let alone speak. When he came up from his air-conditioned quarters to go windsurfing, she walked off in the opposite direction. When she went diving off the back of the boat, he deliberately looked the other way. They read, they sunbathed, they chatted to others, but never once did they address a single word to each other.

'I watched through my field-glasses, completely mesmerised. I had heard the stories, listened to the excuses, hoped that what I had been told was exaggerated or wrong. But clearly it wasn't. The five-year-old marriage, I was forced to conclude, was dead.'

So from the ages of four and two, William and Harry grew up in the care of two parents who were not sharing the same bed, who were more inclined to talk to the press than to each other, and who were also engaging in patterns of systematic deceit. Maybe Diana had not been unfaithful by this date, but she was definitely developing plans in that direction, and she had come to accept the fact that her husband was already doing the same – that the essence of their marriage was a lie.

Barbara Barnes's successor as the two young princes' nanny, Ruth Wallace, lasted only three years in the job. Both boys adored her: Harry called her Nanny 'Roof'. But her closeness to the brothers was not enough – Nanny 'Roof' simply could not stand the ever more bitter warfare between their parents, which, according to different sources, she described as 'difficult to deal with', 'too unpleasant' – or, in one word, 'toxic'. Booking herself a long voyage of recovery up the Amazon in 1989, the nanny would hand in her notice and shake off the poison of the palace. William and Harry could not.

In 1985 Diana's beloved Dr Spock brought out a new edition of his *Baby and Child Care* handbook for parents intended to reflect the new domestic challenges of the times – and prominent among them were marital disagreements that could lead to separation and divorce.

'Most separations and divorces,' wrote Spock, 'involve two people who have become very angry at each other.'

That was unquestionably the case with Diana and Charles, according to Wendy Berry, their housekeeper at Highgrove, where, by the late 1980s, the prince was insisting on spending more and more time.

'I hate you, Charles, I fucking hate you,' Diana screamed at her husband during one confrontation, according to Berry.

'I hate you, Papa. I hate you so much,' William added to the chorus on another occasion, shouting at his father, 'Why do you make Mummy cry all the time?'

Still not ten years old, William was already establishing the pattern of open disdain and aggression towards his father that would mark his early adult life – but more of that later.

The young prince had picked up his nicknames of 'Basher Wills' or 'Billy the Basher' when he joined Mrs Jane Mynors' Nursery School in Notting Hill, not far from Kensington Palace, in September 1985. Noisy, cheeky and defiant of discipline, Wills soon angered his classmates by pushing his way to the front of the dinner queue and getting involved in playground fights. He felt entitled …

'My daddy can beat up your daddy,' he would say. 'My daddy's the Prince of Wales.'

'Basher' went public in the summer of 1986 in Westminster Abbey as a pageboy at the marriage of Uncle Andrew to Sarah Ferguson. After dragging his cousin Laura Fellowes, six, a bridesmaid, down the aisle, the four-year-old 'fidgeted throughout the ceremony', according to Penny Junor, 'rolled his order of service into a trumpet, scratched his head, covered his face with his fingers, poked his tongue out at Laura, and left the Abbey with his sailor hat wildly askew'.

'William's very enthusiastic about things,' explained Diana who was reluctant, like her husband, to be judgemental of their boisterous elder son and heir. 'He pushes himself right into it.'

With neither parent keen to play the disciplinarian, it was left to Nanny Ruth to try to administer some correction. In the autumn of 1987 she yanked the five-year-old home from a birthday party following a tantrum when he had not been allowed to blow out the candles on the cake and had expressed his displeasure by throwing sandwiches and ice-cream around the room. Nanny made him clean up the mess before he left.

By that same autumn of 1987 reports of William's bad behaviour had spread so widely that *Spitting Image*, the satirical TV show, included the five-year-old among its grotesque puppets of the royal family. A juvenile William puppet, dressed in combat gear and armed with a knife and machine gun, was shown wildly attacking a meek and submissive Harry, then just three.

Diana referred obliquely to the issue of her two sons' 'different temperaments' in an interview that year. 'Harry is quieter and just watches,' she said. 'No. 2 skates in quite nicely. But the bad luck about being No. 1 is trial and error, so we're open-minded about William.'

No. 1 and No. 2 … Here was the heart of the problem. Charles and Diana had never hidden from William his future destiny as king – and by being sent to Mrs Mynors' Nursery he had been perversely reminded of this when he was only three. The idea had been that by mixing with 'ordinary' children, the young prince should become more ordinary himself, but the opposite seemed to occur. Everyone from staff to dinner ladies – and not least the other children – knew exactly who William was, and had treated him accordingly, even though they had been told to do otherwise.

When is the right moment to tell an infant that he is destined to be king? Prince Charles had found out at no particular age. 'It's something that dawns on you with the most ghastly inexorable sense,' he said on his twenty-first birthday.

More recently, Prince William and his wife Kate have decided that they would *not* broach the 'king' subject with their firstborn Prince George until a controlled moment of their choice – reflecting William's unhappiness at the haphazard fashion in which the whole business of his royal destiny had buzzed around his head from the start.

'Royal firstborns may get all the glory,' said Diana in one interview, 'but second-borns enjoy more freedom. Only when Harry is a lot older will he realise how lucky he is not to have been the eldest.'

She made a careful point, with Charles's full agreement, that the two boys should be photographed together as equals as much as possible – then sabotaged that by giving interviews in which she dwelt invidiously upon the difference between the heir and the spare.

Out of this mess, however, and after the missteps of his early years, Prince William came to locate positive strength in the knowledge of his weird and formidable destiny. As the rows between his parents intensified; as he wept and shouted at his father; as he found himself taking his mother's side – pushing paper tissues under her bathroom door on one occasion because he could hear her sobbing inside; as he tried to make sense of why the two parents whom he loved no longer loved each other, William came to find consolation in the idea that he would one day be 'king'.

He also found strength in that idea. Many little boys fantasise more or less consciously about brandishing the unimaginable powers of a super wizard or a pirate chief. Well, William really was going to be a king and when that day came, he would be able to exercise the authority that he could already observe his grandmother and father enjoying.

This observation seems to have given the young prince the strength he needed to endure the pain and confusion that any child would feel as his family crumbled around him – the fantasy became William's remedy. 'To young children,' wrote Dr Spock in 1985, 'the world consists of the family which to them is mainly father and mother. To suggest breaking up the family is like suggesting the end of the world.'

By the autumn of 1988, the six-year-old William, dressed in a grey and red uniform and cap, was entering his second full year at the Wetherby Pre-Preparatory School in Notting Hill, and people noticed a new cautiousness about the young prince – a greater sense of control and certainly less elbowing entitlement, with no more complaints about him barging to the head of the dinner line.

The year before, when William had started at Wetherby, was the time when Prince Charles himself had admitted that his marriage had 'irretrievably broken down' and that he had resumed his full-scale intimacy with Camilla. Highgrove housekeeper Wendy Berry got used to seeing Mrs Parker Bowles's car coming up the drive on a Sunday evening soon after Diana had left for London with the boys – and Diana herself was pursuing the same pattern. By 1988 she had started her five-year love affair with Guards officer James Hewitt, who was giving her riding lessons – as well as the boys. The marital deadness observed by James Whitaker on the summer holiday deck of the *Fortuna* had become the reality of the Waleses' everyday London–Highgrove family life.

As the elder brother, William's response to all this had been to grow up very quickly. An intelligent boy, earning good grades at Wetherby, he had begun applying that intelligence to his own life. The trauma of his parents' marriage had matured him early, forcing him to abandon the egotism of infancy and to develop a precocious sense of duty that he applied to

"It's TUESDAY! Your nights are Monday,
Wednesday and Friday."

Charles Griffin, *Daily Mirror*, 1992

his love and support for his distressed mother – but which would also play a role in his vision of himself as a future monarch.

Duty – service to others – is the essence of '*rex iustus*', the just and virtuous king. 'Good King Wenceslas' (AD 911–935) was considered a saint because he went out in the freezing snow around Prague on the Feast of Stephen, the festive day following Christmas Day, when everyone else at court was feasting, in order to help a poor man who was gathering winter fuel.

The once-rambunctious William was becoming more reflective. As he prepared to leave home behind for the challenges of boarding school in the autumn of 1990, the formerly swaggering eight-year-old was a noticeably quiet character – definitely intro-verted. But considering his family crisis and the future destiny that he now took so seriously, the young prince had a lot to be introverted about.

Prince Harry, meanwhile, was moving in quite the opposite direction. Ken Wharfe, bodyguard to Diana and the two boys in the late 1980s, recalls a telling incident when the family were travelling from London to Highgrove for the weekend. According to Wharfe, Harry and his brother got embroiled in an argument in the back seat of the car, with their nanny vainly seeking to referee the dispute.

'You'll be king one day,' said the four-year-old Harry. 'I won't. So I can do what I want.'

'Where the hell did he get that from?' asked Diana.

If the future King William V was already coming to appreciate and act upon his destiny, so was his younger brother. Welcome to Harry the Hellraiser – the don't-give-a-fuck, apparently life-long 'spare'. The meek and submissive 'sweet-natured, shy thumb-sucker' was no more.

So who was now the king of the castle? And who the dirty rascal? The stresses and strains of their parents' marriage had generated in William and Harry a massive and deeply meaning-ful character switch.

10

Exposure

'She had such warmth, she wanted to make people feel special. She realised she was in a unique position and could make people smile and feel better about themselves.'

(Prince William, 22 August 2017)

When James Whitaker, tabloid king of the royal rat pack, sadly set down his field glasses in Majorca in 1986 and privately pronounced his 'death sentence' on the marriage of the Prince and Princess of Wales, he did not, of course, make his thoughts public. The reporter's verdict was based on the couple's apathetic behaviour towards each other on the king of Spain's yacht that summer, but at the time Whitaker filed only a mild and politely questioning story for the *Daily Mirror* – 'Are Charles and Di Still in Tune?'

For the next five and a half years, the flow of Whitaker's lively Charles and Diana narrative would remain consistently breathless and upbeat – like that of every other Fleet Street newspaper.

The Waleses were Britain's best export by far – and if some inside 'sources' whispered to their press contacts that the royal couple had been screaming at each other or were actually sleeping in separate cabins, well, that was not a topic for the front page then, or for any page. It did not make commercial sense to cast serious doubt on the glamorous happiness of this glamorous couple and their two glamorously growing sons. The Waleses sold newspapers. Charles, Di, Wills and Harry were Fleet Street's most reliable good news story in tough Thatcherite times, and the palace's media minders made sure that it stayed that way.

'Look, you guys,' rasped Diana's rough, gruff Australian press officer Vic Chapman at the Majorca media briefing in 1986, 'for Crissakes remember the rules. You don't go out and write *anything*. Otherwise that's it.'

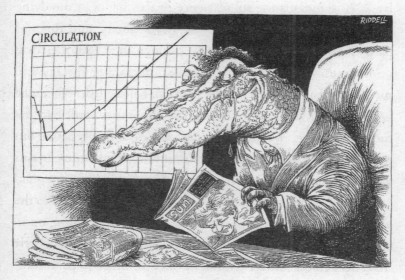

Press 'sympathy' for 'Lady Di'. Chris Riddell, *Observer*, 1996

'That's it' meant no more access to photo opportunities, along with the drying-up of hints as to when you might steal a quick exclusive of Diana buying shoes along the King's Road or taking the boys to Thorpe Park.

'Vic did that sort of "dangling the carrot" the whole time,' recalled the photographer Jayne Fincher. 'He instilled this thing where "If you break the rules ... you will not be getting what I'm planning in three months."'

The jovial Whitaker had to console himself with jokes. When he and some fellow rats managed to persuade the courteous King Juan Carlos to accept their offer to join them for drinks at the Palma Yacht Club, they could celebrate a new nickname for the Spanish monarch – 'Juan for the road'.

By 2020 standards the subservience of the media in the dying days of the Waleses' marriage was extraordinary, and this was partly a matter of changing times. Through the 1980s there was no Internet, which meant no Twitter, Instagram or Facebook to spread scandal – or some muted, barroom half-whisper of scandal – around the world within seconds. The palaces still had the media where they wanted them, with the royal family acting out their allotted parts beneath the proscenium arch whose curtains were strictly controlled by the likes of Victor Chapman.

But on 6 August 1991 the World Wide Web went live to the world. William was then just nine and Harry was coming up to seven. As teenagers and adults they would become the first 'Internet Princes', whose natural instinct would be to communicate with each other, their people and the world via email or SMS text message. Roneo-stencilled press releases would become antiques for them – relics of a bygone paper age. By the turn of the century the two boys would be beavering away on their portable laptops. Then in 2002 Nokia would make it possible for everyone to take photos on their mobile phones. You could become your own paparazzo!

In the early 1990s, however, the old certainties and constraints still prevailed – and there was another, human element to Fleet Street's unfaltering reverence. Most people, and even cynical journalists, still believed that, for all their faults, the royal family behaved to a special standard – that Windsor folk were a superior brand of person who somehow managed to live their lives with extra dignity and class. While a prince might nurse a secret mistress for a decade, for example, he could never possibly nurse fantasies of burrowing up inside her like a Tampax.

But we are getting ahead of ourselves …

The proscenium arch began to crumble in February 1992 thanks to the revelations of a lady who was quite a revelation in herself. Lady Colin Campbell, born 'intersex' in 1949, grew up a boy but had corrective surgery to 'confirm her female status' at the age of twenty-one – George had become Georgie, a glamorous blonde with a wonderfully husky voice who embraced everybody as 'Dawling!' She briefly married Lord Colin Campbell, the younger son of the Duke of Argyll, from whom she parted after just fourteen months, settling in 'fashionable Belgravia' in the 1980s just as the rumours were gathering steam about the problems in the Waleses' marriage.

Lady Colin's rented apartment in Cundy Street was in the same block of flats in which Camilla and Lucia Santa Cruz had started off their London lives – it was where Charles and Camilla had met, in fact. Cundy Street was bed-sit land for the well-connected – and Lady Colin used her connections to great effect.

Jealous fits, bulimia and manipulative behaviour on Diana's part, together with a succession of handsome young male 'confidants' and an empty marriage that was a sham – Georgie picked up all the suggestive rumours that were doing the rounds about the Princess of Wales, and she set them down boldly in her book *Diana in Private*, sensationally serialised in the *Sun* in March 1992, in contravention of Fleet Street's unspoken agreement to keep shtum about royal negatives. By strange coincidence, the acting editor of the paper when it published this markedly pro-Charles and anti-Diana material – 'Marriage Hell of Di' – was Camilla's weekly phone contact, Stuart Higgins.

Lady Colin's allegations caused a storm and the portrait she painted of Diana's less positive side was essentially accurate. But the truth was mingled with elements of sheer fantasy – the rumour, for example, that the princess's former bodyguard and alleged lover Barry Mannakee had been bumped off by MI5 in a motorcycle accident.

But it was not so easy to undermine the credentials of the next author to 'reveal the truth' about the Waleses' marriage. Tough and serious, Andrew Morton (thirty-nine, Leeds Grammar School, Sussex University) was a freelance journalist who had penned some insightful articles on the royals for the *Sunday*

Times. His writing had caught the eye of Dr James Colthurst, an Irish-born surgeon who was Diana's homeopathic and semi-spiritual advisor, and when Colthurst heard that Morton was starting on a biography of Diana, he suggested that the princess should collaborate. The doctor became the go-between.

Using the pseudonym of 'Noah', Morton would send a list of questions to which Diana would tape-record answers. The idea was that his real name should never cross her lips so she would be able to say, hand on heart, that she had never met or even spoken to this man who had decided to write a book about her on his own initiative. Morton later recalled picking up the first tape of the princess's answers to his questions and listening to it in a transport café.

'All around,' he said, 'everyone's eating bacon and eggs chatting away, and I put these headphones on and turn on the tape recorder and listen to Diana talking about "bulimia nervosa", which I'd never heard of, talking about her suicide attempts, talking about this woman called Camilla Parker Bowles. It was like entering a parallel universe – I walked out of that café thinking, Wow, what on earth have I heard? … It was the most incredible outburst of really innermost pain. Rage, frustration, anger – you were swept away with it.'

Morton transcribed it all – dynamite! When a few selected Fleet Street grandees were shown extracts from the text, they could not believe what they were reading. Morton had to produce sworn affidavits from friends like Diana's former flatmate Carolyn Bartholomew before the *Sunday Times* would agree to serialise the book – to be called *Diana: Her True Story* – as well as give assurances that the message had been checked and approved at a higher level. 'You can treat this book,' Morton assured Stuart Higgins of the *Sun*, who had negotiated for subsidiary rights, 'as though she has signed every page.'

Double dynamite!

When Prince Charles read the *Sunday Times* extracts that were faxed to him at Highgrove early on the morning of Sunday, 7 June 1992, he said he could hear Diana herself speaking. The staff, who had sneaked quick glances at the fax machine, were amazed at his calm.

'In the staff areas,' remembered housekeeper Wendy Berry, 'everyone spoke in a hushed whisper, not sure what to say or do. Several ... loyally declared they would never read the book or buy the *Sunday Times* again. But, of course, as the day continued, others made excuses to go out and buy copies of the paper secretly.'

Diana had brought Harry out from London for the weekend, and she finished breakfast early, leaving Charles at the table with his photocopied extracts and their weekend guests, whom Charles took for a courteous walk in the gardens. He then went straight upstairs to the princess's room, carrying the incriminating faxes with him. Within minutes Diana came running down the stairs and out of the house, her face flushed and her eyes brimming with tears, heading back to London with the bewildered Harry.

Seven-year-old Harry was on his own because William, by now approaching his tenth birthday, had started at boarding

Michael Cummings, *Daily Express*, 1996

school nearly two years before. One of the few things on which Charles and Diana had agreed in these troubled times was that Ludgrove, a small family-run boys' prep school set in 120 acres of Berkshire countryside, was the ideal spot for their two sons to begin boarding school, which they would attend between the ages of eight and thirteen. Ludgrove had a tradition of two head-masters working side by side in tandem with their wives in a pastoral fashion that sought to encourage a communal, family ethos.

The school acknowledged that homesickness was a particular challenge to the small boys who were just arriving – 'and if they are homesick,' explains current headmaster Simon Barber, 'there's a massive support network from their own peer group and the adult population.'

Parental separation, divorce and the entire trauma of broken homes provided another focus. Ludgrove made counselling available, and put an emphasis on activities to keep the boys busy – a nine-hole golf course, squash courts, a swimming pool, a music block, art, ceramics, clay-pigeon shooting and a garden plot where each boy could grow his own flowers or vegetables.

'They haven't got the concern about what's going on at home,' explains Barber, 'because they can immerse themselves in what's going on here. It can be easier to be here than at home with all the anguish.'

Another Ludgrove tradition was to keep the boys in touch with the outside world via a daily delivery of newspapers, with current affairs discussed every morning and a test every Saturday. But on 7 June 1992, mysteriously, the Sunday newspapers did not get delivered to Ludgrove School – and there were to be a few other occasions when the headmaster and his wife had to pretend there had been supply problems. They were keen to protect William, as much as possible, from the distress of having to see the story of his parents' failing marriage occupying the front pages.

Here was the new challenge for both William and, to a lesser extent, Harry from 1992 onwards. For the past seven or eight years they had had to experience the pain of their parents' mutual dislike and now the two boys had to cope with this conflict going public, appearing in every lurid detail on television screens and newspaper front pages – with an added dimension. What had appeared in the *Sunday Times* on 7 June that year was more than simple newspaper reporting. It was a deliberate and aggressive exposure of the family's bad blood that had been initiated, shaped and actively promoted by Diana.

The parent who claimed to be so devoted to her children and personally caring of them had had months to think about the effect on them of these revelations – secrets she had never told them yet was now sharing with the world. She had effectively revealed to William, for example: 'I tried to kill us both when I was pregnant with you inside me by throwing myself down the stairs.'

Her True Story was Diana's ultimate weapon in her battle with Charles – a dagger unsheathed, sharpened and aimed quite deliberately at her husband's heart. So if William and Harry felt pain from what the *Sunday Times* revealed to the world in the summer of 1992, that agony had been devised and inflicted upon them by their mother.

11
Camillagate

'Have you no shame?'

(Crowd shout to Prince Charles, early 1993)

'Noah', transport cafés and hush-hush tapes ... The secrets of Diana's collaboration in the creation of Andrew Morton's *Diana: Her True Story* were soon revealed. The public furore led to pressure being put on her friends in a way that she had not anticipated – and particularly on her close friends who had signed affidavits, like her former flatmate Carolyn Bartholomew.

From the moment of the book's sensational serialisation of 7 June 1992, Kensington Palace and Buckingham Palace had been insisting that it was a pack of lies. There might be some small discord inside the royal marriage, conceded the loyalists – these things happen in any marriage – but in no way could this resemble the lurid and tragic mess that had been described. It could only mean that the so-called 'friends' like Bartholomew who had provided material to Morton were liars.

Over the course of the next few days, the pressure shifted heavily onto Diana as Prince Charles, Buckingham Palace – and, it was made clear, the Queen herself – and even John Major in Downing Street were all looking to the princess to distance herself from her friends. She must issue a statement making clear that she disavowed them and all the untruths that they had uttered in Morton's pages.

On the evening of Wednesday 10 June the photographer Ken Lennox of the *Daily Mirror* received a phone call at his Chelsea home. He should head round the corner at once to Carolyn Bartholomew's house, he was told, to be waiting outside at nine o'clock.

'So I shot round there,' recalled Lennox, 'got into the street, parked my car at the top of the street, and ran down, and there was a detective waiting for me who I recognised. And he said, "Can you do your shots from here, Ken?" Which was forty yards away from the front door. And I said, "Yes." So he said, "I'll leave you here and I'll go back and sit in the car."'

At precisely 9 p.m. Carolyn Bartholomew's front door opened as promised.

'Diana stepped out, looked up at me, turned round,' recounted Lennox, commenting later on her punctuality.

'Carolyn came to the door and out onto the front step carrying her baby, with her husband. Diana kissed Carolyn on both cheeks, kissed the baby and kissed Carolyn's husband, looked up to see if I was shooting, walked to the car, got in the car … and looked at me all the way up the street as she drove towards me, giving me a full chance to get more photographs.'

The striking images of Diana's kiss and supportive embrace of her friend Carolyn Bartholomew went round the world the next day. The message was unambiguous. Everything that the Princess of Wales's friends had said to Andrew Morton was true and had her blessing.

Princes William and Harry have never spoken publicly about their parents' catastrophic marriage and the impact that it had upon their feelings and emotional stability. In the twenty-first century the brothers have both become fervent crusaders for mental health. Both have testified movingly about their own psychological pain, talking quite graphically of the mental dislocations they have suffered in the past.

But the pain and the past that they describe is largely related – if and when they agree to give any source for it – to the early death of their mother. Virtually nothing before that. It is as if Diana's death in 1997 provides them with an alibi and a cut-off point. That is when the psychological trouble started, according to what the princes say now – when William was fifteen and Harry was twelve. All their youthful heartache and subsequent mental health problems are dated from that August tragedy in Paris – judging, at least, from the solid examples that they have been willing to provide.

And that is their right. Whatever William and Harry may have confided about events before that, and particularly about the cruel suffering and tragedies of their parents' marriage, to each other, to their families, or to the several therapists that we know they have consulted – that's all private stuff. *Their* business …

*   *   *

Let us move on. The next parental embarrassments to send the two boys cringing mentally behind the bicycle sheds did not, at least, stem from deliberate intention on their parents' part. They were cock-ups, the simple consequence of mindless idiocy – plus a good helping of adulterous animal lust.

In the late 1980s amateur radio enthusiasts – wireless 'hams' – would amuse themselves by listening in to people's private telephone conversations with the aid of a portable radio scanner that you could buy for a few hundred pounds at any Currys or RadioShack-style store. In earlier decades the hams had tended to eavesdrop on police or air traffic control exchanges, but the growing popularity of the new mobile phones offered more inviting targets, like people talking to each other about sex.

By January 1990 Fleet Street was sitting on two such tapes that hams had plucked out of the ether, transferred to tape and sold to rival newspapers for undisclosed sums of money. On one, Prince Charles could be heard burbling various sexual innuendos and complaints to a woman who sounded like Camilla. On the other, Diana could be heard also indulging in sexually suggestive conversation with a man who referred to her affectionately as 'Squidge' or 'Squidgy'.

Phonetic comparison of the Charles tape with Camilla's answer-phone message confirmed that she was the lady with whom the Prince of Wales was giggling. When it came to the 'Squidgy' tape, the suspicion was that the male voice must be that of James Gilbey, a friend of Diana – and evidently a close one.

Stuart Higgins rounded up a posse of some colleagues who accompanied him early one morning to Gilbey's house in Lennox Gardens, Chelsea.

'We told him face to face,' Higgins related in the TV documentary series *Diana: Story of a Princess*, 'fairly aggressively, because we wanted to be provocative, "We have got a tape which we believe contains private conversation between you and the Princess of Wales in which you repeatedly call her 'Squidgy', and it is a fairly intimate conversation." At which point he went completely white, got in his car and drove off.'

Higgins and his colleagues on the *Sun* took Gilbey's silence and horror-struck blanched features as the confirmation they needed – but now what? Just north of Fleet Street, the editors and proprietors of the *Daily Mirror* were asking the same question about the recording that they had purchased, which would come to be known, in homage to the notorious Watergate bugging scandal, as 'Camillagate'.

In neither newspaper establishment could the most cynical of the hacks quite believe what they were listening to. And in 1990 nobody was suggesting that such intimate royal conversation could possibly be published. After confabulations involving editors, proprietors and legal advisors at the highest level, it was decided that these embarrassing tape recordings should never see the light of day, and should be left to gather dust somewhere in a safe.

* * *

Diana's ostentatious kiss and hug with Carolyn Bartholomew changed all that. By endorsing Andrew Morton's intimate revelations in the *Sunday Times*, Diana had invaded her own privacy – and to an astonishing degree. If the Princess of Wales was willing to make public that she had been 'Driven to Five Suicide Bids by Uncaring Charles' – the headline on the opening instalment of the serialisation – what were a few chummy chucklings with James Gilbey?

On 24 August, ten weeks after the *Sunday Times*'s serialisation of Morton's book, the Diana–James Gilbey tapes were duly published in the *Sun*, revealing to the world that the princess answered to the name of 'Squidgy', that Gilbey made her go 'all jellybags', that she referred to her 'other half' derisively as 'His Nibs', that life with Prince Charles was 'real torture', and that she sometimes caught the Queen Mother, then ninety-two, watching her 'with a strange look in her eyes'. With her Sloane Ranger dialogue – the word 'darling' cropped up more than twenty times – and her superficial chatter about shopping and horoscopes, 'the princess comes across,' wrote Cambridge don John Casey, 'as a bird-brained egomaniac'.

Diana also came across to her elder son as a good deal less innocent than William had been presuming.

It seems unlikely that the two princes, then aged ten and seven, heard about 'Squidgygate' when the tape was first published. At the end of August 1992 the family was secluded in the Highlands, in the privacy of Balmoral, where it was probably possible to control access to the news. But the *Sun* had put all twenty-three minutes of Diana's intimacies on an 0898 number for people to phone in and listen to, so neither boy could have remained innocent for long once they got back to school among their fellow pupils.

September 1992 was when Harry – eight years old on the fifteenth – joined William at Ludgrove as a boarder. The Barbers' anti-homesickness programme seems to have worked quite effectively with the younger brother, but trouble was now reported with William. He no longer seemed so happy at the school, and he appeared to have reverted to earlier patterns of aggressive behaviour. There were stories of the elder prince showing off and getting involved in 'a number of scrapes'.

'Squidgygate' was as nothing, however, when compared to what came next. There could be no shielding William and Harry from the ear-nose-and-toe-cringing embarrassment of 'Camillagate' – the six-minute, 1,574-word transcript of their father talking on the phone to his mistress some three years previously, first published in Australia by Rupert Murdoch's *New Idea* celebrity magazine, then reprinted in Britain by the *Sunday Mirror* and the *People*. The conversation was finally picked up by the whole of Fleet Street on 17 January 1993, a few days after the two boys had got back to school from their Christmas holidays.

CHARLES: *I want to feel my way along you, all over you and up and down you and in and out … Particularly in and out.*
CAMILLA: *Oh, that's just what I need at the moment … I can't bear a Sunday night without you.*
CHARLES: *Oh, God.*

CAMILLA: *It's like that programme* Start the Week. *I can't start the week without you.*

CHARLES: *I fill up your tank … The trouble is I need you several times a week.*

CAMILLA: *Mmm, so do I. I need you all the week. All the time.*

CHARLES: *Oh, God. I will just live inside your trousers or something. It would be much easier!*

CAMILLA: *What are you going to turn into, a pair of knickers?* [Both laugh] *Oh, you're going to come back as a pair of knickers.*

CHARLES: *Or, God forbid, a Tampax. Just my luck!* [Laughs] *… My luck to be chucked down a lavatory and go on and on forever swirling round on the top, never going down.*

'Knickers' … 'Tampax' … 'Lavatory' … It is thought that the Mirror Group arranged to debut this shockingly intimate and non-royal material in Australia as a protective tactic against getting sued when it later ran the conversation in its Sunday tabloids in Britain. It was only republishing for British readers, it could argue, what others were already reading around the world. And as Buckingham Palace pondered legal retaliation in January 1993, it realised that would only make matters worse.

The *People* looked back to the monarchy's embarrassments of 1936 to compare Charles and Camilla to the last Prince of Wales and his divorced mistress, Wallis Simpson. 'The British people should have had the right to know what was going on then,' the paper editorialised about the Abdication Crisis. 'You have the right to know what is going on now.'

Abdication did not seem an overwrought comparison to make in the weeks that followed.

'Have you no shame?' shouted one man in a crowd that actually booed the prince when he next appeared in public. Opinion polls showed that disapproval of Charles had doubled in the past two months, with 37 per cent of respondents to a *Daily Express* ICM poll saying that he 'should not succeed if the Queen dies tomorrow'. Seven out of ten of those polled agreed that the Camillagate tapes had caused 'great damage to the monarchy', and 64 per cent felt 'let down' by the prince.

Serious calls were made for Charles to step down from the succession in favour of his elder son, with Princess Anne being proposed as a possible 'Regent' or 'proxy monarch' should the Queen die before William turned eighteen. It was suggested William be invested as Prince of Wales in his father's place.

Diana leapt joyfully to propagate such ideas. 'William is going to be in his position much earlier than people think now,' she had told Andrew Morton. 'If I was able to write my own script I'd say that I would hope that my husband would go off, go away with his lady and sort that out and leave me and the children to carry the Wales's name through to the time William ascends the throne.'

Martin Bashir would push the same question in his notorious *Panorama* interview for the BBC a few years later.

'Would it be your wish,' he asked Diana, 'that when Prince William comes of age that he were to succeed the Queen, rather than the current Prince of Wales?'

'My wish,' responded the princess with one of her coy and

meaningful smiles, 'is that my husband finds peace of mind, and from that follows other things – yes.'

We do not know precisely how Diana broached this explosive and subversive subject with her elder son, but the idea was a simple one to grasp. The boy should not only seek to be a good king. Now William must aim to be a better king than his father.

12

'Uncle' James

'Is it true that Papa never loved you?'

(Prince William, October 1994)

'Tampax-gate' supplied a nasty twist to the tail of 1992, Queen Elizabeth II's *'annus horribilis'* – her 'horrible year', as she described it half-ruefully, half-smiling to the assembled worthies of the City of London gathered in the Guildhall that November to celebrate her forty happy years on the throne. 'Nineteen ninety-two,' she declared, 'is not a year on which I shall look back with undiluted pleasure.'

Andrew and Fergie's separation, the divorce of Princess Anne from Mark Phillips, Andrew Morton and 'Squidgygate', Fergie's toe-sucking and the catastrophic fire in Windsor Castle – after this remorseless succession of embarrassments, the legal separation of Charles and Diana on 9 December would come as almost a footnote. Prime Minister John Major even maintained that the couple's separation would *not* automatically lead to divorce – it was still quite possible, he insisted to the House of Commons,

'I preferred it when she just used to shake hands!'
Tom Johnston, *Sun*, 21 August 1992

that Charles and Diana might be crowned in the future as a 'separated' king and queen.

The ludicrous prospect of the next king and queen of the United Kingdom and Commonwealth turning up to be crowned at Westminster Abbey from their different palaces, then returning home again separately, was presumably intended to assuage the Queen's horror of the 'd-word' harking back to the 1936 abdication of Edward VIII. Divorce had been baked into the British monarchy by King Henry VIII who devised the Church of England to make it possible. In 1820 King George IV launched divorce proceedings in an attempt to stop his wife Caroline, detested by him but beloved of the people, becoming queen.

But Elizabeth II had a personal 'thing' about it. Her Uncle David's liaison with a divorcee had generated such trauma in her childhood that any pretence was now preferable, it seemed, to acknowledging the reality of marital breakdown in the main line of succession.

The December 1992 separation of Charles and Diana kicked off three years of extraordinary hypocrisy in British royal history, with the heir to the throne and his wife setting up separate establishments while still officially 'married' – Prince Charles moving out to St James's Palace, where he could entertain Camilla, while Diana remained in their Kensington apartment which she decided to redecorate to get rid of all traces of her husband.

Diana brought in her friend and healer, Simone Simmons, to exorcise the 'negative energy' that Charles had left behind.

'She wanted me to "let in some light",' remembers Simmons, 'and it certainly needed it. The first time I went there was like walking into a brick wall. I would go into each room and just stand there, focusing on clearing the adverse energy. At the end of the day I was absolutely knackered. The decor was so formal and gloomy – everything seemed to have the Prince of Wales's feathers on it. When I'd finished clearing the bad feelings away, she had it all redecorated in these lovely light, funky colours.'

Diana offered the boys the chance to redecorate their own rooms, and the future king (aged ten) chose blue, while Harry (eight) asked the healer for her opinion.

'Yellow,' replied Simmons. 'It's like waking up in a drop of sunshine.' So Harry had his palace bedroom painted bright yellow as his mother's guru suggested.

Previous page: Happy Families –
The Prince and Princess of Wales
with William, 4, and Harry, 1 year
9 months, in the Wild Flower Meadow
at Highgrove. 14 July 1986.

Left: Prince Charles with Princess
Anne as children in the grounds of
Royal Lodge, Windsor, 1954.

Below: Prince Charles and Lady Diana
Spencer in Buckingham Palace on
their wedding day, 29 July 1981.

Facing: Diana and Camilla Parker
Bowles at Ludlow Races, where Prince
Charles was competing in the Amateur
Riders' Handicap Chase in January
1980. He finished second.

Top: Diana photographed shortly before her death with Harry, 12, and William, 15.

Below: Birthday Parade. Prince Harry, 4 years 9 months, looking out over the Buckingham Palace balcony at the Trooping the Colour ceremony, 17 June 1989.

Facing: First Steps. Prince Harry, 13 months, paces it out at Highgrove, helped by his brother William, 2 years 4 months, 22 October 1985.

Top: Diana presents a polo trophy to her lover James Hewitt at Windsor while William looks on, 1989.

Below: The last photo of Diana, leaving the Ritz Hotel, Paris, with Dodi Fayed on the evening of 30 August 1997.

Left: Princess of Hearts. Diana visits a minefield being cleared by the HALO Trust in Angola, south-west Africa, January 1997.

Top: 'If I walk, will you walk with me?' Prince Philip, Prince William, Earl Spencer, Prince Harry and Prince Charles follow Diana's coffin, 6 September 1997.

Below: 'Mummy'. The wreath of white roses laid on Diana's coffin by Princes William and Harry, 6 September 1997.

'William had a great big poster of Cindy Crawford in his room,' recalls Simmons. 'He was obsessed by her. He asked Diana if he could marry her, so Diana invited Cindy to the palace to meet him.'

The wacky redecoration of Kensington Palace was a metaphor for Charles and Diana's bizarre treading water from 1992 to 1995 – three years of suspended animation when the heir to the throne and his wife were clearly alienated and living separate lives, while the Queen and her loyal prime minister were insisting to the nation that nothing untoward had occurred.

William entered his teens during this period (from ten to thirteen), while Harry went into double figures (from eight to eleven) – formative years in which they experienced how conventional rules did not apply to their family. Thanks to Harold Wilson's Divorce Reform Act of 1969, ordinary British couples who lived separately for two years by mutual consent then divorced automatically. But that emotional logic and release was denied to Charles and Diana – and to their two sons – for the sake of keeping up appearances.

For three years William and Harry were hooked into a royal charade that cut them off from real life.

Simone Simmons says today that the separation of Charles and Diana eventually prompted a degree of reconciliation. But that was not apparent at the time. Charles was determined to get his revenge for Diana's collaboration with Andrew Morton, and he spent much of 1993 organising his private letters and delivering self-justifying interviews to his own chosen mouthpiece, Jonathan

Dimbleby, whose 620-page tit-for-tat *The Prince of Wales: A Biography* was also intended to redeem the damage done to the prince's reputation by 'Camillagate'.

Charles's first broadside came in a TV interview with Dimbleby in the summer of 1994, when the prince admitted to his relationship with Camilla. Immediately afterwards, Diana went down to Ludgrove to talk to the two boys before the end of term.

'William asked me what had been going on, and could I answer his questions?' she later recalled. 'Which I did.'

Was their father's love affair with Camilla the reason why the marriage had broken up, William asked his mother? To which Diana responded with the phrase that she would make later famous on television.

'I said, "Well, there were three of us in this marriage and the pressures of the media was another factor, so the two together were very difficult. But although I still loved Papa, I couldn't live under the same roof with him."'

Asked on a later occasion what effect she thought this explanation had had on her elder son, she replied, 'Well, he's a child that's a deep thinker, and we don't know for a few years how it's gone in. But I put it in gently without resentment or any anger.'

When the Dimbleby biography was published that autumn, William asked his mother directly about the hurtful message of the headlines – 'Charles Bares Soul on Loveless Marriage'. Dimbleby reported their father as saying that the 'overbearing' Prince Philip had 'forced' him into marrying Diana.

'Is it true?' asked the twelve-year-old in manifest distress. 'Is it true that Papa never loved you?'

Harry was also present as his brother posed the question. It seemed clear the two boys had read and discussed every front-page, bold-type repetition of the word 'loveless', and Diana later described how the enquiry and the anguish on her sons' faces as they waited for her answer 'pierced my heart like a dagger. I just wanted to cry.'

But she kept her composure for the sake of her boys – delivering the best response she could manage with an 'answer answerless' that hardly brought much consolation.

'When we first got married,' she told them, 'we loved each other as much as we love you today.'

The two princes' unhappiness at their father's self-justifying biography, however, was as nothing compared to their fury at the publication that same month of another book – *Princess in Love* by Anna Pasternak – the sensational account of their mother's five-year love affair with Guards officer Captain James Hewitt between 1986 and 1991.

Handsome and brave, with an authentic war record to his credit (Gulf War tank commander, Kuwait, 1991, mentioned in despatches), the devil-may-care Hewitt had captivated William and Harry as he had entranced their mother when he started giving her riding lessons in the summer of 1986. The boys had spent long hours on horseback with the captain improving their riding technique, then following him inside the cavalry barracks to experience the thrill of mingling with real-life soldiers in uniform, their horses stamping and whinnying in the stalls.

Hewitt had had his regimental tailor run up genuine khaki uniforms for the two princes, complete with small boots and Guards insignia, teaching them how to march and salute and carry a rifle. It is no exaggeration to suggest that the excitement the two brothers experienced in their time with Captain Hewitt helped to inspire the specific army element in the careers that they would both undertake.

'I'm going to be a soldier when I grow up,' Harry was once heard to declare while clambering into the turret of a tank – and when the time came, the prince joined the Guards, just like Hewitt.

They called him 'Uncle James' and drove down with him and Diana quite regularly to stay in Devon for breaks with his approachable and natural mother Shirley, who ran a riding school. Playing the good guests, the boys would help Diana carry out the dishes after lunch and do the washing up. It made a change from their habitually grand weekend country house destinations – and it was the closest, before their college and military years, that the two boys ever came to the fabled texture of 'ordinary', non-royal family life.

Now, in October 1994, William and Harry discovered from *Princess in Love*, the contents of which were splashed over every newspaper for days, that Uncle James had made love to their mother in a Highgrove four-poster bed while they were on the other side of the door. Hewitt was responding, wrote Pasternak, to a 'cry for help' from Diana, 'like the ghostly cry of a wounded animal … Later she lay in his arms and wept.'

On publication, *Princess in Love*'s first printing of 75,000 copies had sold out in the shops by lunchtime. So not for the first time, William and Harry were confronted by embarrassing intimacies about their mother in the company of the rest of Britain – with an unpleasant extra twist for Harry. Hewitt's square features and ginger-ish red hair prompted a rumour that has dogged the prince to the present day: that the gallant captain, Uncle James, must be his father, since Harry is the only red-head in the royal family.

The suggestion was and is quite impossible. Harry was born in September 1984, meaning that he was conceived around Christmas 1983 (when his brother William was eighteen months old). Diana would not meet James Hewitt for another two and a half years – until the summer of 1986 when Harry was sitting solidly on the back of a pony. And the prince's red hair that provided the basis and the 'proof' of the rumour was, of course, a defining physical trait of the Spencer family.

'A simple comparison of dates proves it is impossible for Hewitt to be Harry's father,' wrote Ken Wharfe, Diana's trusted bodyguard. 'Only once did I ever discuss it with her, and Diana was in tears about it.'

These solid facts did not stop a conspiracy from being hatched in the early 2000s to snatch a sample of Harry's DNA and compare it to Hewitt's – many folk prefer such a conspiracy theory to the old-established truth that grooming people for different roles in life tends to produce different personalities. The plan was to use a 'honey-trap' involving an attractive Argentinian girl who would pluck a hair from the prince's scalp after a polo match. The plot came to nothing, but it is not surprising that its intended victim should ultimately reach the conclusion that the game of being a royal in Britain was not worth the candle.

Still at Ludgrove, Harry, eleven, was relatively shielded from the embarrassments of his mother's *Panorama* interview with Martin Bashir in November 1995 – Diana's final flanking movement in her media battle with Prince Charles. But William, thirteen, viewed the entire programme in the study of his Eton housemaster, Dr Andrew Gailey, and as soon as he saw his mother's face appear on the screen, the prince later related to a classmate, he was overcome with a feeling of dread.

'Friends on my husband's side,' said Diana, explaining her reasons for doing the interview, 'were indicating that I was again unstable, sick, and should be put in a home of some sort. I was almost an embarrassment.'

As she bowed her head archly to the cameras, fluttering her heavily mascaraed eyelashes and speaking in dramatic whispers, 'embarrassment' described the gentlest of the emotions that she must have generated in her watching son.

'There were three of us in this marriage' – William heard again his mother's much-rehearsed complaint, coupled with her wish to be 'the Queen of people's hearts'. The eating disorders, the depressions, the suicide attempts – no detail was spared.

Diana had pre-taped the interview with a BBC crew, and the previous day she had driven down to Eton to warn her son to be ready for strong stuff. But this was more than William had expected – and his mother's candour when Bashir asked about her affair with James Hewitt tipped her son over the edge.

Prince Charles quarantined with coronavirus.
Ben Coppin, March 2020

'Yes, I adored him. Yes, I was in love with him …'

These were hardly the words that any teenager would want to hear drop from their mother's lips – especially when shared with twenty-three million avid viewers around the world. Diana spoke of 'betrayal', and that was exactly what William now felt. Their mother had clearly seen how upset both her sons had been when Charles had confessed his intimacy with Camilla on television the previous year. But here she was doing the very same thing, and even talking about her 'love' for this other man – whom both boys had previously assumed to be simply their riding instructor.

It was too much for the thirteen-year-old. When housemaster Gailey returned to the study to collect his pupil, he found William slumped on the sofa, his eyes red with tears. The prince pulled himself together to rush back to his room. But when, an hour later, Diana telephoned on the house phone, William refused to take the call.

'He hated the idea of everything being on television,' related Simone Simmons, 'and he knew his friends would poke fun at him, which they did. He felt she made a fool of herself – and of him.'

William was in a fragile place. He was only in his first weeks at Eton, having just gone through the college's then notorious initiation rituals. The 'Colours Test', for example, involved learning the names and colours of the school's twenty-four houses and other items of Eton trivia, to be quizzed by a group of prefects who might possibly sit you down beside a bucket containing raw eggs and Worcestershire Sauce. This, they promised boys who seemed too cocky, might be poured over your head if you made any mistakes.

In 1995 £12,384 – the Eton school fees per year – could buy you some high-class bullying.

The consolation that Eton offered after years of communal prep school dormitories was that William could retreat to his own room or 'study' to sorrow in private – and also to reflect. By the time he went home to Kensington Palace at the end of that week to see Diana, he was raging.

'All hell broke loose,' Diana told Simmons the following Monday. 'He was furious ... that she had spoken badly of his

father, furious that she had mentioned Hewitt ... He started
shouting and crying and, when she tried to put her arms around
him, he shoved her away.

'He was really devastated. His anger came from what his
so-called friends at school said to him about it ... Those Eton
boys really ripped into him. They took the mickey out of him
dreadfully.'

Diana was getting a personal taste of how William's intensity
could lead to his notorious rages. The next day he apologised to
his mother for his bad temper, and he presented her with a small
bunch of flowers. But Diana felt that some irretrievable rift had
opened up.

'What have I done?' she kept asking Simmons, as if she finally
realised the ghastly pain and damage that her bitter public
feuding had inflicted upon her sons – and upon William in
particular.

'There was a look of hopelessness on her face,' recalled
Simmons. 'She was still somehow convinced that he would hate
her for the rest of his life ...'

Hate his mother? Or love-hate her? This was the moment when
the thirteen-year-old William seems to have experienced that
decisive act of detachment from the parent that marks the advent
of adult life. The iron had entered his soul. When the question
later arose as to who William would invite to his first Fourth of
June celebrations – Eton's equivalent to Founders' or Parents'
Day – the prince decided that he would invite neither his father
nor his mother.

Instead, he took his older friend and shooting companion William van Cutsem (then seventeen, and today the godfather to William's firstborn George) along with Tiggy Legge-Bourke, his nanny – who, it later emerged in various legal actions, was being openly (and quite falsely) accused in these years by Diana of being Charles's mistress.

'Camilla,' Diana had written to her butler Paul Burrell, 'is nothing but a decoy.'

No wonder the wounded William sought to escape from the pain of his parents' recriminations.

A plague on both your houses!

The young prince was agonised as he tried to take refuge from his parents' poisonous crossfire in the life of a schoolboy. He was mortified by his mother's blabbing and betrayal of trust, but from the playing fields of Eton that winter, he could look up and take comfort in the dramatic sight of his future destiny – the battlements of Windsor Castle looming over the River Thames.

It was in these months of 1995–96 – William's first year at Eton – that the young man would decisively transfer his emotional allegiance away from his warring parents to the more stable and reassuring occupants of Windsor, the Queen and Prince Philip, his grandparents up on the hill.

The lunchtime tutorials instituted by the Queen and her husband's concern for their elder grandson's welfare rescued William. Sitting and talking on those Sunday afternoons with his grandmother in the Oak Room forged the transgenerational axis that has come to dominate and sets the tone for the British royal family to this day.

Diana did not enter this picture. And just as Queen Elizabeth II bypassed the example of her own mother – the too soft and cuddly 'Queen Mum' – to take her direction from her stern and formidable grandmother Queen Mary, whose rigid style she has replicated throughout her reign, so William would bypass the confused and complicated role model of his father Prince Charles. The future King William V would take his personal lead from the severe and determined exemplar of Elizabeth II, formatting himself in his grandmother's image.

One positive consequence of Diana's television interview of November 1995 was that it finally shocked the Queen into winding up the three-year make-believe of the Waleses' never-ending separation. The world noted Diana's famous three-in-the-marriage grievance. But Her Majesty noted how three was turned into four by her daughter-in-law's admission of her love for James Hewitt.

Something snapped. Now even the divorce-averse Elizabeth II realised that the charade had to end. Over the weekend of 16/17 December 1995 the Queen sat down and wrote personal letters to both Charles and Diana insisting that the pair of them should divorce – and quickly too. The letters were hand-delivered to the couple on Monday 18 December.

Three days later on Thursday 21 December the blunt message of the letters – 'Queen Orders Divorce' – was splashed garishly over the front page of the *Sun* with a great deal besides. The Queen and Prince Philip were 'in despair', reported the tabloid, about the very survival of the monarchy following Diana's soul-baring TV performance and had given up hope on their son's ability to resolve the problem with his estranged wife.

It was a massive coup for the *Sun*, winning its editor Stuart Higgins the London Press Club 'Scoop of the Year Award' and a similar accolade from the prestigious *What The Papers Say*.

'There have been many royal scoops this year,' declared the long-running TV programme, 'but none got so near to the centre of power itself – the Queen.'

Well, not quite … The clue to the story's origin came from the fact that this was the only *Sun* world exclusive ever to be bylined directly to its editor, who had, of course, been speaking to another royally connected lady once a week for the best part of ten years.

'So, Mr Higgins, it was Mrs Parker Bowles who gave you the tip-off?'

Mr H – 'I couldn't possibly comment.'

13

People's Princess

*'Not a day goes by when I don't think
about it once in the day.'*

(Prince William, June 2007)

Shortly before midnight on Saturday, 30 August 1997, Diana, Princess of Wales left the Ritz Hotel in Paris with her latest boyfriend Dodi Fayed, son of the Egyptian owner of Harrods, Mohamed Al-Fayed. The couple, who had known each other for little more than a month, were heading for Dodi's apartment near the Champs-Élysées.

Fayed's chauffeur Henri Paul had been drinking heavily since his shift had ended – five aperitifs. Even after he had been asked to chauffeur the couple again, he had ordered himself another Ricard Pastis (an aniseed-flavoured spirit) as the waiting paparazzi mobilised their posse of vehicles and motorbikes to chase the black Mercedes. A few minutes later Henri Paul crashed his precious cargo into a pillar in the tunnel of the Pont de l'Alma beside the River Seine.

* * *

At 1 a.m. the British ambassador in Paris, Sir Michael Jay, phoned with the news to Sir Robin Janvrin, the Queen's deputy private secretary, who was up in Scotland with the family on their annual summer holiday in Balmoral. Dodi and Henri Paul had died instantly, and Diana was seriously injured. Janvrin woke both Prince Charles and the Queen at once, and two hours later Charles received another call – the sad news that his ex-wife had also died. Mother and son conferred together in their dressing gowns. The distressed prince could not decide whether to wake William and Harry, but the Queen suggested that the boys should be left to sleep.

'They're all going to blame me,' complained Charles down the phone to his private secretary Stephen Lamport, following a phone call to Camilla in Gloucestershire and an agonised solitary walk on the moors. 'The world's going to go completely mad, isn't it? We're going to see a reaction that we've never seen before. And it could destroy everything. It could destroy the monarchy.'

The hours dragged slowly by until 7.15 a.m. when Charles felt that he could wake his elder son, who told him that he had not slept well. William had had a disturbed night – and then Charles broke the tragic news of the car crash, and of how every effort to save his mother's life had failed.

William started to cry, embracing his father, while Charles hugged the boy back desperately. As they wept together, William's first reaction was to think about Harry, and to worry how his younger brother would take the dreadful news. He wanted to go with his father to wake his brother up.

'One of the hardest things for a parent to have to do,' Harry later recalled, 'is to tell your children that your other parent has died ... But he was there for us. He was the one out of the two left, and he tried to do his best and to make sure we were protected and looked after. But, you know, he was going through the same grieving process.'

'The shock is the biggest thing, and I still feel it,' said William. 'The trauma of that day has lived with me for twenty years, like a weight ... People think shock can't last that long, but it does.'

When Charles felt that the boys were ready to leave their bedrooms, he told them that their grandparents wanted to see them. Father and sons held hands as they walked slowly down the corridors, a forlorn trio, to the room where the Queen and Prince Philip were waiting. According to the two brothers' subsequent accounts, neither grandparent gave them a hug ...

In London, newspaper editors were frantically trying to recall and reprint their front pages, which had all looked and sounded very clever when the princess was still alive. 'Troubled Prince William,' announced a *News of the World* exclusive on Dodi, 'will today demand that his mother Princess Diana dump her playboy lover.' 'Any publicity is good publicity,' declared the *Sunday Express* derisively of Diana's recent posing on the diving board of the Fayed yacht. 'She seems to relish her role as a martyr.'

While the British public read such perplexing paper coverage that Sunday morning, as radio and TV reported on flashing ambulances in Paris and Diana's wincingly shattered car being towed out of the tunnel, there was a similar disconnect inside

Balmoral. Charles had called the Queen's Flight to transport him to France as soon as possible, only to be asked if his journey was strictly necessary. Should the prince be going to Paris at all, since this incident did not involve the death of a 'royal' personage?

The Queen, it turned out, did not share the national sentiments that were already being expressed by mourners laying bunches of flowers at the gates of Buckingham Palace and Balmoral. Nor did Prince Philip. The royal couple had long ceased being fans of their ex-daughter-in-law and they certainly did not envisage her body being flown home in special dignity to lie in state. On Her Majesty's express instructions, her private secretary Robert Fellowes – Diana's brother-in-law, married to her elder sister Jane – arranged for the body to be sent discreetly to the Fulham Road mortuary used by the royal coroner.

Charles was outraged – both on his own account and for the sake of Diana and his sons. He dived into a bitter slanging match with Fellowes that ended with him shouting at the private secretary, 'Why don't you just go and impale yourself on your own flagstaff?'

Charles turned for help to Tony Blair, the energetic young Labour prime minister who had been elected that summer in a landslide. Unlike the Queen and her husband, Blair and his shrewd press spokesman Alastair Campbell had their fingers very firmly on the national pulse. Talking to the cameras summoned to his local church in County Durham, the premier delivered a clever and powerful statement, apparently on the verge of tears.

'I feel like everyone else in this country today. I am utterly devastated,' declared the prime minister, speaking reflectively and clearly grieving. He was wearing a dark suit and black tie. 'Our thoughts and prayers are with Princess Diana's family, particularly her two sons. Our heart goes out to them …

'We know how difficult things were for her from time to time … But people everywhere, not just here in Britain, kept faith with Princess Diana. They liked her, they loved her, they regarded her as one of the people. She was the People's Princess and that is how she will stay, how she will remain in our hearts and our memories for ever.'

'We must get the boys out and away from the television,' said the Queen as she clicked across the mournful images of the princess being run on every channel. 'We must get the radios out of their rooms … Let's get them both up in the hills.'

Diana's death was a tragedy, but here they were together as a family, away from the crowds and the media in the rugged peace of the Highland landscape where Elizabeth could apply her own favoured therapy in times of trouble – lots of exercise and fresh air. Peter Phillips, Princess Anne's bluff rugby-playing son, took William and Harry out with him on the moors each morning, jollying them along with stalking and the odd fishing expedition – plus lots of mucking around on the brothers' noisy all-terrain motorbikes.

The Duke of Edinburgh took over every evening, gathering the boys and the family round the bulky, wheeled barbecue wagon that was his pride and joy. With its grilling rack and pots and pans stowed neat and shipshape, the wagon would be towed to the shooting lodge selected for that evening's supper. No staff were present and Prince Philip served as chef. Cooking and carving and cleaning up afterwards, the shared rituals of the self-help meal kept the boys busy and made them feel useful. William seemed to be taking it bravely – then apparently he cracked.

'Our worry at the moment is William,' Prince Philip cut in suddenly, interrupting one of the morning funeral arrangement conference calls to London that involved the palace, Downing Street and the Metropolitan Police. 'He's run away up the hill and we can't find him. That's the only thing we are concerned with at the moment.'

Philip had been no fan of Diana, but he was immensely fond of her elder son. He had taught William to shoot, spending hours with him out on the moors and displaying in these days a warm and pastoral care for both his grandsons.

'I can remember, and it sends a tingle up my back thinking about it,' recalled Anji Hunter, Tony Blair's advisor on the conference calls. 'We were talking and then from the speaker phone on the table came Prince Philip's voice, and it was anguished: "These are the boys here. We are talking about these boys – they have lost their mum." It brought it all home to us.'

With William found, Charles walked his sons round the grounds briefing them on the details of the funeral – which he had insisted should take place in Westminster Abbey. At one early stage both the Queen and Charles Spencer had argued for a small, private affair, but after just a day it had become clear that nothing less than the grandeur of a full-scale service and procession through the streets would do, with the coffin being sent out

to start its journey at Kensington Palace in order to accommodate the crowds.

'Is mummy really dead?' Harry, still not quite thirteen, had
asked during the service in the local church which, on the Queen's
instructions, had gone ahead that first Sunday morning without
any mention being made of Diana or the fatal crash that had
happened just hours earlier.

The two boys' nanny Alexandra 'Tiggy' Legge-Bourke proved
a crucial support in these dark days – she was effectively a substitute mother. Charles had hired Tiggy (nicknamed after Beatrix
Potter's motherly hedgehog Mrs Tiggy-Winkle) to play precisely
this role after the 1992 separation – to Diana's fury. *She* did not
need to find a surrogate 'father' to help with the boys, she had
argued derisively – glossing over, perhaps, how she might have
felt if Charles had delegated an active stepmothering role to
Camilla.

'She was part servant, part sister and part mother,' recalls one
royal aide, trying to describe the nanny's special role. She was
Diana without the difficult bits.

'I give them what they need – fresh air, a rifle and a horse,' said
Tiggy. 'She [Diana] gives them a tennis racket and a bucket of
popcorn at the movies.'

To Diana's chagrin, it had been Tiggy who William had invited
to bring a picnic and keep him company in place of his parents
at Eton's Fourth of June celebrations in 1996, following Diana's
embarrassing 'I loved him' disclosures on *Panorama*. But the
nanny was a professional. She had made sure that mother and
son healed their rift over the months ahead, and now her 'jolly

hockey sticks' approach at Balmoral was just what the situation needed.

The Queen herself could have done with some 'jolly hockey sticks' in her dealings with her nation in the days following the death of Diana. Elizabeth II's wish to shield her grandsons from the pain of their mother's death was a worthy reason for taking refuge in the Highlands in the earliest days of September 1997. But her withdrawal also reflected her disinclination to rate the disappearance of the trouble-making princess as any great loss to the monarchy.

Wave of grief – Britain mourns the death of Diana.
Gerald Scarfe, *Sunday Times*, 7 September 1997

The Queen and her husband viewed the epidemic of bouquet-laying as a national nervous breakdown, and Elizabeth II had no intention of getting involved. She would not make any speech of tribute to Diana, nor spend any more time in London than she had to. The Royal Train could take the family down through Friday night for the Saturday funeral, then bring them straight back again afterwards.

'How can we coop the boys up in a gloomy old palace all covered with dustsheets?' asked Prince Philip.

It all came to a head over the flagpole. While Union flags around the country – including those over Windsor Castle and Balmoral itself – were flying at half-mast to mourn the death of Diana, Buckingham Palace itself remained conspicuously bare of any sign of mourning. People understood why the Royal Standard, the luscious confection of heraldic lions and harp strings, was not flying because the Queen herself was not present. But why was no flag at all flying half-mast over the palace?

'I've just been watching *Sky News*,' said Alastair Campbell in a phone call to Robert Fellowes, the Queen's private secretary in London, on Wednesday, 3 September, three days after Diana's death. 'Now, it's just a straw in the wind, but I think they're going to make some mischief over this thing of the flag.'

Sky News had been running dramatic vox pops from the Mall in which mourners laying their bouquets complained about the bare flagpole over the palace and the absence of any sign of royal mourning.

'I hear what you're saying,' replied Fellowes. 'But it's a curious business, the flag at Buckingham Palace. There are certain things, you know, that I can deliver straight away. But I'm not sure it's going to be as easy as it looks, even if it's right, to please the public on this one.'

Fellowes knew his boss. No flag in history had flown at half-mast over Buckingham Palace. The Queen had not done it on the death of her beloved father George VI, and she would not expect it for herself. It was a matter of tradition – something greater than oneself, symbolising for Elizabeth II values approaching the sacred. It was certainly not a gesture to be conceded to the popular media.

'There were times in that week,' recalls one of Tony Blair's staff of September 1997, 'when you could not believe what was coming down the line from Balmoral. You wondered if they were living in the same century.'

Next morning, the papers were aghast at the news that the Queen and her family were staying up in Scotland.

'Show Us You Care,' demanded the *Express*, over a particularly unflattering photograph of a flinty-faced Queen.

'Your People Are Suffering,' complained the *Mirror*. 'Speak to Us, Ma'am.'

As the Queen mulled her breakfast at Balmoral that Thursday morning, Rupert Murdoch's *Sun* had particularly powerful words to offer.

'Where is the Queen when the country needs her?' demanded an open letter on the front page. 'She is 550 miles from London, the focal point of the nation's grief … Every hour the Palace remains empty adds to the public anger at what they perceive to be a snub to the People's Princess. Let Charles and William and

Harry weep together in the lonely Scottish Highlands. We can understand that. But the Queen's place is with the people. She should fly back to London immediately and stand on the Palace balcony.'

Robert Fellowes and Geoffrey Crawford, the Queen's Australian-born press secretary, got on the phone to Balmoral to talk the problem through with Robin Janvrin, then with the Queen herself. There was clearly a need for a change of royal direction – and Elizabeth II got it immediately. Suddenly the details of what flag flew where counted for nothing.

'The Queen has ruthless common sense,' says one of her private secretaries. 'If you can explain clearly why something has to be done, and she agrees, that's the end of the matter.'

A Union flag would fly at half-mast over Buckingham Palace. The Queen's advisors were told to start drafting a tribute to Diana that she would deliver on television. And the whole family would travel down to London next day to spend Friday night in Buckingham Palace. Tiggy began packing the boys' suitcases for rapid departure.

St James's Palace had a surprise waiting for them on that Friday, 5 September. Mountains of flowers surrounded the palace gates – as they did the gates and railings of every London palace – and the limos drew to a halt so that the royals could get out to inspect them and read what had been scribbled on the cards.

'Looking back,' remembered Harry twenty years later, 'the last thing I wanted to do was read what other people were saying about our mother. Yes, it was amazing, it was incredibly moving

to know. But at that point I wasn't there – I was still in shock …
People were grabbing us and pulling us into their arms and stuff.

'I don't blame anyone for that, of course I don't. But it was
those moments that were quite shocking. People were screaming,
people were crying, people's hands were wet because of the tears
they had just wiped away from their faces before shaking my
hand.'

This was contact between royals and public with a raw intimacy that had never been known before. The emotional shock of
Diana's death and the youth of the two boys whom so many had
always looked on as 'their' own children led to traditional boundaries being breached.

'You just felt,' William later said, 'wherever you went people
were watching you.'

At fifteen, the elder brother was at an especially sensitive stage
in his emotional life.

'I remember just feeling completely numb. Disorientated,
dizzy. And you feel very, very confused. And you keep asking
yourself, "Why me?" all the time. "What have I done? Why has
this happened to us?"'

William decided that he had to put his 'game face on', when
all he really wanted to do was cry.

'I just remember hiding behind my fringe, basically,' he recalled
in 2017, 'at a time when I had a lot of hair' – that was a 'joke'
from a young man sensitive about going bald at an early age –
'And my head's down a lot.'

Over dinner that night, talk turned to the ceremony next day.
The faxes had been flying, but it had still not been resolved

exactly who was going to walk behind the gun carriage on which Diana's coffin would be carried. Prince Charles had no doubt that he should walk the long route with both his sons beside him.

But Uncle Charles Spencer did not agree. He was already angry on his family's behalf that his sister's funeral had been hijacked into a royal occasion, and he was particularly opposed to the idea that his young nephews should have to walk the best part of a mile behind their mother's coffin through the streets. Spencer was quite sure that Diana would have been horrified at the idea of her sons having to endure such an ordeal – and felt he had been lied to about the princes walking behind the coffin. He had been told that they had originally asked and had wanted to walk behind their mother.

The earl had argued quite fiercely with their father in a series of angry phone calls that week. One of them had ended with Spencer slamming down the phone on his brother-in-law after 'Charles had said something incredibly rude' about Diana, just days following his ex-wife's death.

Seeking harmony, the Lord Chamberlain's Office had drawn up variable plans envisaging two, three or even four mourners walking in the first rank behind Diana's coffin – on the assumption that Prince Charles and Earl Spencer would definitely walk, accompanied by neither brother (two), either brother (three) or both William and Harry (four).

In the event there were five. As William shied away that evening from the ill-feeling between his uncle and his father, and while Harry remained fearful and undecided, Prince Philip – who had never been scheduled to walk – intervened.

'If I walk,' he asked his grandson, 'will you walk with me?'

'No child should have to do that in any circumstances,' the adult Harry would say in an interview two decades later – then changed his mind when challenged by a subsequent interviewer. Thinking further, the prince agreed that he was happy to have taken up his grandfather's unexpected invitation. What was the alternative – to have been driven in the limos with the ladies?

'It wasn't an easy decision,' remembered William in 2017. 'It was one of the hardest things I have ever done. But we were overwhelmed by how many people turned out, I mean it was just incredible. It was that balance between duty and family – and that was what we had to do.

'I think the hardest thing was that walk. It was a very long, lonely walk. But then again, the balance ...'

There were two big speeches to be made in saying adieu to Diana, and Elizabeth II had to deliver the first of them – into the TV news live from Buckingham Palace at six that Friday evening. William and Harry watched it with the family in a room nearby – with the TV set also showing the thousands of people outside. The Queen was standing with her back to the Mall, so as she spoke the camera was also looking through the window behind her where people were coming and going, still laying their flowers.

'Since last Sunday's dreadful news,' the Queen began, 'we have all been trying in our different ways to cope ... Disbelief, incomprehension, anger and concern for those who remain. We have all felt those emotions in these last few days. So what I say to you now, as your Queen, and as a grandmother, I say from my heart.'

The words 'as a grandmother' had come from Downing Street – from Tony Blair's press secretary Alastair Campbell.

'Alastair was quite tentative about it,' remembers the palace insider who took the call that morning after the draft had been sent to Downing Street. 'He said, "the Prime Minister has only one comment, which is, would it be right for the Queen to say *speaking as a grandmother*?" We grabbed it and used it.'

'I admired her and respected her,' Elizabeth was saying, 'for her energy and commitment to others and especially her devotion to her two boys. This week at Balmoral we have all been trying to help William and Harry come to terms with the devastating loss that they and the rest of us have suffered.'

Next morning at the funeral Charles Spencer made his own thoughts known – having delivered his first message by banning all tabloid journalists from Westminster Abbey. If Buckingham Palace had tried to do that, the outcry would have made it impossible – but there was no gainsaying an angry brother, uncle and indignant ninth earl.

'Of all the ironies about Diana,' Spencer began, 'perhaps the greatest was this – a girl given the name of the ancient goddess of hunting was, in the end, the most hunted person of the modern age.'

Cleverly, her brother claimed for Diana a title higher than saint. She had been 'human', he said, drawing attention to her 'deep feeling of unworthiness' which had helped her speak so directly to her vast 'constituency of the rejected'. To judge how William and Harry have talked as adults about their mother, they were listening very attentively that morning to their Uncle Charles.

And what about the sting that lurked so wickedly in every Spencer tail? As the earl drew his address to a conclusion, he pledged on behalf of his two nephews' 'blood family' – by which he meant the Spencers *not* the Windsors – that he would keep their souls singing so that they would *not* get 'immersed by duty and tradition'. That they would not, in other words, end up as boring old stick-in-the-muds like their father Prince Charles, whose infidelity had betrayed Diana so cruelly from the start, and with whom the earl had been feuding all week.

Charles Spencer has always insisted that he meant no disrespect by what he said in Westminster Abbey that Saturday, 6 September 1997. A few days before the funeral, the earl had actually gone to try it out on his sister in the privacy of the chapel at St James's Palace, reading his words aloud to her coffin.

'I know people will think I'm some sort of fruitcake,' he recalled twenty years later, 'but I do remember hearing almost some sort of approval then – and then I realised actually I probably got the thoughts in order.' Diana herself would surely have said much worse, and there was an anger in her younger brother's tone that captured how millions were feeling that morning. The speech was greeted – astonishingly at a funeral – with a torrent of applause.

It started with the crowds watching on the big screens in the park. The clapping swept down Constitutional Hill, through people's radios and the TV screens, until it reached the abbey and scudded inside through the huge open doors. The applause invaded the vast church itself, rolling irresistibly up the aisle.

People are not supposed to clap at funerals, but this congregation put their hands together wholeheartedly – and eyewitnesses remember Diana's two sons both joining in with the applause. Elizabeth II and her husband, however, did not clap.

The clapping in the abbey on that day was an acknowledgement of many things – of Diana's warmth and human impulses, of her many good works and, above all, of people's recognition that she was fallible. The princess was no saint, and in so many respects she had been an imperfect human being.

But all of Diana's many failings were transcended by her glamour – her sheer glittering magic which embodied the ancient idea of the 'royal touch' that could miraculously heal people of their

'I'd like to be a queen of people's hearts …'
Princess Diana to Martin Bashir, *Panorama*, November 1995.
Peter Brookes, *The Times*, 1 September 1997

ailments and diseases. This was the semi-sacred essence of the 'People's Princess' – that Diana walked the earth as a royal divinity in the tradition of Good Queen Bess, Agincourt's King Henry V or even a right royal monster like King Henry VIII. Those idols had had the royal touch, just as surely as the sad and agonised Charles Mountbatten-Windsor did not.

That glittering magic was Diana's towering legacy to her two sons in September 1997 – and it was also her challenge to them. Could her boys soar as their mother had soared? To this day, William and Harry clearly provide discomfort to Buckingham Palace. The two generate the same mildly extra-terrestrial excitement with which their mother always discomforted the royals themselves and their retainers.

The princes' grandmother the Queen could handle them firmly and astutely – but she and her husband were just about the only people who could. The courtiers of BP, KP and SJP today are certainly at a loss. And William and Harry themselves have so far managed to exercise the same magic over the outside world – at least so long as they have stayed together and have not sought to break up the healing and magical legacy of Diana.

14

Scallywag

*'The problem with my brother is
that he wants to be me.'*

(Charles, Prince of Wales, February 2019)

Here's a question for your next family COVID lockdown quiz – which of the following pranks was played on Queen Elizabeth II by her son Prince Andrew (Mountbatten-Windsor child No. 3, son No. 2 and 'spare' to 'heir' Prince Charles for twenty-two years from his birth in 1960 until the arrival of Prince William in 1982)?

1. Putting itching powder in her bed?
2. Creeping up behind a Buckingham Palace sentry box while his mother was in residence and tying the sentry's shoe laces together?
3. Climbing onto the roof of the palace and manoeuvring the TV aerial to block its reception so that the Queen could not watch her favourite horse race from Sandown Park?

You will be an extremely popular person when you reveal the correct answer – all three! Nobody loses when it comes to identifying the latest act of folly from the monarch's second son who has raised the hazards and handicaps of being a royal 'spare' into an art form.

But let us be fair to Prince Andrew, Duke of York – the helicopter pilot who dodged the Exocet missiles and risked his life in action during the Falklands War in the summer of 1982. His bravery fully entitled Andrew to come home the conquering hero and to clench a rose between his teeth – a princely and endearingly piratical gesture. Then the pirate captain shone again when Windsor Castle caught fire in 1992. Both Philip and Charles were away, and Andrew's shouting out of orders was just what the emergency demanded. His imperious manner has been ridiculed as being very 'Toad of Toad Hall', but in November 1992 Mr Toad's bossiness helped save the Hall.

For many years Prince Andrew was celebrated as the royal family's scallywag – and after 1986 when he married Sarah Ferguson, 'Fergie', the two of them did much to brighten the Windsors' darkening image through some difficult years. It was only later, on his foreign trade missions, that the prince's dubious choice of business contacts came to shadow his reputation. As one Foreign Office official put it, 'Prince Andrew never met an oligarch that he didn't like.'

Elder brother Charles, however, had never been totally 'sold' on his younger sibling. Some said he was jealous of the chance that Andrew had had to display his heroism in action in the

Falklands – and then there was that devilish and unavoidable 'edge' inherent in the dynastic dimension.

Windsor 'heirs' and 'spares' are very much on a par in their earliest years. As 'Little Princesses', Elizabeth and Margaret were virtually equal – until one of them inherited, after which it was all downhill for the younger sister. Charles and Andrew were not so close in childhood, but the cruelty of primogeniture confronted Andrew with the same challenge as his aunt – to carve out some identity, authority and sense of personal value from a lifetime of playing in the reserves. Small wonder that the heir could never help worrying whether his 'spare' was not secretly feeling that 'he wants to be me'.

The 'Way Ahead' group was set up in the aftermath of 1992's disasters to examine what had gone wrong in the '*annus horribilis*' and to come up with reforms for the future – in addition, of course, to improving the fire precautions at Windsor Castle. First assembled by the Queen's confidant and Lord Chamberlain, David Airlie, this informal council of top royals – Elizabeth herself, Philip and all four children, but not yet William and Harry – met a couple of times a year, and its agenda for the summer of 1996 made intriguing reading.

Somehow a *Guardian* journalist had got hold of the plans (and rather approved of them): the idea of giving female royals the same rights of succession as males; abolishing the ban on heirs to the throne marrying Catholics; reforms to royal finances and the payment of taxes; the ending of the monarch's role as Supreme Governor of the Church of England; and a drastic reduction in the style, size and public identity of the entire royal family.

This was Prince Charles's special crusade. In an age of slimming, the future monarch wanted to slim down the House of Windsor. Charles's idea was to reduce the public face of the monarchy to just the sovereign and their consort, plus those children and grandchildren who were directly in the senior bloodline – with no more uncles and cousins to be reckoned up by the dozen, no more aunts.

In a time of austerity, Charles felt that the profusion of royal relatives who spilled onto the palace balcony in all their uniforms and jewellery on ceremonial occasions gave out quite the wrong message. Who knew or cared about these Kents and Gloucesters from a bygone age? And what about the modern Yorks and the Wessexes, for that matter? Charles felt that his brothers Andrew and Edward should step back as part of the slimming process.

The Prince of Wales pursued his theme hard, with Andrew resisting fiercely on behalf of Edward and himself – and particularly his own daughters Beatrice and Eugenie, eight and six in 1996. Andrew saw royal service as the perfect career path for both his girls, and he also pointed out that if Charles really did intend to limit the family workforce in this drastic fashion, it would make a heavy load for William and Harry, which they would surely appreciate sharing with their female cousins. The arguments grew bitter, bringing out into the open all the tensions and jealousies that had long festered between the 'heir' and the 'spare'.

Andrew was the Queen's favourite son – that was the bottom line. Everyone in the family knew it. Elizabeth II had always been uncomfortable with the cerebral and sensitive Charles, forever debating the whys and the wherefores. The gulf between mother and son went back to his very earliest years, when the Queen had been travelling so much in fulfilment of her new monarchical duties – and then found herself, when she got home, just as preoccupied with her racehorses and 'red boxes' of state papers.

As one disenchanted private secretary put it rather brutally in retirement: 'If the Queen had taken half as much trouble about the rearing of her children as she has about the breeding of her horses, the royal family wouldn't be in such an emotional mess … If she'd spent less time reading those idiotic red boxes – to what effect, one asks? – and had taken being a wife and mother more seriously, it would have been far better. Yes, she can handle prime ministers very well, but could she handle her eldest son? And which was the more important?'

It was not his mother but his nannies, Charles told Jonathan Dimbleby with perceptible bitterness, 'who taught him to play, who witnessed his first steps, who punished and rewarded him, who helped him put his first thoughts into words'.

Andrew, by contrast, was the first of the Queen's more favoured second brood – the children she had produced because she *really* wanted them, for personal, not dynastic reasons. But as a consequence of his maternal spoiling, the younger 'spare' had grown up to be an incredibly indulged and self-regarding creature. Like his brothers, he went to Gordonstoun in the wilds of Scotland, but while both Charles and Edward made it to 'Guardian' or Head Boy, Andrew did not. The second son was too much 'the prince', explained the headmaster in a phrase that cruelly summed up just about everything that went wrong with Andrew's subsequent non-military career – from his business and personal dealings with the paedophile Jeffrey Epstein to his embarrassing defence of that relationship on the BBC's *Newsnight* in November 2019. When the *Newsnight* interview ended, the prince actually thought that he had come across 'well'.

Apart from his mother's special favour, Andrew also benefited from the support of his other parent – from whom he had clearly inherited so many of his more forceful character traits. Prince Philip was a supporter of his second son – shielding him, for example, during the 1996 Way Ahead meeting whose details

Prince Andrew interviewed on BBC *Newsnight*.
Ben Coppin, November 2019

somehow found their way into the *Guardian*. After sharp arguments between the two elder brothers, Philip had drawn the gathering to an early close.

But the Duke of Edinburgh would be ill in the summer of 2012 when Prince Charles renewed his campaign to cut down the number of family figures on the palace balcony. On this occasion it was a question of who would step outside to mark Elizabeth II's Diamond Jubilee, celebrating her sixty years on the throne.

Charles had been foiled in 2002 when a score of relatives had been invited onto the balcony to lap up the applause for the Golden Jubilee. But ten years later, in the absence of his father, the Prince of Wales got his way. In 2012 just six people would walk out onto the balcony – the Queen, Charles and Camilla, William, Kate and Harry – a victory for Charles's vision of a slimmed down monarchy with its future built around the talents and energies of his two charming and charismatic sons.

But what if the two brothers happened somehow to fall out? And what if one of them decided to take a hike – to up sticks and go to live in another country? Such a departure would leave only one prince to shoulder all the royal duties and to meet all the demands of an ever more demanding public – not just in Britain but in the wider world. Perhaps the current heir had done just a bit too much slimming.

15

Forget-me-not

*'If we don't feel comfortable pouring our eyes
out in front of thousands of people, then that's
our problem. You know, we've got each
other to talk to.'*

(Prince Harry, 18 June 2007)

For nearly five hundred years the Spencers of Althorp – some twenty generations of them – have been buried in their local parish church of St Mary the Virgin. But in 1997 Diana Spencer, Princess of Wales, was not laid to rest among her ancestors. Her brother had a more private and romantic site in mind – inside a Grecian-style temple on a tree-covered island in the Round Oval lake on his Althorp Estate. As a child, Diana used to skate on the ice there in wintertime.

Here Diana's coffin, draped in a Spencer – not a royal – standard, was interred on the afternoon of Saturday 6 September, attended by just her family and a few others in the aftermath of her funeral in Westminster Abbey. William and Harry had come north on the Royal Train with their father Charles and Uncle Charles – an awkward and strained journey after Earl Spencer's provocative verbal fireworks in the abbey.

The boys planted oak trees in their mother's memory and have since been back to plant more over the years, bringing wives and children as they came along, as well as pots of forget-me-nots, said to have been Diana's favourite flower. On one wall of the temple there is a plaque displaying an extract from her brother's famous abbey speech, giving thanks for 'the extraordinary and irreplaceable Diana, whose beauty both internal and external will never be extinguished from our minds'.

Beside it is a second plaque, bearing the words that Diana herself had uttered in June 1997, just weeks before her death: 'Nothing brings me more happiness than trying to help the most vulnerable people in society. It is a goal and an essential part of my life – a kind of destiny. Whoever is in distress can call on me. I will come running wherever they are.'

These were ambitious words to live up to, and Diana had meant them for just herself. But here, carved into marble, to confront her sons whenever they visited her grave, they blazed out as intimidating challenges to two motherless boys.

William regained his equilibrium pretty quickly thanks to his focus on his role as the future King William V. The prospect of future kingship might discombobulate his neurotic father, but for William it served as a source of strength in these days of sorrow.

Every few Sundays or so William would continue with his weekend walk down Eton High Street and across the bridge into

Windsor. Queen Elizabeth II and Prince Philip performed more healing and effective parenting with their bereaved grandson in those Sunday sessions in the late 1990s than ever they achieved with any of their own children. After lunch the Duke of Edinburgh would execute his discreet post-prandial vanishing act, leaving the sovereign to share her heart and secrets with her teenage protégé.

Did Her Majesty encourage her grandson to say his prayers in these days of difficulty? The Queen is known to kneel every day beside her bed, just as surely as her daughter-in-law Meghan bows her head in Agape meditation with each dawn. Elizabeth II is a dedicated Christian who would regularly invite the American evangelist Dr Billy Graham to lunch with her when he brought one of his crusades to Britain. Theologically the Queen had more in common with the fundamentalist preacher-man than with many of her archbishops of Canterbury, and she surely prayed for the spirits of both her sorrowing grandsons. We do not know – we shall probably never know – the content of her Sunday heart-to-hearts with the teenage William. But she did influence the boy – subtly.

'It's very much the case that she won't necessarily force advice on you,' William revealed a dozen years later, talking to the Queen's 2011 biographer Robert Hardman about the influence of his grandmother. 'She'll let you work it out for yourself. She's always there for a question or two – for whatever it is you might need. But, just as she probably had to, she feels that you have to work it out for yourself, that there are no set rules. You have to make it work. You have to do what you think is right.'

This grandmotherly challenge helped steer Prince William through his remaining years at Eton. He noted how the Queen had had 'to carve her own way', so he was not scared to do the same. It gave the young man a moral compass and a purpose. William was popular with his school mates, developed steady friendships that have lasted to the present day, and garnered twelve GCSEs – with A grades in English, history and languages. When it came to his A-levels he knocked out an A, a B and a C – hardly stellar grades, but quite respectable.

William had decided early that he did not, in fact, want to go to Oxford or Cambridge like his father and Uncle Edward, who had both sneaked in with undistinguished exam results. Diana had planted a healthy anti-elitist instinct in both her boys. So William would opt for St Andrews on the east coast of Scotland – where he would soon meet the young Ms Middleton who had so happily opted for the same academic destination.

From Eton to Kate! Give or take the odd gap year, plus a session in the military, that just about covers the story of one young prince's early life. The progress of William's younger brother, however, did not prove so smooth …

Prince Harry's unhappiness in the months following the death of his mother was compounded by an especially skewering humiliation when he returned to school. He was held back for a year. The prince had not measured up to his Common Entrance exam requirements, so while his friends skipped off to Eton, Harrow and their other public schools, Harry, thirteen on 15 September 1997, was stuck at Ludgrove having to repeat his studies and endure the pitying glances of the younger generation who were now his contemporaries.

This was partly Diana's fault. Harry would have been welcomed by all manner of British public schools, but his mother had been set on her younger son joining William and the elite at Eton College.

'If he doesn't go there,' she told the author Ingrid Seward, 'everyone will think he's stupid.'

That, sadly, was exactly what most people *did* think about dear Prince Harry. Nobody ever imagined that he was a Brain of Britain. The young man had so many other good qualities – his vigour, his warmth, his horsemanship. 'He's very artistic and sporty and doesn't mind anything,' Diana told Seward protectively.

On car journeys Prince Charles would try to sharpen the geographical knowledge of his younger son by testing him on the world's capital cities, along with his maths – which had always been a challenge for Charles himself. Charles had failed his maths O-level at his first attempt.

The Prince of Wales came to feel that Eton was simply beyond the intellectual reach of Harry and for a time Diana had agreed, prompting the two parents to research a series of alternatives – posh schools for thickos. But William protested. He insisted that his brother would be happiest joining him at Eton – that's what Harry had told him he really wanted to do, so that's what William wanted too.

Here was an early example of William putting his arm around his younger brother. There was no sign at this stage of their lives of William feeling that his royal destiny should take him in a different direction from Harry. By the mid-1990s both brothers had suffered a decade of parental disharmony and this seems to have pulled them together. Even before Diana's death, the brothers were quite sure that they wanted to spend their school days in each other's company if they possibly could.

So that had left Harry with the challenge of Eton's relatively stiff entrance requirements which, unlike Oxford or Cambridge, the school was not prepared to relax, even to recruit another Windsor. Hence the extra year at Ludgrove, additional tutoring, less partying and more swotting.

But Prince Charles did have a reward in mind for all this academic effort – an encounter with the Spice Girls, then Harry's favourite group, as well as a meeting with Nelson Mandela. The new teenager had been scheduled to spend the October half-term of 1997 with his mother, since Charles was booked for the official five-day tour of South Africa, Swaziland and Lesotho that involved these Spice Girls/Mandela encounters.

'Harry's half-term at Ludgrove is coming up in October,' explained Charles to his old friend and polo-playing companion, Geoffrey Kent. 'He was meant to spend it with his mother.'

Kent had the solution. Co-founder of the Abercrombie & Kent travel empire, Kent was credited with inventing the modern luxury safari on which clients shot with a camera not with a gun – and could enjoy a chilled bottle of water or champagne in their tent at night. When half-term arrived, Kent whisked Harry away for a safari in Botswana, the former Bechuanaland to the north of South Africa, an 'absolutely airtight and low-profile' trip –

while leaking to the press a false itinerary for a Tanzania expedition that got the paparazzi camping out around Kilimanjaro 1500 miles to the north-east.

For three days Harry cruised undetected in an open-top Land Rover with his schoolmate Charlie Henderson, in the company of just Tiggy Legge-Bourke, a bodyguard and Kent. The party canoed and fished in the Okavango Delta, home to thousands of elephants, rare birds, and plenty of leopards and lions.

One morning before dawn, Kent took the doors off the helicopter and strapped Harry in tightly so he could look out and get the full flavour of an African sunrise as they swooped down over the Okavango.

'Have you got special permission to take the doors off?' asked the prince.

'No, Harry,' replied Kent. 'We are out of touch, so enjoy it' – an answer still possible in those days when Internet connectivity had barely started in Africa.

It was Harry's first taste of Africa, its people and its wildlife, and it proved the beginning of a love affair. Inspired by his days and nights camping under the stars in Botswana, he would come to make animal conservation one of the burning causes in his adult life – and when, in July 2016, the prince was introduced on a blind date to the US actress Meghan Markle, he would invite her to fly off with him on an instant trip to Botswana.

Kent's secret safari yielded an extra dividend – or maybe it was the Spice Girls and Nelson Mandela that did the trick. On Harry's return to Ludgrove, the prince was spotted actually visiting the school library! The thirteen-year-old knuckled down to his studies as never before and at the year's end he succeeded at Common Entrance with the 65 per cent grade that he needed to gain entry to Eton – including passes in both geography and maths.

Prince Charles's hope that his second child might replicate the special sibling partnership that he had enjoyed with Princess Anne had not, of course, worked out exactly – William and Harry were no brother and sister act. But by their teens, life and death had forged them into a pair of mutually supportive companions – and this partnership took clear shape when Harry joined William at Eton in the autumn of 1998. Harry had gone the extra mile to reach the level of his higher-achieving brother and they now enjoyed two of the most closely interlinked years of their lives.

For security reasons, the princes were placed in the same house – Manor House – in the care of the fatherly Andrew Gailey, and William took pleasure in showing his brother around the house breakfast room, where boys could make coffee and toast for themselves in the mornings. Dr Gailey had installed a pool table and was relaxed about the boys hanging posters of their favourite models and movie stars above the scruffy oversized sofas around the common room walls.

They were allowed pin-ups in their rooms too. William had opted for Claudia Schiffer and, inevitably, for Cindy Crawford. Harry opted for the African-American actress Halle Berry – a Meghan Markle lookalike, some would later maintain with hindsight – in the middle of a spectacular red and orange psychedelic wall-hanging. Both boys had framed photos of their parents beside their beds.

William had established a close and trusted circle of friends at Eton and Harry was invited to join them. His year's delay at Ludgrove had somewhat severed the prince from his own contemporaries, so quite a few of his expanding social circle were a full two years older than him – making it likely that the fourteen-year-old would be introduced to temptations that were ahead of his years. Harry's bright self-confidence was misleading – he was not as grown up as he appeared.

On regular Sundays Harry joined William for the walk along Eton High Street and across the bridge to lunch or tea with their grandparents, and many of their weekends would be planned around activities with Tiggy or a friend of hers, Mark 'Marko' Dyer, a burly, red-headed former Welsh Guards officer who had been an equerry to Charles for a spell. Dyer knew the royal ropes and his later career would embrace the creation of two of south-west London's more successful gastropubs, the Sands End and the Brown Cow, which became popular venues for the 'Glossy Posse' smart set with whom Wills and Harry ran. The Sands End would also become one of Harry's secret rendezvous during his courtship with Meghan.

Many weekends were spent at Highgrove, which had now become the brothers' full-time home base. For security reasons Prince Charles had had a bombproof shelter constructed in the cellar, and for teenage amusement reasons he allowed his two sons to adapt it into a disco-rumpus room – 'Club H', a black-painted dungeon-discothèque scattered with scruffy Manor

House-style sofas, where Harry and William could entertain their school friends on holidays and at weekends. Club H featured a well-stocked bar – here was the first temptation for the young Harry – along with a state-of-the-art sound system that made every floor of the two-hundred-year-old building quiver.

Club H turned Highgrove into quite the hot spot when Dad happened to be away – which was an ever more frequent occurrence. What with the prince's busy workload as heir, his extracurricular campaigning for good causes like ecology and his personal extracurricular activities with Camilla whom he could not yet bring 'home', Charles had not lived up to his promise to be a full-time hands-on father.

The popular image of the heir to the throne 'talking to his plants' caught the public imagination as encapsulating Charles's detachment from the real world. It could also sum up his role as parent, mooning around the conservatory while his sons jived it up in the cellar. Club H became the focus of the two brothers' teenage lives, and although their basement activities appeared to be private, they would lead to some very public embarrassments for Harry.

In their father's absence, William 'relaxed' as intensively as Harry did – in fact, the sixteen-year-old was already a steady drinker. Club H had been very much the elder brother's inspiration, with Wills' older friends largely setting the social pace for Harry. And if Prince Charles did happen to be at home, the two brothers and their friends could all pile out together to the Rattlebone Inn in the village of Sherston five miles away.

It was illegal in British pubs then, as now, to sell alcohol to anyone below the age of eighteen, but in those years the landlord of the Rattlebone turned a blind eye to underage drinking – and the inn also allowed its young royal patrons to engage in after-hours 'lock-ins', where, it would emerge, cannabis was smoked. The cars of the royal bodyguards waiting outside meant that the local police were hardly likely to stage a raid. So this village pub also became, in a sense, 'private' royal property.

These were the years, when he was as young as fourteen or fifteen, when Prince Harry started to drink alcohol in serious quantities. He loved to swill it down like his brother, reported friends. And some of the Rattlebone circle also began sampling exotic substances.

At Eton the prince had already earned the nickname of 'Hash Harry' on account of the smoky aroma that sometimes emanated from his room, and it was not long before these cannabis rumours reached journalists who were rooting around Highgrove for scandal – specifically the *Sunday Times* and also the *News of the World*, whose editor Rebekah Wade (later Rebekah Brooks) had mounted an investigation into the young princes' activities in Gloucestershire.

In the mid-1990s new rules on the reporting of the young royals were being negotiated by Britain's Press Complaints Commission (PCC), whose director Mark Bolland would move on to join Prince Charles's staff in 1996. Chastened by the death of Diana, most newspapers had formally agreed that William and Harry would be neither photographed nor reported on – official photo ops aside – as long as they remained in full-time education.

It eventually became clear that the princes' protection officers knew all about their charges' after-hours drinking. But they had agreed that their responsibility began and ended with their guarding and protection duties. It was not their job, they felt, to act as surrogate parents nor to exercise moral judgements on William and Harry – though it has never been made clear how serving police officers could have connived in the breaking of the law when it came to after-hours lock-ins and the smoking of illegal drugs.

In the late 1980s the authorities at Scotland Yard had become worried about the personal relationships that some royals had developed with their long-serving protection officers. There had been the suspicion of an affair between Diana and her 1985/86 bodyguard Barry Mannakee, and a certain jealousy of the more appropriate family relationship that she and her sons developed over the years with SAS-trained 'Uncle Ken' Wharfe. The Yard had changed the system so protection officers were shuffled round in short tours of duty specifically to prevent such cosiness developing.

Prince Charles had protested against the change. He had no objection to protection officers playing a semi-parental role with his sons – and certainly some quiet words of warning in the right ears might possibly have avoided what happened next.

The problem came to a head as early as August 2000 after William, now eighteen, had departed Eton and headed off to Belize for the start of his gap-year adventures. Lonely and left to his own devices, Harry, still only fifteen at that date, began getting stoned to excess, continuing his pot-smoking at Club H and at the Rattlebone throughout William's absence in 2001, until someone – a member of the Highgrove staff, it is thought – finally took the responsibility of warning Prince Charles what was going on.

The timing of what happened next is confused, but it is known that sometime in June or July 2001 – several weeks *before* Charles was made aware of his son's problem in August or September – Mark Dyer had escorted Harry on a cautionary low-key visit to the Featherstone Lodge rehabilitation centre in Peckham, south London. There the prince had spent a couple of hours talking to a number of 'buddies' – former heroin and cocaine addicts whose tales of their own personal drug disasters were intended 'to teach Prince Harry about our work', according to Bill Puddicombe, the head of the organisation that ran the centre. The buddies also briefed their visitor on 'the consequences of taking drugs'.

But when the *News of the World* broke the story in January 2002 – 'Harry's Drugs Shame' – it was suggested that Prince Charles had personally organised this rehab visit at a *later* date as some sort of therapy to provide his son with what the paper described as a 'short sharp shock'.

'This is a serious matter which was resolved within the family. It is now in the past and closed,' Charles declared in an official statement, with his mother backing him up. 'The Queen shares the Prince of Wales's views on the seriousness of Prince Harry's behaviour and supports the action taken,' said Buckingham Palace. 'She hopes the matter can now be considered as closed.'

The *Sunday Times* and the *News of the World* had been investigating Harry's pot-smoking and under-age Rattlebone activities for several months to compile a 'Gloucestershire dossier', since the *NoW*'s Rebekah Wade knew she needed firm evidence of illegal activity to override the press agreement not to report on the private lives of the boys. The PCC felt compelled to agree, and in the complex negotiations that followed with Prince Charles's office – where the PCC's former boss Mark Bolland now controlled the PR machine – it had been resolved to reframe the story, when published, to give the impression that it was Prince Charles, not Mark Dyer and his office, who had organised the rehab trip.

This twist of timing turned a narrative that might have suggested parental out-of-touchness into a fable of fatherly redemption, with the *News of the World* actually praising Charles's 'decisive intervention' in an editorial headed 'Courage of a Wise and Loving Dad'.

'Unfortunately, this is something that many parents have to go through at one time or another,' one 'senior aide' to Prince Charles remarked, and the media took its cue from this. 'No one in our society is immune from the problem of drugs,' opined the *Mail on Sunday* forgivingly.

'Households right across the country waking up to this story,' declared Liberal Democrat leader Charles Kennedy, 'will probably have had very similar experiences with their own teenagers.'

* * *

This masterpiece of damage limitation had been the work of Charles's new PR supremo Mark Bolland, who would disclose a few years later that 'the sequence of events' producing this largely favourable reaction to Harry's drugs scandal had been 'distorted'. He himself, he admitted, had been the sympathetic 'senior aide' quoted in the article.

Six years earlier the *Sun*'s historic 'Queen Orders Divorce' scoop of December 1995 had been accompanied by another leak from Charles's office – 'Charles Will Never Wed Camilla'. In this apparently binding commitment, the Prince of Wales acknowledged that 'the British people would never accept Camilla as their Queen' and declared that he was 'NOT prepared to put the woman he loves before his duty to the nation'.

'He has a sense of duty,' explained a friend, 'and that's all he is concerned about. He's not about to run off and marry Camilla.'

'Should there be a divorce,' confirmed Allan Percival, Charles's official palace spokesperson, for the record, 'the Prince of Wales has no intention of remarrying.'

But within months of issuing these apparently irrevocable promises, Charles had started assembling friends, lawyers, eminent journalists and PR consultants in high-powered councils of war that were intended to achieve precisely the opposite result – to reverse the way in which the media and the public viewed both himself and Camilla so that the couple could marry.

'I'm not this awful person,' complained Mrs Parker Bowles at one such gathering, expressing her annoyance at the popular sainthood attributed to Diana – still very much alive in 1996 – in contrast to Camilla's own stereotype as a scheming, cigarette-smoking adulteress. 'I just wish someone would do something about it.'

That someone proved to be Mark Bolland whose name had come up one evening at one of Charles's strategy dinners at St James's Palace. The young chairman of the Press Complaints Commission – comprehensive school-educated and just coming up to his thirtieth birthday – was praised by a PCC colleague for his high-powered charm and mental nimbleness, and for the fact that he was not a PR executive. The press was more likely to regard him as one of their own.

When Charles met Bolland in July 1996, he was won over. The prince invited Bolland to join his staff where his principal objective, in the words of Charles's 2018 biographer Tom Bower, would be 'to reverse Camilla's image as his privileged, fox-hunting mistress, to make her acceptable to the public and overcome the Queen's hostility to them being together'. An important part of the job would be to improve Charles's public image as the caring and concerned parent to Diana's children – and an extra point in Bolland's favour was his reputation for being irreverent and entertaining.

'If you don't have fun in the job there's no point in it,' Bolland said to his new boss when they met. 'It doesn't all need to be so terrible. Things can get better.'

'If you say so,' said the prince.

16

Killer Wales

'Everyone gets themselves into trouble at some point. It's how you learn from it.'

(Prince Harry, October 2020)

In the years around 2000 William and Harry liked to joke about the high-powered manoeuvrings with which Mark Bolland masterminded his apparently impossible PR campaign to make Camilla Parker Bowles a re-marriageable item for their father. In fact, Charles's assistant private secretary (rapidly promoted to deputy in 1997) achieved his goal with surprising speed in April 2005 – the marriage of the Prince of Wales and his lady-love to general public acceptance, if no special enthusiasm.

The boys humorously dubbed Bolland 'Lord Blackadder' after the scheming and manipulative anti-hero of the long-running *Blackadder* TV series starring Rowan Atkinson – all sneeringly curled lips and sinisterly arched eyebrows.

But Harry was not laughing in January 2002. For whose reputation had Lord Blackadder actually worked to save? 'World

Exclusive – Harry's Drugs Shame'? Thank you very much, dear Mark. Dad might have emerged from the story smelling of roses, but it was Harry who was typecast as the 'Bad Boy of Buckingham Palace' or 'Boozy Harry'.

This was the beginning of the popular media stereotyping that would eventually contribute to Prince Harry's departure from Britain – while the other face of that stereotype was, of course, the impeccable image of his perfect elder brother, golden boy Prince William. There were even newspaper stories suggesting that it was William who should get the credit for intervening at his father's request to 'save' Harry from his youthful over-indulgence.

It was a complex story, since Harry had certainly lost his way in 2000 and 2001 when the brothers' two-year Eton partnership ended, while William disappeared to pursue his gap year around the world. In the absence of William's companionship, the younger brother had turned to false companions.

But it was William who had opened the first bottles behind the well-stocked bar in the cellar of Highgrove and had led the group forays to the Rattlebone Inn after hours. William was the blue-eyed glamour boy at the centre of the Glossy Posse, pouring out the drinks and inspiring all the revels that would coax his younger brother – a full two years and three months younger, still a child in many ways – into errant and self-destructive habits. 'So that's why they call it "Highgrove"!' was a joke from the left-wing *Observer* that applied to both brothers. But it actually applied rather more to William, since he had been the Lord of Misrule and the driving spirit behind the entire seductive fantasy of Club H.

Both Charles and William, father and elder son, could move on smoothly from 'Harry's Drugs Shame' towards the grand and glittering roles that the dynasty and public opinion required of them. They were in the clear. For all the media's alleged thirst to reveal 'the truth' about the scandals of Highgrove, Britain's tabloid newspapers *never* put anything seriously discreditable on the record about the future King William V. The heir was the 'King of the Castle', and it was Harry who was cast as the 'dirty rascal'.

Charles's much-schemed-for marriage to Camilla was nearly derailed by the couple's unashamed passion for fox-hunting, which had come to be shared by both William and Harry. The fact that their father had used the controversial blood sport as one of his alibis when deceiving their mother did not seem to diminish his sons' enthusiasm for the hunt, nor for the other countryside pursuits that were becoming matters of public and political contention in the years around 2000.

William had been just four when his father took him shooting for the first time at Sandringham with ex-King Constantine of Greece and Spain's King Juan Carlos. The boy was armed only with a toy silver pistol, but animal rights campaigners were appalled. 'It is horrific for a child of his age to be indoctrinated into slaughter,' complained Beki Barthelmie, a committee member of the local RSPCA (Royal Society for the Prevention of Cruelty to Animals).

Two years later (in 1988) it was Harry's turn when, also four, he joined his father on another Sandringham shoot. 'I think

[Prince Charles] has been highly irresponsible,' declared James Barrington, executive director of the League Against Cruel Sports. 'He is brandishing a deadly weapon. It is showing young Harry the glamorous side of guns.'

Charles was undeterred. Field sports provided precious moments of personal bonding with his boys – just as shooting and fishing had been rare and shared pleasures in his own often complicated relationship with his father. Now Charles found a way to get close to William and Harry as they pursued wildlife together.

According to Darren McGrady, personal chef to the Waleses in the mid-nineties, when William and Harry were entering their early teens, 'The boys loved being in the countryside, especially Balmoral with their Granny. They were always out shooting, hunting and fishing. They'd go out at night with their torches and come back with a couple of rabbits which I'd chop up and serve to the corgis.'

Diana was ambivalent about her sons' hunting enthusiasms. She had no particularly strong feelings on the politics of field sports.

'I don't know why I'm always portrayed as an "Anti",' she told the writer Ingrid Seward, 'because I'm not. After all, I was brought up in the country.'

But she did get upset when William and Harry came back to see her after one weekend with Charles that had included the shooting of rabbits.

'I can't believe that my sons have blood on their hands,' she said to Simone Simmons.

According to Simmons, the princess was upset the boys should be introduced to shooting at such a tender age and she made her feelings clear to them.

'You should both be ashamed of yourselves,' she said. 'It's wrong to kill little animals. I shall now call you both the "Killer Wales".'

The two boys laughed.

'Don't laugh,' Diana responded sharply. 'It's not funny. You've been involved in the murder of some innocent creatures. A little rabbit is not doing harm to anybody.'

'Talk about going red,' recalls Simmons. 'It made both of them very ashamed – well, for the time being. But it wasn't long before they were out hunting with their father again.'

Trying another tack later, Diana tried to warn her sons of the wider image complications of their countryside passions. Her 'Diana antennae' were cannily aware of the general public's ambivalence on this highly sensitive subject.

'Remember,' she told them realistically – and not without a degree of cynicism – 'there is always someone in a high-rise flat who does not want you to shoot Bambis.'

In her awareness of how the general public felt about fox-hunting Diana was more cautious than the two boys' father. Prince Charles made little secret – and was almost reckless – in his opposition to the strengthening political campaign that fox-hunting should be banned.

Anti-blood sport sentiment had taken a major step forward with the election of Tony Blair's Labour government in 1997, and Charles openly welcomed the creation of the Countryside Alliance in that year to fight back against the trend. 'Give rural Britain a voice' was the motto of the Alliance, arguing that hunting reflected a legitimate tradition of British farming life and was not the socially exclusive and bloodthirsty depravity depicted by ignorant lefties and townies.

Charles could not have agreed more, and he encouraged his sons in the same belief. In October 1999 he was accused by the League Against Cruel Sports of making a 'political statement' when he very obviously took his boys out with him on the first day of the fox-hunting season. William, seventeen, joined his father with the Beaufort, while Harry, fifteen, followed on the pillion of a trials motorbike.

In the year 2000 Charles was offered and wanted to accept a position as 'Patron' of the Countryside Alliance, which was gathering ever more support for its anti-government campaign. Mark Bolland swung smartly into action, enlisting the help of private secretary Stephen Lamport to put the dampers on such a politically provocative act. It would have been a disastrously partisan gesture for the heir to the throne – not to mention the fresh scrutiny it would have invited of Camilla's fox-hunting activities.

Charles grudgingly yielded ground, but he intensified his campaign to make Prime Minister Tony Blair change his mind in a sequence of fiercely argued personal letters that he addressed to both Blair and other ministers. To their recipients they were known as the 'black spider memos' – since they were often written or finished off in Charles's own wandering hand with a jerkiness that suggested they had been scribbled quite late at night.

'You'd never have a handwritten letter from his mother,' reported one member of the government, 'but you sure have them from him. That's his way. He underlines a lot. There are quite a lot of exclamation marks, quite a lot of quite passionate language.'

'Sometimes critical, always questioning,' reported the *Telegraph* in September 2002, 'these letters have been landing on the desks of successive government ministers for more than two decades.' In one such memo Charles expressed his agreement with farmers who told him they were being more victimised on this issue than 'blacks or gays'.

'Charles has got a bloody cheek writing to the PM in such inflammatory tones,' declared one Labour minister. 'To compare fox-hunting to ethnic minorities defies belief. The man has lost all sense of proportion.'

Charles remained defiant. 'The Prince may well have written to the Prime Minister about fox-hunting,' confirmed one of his spokespeople without apology. It was no secret that the prince wrote regularly to a range of ministers to express his thoughts, particularly when he had been out for the day talking to people on public engagements.

When the existence of the 'black spider' missives was disclosed in 2002 – their full contents were later revealed after more than a decade following a lengthy legal battle – Charles was dubbed 'Angry of Windsor' and the 'Prince of Wails'.

* * *

Feelings reached their height in September 2002 when the Countryside Alliance planned a 'Life and Livelihood' march through the centre of London.

'If Labour bans hunting,' Charles was overhead complaining that autumn, 'I'll leave Britain and spend the rest of my life skiing.'

Once again Mark Bolland intervened. Charles had provocatively given his staff permission to join the three hundred thousand people who were due to demonstrate in favour of fox-hunting on 22 September. But he acknowledged that he could not possibly take part himself and he prevailed on Camilla, William and Harry to keep their heads down as well.

William had delayed his return to his second year at St Andrews University to join his friends on the march, led by Luke Tomlinson, a polo-playing companion with whom William and Harry had been close since childhood. The Tomlinson family owned the Beaufort Polo Club. Now William had to be content with going up on to the roof of St James's Palace to follow the marchers' progress, using his mobile phone to call through his support to Tomlinson and the others in the streets below.

Camilla, for her part, made a point of attending the post-march party organised by the novelist John Mortimer's campaigning second wife Penny Gollop, founder of the Leave Country Sports Alone pressure group. Throughout these weeks Mrs Parker Bowles had kept her Countryside Alliance sticker prominently displayed on her car windscreen.

* * *

It is difficult to imagine that Charles and Camilla would have been able to marry at Windsor in April 2005 with relative public acceptance if either or both of them had stepped out on to the streets of London in such a gesture of anti-government defiance two and a half years earlier. As for William and Harry, the modern champions of wildlife preservation, they must be thankful that their current CVs do not feature footage of them marching with demonstrators chanting in favour of the hunting and dismembering of wild mammals by trained packs of dogs.

The brothers had Lord Blackadder to thank for that contribution to their reputational preservation, but William still insisted on making his feelings clear. The Hunting Act finally passed through the House of Commons on 15 September 2004, but not before two young protesters dressed in fluorescent jackets burst into the chamber – the first invaders of the hallowed space since 1641 on the eve of the Civil War.

One transgressor was Otis Ferry, the twenty-one-year-old son of pop singer Bryan Ferry. The other was Luke Tomlinson, twenty-seven, William and Harry's close friend. Each offender, along with six accomplices, was fined £350 under the Public Order Act and given an eighteen-month conditional discharge. In a curious pre-figuring of the Washington DC Capitol invasion of January 2021, the eight plotters had taken advantage of an angry demonstration outside the legislature by thousands of their fellow supporters to sneak their way into the building.

The Hunting Act received royal assent on 18 November 2004, but it was not due to come into effect until 18 February 2005 – allowing Prince William, then twenty-two, to make one last gesture. On 3 January 2005, he dressed in his hunting jacket and hard hat to join the Beaufort when it rode out for one of its last full-scale hunting expeditions, authorising a spokesman for the hunt to make quite clear: 'I can confirm Prince William joined us for the meet today.'

There were certain issues on which the future King William V knew his own mind and he was not afraid to let the world know it.

17

Wobble

*'I just want to go in there and
get my asparagus, or whatever.'*

(Prince William on shopping in St Andrews,
BBC, 19 November 2004)

It was early in 1998, within months of his mother's death, that
William, still only fifteen, had decided that he must get to
know Camilla. When Diana's friends found out about it, some
of them felt that her elder son was betraying her memory – but
William was already a pragmatic and unsentimental young man.
He saw this as his obvious next priority. The purposeful teenager
realised and accepted that the woman, whom his late mother had
hated with such a passion, now occupied a place at the heart of
his father's life. So like it or not, that put Camilla at the heart of
his life as well.

'Eighty per cent of the boys at Eton have stepmothers,' ran
the gist of his reported explanation to one friend. His estimate
sounds a huge and exaggerated assemblage of stepmothers to be

concentrated at any one school or college, but the point remained – why shouldn't the prince move ahead to meet up with the new woman in his father's life? Of the two brothers, William was the one who had inherited Diana's cunning and hard-headed realism.

Out at Highgrove William tried following the hunt on one occasion when he suspected that Camilla was riding with the Beaufort. He had chased after the riders on his beloved quad bike, but his quarry proved elusive. In the months following Diana's death, Mrs PB – whose horse was now kept and cared for at Prince Charles's stables – was officially 'vanished' from public view by her minder Mark Bolland. It was part of his strategy that Camilla should become a non-person for a spell, so whenever she dared to venture out with her hunting friends, her hardhat was pulled down low over her forehead.

Then in the spring and summer of 1998 the lady resumed her visits to St James's Palace – and William made his move. One Friday afternoon in June, just a week or so before his sixteenth birthday, school ended early and the prince headed up from Eton to meet some friends in London – phoning his father with feigned casualness to say that he would be dropping in for a change of clothes.

Panic at the palace! As Camilla subsequently related – via Bolland, the channel for all the 'human interest' stories that were now let slip to humanise the scheming adulteress – her first instinct was to bolt when Charles told her that Wills was on the way. But she powdered her nose, put on a brave face and smilingly bobbed William a curtsy.

Oh, the miracles that can be accomplished over an old-fashioned cup of tea! It was William who led the conversation, Camilla recalled, trying to put her at ease with Gloucestershire talk of horses, the hunt and polo. How was Tom (her son who was also Charles's godson) getting along since leaving Oxford?

After half an hour of the professional chit-chat in which the prince was already quite practised, the ever-composed teenager made his excuses and left for the movies. William appeared quite unruffled by the encounter – but the momentous meeting had left Camilla, by her own account, 'trembling like a leaf'.

'I really need a gin and tonic,' she said – and promptly poured herself a double.

Harry proved yet more relaxed about his meeting with the wicked stepmother. It was over tea again – this time at Highgrove a month or so later in the company of Tom and Laura Parker Bowles, Camilla's two slightly older children, at twenty-three and twenty, with whom William and Harry had already spent some time the previous Easter.

Camilla would report that Diana's younger son had looked at her 'suspiciously'. But, as with William, the encounter apparently piqued her own anxieties more than it did the laidback juvenile – at least according to another story leaked to 'normalise' Camilla as part of the narrative of the Diana-less family.

'Whatever makes you happy, Papa,' was the standard response of both Diana's boys to Charles's efforts to construct a new domestic circle around his now ever more present companion.

NATURE NOTES

Potted   *Potty*

Avoid planting near snapdragons

Fig.1

Camellia *(Paramour carolus)*
This old favourite wilts in the glare of The Sun, preferring the shade, but can adapt eventually to a more exposed position with careful nurturing.

Prince Charles photographed with Camilla in public for the first time.
Peter Brookes, *The Times*, 30 January 1999

The brothers did not feign great enthusiasm, but they expressed no hostility either.

In this summer of 1998 Harry was basking in his recent success at Common Entrance, and as he got ready for Eton his father told him that he wished to broach 'an important conversation'. The time had come, Charles felt, to tackle the unpleasantly rumbling 'Hewitt Question'. Harry's new, more grown-up friends at the school might tease him, the prince worried, about the story of Diana's long relationship with 'Uncle James' – which Harry obviously knew about – along with the rumours that the red-headed Captain Hewitt was Harry's 'real' father.

We do not know whether this unsettling suggestion of Harry's paternity had come the thirteen-year-old's way by this date – we get the story of this highly intimate encounter from Angela

Levin, who interviewed Prince Harry in 2017. According to Levin, Charles's concern was to reassure his son 'that without doubt he and not Hewitt was his father' – and presumably Charles emphasised how the calendar made the rumour quite impossible, since Hewitt had not met Diana until two years after Harry's birth.

'Harry listened carefully,' according to Levin, who sources this story to 'someone who wants to remain anonymous'. But the prince 'didn't say a word either while his father was talking, or when he had finished'.

This was hardly surprising. What words could any of us conjure up if one of our parents suddenly presented us with the practical details of such an intimate topic? The young teenager's silence could well have reflected Harry's frequent problem during these years – being confronted with an issue that was simply too grown up for him.

But Harry may also have been wondering why, just at the moment when his father was attempting to reconcile his son to his longstanding mistress – the source of such family pain and distress – he should choose to bring up the subject of Diana's infidelity.

Prince William's career at St Andrews University could scarcely have got off to a worse start – and he had his family to thank for that. The massed cameras were all waiting on 24 September 2001, to see the nineteen-year-old prince arrive in the Scottish seaside town to commence his history of art studies, in a state of some anxiety.

'I think he was really nervous when he arrived,' recalls Colleen Harris, Charles's press secretary, the first black senior official to be employed by any of Britain's royal households. 'All the press were there – cameras from all over the world – and it suddenly hit him. He was very unsteady for a little while after that. He'd had a fantastic "gap year", going anywhere on the globe that he'd wanted and suddenly he was stuck here in this corner of Scotland, not knowing anybody, just one or two guys from Eton whom he didn't know that well, and he was very much alone.'

Harris had given strict instructions that the media should pack up their bags and leave the moment they had got their agreed photo op shots of the prince starting his studies, and when everything seemed calm she handed over to Niall Scott, the university's press officer. Scott was now in charge, she made clear, and if he should spot anyone wandering round 'with anything larger than an Instamatic', he should feel free to run them out of town. The police would back him up and if there were any problems he should give her a call. St James's Palace was worried about defending the privacy of all the students at St Andrews – since the object of the entire exercise was to enable normal college life for the prince.

'William was very sensitive to that,' Scott recalled. 'He knew the unsettling effect his presence could have and was keen that it should all be quietened down.'

But hardly had the last TV truck disappeared when Scott looked out of his window to see a full-scale camera crew setting up to film.

'What are you doing?' he asked – to be told, 'We're Ardent – here's our card. We're making an A-Z of royalty for an entertainment channel in the States and we're waiting to film William coming out of his lecture.'

Ardent Productions, they explained, was a TV company owned by Prince Edward. Prince Edward? Yes, that was the one! William's own uncle was breaching the carefully negotiated embargo that was being observed by the world's media.

Colleen Harris had not quite left for London, and she could not believe it: 'They kept saying they had permission to be there, and I said, "Well I'm the person who would give you permission and I haven't – so you can't be here."

'"No," they said, "we've got permission from Prince Edward." They just wouldn't go away.'

In London Prince Charles was reported to be 'incandescent' with rage. The air was said 'to have turned blue' when the prince heard that his own younger brother had invaded William's privacy.

Prince Edward and his wife Sophie, the Earl and Countess of Wessex, had not made a success of their attempts to be modern working royals. Sophie had recently been conned by the 'fake sheikh' reporter for the *News of the World*, Mazher Mahmood, whom she believed to be a potential client for her PR company. In their conversation, the countess had talked disrespectfully about the Queen as the 'old dear' and derided the grandeur of the then prime minister by calling him 'President Blair'. But the Wessexes seemed afflicted by a certain grandeur themselves when they went round to St James's Palace to apologise personally to Charles for Ardent's antics in St Andrews. They explained that they had walked round to SJP through the park 'to give pleasure to the people'.

William's experience of St Andrews University barely recovered from that ill-omened beginning. He had not anticipated quite how 'boring' – his word – life in a small Scottish seaside town could be. Highlights of the week included shopping in the local Tesco, while his social life was clouded by everyone's awareness of his celebrity. As the prince was drinking one night in a bar soon after his arrival, a passing female student gave his bottom a pinch – to which William responded with a look of sharp disdain. 'He was *not* impressed,' said one final-year student who witnessed the incident.

William Wales, as he asked to be known, played water polo and football on Wednesday afternoons, returning every night to his highly secure but cell-like accommodation in the St Salvator's hall of residence – 'St Sally's'. As the term progressed, the winter weather soon grew cold, grey and austere, and he found it difficult to make new friends. He missed his brother too.

There simply was not the 'buzz' at St Andrews that William was used to, and he fled the campus as often as he could the moment work ended on a Friday. By media count, the prince spent only two of his first thirteen term-time weekends in St Andrews, voyaging all the way to London or Highgrove in search of social life, at no little inconvenience and expense. He had to journey with a bodyguard and usually a driver for four hours or more each way – and that was if he travelled by air.

Academically, the prince did not find his history of art course all it was cracked up to be either. Its workload was more than he had expected – and under the Scottish system he was sentenced to a full four years to get his degree, not the three years he would have faced in England.

When William got home for Christmas that December of 2001, he told his father that he wanted to leave St Andrews. He was miserable. He had had enough of small town life – and all the travel arrangements that he needed to escape it. He asked Prince Charles to arrange some plan of withdrawal and transfer, possibly to Edinburgh as being more 'cosmopolitan' – or to some university in England or even Italy or the United States – and his father agreed to enable the change. Charles asked his private secretary, Sir Stephen Lamport, if he could come up with a 'strategy' of extrication and transfer for his son.

Lamport conferred with spin doctor Mark Bolland, now ranking as his deputy private secretary, and the pair were horrified. They protested strongly to their boss, remonstrating that some way must be found to keep his son at St Andrews.

'It would have been a personal disaster for William,' said one of them later. 'He would have been seen as a quitter.' Bolland feared a repeat of the debacle that had followed Prince Edward's decision to opt out of the Royal Marines – an act of surrender that damaged Edward's reputation for years.

'William needs to knuckle down and not wimp out,' was Prince Philip's robust and reported response as his grandfather.

Then there was the prospect of an 'even bigger' disaster for the monarchy – the likely political and social fallout in Scotland, where much had been made of the heir to the throne coming to study north of the border. For William to forsake Scotland's premier college after four months, Lamport and Bolland argued to Charles, 'would be taken as a snub by the Scottish people'.

'It would have been a PR disaster for St Andrews if he had left after one term,' said Andrew Neil, the journalist and editor who was, at the time, Lord Rector at St Andrews, 'and we worked very hard to keep him.' The phone lines hummed between the university and St James's Palace, with Lamport and Bolland bringing in Andrew Gailey, William's former housemaster at Eton.

'It was really no different from what many first-year students go through,' Mark Bolland recalled. 'We approached the whole thing as a "wobble" which was entirely normal. St Andrews had a flexible course structure, and when they heard that William might be happier majoring in geography, they made sure there were no roadblocks.'

'He got "the blues" – which happens,' said Andrew Neil. 'We have a lot of public-school boys who get up here, and by November when the weather gets grey and cold, wish they were back home. William was a long way from home, and he wasn't happy.'

In the end the two royal aides prevailed on Charles that he needed to demonstrate more fatherly backbone. It was not quite Charles's way to talk of 'knuckling down', Prince Philip-style, but in the course of a long parental heart-to-heart over Christmas he managed to persuade his son to think again.

'I don't think I was homesick,' William later admitted. 'I was more daunted. My father was very understanding about it and realised I had the same problem as he had probably had. We

chatted a lot, and in the end we both realised – I definitely realised – that I had to come back.'

So in January 2002 William headed back to St Andrews, resolved
to try again, and he was soon making good progress in two new
directions. The prospect of switching to geography made his
academic work more appealing, and socially he started investigating the possibility of renting a flat in the town with friends the
following September. This would release him from the confines
of his 15 ft x 15 ft 'cell' in St Sally's and give him a taste of why
he had really come to university – to enjoy some flavour of 'ordinary everyday life' with his contemporaries.

But in St James's Palace, Mark Bolland had been reflecting.
Just a few weeks earlier, he had successfully turned the *News of
the World* story of 'Harry's Drugs Shame' to Prince Charles's
great advantage (if not to Prince Harry's). Now he saw a way to
boost Charles's image still further as the concerned and caring
parent of Diana's elder son – the future king. On 3 March, just
as William was recapturing his momentum at St Andrews, the
Daily Mail ran the dramatic revelation (from an 'unnamed'
source, naturally) that 'William Wants to Quit "Boring"
College'.

As with 'Harry's Drugs Shame', Prince Charles emerged from
the article as the hero of the hour. Far from consenting to
William's wish to leave St Andrews – which had been Charles's
first instinct until Lamport and Bolland made him think otherwise – the Prince of Wales was presented as a wise and firm father
who had urged his son 'to "stick with it" and not abandon his

four-year degree in history of art'. Describing how William's worries had started the previous summer before he left for Scotland, the *Mail* revealed – in a detail that can only have come from Bolland – that Charles had cancelled a week's holiday planned with Camilla and the king and queen of Jordan so that he could spend more time with his son.

William meanwhile was portrayed as a spoiled and over-privileged wimp.

'Frankly, he was feeling sorry for himself,' commented one 'anonymous' unknown, without much sympathy, in a follow-up article next day that pointed out how 'William continues to spend most of his spare time at Highgrove … He needs to throw himself into the social scene [in St Andrews] a bit more.' The prince was too stand-offish – 'snobbish' was the implication. When he went to pubs like the Westport Bar, 'he has an arrangement to sit at a table behind a pillar'.

'We respectfully suggest,' wrote the *Guardian* in one of several less than sympathetic follow-ups spawned by the leak, 'that spending a night staring at a pillar may not be the optimum way to a splendid evening.'

18
Kate's Hot!

'That's kind of almost why I waited so long …
I'm trying to learn from lessons done in the past.'

(Prince William, 17 November 2010)

Tuesday, 26 March 2002. The date has passed into royal folklore – it was the moment when Prince William first set eyes on Kate Middleton in her underwear sashaying down a fashion runway at St Andrews University.

That was the start of it all – the royal romance, the televised marriage celebrated by millions, the birth of three babies and, eventually, looking into the future, the prospect of this couple sitting side by side on their thrones as king and queen. Everyone agrees that it all started on that catwalk in an austere and draughty Scottish student union – even the lovebirds themselves, who do not normally like to confirm or deny such private matters.

* * *

But it was not quite as simple as that sounds ...

We now know that Tuesday, 26 March 2002 was, for a start, very far from being the first time that Kate and William had encountered each other. Catherine's deep-digging biographer Katie Nicholl demonstrated in 2013 how the couple had almost certainly met while they were still at school – Wills at Eton and Kate at Marlborough College, where a number of her girlfriends were paid-up members of the Glossy Posse of Berkshire–Gloucestershire socialites who partied with the princes. As such, the Marlborough girls had been regular visitors to the gatherings at Highgrove's Club H in its 1999–2000 heyday, and two of Kate's very closest friends, Emilia d'Erlanger and Alice St John Webster – what wonderful posh old names! – were without doubt inner members of the 'William set'.

'We all knew as teachers that that year group was moving in "royal" circles,' recalled Kate's Marlborough housemistress Ann Patching to Nicholl. 'They were friends.'

That would definitely help to explain why Kate had switched her university application to St Andrews in August 2000 when she heard that William was going there – as much to be with the circle that would gather around William as with the prince himself. Then, while finishing off her gap year in the summer of 2001, Kate got a job on a yacht based in the Ocean Village Marina in Southampton, where her fellow deckhands ribbed her about making a beeline for William when she got to St Andrews.

'Obviously you might meet him,' said her first mate, Paul Horsford. To which Kate replied in a matter-of-fact fashion, 'I've already met him once or twice before.'

Kate gave no more details and would not be drawn, related Horsford to Nicholl. '[Kate] was always very professional and very private – and very careful with what she said.' In olden days young ladies were advised to keep themselves 'tidy' in a virginal sense if they were aiming to secure a high-profile husband. Nowadays the intimacy that matters is to avoid getting too close to the press.

The couple clearly saw a lot of each other once they reached St Andrews as fellow students on the smallish history of art course in the autumn of 2001. When William could not attend lectures, Kate sometimes took notes on his behalf, and both were residents of the same old Gothic-looking hall of residence – 'St Sally's', with rooms quite close to each other. They ate in the same hall for meals. They were in groups that tended to breakfast early together, with Kate and William always going for the 'healthy' selection: muesli and fruit, not bacon and eggs – and certainly no kippers.

When Wills got back to St Sally's early in 2002 after his Christmas 'wobble', the prince felt he knew Kate well enough to invite her to join the house-share that he was putting together for that September with fellow Etonian Fergus Boyd and another female student, Olivia Bleasdale. This seems a strangely decisive initiative for the cautious William to have taken. No one would extend such a personal and year-long commitment to a person they do not feel they know and also trust – and if you are William Wales you make sure to select someone you feel quite confident will not blab to the newspapers, nor to anyone else.

So here was the first reason why Catherine Middleton is due one day to become Queen Catherine the Sixth. She has all the attributes of the perfect flatmate – steady and reliable, clean and tidy, good company but not too gossipy, smiling and upbeat, and a fluent but not over-chatty conversationalist who could be relied upon to invite her attractive friends to your joint parties. She would never be too loud over breakfast next morning – and she was always good for the rent.

When it comes to the sex bit and the functioning of boyfriend–girlfriend relationships in such a modern university flat-share, readers of an older generation (like the author's) should be aware that nowadays these emotional complications are more unlikely than likely to feature in student friendship groupings. Fergus Boyd, for example, already had a girlfriend at St Andrews, Sandrine Janet, whom he would later marry but with whom he chose not to share a flat at uni.

Here's another question about that historic encounter at the fashion show … Having laid out all we know about the serious and purposeful young Kate Middleton being so 'professional' and 'private' and 'careful' – a real buttoned-up little William in many ways – aren't we somewhat surprised to discover her sashaying down a catwalk in her underwear?

And what about the prince? Have we ever heard of Prince William willingly sitting down in the front row of a fashion show before or since? Which brings us to the extra ingredient in our story, the urgent common cause that brought William and Kate to that student union hall early in 2002 in an atmosphere of unusually high emotion – the tragic catastrophe of the 9/11 attacks on America that had occurred only a few months earlier, just as the St Andrews students were starting their academic year.

This DONT WALK charity gala of March 2002 was their response – a fundraising effort for the families of the nearly three thousand victims of Osama bin Laden's attacks. The name DONT WALK was taken from the famous, apostrophe-free pedestrian crossing signs in New York, and some four hundred female undergraduates had rushed to volunteer for the fashion parade that the hastily assembled charity committee had thrown together. Someone had used their parental connections to pull in Yves Saint Laurent as a sponsor and other smaller fashion houses followed – among them the up-and-coming designer Charlotte Todd.

Wealthy male undergraduates were pressed for the £200 or so that it took to rent a front-row table and William was one of these – though he carefully paid the money through a friend. No one knew that he was planning to attend, and Colleen Harris, Prince Charles's press secretary, had even assured Niall Scott, the St Andrews press officer, that William would not be there. As a consequence Scott had encouraged the media to flood into the dramatically lit hall to help generate all the photos and publicity that this spectacularly worthy cause – the issue of the moment – deserved.

'Five minutes after I'd opened the union doors to the press,' Scott recalled, 'William walked round the corner with his mates and into the hall and sat down at the table right at the end of the runway. The press thought they'd died and gone to heaven.'

Scott reckoned that he might be destined for a slow and painful death at the hands of Colleen Harris with *no* chance of heaven when the royal press officer found out what had happened. But when he called London in a panic, Harris was only mildly displeased – 'She is about the calmest woman I have ever met,' Scott said. 'That was when I learned that William, on occasion, would lead even his most trusted minders a merry dance.'

Backstage, Catherine was also making merry. DONT WALK had captured the imagination of the entire campus. Only the very hottest chicks had been selected to rehearse and parade – and Kate was determined to dazzle for the cause.

Take a look at the photo of her in the second picture section – does that look like a conventional dress to you? It was, in fact, a long see-through petticoat-style skirt designed by Charlotte Todd to be worn from the waist down with some chunky knitwear round the shoulders. But at the last minute Kate had decided she would not wear the shift around her waist as a skirt – she discarded the knitwear and hoiked the blue silk belt up above her boobs to create a transparent mini-dress, with her black bra and knickers showing through.

That is how she emerged and paraded down the catwalk to raucous cheers. No wonder William was impressed!

'Wow,' he whispered to Fergus Boyd, 'Kate's hot!'

Here was a fresh dimension to William's solid, reliable lecture-note-taker and future flatmate that he had not expected – well, not this soon at least. The urgency of the 9/11 cause created an atmosphere that night which pushed the boundaries for all concerned – helped by liberal quantities of Red Bull, according to one participant.

DONT WALK would go on from this 2002 debut to be repeated annually at St Andrews, becoming the most successful student-run charity fashion show in the UK. Over the years it has raised more than £300,000 for good causes from ecology to homelessness, with DONT WALK (still minus its apostrophe) coming to mean 'Don't walk on by ...'

So the couple's personal spark had been lit at a charity occasion of the very type they would spend their lives encouraging and attending – and 9/11, which dominated those early years of the century so tragically, had another consequence. The US and UK governments would shortly send troops to clear Bin Laden and his followers out of their safe havens in Afghanistan – and in due course Prince Harry would serve in that war.

That March evening at the DONT WALK after-party, William and Kate were seen with their arms around each other. This had happened before – just a month or so into their first term together at a party at which William was getting seriously hit-upon by a pushy female student. The prince was being really polite, but he couldn't shake her off, and the girl did not get the hint – until suddenly Kate appeared out of nowhere behind him and put her arms around William.

'Oh sorry,' he said, 'but I've got a girlfriend', and he and Kate went off giggling together.

'Thanks so much,' he mouthed to her.

'Kate was the only girl in the room who could have done that,' commented Laura Warshauer, an American history of art student who described the incident to Katie Nicholl.

The episode showed extraordinary self-confidence on Kate's part and was an example of how the couple must have been friends – 'mates' perhaps, if not boyfriend and girlfriend, from their very first days at St Andrews. That started to change from the 26 March 2002 fashion show, which was not so much the date of an encounter as a refreshing of the screen – the revealing of a new Kate. The couple were also seen kissing towards the end of the DONT WALK after-party and making no attempt to hide it, although one source thought they did see Kate pulling away slightly. During the first term she had had a boyfriend, Rupert Finch, an attractive fourth-year law student, whom she had been seeing less of since the Christmas vacation.

Now William and Kate definitely became an 'item', even if friends were not sure of the details – it was not considered 'friendly' to probe – and the outside world knew still less.

'After the event,' recalls Simon Perry, London editor for *People* magazine, who visited St Andrews several times in 2002, 'it became clear that the March fashion show must have been some sort of turning point. But at the time we had no idea at all. We could not tell who was who.'

Kate Middleton was very good at keeping herself out of the papers, not least because her St Andrews friends were so close and loyal – and that loyalty extended across the student body as a whole. A decade or so later, after the couple had finally got married, details would start to creep out about the events of 26 March 2002, since the fashion show had turned out to be historic in its way. But at the time there was silence. Whether or not they had ever encountered William personally – and many had not

– St Andrews students took pride in keeping their traps shut. Those who had mobile phones texted warnings when they suspected that journalists and snoopers were in town.

'We saw William that spring and summer with various friends, male and female,' says Simon Perry. 'But it was not until the autumn of 2002, when their flat-share started, that we could begin to put names to faces – and even then it was not obvious that William was specially with Kate, rather than with, say, Olivia Bleasdale.'

Conspiracy and pretence had been built into the essence of William and Kate's relationship from the start. It had to be – vis-à-vis the outside world. Through the academic year of 2002–3 the two of them would emerge from 13A Hope Street at different times most mornings, heading in different directions. William's post-wobble subject switch to his geography major, with an entirely different faculty building and timetable, made this separation easier. But even when the couple socialised together in the evening, meeting up for meals or drinks or parties, they always seemed to be mixed and mingled with different groups of friends, among whom they jostled and joked and talked quite independently. There was nothing remotely lovey-dovey on display.

William had been trained in this sort of deception since childhood – it was embedded in the very nature of royal life. Catherine took to it immediately.

Love certainly did strike at some time during that Hope Street flat-share of 2002–3 – the couple acknowledged as much in their engagement and wedding interviews. And it intensified in the following academic year when they moved to a romantic house on the Strathtyrum Estate near the famous St Andrews Golf Course. Hope Street had been a modest grey stone terraced house, where William and his friends had occupied the upper two floors – an absolute nightmare for William's protection officers, who had had to fit bulletproof windows and a bomb-proof front door.

Balgove House stood in its own grounds with some two acres of wild meadow surrounded by a six-foot-high stone wall. William said it was just like a miniature Highgrove – and only a quarter of a mile from the St Andrews campus! Here Kate became Queen of the Aga, presiding over a household of three men – Wills' friends Oli Baker and Alasdair Coutts-Wood were their new housemates – and they quickly earned a reputation for hosting premier parties.

By the end of 2003, rumours had started to circulate that William and Kate were a serious couple, and Kate made the mistake of confiding their romance to her mother Carole. Carole herself was perfectly trustworthy, but that Christmas she could not help passing the news on to her brother, the garrulous Gary Goldsmith – who was so delighted that he started a new year business meeting by pushing a note across the table to a colleague: 'I think I'm going to be the uncle of the future Queen of England!!!'

In fact, the Middleton/Goldsmith dam held water. The revelation came more predictably, and catastrophically, from the tabloid press. At the end of March 2004, William could not help getting affectionate with Kate on a ski lift, stealing a kiss during the family's annual skiing holiday in the Swiss Alps at Klosters, and the *Sun* ran the photographs in a front-page story on 1 April 2004 as a 'World Exclusive': 'Finally ... Wills Gets a Girl: Prince & Kate So Close in Klosters.'

'Fuck!' exclaimed William in fury when his friend Guy Pelly showed him the paper. 'They have no right. We have an agreement!'

In fact, the palace had *two* carefully negotiated agreements in place with the British press. There was the fundamental pact applying to both boys – and, in this case, to Wills' 2001–5 sojourn in St Andrews – that they would not be photographed without their consent during their full-time education. Then Prince Charles had taken the further precaution, through his new press officer Paddy Harverson, of negotiating a second deal to ensure specific privacy during the royal skiing holiday, in return for which Charles and William had posed for pictures when they arrived – rather charming, affectionate ones, as it happened, in which William had put his arms around his father, ragging him fondly.

The *Sun* made no attempt to deny these agreements and issued no apologies. Editor Rebekah Wade argued rather that the pictures had been published in a higher cause, since William was now fully adult – twenty-one the previous year – and one of his girlfriends could well become queen one day.

'Her subjects will be entitled to know all about her,' argued Wade. 'Our story about Prince William and his girlfriend Kate Middleton is 100 per cent true. Therefore, there is a strong public interest in publishing these delightful photographs.'

Wade had a point – and then her rival tabloid, the *Mirror*, weighed in with more evidence confirming that William and

Kate were a serious item. The paper cited plausible St Andrews sources showing that the couple had been romantically involved for months, and in the ensuing stand-off, Clarence House stumbled. Its royal briefers wandered into excessive detail, arguing that while the couple may have shared student accommodation for eighteen months, they had not actually shared a bed and didn't 'live together' in the way that that phrase was popularly understood.

Too much information …

'Look, I'm only twenty-two, for God's sake!' exploded William when asked in 2004 about his marriage plans. 'I'm too young to marry at my age. I don't want to get married until I'm at least twenty-eight or maybe thirty.'

So, dear Catherine, that means you've only got eight years to wait …

William's wariness derived from the example of his parents' disastrously failed marriage. By this point he was old enough to have dipped into several of the vast library of books about Diana and to have glanced at some of the newspaper articles on her – though he hated them all. He had also begun to get a taste of the remorselessness of the royal system, and he was determined not to be prematurely pressured towards the altar as his mother and father had been.

So in the summer of 2004, with just a year to go until his graduation, William rather welcomed the mischievous suggestion of Guy Pelly that he might leave Kate at home and join his friend on a 'boys only' sailing trip to Greece. And Pelly being

Pelly, the best friend made another suggestion: that the yacht might be staffed and operated by an all-female crew. Kate was not impressed and she made sure William knew it.

Mischief was Guy Pelly's middle name. He had been one of the original and most rowdy ringleaders of the Glossy Posse and a stalwart presence at Club H. As the son of Diana's friend Lady Carolyn Herbert, Pelly had been close to both princes from childhood. When St James's Palace had wanted to suggest a 'bad influence' who might have led Harry astray in his 2002 'Drugs Shame', it was Pelly's name that it floated to the newspapers – most irresponsibly, as it turned out. Pelly had actually been in Australia in the weeks when the *News of the World* was gathering its incriminating evidence of Harry's pot smoking. But this did not save him from being asked to leave Cirencester's Royal College of Agriculture, after which he had had to redirect his land management studies via Newcastle University.

The naked injustice of this, and the good-humoured fortitude with which his friend had picked himself up and moved forward, had endeared Pelly to Prince William still further. There was – and is – a case for saying that Guy Pelly is the oldest and closest male friend of our future king. Never underestimate a man who is wise enough to play the fool. When Pelly went into the night-club business in his twenties, both William and Harry would make a point of visiting their mate's *boîtes* regularly until they all got established. And in 2018 William would invite his friend Guy to be a godfather to his and Kate's third child, Prince Louis.

It did take some time, but Catherine's acceptance of Pelly's godparenting showed how she had moved on from the all-male cruise suggestion that she certainly had not welcomed in the summer of 2004.

'At the time I wasn't very happy about it,' she admitted to ITV's Tom Bradby in 2010. 'But actually it made me a stronger person. You find out things about yourself that maybe you hadn't realised.'

'In that particular instance, we did split up for a bit,' agreed Prince William. 'We were both very young. It was at university. We were both finding ourselves as such and being different characters and stuff. It was very much trying to find our own way, and we were growing up. It was a bit of space and a bit of things like that, and it worked out for the better.'

Catherine found her own space that summer on some French leave with a group of St Andrews friends staying at Fergus Boyd's parents' house in the Dordogne, plus some quality time with the ever-supportive Middletons. She and William had committed to go back to Balgove House again for their fourth and final year, so the end of September 2004 found them reunited – and actually stronger, on reflection, for the time spent apart.

Now William's joke about living in a mini Highgrove came to pass again as the reunited couple moved back in to Balgove and hit their stride for their concluding terms at St Andrews – they had final exams the following summer to cram for. Both were committed and serious students, and Balgove's relative isolation gave them the chance to get their swotting done.

But that did not stop them entertaining in some style. The couple's occasional dinner parties in their dining room with its rustic open fireplace and long mahogany table that seated no fewer than seventeen became sought-after invitations. Kate had organised some bright red and white gingham curtains, while William's contribution was a glass-fronted champagne fridge and a large oil painting of his royal grandmother who presided solemnly – though surely with a mild touch of satire – over the festive gatherings.

In the summer of 2005 William and Kate certainly graduated from St Andrews with a first-class degree in memorable entertaining – and they had performed well academically. Each had earned a distinguished upper second-class degree – a 2:1, that token of hard-working intelligence without the eccentricity of genius.

'You will have made lifelong friends,' declared Vice-Chancellor Brian Lang in his farewell address. 'You may have met your husband or wife. Our title as the top match-making university in Britain signifies so much that is good about St Andrews, so we rely on you to go forth and multiply.'

19

Kate's Not!

*'You go through the good times. You go through
the bad times – both personally and within
a relationship as well.'*

(Kate Middleton, 17 November 2010)

Camilla had confided to Kate the secret of hanging on to a busy prince: fit your timetable – well, basically your whole life – around his. But after St Andrews University, William's timetable was proving rather un-fit-roundable. His next destination was the Royal Military Academy at Sandhurst, where he was due to spend the best part of 2006 training to be an army officer – the start of his plan to do stints in all three military services whose commander-in-chief he would become as king. Marriage had not been included in that schedule.

In the meantime, the prince, twenty-three in June 2005, undertook his first solo royal tour abroad when he flew to New Zealand to represent the Queen at the sixtieth anniversary of Allied victory in the Second World War. Happily, the British

Lions rugby team were touring the islands at the same time, which made for a lively ten days of engagements – rendered all the livelier by screaming crowds of hysterical young women. Kate followed her boyfriend's progress – and the screaming – via the evening TV news bulletins at home.

While Kate's medium-to-long-term objective was quite simple – to lead William in handcuffs to the altar – for the time being she had to devise her own independent career path as camouflage. This was a matter of both personal and public tactics. In neither respect would it help Ms Middleton to appear the slightest bit needy – and of course there was the ultimate and unthinkable possibility that she might end up getting dumped! In that event, the woman who would be known for the rest of her life as the girl-that-Wills-let-go would unquestionably need a plausible career to provide clear shape to the rebuilding of her non-royal identity.

Party Pieces provided the model. With the help of her parents, Kate set about trying to create her own company that would design and sell high-quality but reasonably priced children's clothes online. She would try her hand as a businesswoman. The would-be fashion executive toured Britain looking at samples and flew to Milan to check out possible manufacturers. At the same time, her parents set her up in her own Chelsea flat within safe range of Sloane Square – one never wants to live too far from Peter Jones.

* * *

9 April 2005: The marriage of Prince Charles to Camilla

That September 2005 William started his own domestic royal duties when he became the patron of Centrepoint, Britain's largest youth charity for the homeless. Here was an opening move that was very much in the footsteps of Diana – in due course the prince would venture out into the streets of London at night to see what it was like to sleep rough with the homeless. William also expressed his developing wildlife interests by becoming a patron of the Tusk Trust, an African conservation charity based in the UK. These were significant preludes to the adult prince's style as a working royal, and the press nodded towards them politely, while continuing to focus on what really interested them – his love life.

Following Charles and Camilla's marriage the previous April, the now openly acknowledged romance between William and Kate had become Britain's top royal story, with a succession of pundits confidently predicting the imminence of their marriage. William Hill and other bookmakers had started accepting bets on the date of the wedding, and the couple themselves were said to keep a calendar of the media's marriage projections in Kate's kitchen, where they took amused turns over breakfast to add the ticks. Woolworth's was even reported to have designed a set of William-and-Kate china.

The prince's father and grandmother knew this pattern of public interest all too well, but they were both warmly in favour of Kate as their latest recruit. Charles sent her a personal invitation to his November 2005 birthday party – a definite sign of approval – while the Queen invited her to join the traditional family Boxing Day shoot at Sandringham. William had been giving his girlfriend shooting lessons and he would present her with a set of binoculars that Christmas.

There seemed every reason to expect the announcement of a royal engagement before too long. But the twenty-three-year-old who would have to get down on one knee and actually make the proposal remained as adamant as ever about his long-term schedule of 'no marriage before thirty'. William was not going to repeat his parents' mistakes – and his upcoming year at the Royal Military Academy intensified the complications. In itself Sandhurst would constitute a year of all-consuming, twenty-four-hour-a-day activity, and the prince was hoping to follow that with a posting to the elite Blues and Royals Guards regiment, towards which Harry was also moving. There was no space in this timetable for all the frivolity and folderol of a grand royal wedding.

Through his tough year at Sandhurst the prince appeared in public with Kate from time to time – at a polo match where the couple were spotted kissing, and more formally at the marriage of Camilla's daughter Laura that summer. Then in December 2006 Kate sat in the front row at Sandhurst beside her parents at William's final graduation smiling proudly like a young wife or fiancée – except that she wasn't.

The tensions behind the scenes had been growing. Kate was less than a month away from her twenty-fifth birthday, and the couple had been dating seriously for the best part of five years – time enough, surely, for any reasonable boyfriend to commit. When William invited her to join him that year at Sandringham for the royal family's traditional Christmas lunch, she refused. It was the first time the Queen had ever extended such an invitation to an unregistered 'girlfriend', but Kate had her own take on that break with tradition: she would go to Sandringham on Christmas Day only when she *had* been registered and had a ring to prove it. She went off to Scotland to spend the holiday with her family instead.

Pressurising William, however, was not the way to make him change his mind. The prince's time away from Kate and the intensity of his RMA training had affected his thinking. The newly commissioned officer had begun to worry whether he had not, perhaps, found the right girl at the wrong time. His fun-loving fellow cadets at Sandhurst had demonstrated how much living he still had to do before he settled down. The *Spectator* had recently run an article anointing Kate as 'The Next People's Princess', and that had raised all the old anxieties about his parents' over-rapidly-arranged marriage.

William turned to his father and grandmother for guidance. The Queen had grown very fond of Kate, but she did not wish to interfere – and there were the lessons of the relatively brief courtships of Charles, Anne and Andrew. All their marriages had ended in disaster. She told her grandson that he should not rush into a commitment if he was feeling any doubts – and his father advised the same. Equally fond of Kate, Prince Charles was not happy with the idea that William might be seen by public opinion to be 'stringing her along' – and having himself been pressured into marriage by his father, he did not want to follow that path with his elder son.

Kate's birthday on 9 January 2007 was marked by the arrival of the largest scrum of photographers yet seen outside the door of her Chelsea home, waiting for the 'pre-engagement' or 'engagement day' photo that had been widely predicted. When Kate came out that morning she looked positively frightened. Charles was by this point providing her with a car and driver, but she received full royal protection only when she was in William's company, and here she was on her own, with William down on the south coast somewhere near Bournemouth on his latest army training course. It might be her birthday, but she did not offer the press her usual bright smile – and as she headed alone to work, it was clear that she was feeling under pressure.

William, meanwhile, was enjoying the life of a hard-drinking army officer. Not for nothing was his new regiment known as the 'Booze and Royals'. The prince was spotted in London dancing wildly at Boujis and at Mahiki, Guy Pelly's joint, and also in Bournemouth, where one of his dancing partners described the experience vividly.

'He has big, manly hands,' reported eighteen-year-old Anna Ferreira, a glamorous Brazilian brunette who described herself as a student in 'international relations'. 'And certainly he knows what to do with them … I was a little bit drunk myself.'

Royal biographer Christopher Wilson commented on the 'laddish' culture of the British army officer that had clearly seduced William. 'They take a light-hearted approach to the opposite sex,' said Wilson. 'The most important thing is bonding with men because you might need them under fire, whereas women are seen as adornments and people to have sex with.'

That might be shrewd sociology – but for Kate the problem was emotional not academic. On 11 April she excused herself from a meeting at Jigsaw, the fashion store with which she had recently started working, to take a call from William in a conference room out of earshot of the other buyers. She shut the door for more than an hour. When she rejoined the meeting, she was single.

The Middletons rallied round. Mum whisked her daughter off within days on a trip to Dublin to support an artist friend at the opening of their private view, then rounded off the cultural adventure with a tour of the National Gallery of Ireland. Brother

James escaped with her to Ibiza, and back home again there were reports of William's 'ex' being sighted enjoying herself on the London party circuit. Guy Pelly proved an unexpected ally, inviting Kate to Mahiki – and quietly advising her to give Wills some space.

Ms Middleton was not going to be seen as defeated. As the mornings got lighter she started heading out for the Thames to practise with an all-female dragon boat crew. Twenty-one-strong, the young women called themselves the Sisterhood – 'an elite group of female athletes on a mission to keep boldly going where no girl has gone before'. Their ambition was to paddle the twenty miles across the Channel from Shakespeare Beach in Dover to Cap Gris-Nez to raise money for children's hospices, and it was undoubtedly a good cause. But from Kate's point of view, her mission was to convey a very definite message to the world too – and to one particular person.

That person got the message quicker than he or anyone else expected. William found the dating difficult, for a start, when a surprising number of young women from his circle turned him down flat. They could suss out the truth about where his heart lay, even if he himself could not. Suddenly young students from Brazil no longer seemed so glamorous, and the prince missed his family – which by now meant the Middleton family. One pillar of William's year at Sandhurst had been his regular Friday night escapes to Bucklebury, where he could collapse and be mothered by Carole – and also fathered by the quiet and affectionate Michael who, whisper it, could provide a better ear for confidences, on some issues, than Prince Charles.

William had actually had his quad bike transferred from Highgrove to Bucklebury – he felt so much at ease being part of the Middleton clan. Their warm domestic closeness was something he had never known before. So often when he and Harry had been theoretically 'at home' with Dad, Charles had really been doing business over dinner, while the two boys ate alone. William had also become attached to the Middletons' upper-middle-class habit of renting villas for summer breaks around the Med – and to this day that remains a feature of the Cambridges' summers. He is the first and only senior British royal to vacation annually as the guest of his non-royal in-laws on foreign summer 'hols' like ordinary folk – sometimes flying privately, but also flying budget in the back of the plane like everybody else. Small wonder then, in April and May 2007, that the phone calls should resume.

'I don't think it's really over,' one Middleton pal had whispered to *People*'s Simon Perry on the April day that the break-up first became news. 'I don't think this is the last you'll see of the two of them.'

And so it proved. On 24 June 2007, just ten and a half weeks after the Jigsaw conference room phone call, the tireless Katie Nicholl revealed in a 'World Exclusive' on the front page of the *Mail on Sunday* that 'Wills and Kate Are Dating Again'. She also disclosed some juicy details – the couple had been seen kissing and dancing closely at a party in William's barracks in Bovington, Dorset.

'They couldn't keep their hands off each other,' reported Nicholl on the testimony of 'eyewitnesses' at the party. 'But

William didn't care that people were looking. At about midnight, he started kissing and smooching her. His friends were joking they should "get a room", and it wasn't long before William took Kate back to his quarters.'

Nudge nudge, wink wink – just what we all like to read on the front page of our Sunday newspaper! But Nicholl was engaged in some serious business – and on behalf of some people who were clearly serious. The reporter had spoken to sources who were representing both William and Kate and who wanted the world to know that the couple were back together again and were working out how to move forward on a new basis.

The break-up had happened, explained Nicholl, because of 'William's unwillingness to commit to a long-term relationship and, ultimately, marriage'. But now things had changed. 'I understand that William has told Kate he is very serious about getting back together … William wants to make things work and said that if they get back together, it will be the real thing.'

For her part, Catherine explained – through another helpful friend, of course – that 'she absolutely loves William', but that she 'is thinking about things … It is the toughest decision of her life … She knows if they do get back together, there'll be no turning back. There will have to be an engagement and then marriage.'

Hmmm, so here was the m-word again … A friend of the prince's was very happy to confirm for the record that 'William hasn't stopped pining for Kate since they split up. He keeps saying she's an amazing girl and the best thing to happen to him. He's definitely serious about getting back together.'

So this was it, the essence of a new personal life-and-love arrangement between Prince William and Catherine, all laid out in black and white in the self-same fashion in which both Diana and Prince Charles – in his Mark Bolland days – had leaked out the details of their personal love-styles via helpful 'friends' and briefings to newspapers.

Katie Nicholl has since confirmed that, as well as talking to close friends of both William and Kate in June 2007, she had spoken to a 'senior palace aide' while preparing the story and had been 'given the nod'. If Kate agreed to resume her relationship with William, it would now be on a solid new basis that was mutually agreed to lead to an engagement – and eventually to marriage.

It might take a long time. Catherine might have to put up with media derision for hanging around playing 'Waity Katie' – but Prince William had finally made up his mind. He was ready to commit. The young man still had his stints to do in both the navy and the air force. In civilian life, he wanted to develop his charity profile as well – and there were definitely ways that she could help him with that. There might also be engagements and foreign tours representing the Queen on which Kate still could not accompany him. She was going to have to be very patient indeed.

But at last Ms Middleton knew where she stood. She trusted the word of the man she loved who, for all sorts of reasons that she had come to accept, felt that he could not commit to marriage before he was thirty years old – and in the end, after three more long years, her trust would be repaid. At the end of a safari holiday in Kenya in October 2010, on the shores of Lake Rutundu, William got down on one knee and extended his hand to offer Kate the beautiful and famous diamond-and-sapphire cluster engagement ring that had been worn by his mother. He had told neither his father nor his brother of his intention to propose to Kate at that particular time and place – though he had spoken to Harry to make sure that his brother was quite happy for Kate to take possession of their mother's fabulous ring when the time came.

On 16 November 2010 the engagement was formally announced of Ms Catherine Middleton (twenty-eight) to Prince William of Wales (then also twenty-eight). Far from being 'Waity Katie', the dragon boat oarswoman had managed to rush her prince forward by two whole years.

'So,' asked Tom Bradby, ITV's political editor, on the engagement night, discussing the 2007 separation that had transformed the royal couple's relationship – did that ten weeks or so of break-up provide 'a chance to re-centre yourself'?

'Yes,' replied Kate. 'Definitely, yes.'

'You were obviously upset when you split up,' continued Bradby, 'but all your friends [on both sides] talk about there being a very substantial love that has built up over a period of time that's part friendship – and more than that.'

'Well,' replied Kate, 'I think if you do go out with someone for quite a long time you do get to know each other very very well. You go through the good times. You go through the bad times – both personally and within a relationship as well. I think …

you can come out of that stronger and learn things about your-self.'

Discussing the pain of past emotional break-ups provided a striking new dimension in official royal engagement and marriage interviews – and it was a definite improvement on 'whatever "in love" means'. Tom Bradby had even discussed that particular hazard with William and Kate in the course of several hours of preparation and rehearsal for the interview, and William cleared the hurdle with aplomb.

'The timing is right,' he said. 'We are very very happy.'

The prince also interrupted when Bradby turned to Kate and asked, 'You've had a long time to contemplate this moment?'

'Let's not over-egg the "long" bit,' joked William.

The informal tone of the interview reflected the closeness that had developed between William and Bradby since the journalist had served as ITN's rather reluctant royal correspondent in the early years of the century. Invalided home from Jakarta, where he had been hit in the leg by a bullet while covering a demonstra-tion, Bradby – who had recently become a father – had asked for a job 'that didn't involve getting shot', and the royal beat had been the only one available. The young journalist came to the assignment with as little enthusiasm for princes as they felt for the press, but from that unpromising beginning, a friendship had flowered.

Though a decade and a half older than either William or Harry – with whom he would also become friendly – Bradby had a youthful energy that brought him close to the young men, as well as the empathy of a fellow toff who was so bright he could have gone to grammar school. Bradby's public school, Sherborne in Dorset, was even older than Eton – more than seven centuries older, founded in AD 705 by St Aldhelm – with a rural modesty that gave it more class.

Bradby totally 'got it' when it came to his coverage of the royal family. 'It's really about *us*,' he once said, 'and why we project so much onto them.' He was a clear cut above the majority of the royal rat pack – and his personal closeness to the princes also led to a coup that had remarkable consequences.

One day in 2005 William had phoned Bradby, by then ITN's political editor, to let him know that he had come up to London and would Tom fancy meeting for a beer? The prince wanted to discuss pulling together the videos of his gap year, and the next day Bradby was astonished to discover the details of all this printed in the *News of the World*. He had not discussed the project with anyone – not even his wife, the jewellery designer Claudia Bradby – and when he did meet up with William the prince said just the same. He had not spoken to anyone either.

Some sort of eavesdropping or phone-hacking seemed to be the only, if scarcely believable, explanation. So William's office contacted the police, and eight months of inquiries would lead to the arrest of a freelance private investigator, Glenn Mulcaire, along with Clive Goodman, the *News of the World*'s royal editor. Both men pleaded guilty to illegally intercepting phone messages, for which they were respectively sentenced in January 2007 to six months and four months in jail. The police eventually presented evidence that, in the course of this intrusion, Prince Harry had been hacked 9 times, Prince William 35 times, while Kate Middleton – beginning in December 2005, soon after she had left St Andrews when she was just starting work – had had her phone hacked on no fewer than 155 occasions.

These extraordinary figures came out of a later trial resulting from the discovery that the *News of the World* had been phone-hacking far beyond the royal family, including numerous celebrities (Elton John, Uri Geller, Hugh Grant, Elizabeth Hurley, Jude Law, Heather Mills) and the voicemail of missing British teenager Milly Dowler who was later found murdered. The deletions of Milly's voicemails in 2002 – when Rebekah Wade was editing the paper – had resulted in the missing girl's parents being led to believe that their daughter was still alive.

Such was the public outrage at these revelations that in 2011 Prime Minister David Cameron announced a wide-ranging inquiry into the British media, and the briefly shame-faced proprietor Rupert Murdoch felt compelled to shut down the *News of the World*. The disgraced newspaper ceased publication on 10 July, after nearly nine thousand issues spanning 168 years, printing a full-page apology for its involvement in the hacking scandal.

This destruction of the detested 'News of the Screws' came just ten weeks after William and Kate's marriage of April 2011, and it provided William, in particular, with the sweetest wedding present of all. Finally he and Harry (and Kate too) had secured some sort of revenge over the hated media rat pack that had killed their mother and made their own lives such a misery for so many years – with the particular piquancy that this involved the humiliation of the very newspaper that had gloried in 'Harry's Drugs Shame'.

This had all stemmed from William inviting his mate Bradby for a beer, and it cemented the friendship and position of the newsman in his life at that time, and in Harry's too. It would be in the course of a Tom Bradby interview in 2019 that Harry would reveal that the two brothers found themselves on different paths.

The marriage of the new Duke and Duchess of Cambridge on 29 April 2011 was a triumph, poignantly staged in Westminster Abbey. How brave of William to have chosen the aisle where he had processed behind his mother's coffin! Playing their various wedding roles in the abbey presented such conflicting emotions for Diana's sons and for the entire royal family – a moment of both challenge and renewal.

The wedding service with which the gathering contrasted most strikingly was the marriage of Charles and Diana in St Paul's Cathedral thirty years earlier, almost to the month. Here was the elder product and survivor of that marriage – the vindication of the tragedy, in a way – with the same sapphire and sparkling diamond ring on the bride's finger symbolising the emotional commitment at the heart of the ceremony, but representing such very different realities.

By one count Charles and Diana had only been on thirteen dates before they got engaged. William and Catherine, by contrast, were finally tying the knot after nearly a decade of firm commitment – while also making sure about each other. They had had the foresight to arrange their separation *before* they announced their engagement.

After their May 2011 honeymoon in the Seychelles, the couple set off the following month for their first major foreign assignment – a tour of North America, starting in Canada where anti-royal sentiment had been festering for some time. The dominion was quite happy to remain part of the British Commonwealth, but to retain Britain's Queen as head of state seemed a nonsense to more than 60 per cent of Quebecers, with some 40 per cent of English-speaking Canadians in agreement.

Within days of their arrival by British Airways – 'So they fly commercial like the rest of us!' – the Cambridges had turned that sentiment right around. Cheering crowds welcomed the glamorous young couple to Ottawa and on across the country westwards to Calgary, where an enterprising pollster thought to enquire how a sample of 1,005 people felt about the royal succession. This group were much happier than they had previously been about the idea of retaining the British monarchy, with 56 per cent actually saying they would prefer William to succeed the Queen, compared to just 26 per cent who supported the prospect of Charles as a future king.

Here was a dilemma for the years ahead. The more popular and successful Catherine and William became, the more they pushed Charles and Camilla into the background.

20

Line of Duty

*'I was in the military for ten years, so I'm more
normal than my family would like to believe.'*

(Prince Harry, March 2020)

Boujis, Mahiki, Club H – there was seldom a shortage of
venues for the perpetually partying princes. And then, in
January 2005, along came 'Colonials and Natives', the politically
incorrect theme of a fancy dress celebration planned for the
twenty-second birthday of their friend Harry Meade – son of
Princess Anne's one-time boyfriend Richard Meade, the Olympic
gold medallist event rider.

Guy Pelly said he would accompany the boys down to Maud's
Cotswold Costumes to select their outfits. Guy himself rather
fancied going as the Queen – 'My husband and I take great pleasure in each other …' After a few drinks, Guy could do a very
good Queen Elizabeth II.

But was Granny a colonial or a native? Looking through the
available garments on Maud's rails it was difficult to pick out

costumes that really fitted the declared – and magnificently dodgy – theme of the party. In the end William opted to go as a lion – or was it a leopard? – with tight black leggings and furry paws. As for Harry, he chose a khaki-coloured uniform that, he later explained, he selected for the sandiness of the shirt: he thought it complemented his ginger colouring. The trouble was that the shirt's left sleeve was encircled by a bright red and white armband bearing a stark, black Nazi swastika.

The rest, sadly, is history. If there was one incident in the youth of Prince Harry that would be taken to represent his wild, foolish and unjudged side, it was that Nazi costume. A sneaky fellow guest used their mobile phone to snap a photograph of the prince, beer in one hand, cigarette in the other, and a few days later, there was Harry parading on the front page of the *Sun* of 13 January 2005 looking like a member of Rommel's Afrika Korps.

'Harry the Nazi' read the headline – 'Prince's Swastika Outfit at Party'.

Just about a year after this, by then a cadet training at Sandhurst, the twenty-one-year-old would generate another set of similar headlines. Delayed and bored in an RAF departure lounge while awaiting his flight home from a military exercise in Cyprus, Harry got hold of a video camera and panned it around the sleeping faces of his fellow officer cadets.

'Ah,' he could be heard to say quietly, homing in on one fellow Sandhurst comrade, 'our little Paki friend Ahmed!'

If this remark was overheard by Cadet Ahmed Raza Khan, who would later be awarded the Best Overseas Cadet prize at

Sandhurst as the prelude to a distinguished career in the Pakistani army, he did not react at the time.

And that was not all … In another sequence filmed at night, Harry greeted a fellow cadet who was wearing a camouflage hood with the salutation, 'Fuck me, you look like a raghead!' – 'raghead' being army slang for Taliban and al-Qaeda fighters, as St James's Palace had to explain with some embarrassment when the videos became public.

'All is good in the empire,' Harry was heard to comment, chuckling, on several occasions, as film shot by some other cadet showed the prince kissing a comrade and asking another whether he felt 'gay', 'queer', or 'on the side'.

Harry then conducted a mock military briefing, dressed in combat gear, cigarette in hand, pretending to finish off a mobile phone call to his famous grandmother before he started. 'I've got to go, got to go!' he said. 'Send my love to the corgis and Grandpa … God Save You!'

At the end of the briefing, he asked his colleagues if they had any questions, to which one responded, 'Are your pubes ginger too?'

'Yes,' replied the prince laughing. 'They are!'

The national response to both these cringeworthy episodes when they hit the media in 2005 and 2009 was predictably one of outrage, led in January 2005 by the Israeli foreign minister and numerous Jewish organisations. They were understandably incensed by the unthinking crassness of the prince's behaviour just two weeks before Holocaust Memorial Day. On 27 January Harry's uncle, Prince Edward, was due in Auschwitz to represent the Queen at a ceremony marking the sixtieth anniversary of the liberation of the death camp.

'I'm very sorry,' said Harry in a statement released immediately, 'if I caused any offence or embarrassment to anyone. It was a poor choice of costume and I apologise.'

'A poor choice of costume'? The prince's apology could surely have displayed more understanding of his disastrous frivolity and ignorance.

But there was an element of ritual to this public outrage too. Harry's behaviour was deemed 'totally unacceptable'. Everybody had to have their say – the leader of the Tory Party, the statutory anti-crown left-wing MP, a former armed forces minister, plus the inevitable 'royal expert' filmed outside some palace or other, a royal 'talking head' – among whom was this author at the time, not striking a very sympathetic tone, as I recall. All of us were eager for our forty-five seconds of indignation and screen time – and all of us were missing the point entirely.

Was Harry really a neo-Nazi, as one Labour MP alleged? Obviously not, since he would fall in love with and marry a woman of mixed-race origin, and it is difficult to imagine that anyone really believed it at the time. The boy was naughty, not Nazi – naughty, but reasonably nice – as Harry's Sandhurst comrade, the now wide-awake Ahmed Raza Khan, wasted no time in telling the *Sun*: 'We were close friends when we were training,' he said, 'and I know he is not a racist … [He] called me by a nickname which is usually very insulting, but I know he didn't mean it that way.'

By January 2009, when the *News of the World* broke the story, Harry and Khan had both long departed Sandhurst and, by that date, had also seen active service in Afghanistan fighting the Taliban. They had both killed and had risked being killed, and they discussed their experiences together when Harry rang his friend to apologise.

'Forget about it,' said Raza Khan.

Yes, indeed. But let us not forget the main point. Foolish and thoughtless though Harry may have been at the age of twenty-one and twenty-two, he was the victim of a national process that has to be seen as a mutual popular conspiracy. The young man had been typecast – categorised as the court jester.

In 2006 there were dozens of other young men going to Sandhurst who talked about 'Pakis' and 'ragheads'. We know that

Prince Harry complains at press 'abuse and harassment' of Meghan Markle. Peter Brookes, *The Times*, 9 November 2016

from all the giggling on the video by his fellow cadets – who today are senior officers in our upstanding British army. Some of this future military elite might even have been willing to dress up in Afrika Korps uniform for a laugh – and we certainly know that when Harry turned up at the home of Richard Meade in January 2005, there were several hundred horsey folk who smiled and nudged at the young prince's costume complicitly. There is no record of any of them dashing their champagne glass to the ground with a cry of 'totally unacceptable!'

Most clearly of all, we know that Harry chose his costume in conjunction with his elder brother the future King William V, who laughed all the way back to Highgrove with the younger sibling he was supposed to be mentoring – and then onwards to the party together. But did a single newspaper or Sunday morning commentator remark on Prince William's role in the debacle?

We are back again to the personal, social and national stereotyping that we noted at the time of 'Harry's Drugs Shame' in 2002. It was the function of the elder brother to be perfect, whether he truly was or was not, and it was the function of the younger one to make the rest of us laugh or complain or feel disapproving – and at all events to make us feel thoroughly superior to the poor clueless kid.

This was the role that all of us shaped for Prince Harry over the years every time that we scoffed at a newspaper picture of him playing the court jester – and thus encouraged the papers to print still more. Harry's departure from Britain in March 2020 has become known as 'Megxit' and his relationship with Meghan Markle undoubtedly played a role in that decision – we will be looking into all of that very closely. But Meghan was not the original factor in Prince Harry's decision to get shot of his family – he already had very solid reasons to get shot of the rest of us with our patronising laughter.

In January 2005, following the 'Colonials and Natives' costume fiasco, we now know that Prince Harry was drawn to re-evaluate his elder brother's involvement and the unfairness of William's subsequent emergence smelling of roses. It made Harry feel alienated. Friends recall 'no-speaks' and quite a serious rift between the two brothers at the time – as there had been after the 'Drugs Shame' of 2002, when Harry had first started to realise the price of playing the functional scapegoat. On that occasion he – and Guy Pelly – had shouldered all the blame for the wild antics of the Rattlebone crowd, when the real Rattlebone ringleader had been William.

'For the first time their relationship really suffered, and they barely spoke,' said one former aide, speaking to Katie Nicholl. 'Harry resented the fact that William got away so lightly.'

William himself felt guilty, confiding in his St Andrews tutor, John Walden, that he was 'having a bit of a crisis'. But the ability and the willingness of the brothers to keep talking to each other at this age helped them both to move on – and while William had his geography exams to worry about, Harry had Sandhurst.

That summer of 2005 saw the perpetual 'spare' setting off to the Royal Military Academy to start his officer training. On arrival, along with every other cadet, Harry had his head completely shaved and was assigned a room not much larger or different in character than a prison cell. He was given his own iron and ironing board, which he had never used before – and he later admitted that Sandhurst was the first time in his life that he wielded a lavatory brush.

At 5 a.m. every morning the prince would jump out of bed with his fellow cadets, all brushing their teeth and tidying up around themselves, folding their shirts and jumpers into perfect A4 rectangles. Socks had to be rolled into special balls that made them look like smiley faces, and clothes were organised in their wardrobes by colour. By 6 a.m. Cadet Wales and his fellows had to gather in the corridor outside their room to sing the national anthem – no jokes now about God saving Granny.

The young man revelled in all this – in living a life just like everyone else's.

'I wasn't a prince,' he said. 'I was just Harry.'

He was plain Officer Cadet Wales – with no bowing or scraping. For these forty-four weeks of obeying orders without argument and getting bossed around, Harry could take a few steps towards being ordinary and learning how the real world worked.

'If you want to be a success you have to be a team player,' he later told Angela Levin. 'You get taught in the army that you can't get anywhere without the support of other people. I agree.'

On 12 April 2006 the twenty-one-year-old prince marched stoutly in the Sandhurst passing-out parade, now Second Lieutenant Wales in the Household Cavalry, Blues and Royals. For the first time in fifteen years the Queen had come to take the Sovereign's Parade in person, since not only was Harry graduating,

William had joined Sandhurst a few months earlier as a regular cadet – which meant that he actually had to defer to his younger brother.

'He is determined not to salute me,' said Harry. 'But it is the army and you have got to do things.'

The next step for most of Harry's fellow graduates involved service in the Iraq war, and Harry was intent on joining them.

'There's no way I'm going to put myself through Sandhurst,' he said, 'and then sit on my arse back home while my boys are out fighting for their country.'

Harry joined the Household Cavalry training course for Iraq with a group of Blues and Royals, but the news of his plans soon found its way into the newspapers – drawing an almost instant response from the battlefield.

'We are awaiting the arrival of the young, handsome, spoiled prince with bated breath,' declared Abu Zaid, commander of the Malik Ibn Al-Ashtar Brigade. 'He will return to his grandmother – but without ears.'

The Shia leader boasted that his spies would have no trouble locating the prince within weeks of his arrival, and General Sir Richard Dannatt, chief of the general staff, regretfully agreed. The threat could not be ignored, and on 16 May 2007, just days before his departure for Iraq, Harry was informed that his deployment had been cancelled. When the news became public, many felt relieved, but other voices complained that all the prince's training had been a 'waste of public money'.

The young man was understandably depressed. 'If I'm going to cause this much chaos to people,' he said, 'then maybe I should just, well, bow out and not just for my own sake, for everyone else's sake.'

'It was a very low point in [Harry's] life,' recalled a colleague at the time, 'because he felt as though everything he'd trained for had been a waste of time.'

Richard Dannatt let it be known to the Queen that he would manage it better next time, liaising with Major Tom Archer-Burton who had become something of a mentor to Harry at Sandhurst and was helping him through the early months of his career.

Archer-Burton was 'the only man capable of telling Lieutenant Wales to do press-ups', in the view of one contemporary Sandhurst witness, 'or stand on one leg for as long as he feels necessary.'

Major Tom became the supervisor of organising Harry's next assignment – to Afghanistan. The prince would be the first member of the royal family to serve in a warzone since his Uncle Andrew flew helicopters in 1982 in the Falklands War. As a family man, a philanthropist and a committed Christian, Archer-Burton would also be credited with gently helping move Harry along from costume parties and racial jokes, stimulating the young man to deeper spiritual reflection in his personal life.

Travel plans were discreetly set in motion, and that December 2007 found the prince on active service at last – in Afghanistan. '[The Queen] was very pro my going then,' Harry commented later, 'so I think she's relieved that I get the chance to do what I want to do. She's a very good person to talk to about it. Her knowledge of the army is amazing for a grandmother. I suppose it's slightly her job.'

That Christmas Elizabeth II bowed her head over the table and led prayers for the absent Harry as the rest of the family sat down for lunch in Sandringham. Harry himself was eating goat curry at the time, he revealed – and the prayers were needed. Sergeant Tom Pal from an anti-tank platoon, recalled meeting up with Lieutenant Wales shortly afterwards.

'I was sitting chatting with ... Prince Harry about random stuff,' he said, 'when the camp was hit by a Chinese 107mm rocket ... Whoosh, bang, wallop!' The rocket struck a 'breath-stopping' fifty metres from where the prince and Sergeant Pal were sitting, and they rushed to put on their protective body armour and helmets.

'At that time of year where we were working, it was pretty mental,' said Pal. 'Various checkpoints were getting attacked every single day.'

Harry had been assigned to serve as a forward air controller in some of Afghanistan's most remote and dangerous areas, responsible for controlling military air movements from the ground and calling in lethal air strikes on Taliban positions – killing the enemy, in other words.

Miguel Head was the defence ministry official in charge of keeping Harry's presence in Afghanistan out of the newspapers. In 2006 Head had tried and failed to smuggle Prince William out to the war in Iraq, and he was determined to do better with Harry – creating a taskforce of newspaper editors and broadcasters that he later described as 'the circle of trust ... we were very transparent about everything'.

'Look, this is going to happen,' Head told the group of media bosses in late 2007, speaking on behalf of Des Browne, the Labour defence minister of the day. 'We don't know how it's going to happen, but we want it to happen … So let's discuss how it might work for you.'

To start with the BBC caused trouble – news censorship during a major war would be 'against our editorial guidelines', it felt. But Head explained that this project was about more than letting one young prince go out to play war games. Harry had trained seriously for several years. He was a professional army officer, and he had the rights of any other citizen and officer to do his national duty – and to set an example to others.

'The competitive nature of the media,' recalled Head a dozen years later, meant that none of the editors wanted to be seen as 'the bad person'. Prince Harry was enormously popular – he was still very young.

'It had been only ten years since Diana, Princess of Wales had died,' Head would remember. 'There was still a very strong sense in the country of the public, in effect, bringing the two young princes into their arms and saying, "We will look after them – and You Press, you had better keep your hands off them! Don't you dare do to them what you did to their mother."'

The reporting blackout that was finally agreed on Harry's Afghanistan activities did not involve lawyers.

'It was a gentlemen's agreement,' said Head. 'But it was written down on paper. It was codified about who would get access to what' – along with the details of which reporters and broadcasters would conduct a succession of interviews that would be retained to be broadcast at the end of Harry's assignment, which in the end would last for just seventy-seven days.

Eleven weeks was less than he had been hoping for, but, when events failed to go according to plan, it was more than might have been feared. After just four weeks, *New Idea*, the indefatigable Australian magazine that first published the 'Camillagate' tape in 1993, now discovered that Prince Harry was on active service with the British army in Afghanistan. Not being part of the UK agreement nor even being aware of the blackout, *New Idea* posted the story on its website.

'We saw this in the press office,' recounted Miguel Head, 'and thought, Oof! This is it! It's over, four weeks in! It's done.'

But the defence ministry held its nerve. These were still early days for the Internet, before many publications had started distributing content online, and relatively few people then were looking to the Web as their main source of news. The *Sun* spotted the story straight away, and it contacted the ministry privately. But the British tabloid did not want to break the agreement unilaterally.

'There was still a sense,' said Head, who shared the problem with the whole of the taskforce, 'that nobody wanted to be the first to go.'

Miraculously, the blackout held for six more full weeks – until the Drudge Report, an investigative US website that had broken the Monica Lewinsky scandal, stumbled on *New Idea* and unhesitatingly ran the story on 28 February 2008.

'It went BOOM! on the website,' remembered Head – though it was not so much the American muckrakers as their Australian magazine source that got into trouble for the revelation. 'Poor old *New Idea,*' he said. 'This little known, very friendly magazine in Australia, came into the worst criticism – particularly in Australia where the monarchy is very popular … They had published the scoop of the century and just didn't realise it!'

When the news broke, Harry was in a remote base near the front line in Afghanistan, and he had to be helicoptered straight out and back to the main British base in the country, where he was put on an aeroplane for Britain, landing at RAF Brize Norton that night. Miguel Head had organised a small group of journalists to greet him.

'He was very upset, actually,' recounted Head. 'He was really down. I wouldn't describe him as angry – he's far more mature than that and he understood why it had happened. He was just very sad about it. In that time, you develop such a close bond with your troop. And it's a job that he evidently was very good at and passionate about. To suddenly have to cut it short, in the middle of a day as well … It was very sudden.'

Head was touched that Prince Charles and Prince William had both come out to the airfield too.

'It was the first time I realised – that I saw with my own eyes –' Head said, 'the closeness of the relationship between the two brothers. Think about the mixed emotions Prince William would have had, because *he* wasn't allowed … *He* never got to go. So he would have known how Prince Harry felt, and he was very protective of him.'

To the west of Oxford, RAF Brize Norton was the airfield to

which many Afghanistan casualties were being repatriated, and Harry shared an aircraft with three seriously wounded men being flown home, one of them still in a coma and clutching pathetically at the piece of shrapnel that the surgeons had removed from his head.

'As I was waiting to board the plane,' Harry later recalled, 'the coffin of a Danish solider was loaded on by his friends ... The way I viewed service and sacrifice changed for ever.'

The sobering experience of the long flight home with his dead and wounded comrades proved to be the inspiration for Harry's Invictus Games for disabled veterans.

'Those are the heroes, not me,' the prince would insist, 'the ones who have lost limbs and will never be able to live a normal life again.'

The prince was still wearing his combat gear, all covered in desert sand on 1 March 2008, and as he sat down to talk to the press it was clear that he was exhausted. He had not washed for a day and a half and he was obviously very upset as he tried to absorb the reality that, yet again, something he really cared about had been torn from him.

Miguel Head and his media colleagues had carefully agreed a list of questions for the prince to answer on his return, but the interviewer had got only two or three questions into the list, when Prince William suddenly stood up at the back of the room. He had been seated behind Head, and as the ministry man turned to look, he saw the older prince making a cutting motion with his hand across his throat – saying, in effect, 'This is over.'

'It was simply a brother,' explains Head today, 'realising that at that point nothing was more important than his brother's welfare – and none of the other agreements mattered … It says something about the closeness of the two brothers and their authenticity, as well. They will not fake who they are simply to play a game, or to go along with other people's expectations. And they are perfectly courteous and loyal, and they will abide by agreements up to a point. But they will come to a point where they say, "Well, actually …"'

Miguel Head looked at Prince William, then he looked at the media folk he had assembled and with whom he had been negotiating for weeks.

'And I think, I have a split-second choice here. Do I go with this very carefully calibrated agreement with the broadcasters and just say to Prince William, "No, I'm sorry – this has got to continue"?'

Or should he go along with Prince William, the future king whom he has never met before?

'And then I looked at Prince Harry and thought, You're exhausted. This is not the time or the place for you to be here doing an interview.'

So Head did something he had never done before – he turned to the media pack and just wound up the press conference. He flatly told them it was over.

'Prince Harry looked at me,' recalls Head. 'I remember the relief on his face and he left the room.'

Then Miguel Head got screamed at – 'I mean, literally screamed at' – by the BBC producer who had been conducting the interview. But the prince had, in fact, given coherent and reasonably lengthy answers to the few questions that had been put to him. With the footage of Harry's arrival, there was more than enough to put together a solid bulletin at the top of the news.

Embracing each other fondly, the two brothers walked off with their father into the night.

21

Fantasy of Salvation

*'Every year we get closer, and we've even resorted
to hugging each other now after not seeing each
other for long periods of time.'*

(Prince Harry, January 2006)

During his 2004 gap year between school and Sandhurst, Harry had worked and played in several countries around the world, rather in the fashion that William had travelled four years before. The younger brother enjoyed memorable experiences in Australia, Botswana and Argentina (lots of polo) – but his greatest involvement came during the final two months he spent working in the landlocked southern African enclave of Lesotho.

It was late 2004. Harry was nineteen rising twenty that September, and he was immensely impressed by the kindly and bespectacled younger brother of Lesotho's king, Prince Seeiso, thirty-eight – a 'spare' who had found a role for himself in charity work, particularly with disadvantaged and Aids-struck communities.

'I met so many children,' recalled Harry, 'whose lives had been shattered following the death of their parents – they were so vulnerable and in need of care and attention.'

It was his first prolonged, thought-provoking contact with the practical consequences of the HIV/Aids pandemic that had become such a crusade for his mother in her final years. Again and again as he travelled with Seeiso, who rapidly became a friend, the prince encountered community projects whose work was inspiring, but which could not raise funds from western sources because they did not have the book-keepers to demonstrate how their money was being spent. Talking to Seeiso, Harry decided to set up a charity that could generate and handle the money flow correctly, and he named it after his mother's favourite flower.

'We came up with the name Sentebale, which means "Forget-me-not" in Sesotho, the language of Lesotho,' he explained. 'This charity is a way in which Prince Seeiso and I can remember our mothers who both worked with vulnerable children and people affected by Aids. I really feel that by doing this I can follow in my mother's footsteps and keep her legacy alive.'

Sentebale was formally launched in April 2006, the same month that Harry graduated from Sandhurst, and the following month, William and Harry announced the founding of the Princes' Charities Forum as a way of bringing all their developing and varied charitable interests under one single brotherly umbrella.

Prince Charles had started his immensely successful Prince's Trust with the £7,500 severance pay that he received on leaving the Royal Navy. Now as they entered adult life his sons decided to follow his example – and it does not seem to have occurred to either of them in 2006 that they should *not* work together. They were brothers. Brotherliness had fundamentally shaped their lives and visions at this age – it was their joint identity that the outside world found very charming.

They had always played as a pair. Now they got philanthropic as a pair, funding their forum with what was described as 'a six-figure sum' from their personal fortunes – largely the money left them by their mother. Both their father and mother, explained William, had instilled in them 'from the word go' that with their great privileges in life went 'an absolute responsibility to give back'.

The tenth anniversary of Diana's death was approaching, and it was the perfect opportunity for her sons both to remember their mother and to raise funds for the causes that she and Charles had championed – as well as one special brotherly cause of their own. Alongside help for disadvantaged young people in memory of Diana, and support for climate change initiatives in homage to Charles, William and Harry agreed that a final third of the money they raised should go to the armed forces.

On the face of it, war was a curious third corner to their charitable triangle: helping the young, saving the planet – and killing people. But the brothers were thinking of veterans and the wounded. They did not say it – perhaps they did not even realise it – but the comradeship and parental authority of the armed forces had given both brothers more of a family life than their own parents ever had.

William and Harry raised £1.2 million for their three causes, spread over eight charities, in a Concert for Diana held at Wembley Stadium on 1 July 2007. It would have been her forty-sixth birthday.

'It's a little bit funny, this feelin' inside' – Elton John sat down at the piano to kick off the proceedings with his hit 'Your Song' in front of a giant tableau of Mario Testino's haunting black and white photographs of Diana that had been beamed onto the stage backdrop. Then Tom Jones demonstrated that he could still rock at the age of sixty-seven, getting the sixty thousand strong crowd to their feet, including both the princes and their largely female companions in the royal box – *'You don't have to be rich to be my girl!'* Maybe the lyrics meant something special to Kate Middleton, who was appearing in public with William that day for the first time following their three-month break – and hence was the main focus that afternoon of all the telephoto lenses in the press enclosure.

Duran Duran, Status Quo and Kanye West – the line-up of performers at Wembley that day showed the pulling power of Diana's name that her sons had now inherited. The money kept rolling in, and in September 2009 would enable the formal establishment and launching of the brothers' own joint charitable organisation – the Foundation of Prince William and Prince Harry.

'We feel passionately,' said William at the time, 'that working closely together with those who contribute to our foundation, we can help to make a long-lasting and tangible difference.'

'We are both massively excited,' echoed Harry. That summer of 2009 had seen the brothers living together for what would prove to be the last time – in a rented cottage close to RAF Shawbury in Shropshire where they were both training for their licences on Lynx helicopters at the Defence Helicopter Flying School. Aged twenty-seven and twenty-four, the two brothers were still on the very best of terms – and on the best of form in front of the cameras.

'Bearing in mind I cook – I feed him every day – I think he's done very well,' said William jokingly – or half-jokingly. 'Harry does do washing-up, but then he leaves most of it in the sink and then I come back in the morning and I have to wash it up … I do a fair bit of tidying up after him. He snores a lot too. He keeps me up all night long.'

The interview had been organised by PR man Miguel Head, who was now working directly with the brothers. Following his impressive handling of Harry's time in Afghanistan, Head had been lured away from the Ministry of Defence by William and Harry to become their first joint press secretary – it was another example of the personal web of partnerships that they were developing together.

'Oh God,' responded Harry, 'they'll think we share a bed now! We're brothers, not lovers!'

The younger prince vowed it would be the 'first time, last time, we'll live together' – with William observing acidly, 'It's been an "emotional" experience.'

Becoming serious, Harry put in a bid to get out to Afghanistan again. '[It] would be fantastic,' he said, 'and my best chance is to do it from a helicopter … I'm a bit of a Lynx lover since I started this course.'

Still more than a year from getting engaged to Kate, his elder brother agreed, expressing the hope that he too would be able to see serious action before long.

'I didn't join up to be mollycoddled or treated differently,' said William. 'As far as I am concerned, in my eyes, if Harry can do it, then I can do it.'

Prime Minister Gordon Brown did not agree. There were immense government benefits to be derived from handsome young princes undertaking military service – whether by helping to legitimise Britain's controversial Afghan adventure or by raising troop morale and encouraging recruitment. 'The virtuous circle' was how General Dannatt described the mutual hook-up by which the royals and the military supported each other.

But the risks of dangling a future king in front of the Taliban were too great, not least since that would also endanger the soldiers around him. 'Mollycoddling' proved the only option. William's helicopter destiny became domestic – and heroic enough, in all conscience, as he started to work in Search and Rescue on the island of Anglesey. In 2013 the heir moved to the Air Ambulance Service in East Anglia, where he settled with Kate in Anmer Hall on the Sandringham Estate and started raising their family. William would delay his royal duties in order to spend several years working as a full-time helicopter rescue pilot.

It was Harry who went to Afghanistan for a second tour of active duty. War was the perfect assignment for a royal reserve – one of the rare perks of the job. The survival of the heir could not be risked, but the life of the 'spare' was dispensable. Harry had qualified as an Apache helicopter pilot in April 2011, the same month that William and Kate got married, and he was deployed to Helmand Province over Christmas 2012.

So once again the Queen said prayers for Harry over a Christmas lunch at Sandringham – while the prince put on a Santa hat to cook breakfast for his crew, then queued for his turkey dinner alongside the thousands of other servicemen and women who were deployed in Camp Bastion. His father had sent him some Highgrove honey for Christmas and a box of Cuban cigars – which Captain Wales promptly traded for sweets and chocolates with his fellow officers.

This time the prince completed his full eighteen-week tour at the battlefront without interruption, enjoying military success with his combat unit that was averaging two Taliban kills per week. Harry was proud to have made his own first kill within a few weeks of arrival, attributing his success to his skill with computer games.

It was 'a joy for me,' he explained in his pooled press interview, 'because I'm one of those people who loves playing Play-Station and Xbox. So with my thumbs, I like to think I'm pretty useful.'

Linking the killing of people to PlayStation 'joy' would not be well received when Harry got home, but the soldier prince was unapologetic.

'Take a life to save a life,' he responded stoutly to his critics. 'That's what we revolve around. If there's people trying to do bad stuff to our guys, then we'll take them out of the game.'

'I'm not here on a free pass,' he continued. 'Our job out here is to make sure the guys are safe on the ground, and if that means shooting someone who is shooting them, then we will do it.'

Speaking in the aftermath of another tabloid exposé, Harry was feeling especially anti-press. While enjoying a pre-combat spree with friends in Las Vegas, he had got involved in a game of strip snooker – billiards or pool in American parlance – miss a shot and you have to take off an item of clothing. It had been a hot night and since Harry started the game wearing only swimming shorts, it hadn't been long before he was completely naked – and was rushing to the rescue of a young lady who was similarly bare. Naked pool!

The resulting tableau was captured by the inevitable mobile phone and appeared shortly afterwards on the muck-raking US website TMZ. Within hours the grainy pictures of the naked prince cupping his 'crown jewels' had gone viral.

Prince Charles's lawyers tried to keep the worst pictures out of UK papers on privacy grounds – Harry had been in a private hotel room, with a reasonable 'expectation of privacy'. But the images were syndicated internationally, and then the *Sun* broke ranks under the headline 'Heir It Is'. There was a clear public interest, argued the paper, in Britons seeing what everyone else in the world could see.

Prince Harry was approaching twenty-nine years of age when his strip pool pictures hit the papers in August 2012 – a full decade since his 'Drugs Shame' story of 2002 and nearly eight years since the swastika scandal of 2005. So how much progress had this young man really made?

For the last two years of his twenties, Harry would later confess, his life had slipped sideways into 'total chaos ... I just didn't know what was wrong with me ... I had probably been very close to a complete breakdown on numerous occasions.'

William came to the rescue, urging him to seek professional help.

'My brother was a huge blessing,' Harry recalled. 'He kept saying, "This is not right, this is not normal – you need to talk about stuff."'

Working with Kate, William had recently been developing his involvement and contacts in mental health. It had always been an interest of his, but by then he was engaging in the cause more strongly, serving as an ambassador for the charity Heads Together, and he helped Harry to find a specialist he could talk to.

'I started to have a few conversations,' remembered Harry in 2017, 'and actually all of a sudden, all of this grief that I had never processed started to come to the forefront and I was, like, "There is actually a lot of stuff here that I need to deal with."'

So much of it went back to the 1997 death of Diana, of course.

'I can safely say,' he admitted, 'that losing my mum at the age of twelve, and therefore shutting down all of my emotions for the last twenty years, has had quite a serious effect on not only my personal life but my work as well. I thought that thinking of her was only going to make me sad and not going to bring her back. So from an emotional side, I was, like, Right, don't ever let your emotions be part of anything.'

Harry confessed that he had been 'sticking my head in the sand, refusing to ever think about my mum because why would that help? ... I was the typical 20-, 25-, 28-year-old going around going "Life is great. Life is fine."'

Which helped to explain the difficulties that he had been experiencing with girlfriends ...

Prince Harry was famous – notorious some might say – for his array of glamorous female companions. You can find entire websites devoted to the subject, complete with exotic photographs and details of assignations. But in the B.M. (Before Meghan) years, just two young women really made an impact – Chelsy Davy and Cressida Bonas. Both were strong, stand-up characters of substance and style who stood by their man when the going got tough, but in the end they both fell by the wayside.

Chelsy Davy was a bright and bouncy white Zimbabwean lawyer and businesswoman whom Harry had met in his school days. Chelsy had been at Stowe School where her friends knew Eton boys and introduced her to the prince – it was the start of an on-off relationship that would last more than half a dozen years.

'I would love to tell everyone how amazing she is,' Harry said in his twenty-first birthday interview in 2005. 'But once I start talking about that, I have left myself open.'

Earlier that year, Chelsy had broken off from her studies in Cape Town and had flown back to England expressly to support Harry in the aftermath of his swastika armband disaster. She was a true friend – funny and tough, with the ability to laugh her boyfriend out of his insecurities. Initially she had been willing to tolerate the downsides of a royal relationship which even followed her home to South Africa, where photographers would put tracking devices on her car, and she appears to have accepted the reality that while she was away her prince might seek other companions.

In April 2006 Chelsy was at Sandhurst to celebrate Harry's graduation as a second lieutenant, dancing passionately with him at the ball that night, wearing a much-remarked-upon backless turquoise satin dress. Dancing beside them that evening was William with his St Andrews girlfriend Kate Middleton – but while Kate would last out the bumpy royal marriage course, Chelsy would not. In 2011, after more comings and goings, she finally decided to go – and it was, ironically, Kate and William's grand and glorious wedding that spring that did it for her. According to a friend, she told Harry that she could never make the sacrifices she had witnessed Kate making, particularly when it came to moulding her life around the unremitting attention of the press.

'It was so full on – crazy and scary and uncomfortable,' she told *The Times* later.

That was the very same verdict arrived at by serious girlfriend number two, Winchester-born Cressida Bonas, another intelligent and enterprising blonde (also educated for a spell at Stowe) who dated Harry from 2012 until 2014. A rising actress, Cressida did not enjoy the critical remarks that she could hear people making behind her back when she walked down the street in London – she felt that the fame of her relationship with Harry had put her 'in a box'. In 2014 she was said to have been 'completely spooked' after watching the TV coverage of William and Kate touring New Zealand and Australia with baby George in tow – that was not the way she would want to enjoy her eight-month-old son, she regretfully explained to Harry.

Both women blamed the royal system for their eventual disenchantment and disengagement. They did not – politely – suggest any dissatisfaction with Harry himself nor his fondness for strip snooker or pool parties and the possibility of dalliance with any ladies who might present themselves at such occasions.

But Cressida did complain to friends about Harry's neurosis concerning the media. He would rant and complain, she related, about paparazzi lurking where clearly there were none. The prince, she came to feel, was a damaged and self-obsessed young man, and in 2017 when he announced his engagement to Meghan, Cressida posted a cryptic quotation that can be read on her Instagram page to this day: 'No matter how educated, talented, rich or cool you believe you are, how you treat people ultimately tells it all.'

These were damning words – and Charles might later come to ponder their truth when his son started issuing public pronouncements on the quality of his father's parenting.

As Prince Harry entered his thirties, Diana and Charles's second-born could pride himself on much. His Sentebale charity in Lesotho was going from strength to strength, and in September 2014 his Invictus Games – the Olympics for injured veterans inspired by his moving 2008 flight home from Afghanistan – had proved a stunning success when it made its debut in London.

'*Invictus*' is the Latin for 'unconquered' or 'undefeated' – and the younger brother could surely claim to be that. His personal therapy was working.

But Prince Harry was also preparing to leave the army because he felt that his military career had nowhere to go. He had lost his position as number-one companion and counsellor to his elder brother. Kate had – quite rightly – taken over that function for William, and she was also accompanying her husband in a new direction: towards his role as senior heir and king. The 2013 birth of their son Prince George – with Charlotte and Louis to follow – had wiped out Harry's 'spare' status in the succession to the throne, and a life of partying could no longer deliver for the prince in the way that it once had. When it came to his love life – those ever-available women – Harry was clearly seeking something deeper and more satisfying than availability. Here was a young man in search of a purpose – in search of a saviour, in fact.

22
White Knight

'There comes a time when you think,
Right, now's the time to settle down.'

(Prince Harry, May 2015)

Prince Harry met Meghan Markle, star of the US TV legal drama series *Suits*, early in July 2016, while she was taking a break in London from filming in Canada. Their blind date had been arranged by a mutual friend.

'I didn't know much about him,' Meghan later explained to the BBC, 'so the only thing that I had asked [our mutual friend] when she said that she wanted to set us up, was, "Well, is he nice?" 'Cause if he wasn't kind, it just didn't seem like it would make sense.'

Harry passed the kindness test with flying colours.

'We met for a drink,' said Meghan, 'and then I think very quickly into that we said, "Well, what are we doing tomorrow? We should meet again."'

At the Kensington Palace photo call following their engagement announcement sixteen months later, Harry was asked when he had decided that Meghan was 'the one' – and he replied without hesitation, 'The very first time we met.'

After their second date in London, Harry invited Meghan to accompany him on a trip to Africa the following month.

'I managed to persuade her to come and join me in Botswana,' he said, describing the early days and nights of their romance, and how the two 'camped out with each other under the stars. Then we were really by ourselves – which was crucial to me to make sure that we had a chance to get to know each other.'

'To make sure that we had a chance to get to know each other …'

Here was the challenge for both of these fresh-encountered lovers. The delight and passion – their sheer, unbridled attraction towards each other, physical and emotional – went without saying. But the stakes were high. Harry, thirty-three in 2017/18 – a full five years older than William had been when he got married – was well aware of the royal obstacle course that lay ahead for his sweetheart and had brought down his mother.

Already Harry could sense in Meghan the quirks and originalities that made her such a similar character to Diana – extrovert and show-off-y, impulsive, unpredictable, loving and also revolutionary. She was a changer not a conformist, his 'white knight' who fought her battles with the same non-royal – indeed, those temptingly *anti*-royal – qualities of his mother. This woman's feet were not for binding, and Harry had no wish to inflict Diana-style tortures upon his newly discovered soulmate. He relished the chance to build Meghan into the Diana that death had denied.

As for Meghan, she had been married and divorced before – with Trevor Engelson, a genial Hollywood producer and talent manager to whom she had stayed wed for just two years (2011–13). This meant that Meghan could be described (whisper it!) in exactly the same dreaded terms as Wallis Simpson who had shaken the British monarchy so drastically eighty years earlier – she was 'An American Divorcee'!

British tabloids would not be slow to make the comparison.

After all the scandal of Prince Charles's messy divorce and remarriage to Camilla, Meghan's relatively quiet and civilised separation from Engelson – with whom she remained on good terms – presented no obstacle to Harry and Meghan proceeding rapidly to the altar. Sometime during that first summer and autumn together in 2016 Harry introduced his girlfriend to both his father, who thoroughly approved, and his grandmother, who was reported to feel just the same. According to one source, the Queen was 'delighted to see Harry in a loving relationship'.

The problem was older brother William. Wills *said* that he liked Meghan personally – as did his wife Catherine. The press stories of war between the two womenfolk were certainly off beam – Meghan and Kate actually got on rather well at the start. They might not be best-buddy material, but here they found themselves, sister-outsiders in their extraordinary royal situation, and both of them cool professionals, treating each other with mutual respect. Each was far too canny to make an enemy of a prospective sister-in-law – it only made sense to be friends.

The fundamental conflict was between the two males who had known each other all their lives and had never hesitated to tell each other exactly what they thought and felt. William worried that his brother was moving too fast in his courtship – and he did not shrink from saying as much when Harry started talking about getting hitched to Meghan quite soon.

'This all seems to be moving rather quickly,' William was said to have remarked to Harry doubtfully, on the testimony of one friend. 'Are you sure?'

'Don't feel like you need to rush this,' William told Harry according to sources who were close to the younger brother. 'Take as much time as you need to get to know this girl.'

William couldn't understand how Harry could contemplate marrying this still unknown and untested quantity less than two years after their first meeting. It went against his every instinct – and his own track record. If 'Waity William' had taken a decade to test out and approve his life partner, surely his younger brother could ponder his options for just a year or so more?

But 'Waity William', of course, took so long to commit to Kate for the sake of the monarchy. He had been auditioning her for a job all those years. So Harry could not help but wonder whether Wills was really concerned about his personal happiness – or whether he was, once again and as per usual, thinking about the make-up and fortunes of 'the Firm' whose boss he would become one day?

Harry also took offence at William's use of the words 'this girl', which struck him as 'snobbish', and he was tired of William's assumption that he knew better as an elder brother. His response was a brusque and offended push-back – and after several more peppery reactions, William turned to his uncle Charles Spencer for help. From time to time Diana's younger brother had played something of an honorary godfather to both boys in the years since the death of their mother, and he agreed with William to see what he could do.

The result of the Spencer intervention was an even more bitter explosion, however. Once again Harry refused to slow down. He didn't blame his uncle. He understood why Diana's brother should want to help. Yet he was furious with William for dragging other family members into the row – and he would still be feeling mistrustful a year later when the two brothers donned their smartest dress uniforms for Harry and Meghan's wedding day.

Looking at the once-fond friendship and now-sad feud between Harry and William – with its echoes in previous generations of the sisters Margaret and Elizabeth and then the brothers Andrew and Charles – we find ourselves faced for a third time in the reign of Queen Elizabeth II with a personal and emotional souring between heir and 'spare'. The pattern is always the same. Childhood closeness and naïve fondness are changed to adult alienation by the functional difference between the pair, since the moment inevitably arises when, for one reason or another, the elder sibling feels they must pull rank.

Personalities also play their role, however – and here we move to less solid ground, for some accounts of this early showdown between William and Harry played up deeper questions. The older brother could sense, it is alleged, and did not trust the long-term ambitions of this American over-achiever.

'William told his brother they knew nothing about her background, her intentions, what she was really like,' according to Emily Andrews in the *Sun*.

Not surprisingly, this questioning of Meghan's personal reliability was not directly confirmed in those early days by either of the only two people who could possibly know what was really said in their brotherly confrontation. Friends pushed William to give chapter and verse. Surely he had some doubts from the start about this loud and elbow-y female already nicknamed 'Me-gain' by critical palace staff and about the way that Harry had been transformed into a different person by her touch?

But in the days before the couple married, William refused to be drawn. Brotherly loyalty endured. One close friend pressed him hard on the subject and could get nowhere.

'All he would say in his stuttery way was, "Harry has gone too fast on this."'

At the end of February 2018, William, Kate, Harry and Meghan appeared on stage together for the first time to launch their Royal Foundation Forum. The newspapers hailed them as the 'Fab Four'. Harry and Meghan were now 'official' because they had got engaged three months earlier and were due to marry in three months' time.

The Royal Foundation was the joint charity arm that Diana's two sons had established in 2011 to co-ordinate their mother's legacy and their charitable work for their three core causes – veterans, child development and conservation. Over the years these had extended to a fourth objective, mental health, and Meghan was keen to add her feminist dimension to the work. Harry welcomed her to the group.

'I'm personally incredibly proud and excited,' he said, 'that my soon-to-be wife, who is equally passionate about seeing positive change in the world, will soon be joining us with this work.'

William then welcomed Meghan to the family in a more official fashion, adding how 'delighted' he was for her to be joining the team, and Kate backed her husband up with a round of personal applause.

What good actors they all were ...

'Working together as a family,' came a question, 'do you ever have disagreements about things?'

Cue nervous laughter. The two women looked at the ground saying nothing, using their hair to hide their faces – and their true emotions, presumably. Harry held on to Meghan for some mutual support. It was William who said quite directly, 'Oh, yes' – inspiring his brother to make a joke. There were so many clashes, said Harry, that 'they come so thick and fast'.

Had these disagreements been 'resolved'? the questioner persisted. To which William replied facetiously, 'We don't know!'

* * *

Previous page: Prince William, 17, in his final year at Eton, June 2000.

Below: William and Kate, both 23, on their graduation day at St Andrews University, June 2005 – photographed by the Middleton family.

Facing: Kate Middleton, 20, at the student fashion show, St Andrews University, where she caught the eye of Prince William, 26 March 2002.

Top: Prince William and Kate on their wedding day, 29 April 2011.

Below: Fresh from the Registry Office. Prince Charles and Camilla on their wedding day in the White Drawing Room at Windsor Castle, 9 April 2005.

Facing: Son and Heir. Prince William and Kate on the steps of the Lindo Wing, Paddington, following the birth of Prince George, 23 July 2013.

Top: Harry, Meghan, Kate and William 'together' at the Royal Foundation early 2018.

Below: David Cholmondeley and wife Rose Hanbury greet William and Kate at their fundraising dinner for East Anglia's Children's Hospices in June 2016.

Inset: Rose Hanbury, 34, at a charity function in London, October 2018.

Top: Kate and Meghan enjoy Wimbledon together, women's singles final, 13 July 2019.

Below: Where's Archie? No sign of the Sussex family in the Queen's 2019 Christmas broadcast.

June, 2019. Prince William holds his youngest child Louis on the balcony of Buckingham Palace for the Trooping the Colour ceremony with Catherine and their elder children George and Charlotte.

By now – early in 2018, a few months before her wedding – Meghan was based and operating out of Kensington Palace like any other royal, even though not yet officially part of the central core of the working royal family. For some time she had been allotted staff to help her from the pool of 'courtiers' serving William and Harry in their joint office.

'Courtier' is a word whose meaning has evolved over the years. In his classic *The Book of the Courtier*, published in 1528, Baldassare Castiglione described a class of elegant and mildly foppish ladies and gentlemen who strolled and danced attendant around the largely absolute rulers of Europe's Renaissance kingdoms and principalities.

Over the generations the more political and purposeful of these made themselves useful as advisors and administrators to their royal bosses – the classic examples being William and Robert Cecil, father and son, who became effectively prime ministers to England's Queen Elizabeth I and then her successor King of Scotland and England, James VI and I. Since they dealt with all the paperwork they became known as 'secretaries' or private secretaries – though the essence of their job was to manage the public face of their royal master or mistress, and they exercised a great deal more power than their secretarial title might suggest.

By the twenty-first century these figures – by now salaried career employees largely recruited from Britain's Civil Service and Foreign Office – were still running the households and work of the essentially ceremonial monarchy. Each royal could count on their own private secretary who supervised an office that also included a press or communications secretary, as well as equerries and ladies-in-waiting ready to help out with the practicalities of their public engagements – from picking up the posies to composing the speeches.

In March 2021 Meghan would proudly confess to her friend Oprah Winfrey that she had not googled nor done any home-work – 'I did not do any research' – to investigate the compli-cated royal set-up she was entering. 'I would say I went into it naively.'

Meghan complained to Oprah that, apart from her supportive chats with Harry – 'Everything we thought I needed to know, he was telling me' – she received no proper instruction from what she called 'the institution'.

'I didn't fully understand what the job was – what does it mean to be a working royal? What do you do? What does that mean? … There was no way to understand what the day-to-day was going to be like.'

These complaints were directly contradicted in August 2020 by Omid Scobie and Carolyn Durand, the chroniclers to whom the Sussexes, their friends and staff supplied the information for their revelatory and largely 'approved' volume *Finding Freedom*.

'Harry insisted his fiancée have a dedicated team to assist her in learning all the ins-and-outs of royal life,' explained the two scribes. '"Harry wanted staff that Meghan could truly trust in all situations".' And the writers went on to describe this trusted team: Amy Pickerill, who would become Meghan's assistant private secretary; Heather Wong, who had previously worked in the Obama administration as Secretary of Public Affairs at the US Department of Homeland Security; Edward Lane Fox, Harry's private secretary and a former captain in the Household Cavalry, known after his initials as 'Elf'; and Jason Knauf, a conscientious young American PR man whom the royal brothers had poached from the Royal Bank of Scotland and who had started his career as a media advisor to the government of New Zealand.

This impressively multi-national and loyal team came to refer to Harry as 'PH' while Meghan was 'M'. At the outset they organised several meetings, according to a courtier, 'to make sure she was supported in carving out the right role for herself in the family on empowerment, [and] other issues she cared about, so she had the right resource support'.

Scobie and Durand were at pains to point out that Meghan was given exactly 'the same informal training Kate had embarked upon following her engagement to William'. This was 'a series of instructions that covered everything from how to most gracefully

Johannes Leak, *Weekend Australian*, 9 March 2021

exit your chauffeured sedan while wearing a pencil skirt, to when to curtsy to members of the family several rungs up the hierarchy from you'. As Meghan underwent her tuition, in the judgement of the two authors, she 'was connected to a team of experts'.

Meghan, however, complained to Oprah more than once during their TV interview that the royal 'institution' did not give her the total back-up she needed – 'We weren't being protected' was her much-repeated refrain.

Here again the loyal Scobie and Durand flatly contradicted her. The future duchess 'underwent an intense two-day security course with the SAS [Special Air Service], the British Army's most elite regiment,' they related. 'The training – which all senior members of the royal family, except the Queen, have completed at SAS headquarters in Hereford – is preparation for all high risk security scenarios, including kidnapping, hostage situations and terrorist attack.'

Meghan's tough SAS tutors took her through 'a staged kidnapping where she was bundled into the back of a car by a "terrorist", taken to a different location and then "saved" by officers firing fake guns (the kind used in Hollywood filming) for realism.'

Kate did not undergo this intense SAS training until after her wedding to William, wrote Scobie and Durand. But Meghan received special treatment. Her training course was brought forward specifically for her benefit, since she and Harry had received an especially high number of threats – and the instruction in self-protection could scarcely have been more thorough. During the mock kidnapping, 'Meghan was even taught [how] to develop a relationship with the enemy.'

Could this have been where Meghan learned the tone and posture of pleading that she demonstrated so effectively talking to Oprah for more than two hours – and to millions more around the world in March 2021? Could it have been the kidnapping experts of the Special Air Service (motto: 'Who Dares Wins') who taught the duchess in their days together at Hereford how to convey such a convincing impersonation of helplessness – and how to deploy her self-pity to such dramatic effect? Three years later Meghan would certainly offer a brilliant impression of a hostage begging for liberation on primetime television – and the world would come rushing to rescue her.

At numerous points in Scobie and Durand's favourable biography there are remarks and contributions from 'a source' whom many critics and observers have said could only have been Meghan herself – and this was one of them. At this point in the narrative the 'source' explained how the mock kidnapping staged by the SAS had been an 'extremely intense and scary' ordeal for Meghan, but how it was an experience that 'she was grateful to have gone through'.

Harry had been insistent, according to this same 'source', that Meghan's staff should all be loyal and supportive 'people that, no matter what, would have both their backs', and *Finding Freedom* went into great detail about the various team members working to guide their beloved boss 'through the potential landmines, and comforting her when the public criticism grew to be too much'.

Amy Pickerill – 'or "Pickles" to friends' – was chief among these. This high-powered University of Nottingham graduate and former media relations manager was described as 'Meghan's right-hand woman', and she took the lead in the organisational details of the dream wedding of May 2018.

So it was strange that just two months before the wedding to whose workings she was so vital, Pickles announced she would be leaving the Sussexes' service – and she was not the first to depart. A hitherto loyal and unnamed personal assistant of Harry's had already left within months of Meghan's arrival, to be succeeded by Melissa Touabti, 'a hugely talented person', according to one of her colleagues, who had fitted in well and who, like Pickles, was playing 'a pivotal role in the success of the royal wedding'.

But soon after Touabti's arrival Meghan asked her new PA to order some personally embroidered red blankets for the guests at a Sandringham shooting party that Meghan was hosting for a group of Harry's friends. When the blankets arrived, however, they were not the right shade of red for Meghan, and by several accounts the duchess 'went mental' at her hapless PA. Melissa Touabti was alleged to have been 'traumatised' by her boss's behaviour and decided she could take no more. She promptly walked away from her high-profile royal service.

But there was another side to this story, according to Scobie and Durand. The duke and duchess had already grown 'dissatisfied' with Melissa's work, they wrote, and explained they 'were not disappointed when she left' – though the joint authors do not appear to have checked Melissa's own version of events with her. They also spelled Touabti incorrectly as 'Toubati' when they noted the unspecified disappointment of the Sussexes.

In the months that followed, the other members of the specially assembled support team made their excuses and departed. Like Pickles, Edward Lane Fox announced his departure before the wedding and stepped down soon afterwards. Jason Knauf lasted until the following spring, when he switched horses niftily to enter William's service, while Heather Wong left in September 2019. It was a strangely high rate of staff departure. Most KP courtiers were noted for the comparatively long tenures of their comfortable and prestigious jobs. But it looked as if employees could not wait to escape service with Harry and Meghan – and those who left formed themselves into an informal fraternity that they titled the 'Sussex Survivors Club'.

There had clearly been a clash of cultures. In the long tradition of royal service there was a sense in which the courtiers were always the rulers of their royal masters and mistresses. The apparently servile underlings were the true scriptwriters and choreographers of the royal melodrama – hence the paradoxical streak of humility characterising the more successful members of the British royal family.

Meghan was a professional performer herself, of course, schooled in Los Angeles where every production was built upon the very opposite principle – the pre-eminence of the star and his or her overweening demands. This unashamed autocracy, in which Baldassare Castiglione would have felt very much at home, was embodied in the daily studio 'Call Sheet' with its stark distinction between those who were 'Above' or 'Below the line'. Divas ruled the military-style sets that generated Hollywood movies and TV shows – with aides, hairdressers and make-up artists trembling at their every whim.

This inversion of the British system is evidently what Rachel Zane, star of *Suits*, brought with her to Kensington Palace in 2017. Under pressure to perform herself, Meghan apparently placed her palace staff under undue pressure, and within a few months cracks and strains started to emerge. There were stories of 'Hurricane Meghan' spraying out demanding emails with the dawn and expecting her staff to be awake to answer them – at five in the morning! There were allegations of shouting and weeping that had had aides and secretaries retreating in tears.

Meghan's friends, her lawyers and her American PR staff have always rejected these allegations stoutly, while their British team have dismissed the accusations of bullying as a 'calculated smear campaign'. But there has been no detailed denial of the specifics and they have offered no explanation for the unusually high rate of turnover among the Sussex staff.

'I think it's really good we've got four different personalities,' said Prince Harry optimistically in February 2018, when the 'Fab Four' appeared together to launch their Royal Foundation Forum. 'We've all got that same passion to want to make a difference … Working as a family does have its challenges, of course it does … But we're stuck together for the rest of our lives.'

That long-term commitment would soon prove over-ambitious, but for the moment the royal foursome seemed set fair with all the excitement of the wedding on the horizon.

It was announced that Meghan would now join Harry, William and her future sister-in-law as a fourth trustee, and the newcomer expressed the hope that the foundation might extend its support to the women's empowerment movement that was developing in the US from the recent Harvey Weinstein sexual harassment scandals.

'Right now,' said Meghan, 'with so many campaigns like #MeToo and #TimesUp, there's no better time to continue to shine a light on women feeling empowered and people supporting them.'

Everybody nodded approvingly. Yet no one – neither on the stage, nor in the audience, nor even in the attentive and critical press pack – appeared to realise quite how revolutionary was this suggestion that Meghan was making. Created in America only the previous month and linked to #MeToo, #TimesUp was a $13 million legal defence fund seeking legislation to discipline and punish companies that tolerated sexual harassment.

Legislation meant politics – and in royal terms politics was simply taboo. It was a total no-no for the British royal family to endorse any cause, no matter how virtuous, that could be seen to take one political side against another. At the time of writing royal organisations like the Queen's Commonwealth Trust have endorsed the objectives of the Black Lives Matter movement – but the royal family and the foundations it supports can never endorse sit-in protests or the tearing down of statues.

So here was another profound reason for the rift that would divide William and Harry and come close to shattering the House of Windsor in less than two years. Ms Meghan Markle didn't just want to do good in the world – she wanted to change the world.

23

This Little Light

*'Your sense of self-worth becomes really skewed
when it's all based on "likes".'*

(Meghan Markle discusses social media,
October 2018)

In the early months of 2018, Meghan Markle had a wedding to organise, and as the wedding day approached temperatures rose over what the bridesmaids should wear.

'It was a really hard week of the wedding,' Meghan later recalled in her March 2021 interview with Oprah Winfrey, 'a few days before the wedding …'

Meghan had met with Kate, her soon-to-be sister-in-law, for some last-minute adjustments to the costumes of the brides-maids, Kate's daughter Princess Charlotte, three, and five other well-born little girls, aged two to seven.

Some sort of disagreement arose between the two women – 'About flower-girl dresses,' as Meghan later described it, 'and it made me cry … It really hurt my feelings.'

That is all we know about the substance of the argument. Some said the quarrel was over whether or not the little girls should wear tights, with Meghan suggesting that the girls should go bare-legged – and if that was the case, photographs of the big day suggest that Meghan got her way.

But the issue that engrossed the world was who made who cry? When stories of the confrontation hit the British newspapers six months or so after the wedding, it was reported that Meghan had left Kate 'in tears' over her 'strict demands' with regard to the flower-girl dresses.

Meghan flatly denied this, however, when talking to Oprah.

'No, no. The reverse happened. And I don't say that to be disparaging to anyone … She was upset about something but she owned it, and she apologised.'

Oprah looked puzzled as she tried to establish the truth nearly three years later.

'This was a really big story at the time, that you made Kate cry. Now you're saying you didn't make Kate cry – Kate made *you* cry. So we all want to know what would make you cry? What were you going through?'

At this crucial moment in Oprah's primetime 'Tell-All' interview Meghan refused to tell anything at all. Kate was 'a good person', she said, '… and I've forgiven her.'

The issue was all a matter of how poorly her palace PR team handled the controversy and the malice of the tabloid press: 'They really seemed to want a narrative of a hero and a villain.'

The same issue had cropped up a few months earlier when it came to the bride's choice of her tiara.

Sometime early in 2018 Meghan went to Buckingham Palace to review tiaras from what many experts consider the most fabulous collection of personal jewellery in the world, to examine them with its owner – the Queen. As so often, there are differing versions of how events unrolled.

Unconfirmed by the palace – but not denied – we are told that the Queen had not felt able to agree to Meghan's initial choice, a beautiful emerald headdress that was said 'to have come from Russia'. This was code for a sensitive origin, meaning that the treasure was one of those that had found its way into Windsor hands through 'undefined' not to say dubious channels – and for an undisclosed price – in the aftermath of the Russian Revolution. There was scandal attached. For this reason, the emerald tiara was seldom, if ever, put on public display, and it would suit neither the palace nor Meghan herself that spring if newspapers started speculating about precisely which Tsarist princess had worn the tiara and how she had been assassinated.

Unfortunately Harry's ignorance of both history and family tradition meant that he had no understanding of this subtlety. Not for the first time, nor sadly the last, the word 'no' pushed a button inside him, and he flew into a rage. There were dressers and flunkies present, guarding and organising the jewels, so it was inevitable that his now-famous exclamation should find its way to the outside world – 'What Meghan wants, Meghan gets!'

The command was addressed, apparently, to Angela Kelly, sixty, the Queen's formidable dresser, credited with her snappy late-life fashion revival, and also the curator of HM's jewels. The no-nonsense daughter of a Liverpool dock worker, with a Scouse

accent that made her sound like one of the Beatles, Kelly –
'AK-47' as she was known to palace staff on account of her
uncompromising manner – took no hostages. She upbraided
Harry in no uncertain terms, and the Queen – to whom AK-47
was said to be a friend as well as an aide – took her side.

'Meghan cannot have whatever she wants,' she was reported to
have said. 'She gets the tiara that she's given by me.' Meghan had
arrived in London expecting a starring role and discovered that
in terms of royal precedence she had been allotted a walk-on part.

Accounts differ as to whether the exchange took place in the
presence of the sparkling tiara itself, plus Meghan, or whether
Her Majesty administered her reproof to her grandson later. The
official outcome, however, was another beautiful headdress of
safer and more respectable provenance for Meghan to wear on
her wedding day – Queen Mary's classic art deco Diamond
Bandeau featuring no fewer than eleven sections of glittering
diamonds and platinum.

Queen Mary (1867–1953) – 'May' to her intimates – had
been Elizabeth II's stern grandmother, the first ever queen consort
of the House of Windsor after its creation in 1917. Upright and
unbending in posture and family life, her older courtiers and
relatives saw unmistakable echoes of 'May' in the style that
Elizabeth II would adopt whenever she wanted to look inscruta-
ble – 'She's having a "Queen Mary" day.'

With its central brooch of diamond flowers, Queen Mary's
tiara would make Meghan look literally dazzling as she walked
down the aisle – definitely a queen for the day.

*   *   *

The challenge would be getting her there, since aisle-duty lay in the hands of her father Thomas, whose behaviour to date had appeared exemplary.

'I think it's wonderful,' Thomas Markle had told the press when news of the couple's engagement had been announced in November 2017. 'I think they're [a] very good match, I'm very happy for them, Meghan and Harry ... I love my daughter very much. Harry's a gentleman.'

Meghan had kept her father well-informed about her developing relationship, speaking to him quite regularly and introducing him to Harry over the phone. But life had not been kind to the Emmy-winning lighting director of *Married ... with Children*. Money troubles had driven him south of the border to the modest seaside resort of Rosarito in north-west Mexico, where he had been surviving with some difficulty on his savings, and subsidies from his daughter – Meghan had propped up her father to the tune of some $20,000–$30,000 from her earnings by one estimate. In 2016 Thomas Markle had filed for bankruptcy.

The money worries of the heavy-set seventy-three-year-old made him vulnerable to the wiles of the tabloid paparazzi – and in the spring of 2018 one duly came calling in the form of Jeff Rayner, forty-four, a successful British-born photographer who had driven to Rosarito in his Porsche from Los Angeles. Rayner offered Thomas a cut from the syndicated sales of some staged pre-wedding photographs he proposed to take of Markle getting ready for his big day as father of the bride – being measured for his wedding suit, for example, browsing a book of British landmarks while drinking a coffee in Starbucks, and working out with weights to get in shape for his walk down the aisle. The deal would be worth as much as £100,000 by later estimates and Markle spent a day posing for Rayner to produce a set of quite charming shots.

The problem was that another tabloid team was on to the ruse, using CCTV cameras to capture images of Rayner and Markle faking their pictures together, and showing how the 'tailor' allegedly measuring Markle was a young assistant from a nearby party goods shop, while his working out with weights had been shot on a litter-strewn waste tip that no one in their right mind would exercise in unless they were trying to stay away from prying eyes.

On 13 May, less than a week before the wedding, the *Mail on Sunday* revealed the entire embarrassing scam – which was seized upon and amplified by Britain's newspapers and by broadcasters around the world. Yet again Harry's life had been tainted by the tabloid media, and the wedding joy of his wife-to-be had been poisoned as well.

Recently released court documents show Meghan and Harry reacting with surprising calm the next day when they received a text message from Thomas explaining that he could no longer attend their wedding and that he would be issuing a public apology. But then he shut off his phone, failing to answer his daughter's calls, leading Harry to tap out the following text message of Monday 14 May, filed in court papers in London in the spring of 2020:

Tom, Harry again! Really need to speak to u.

U do not need to apologize, we understand the circumstances,
    but 'going public' will only make the situation worse.

If u love Meg and want to make it right please call me …

Meg and I are not angry, we just need to speak to u.

Thanks …

Any speaking to the press WILL backfire trust me Tom …

On receiving this text Thomas Markle did not respond. But he did issue a public statement later that same day through the celebrity website TMZ, which pays contributors for 'interesting' items of news. Thomas reported that he had suffered a heart attack and was going into hospital for emergency surgery – while keeping his phone shut off so that neither Meghan nor Harry could get through to him.

'I've been reaching out to you all weekend,' texted the frustrated Meghan on Tuesday 15 May, 'but you're not taking any of our calls or replying to any of our texts … Very concerned about your health and safety …'

Markle did not respond to his daughter for a full two days following his TMZ announcement, finally texting her on Wednesday 16 May to confirm that he wouldn't be able to attend the wedding since his doctors would not allow him to fly. Thomas went on to wonder who would be giving her away in his stead, telling Meghan that if she really needed him, then he would get out of bed and come just the same.

Thomas Markle was clearly desperate. But so were Meghan and Harry, and the window into their anguish was opened in

April 2020 by the papers lodged in the legal dispute between the royal couple and Associated Newspapers over the highly personal letter that Meghan would later send her father – three months after the wedding, in August 2018 – summing up her feelings about their unhappy rupture and bidding him farewell. The *Mail on Sunday* published extracts from this letter on 10 February 2019 without securing Meghan's consent – hence the lawsuit.

Meghan would win her case spectacularly on privacy grounds in February 2021 and the documents submitted made fascinating reading. Thomas may have 'told the claimant he loved her', runs one such paper, 'and wished her the best', but the stress he was placing on his daughter was extraordinary. To inform Meghan (and the rest of the world via TMZ) that he had suffered a heart attack but then deny her any means of making contact to see how he felt was surely no way to treat his daughter at any time – let alone in the tense and challenging days before her wedding.

Harry could not stand idly by. That same Wednesday 16 May, three days before his wedding to Meghan, he composed an angry text message to his would-be father-in-law complaining, among other things, that Thomas had not answered more than twenty phone calls they had made to him, 'admonishing Mr Markle for talking to the press and telling him to stop'. Failing to ask how the heart operation had gone, how Markle was feeling and conspicuously failing to send him any good wishes, the prince also accused Thomas of 'causing hurt to his daughter'.

Now Markle did respond curtly, according to the court papers. 'I've done nothing to hurt you Meghan or anyone else,' he messaged, saying that he knew 'nothing about 20 phone calls'.

And he shot off a particularly bitter zinger: 'I'm sorry my heart attack is any inconvenience for you.'

Meghan didn't hear directly from her father again. Phone records show that Thomas did eventually try to call her on the morning of her wedding, Saturday 19 May, but at 4.57 a.m. British time – just after dawn – and the call went unanswered. According to the legal documents, father and daughter did not speak thereafter.

'Yes, of course,' responded Prince Charles, when Harry asked if he would step in for Meghan's father and walk her down the aisle of St George's Chapel on her wedding day. 'I'll do whatever Meghan needs and I'm here to support you.'

In fact, Meghan walked down most of the aisle by herself on that day at Windsor. Feeling herself to be a proudly independent woman, she felt she had a proud point to make. Wearing Queen Mary's Diamond Bandeau and trailing her happy gaggle of bare-legged bridesmaids behind her, she met up with Prince Charles at the end of the nave, whence he escorted her into the private royal chapel and handed her over to his son.

'Thank you, Pa,' said Harry.

So that made 'Pa' one of the heroes of the day – and the other was the Reverend Bishop Michael Curry of Chicago, head of America's Episcopal Church. Curry had been invited by Meghan and Harry to deliver the sermon and he chose to give it on the 'healing power of love'.

'He did it black,' reported the *Guardian*, 'with music in his arms and rhythm in his voice.'

Wedding day of Prince Harry and Meghan Markle.
Peter Brookes, *The Times*, 19 May 2018

The bishop had been asked to preach for six minutes. But inspired by the occasion, and departing from the prepared text on the iPad that he was waving in front of him, Curry went on for fourteen.

'What a fucking time to try out that much new material!' responded one user on Twitter. '[I'm] reeling from that preacher's performance.'

So was the entire congregation. Bewilderment, giggling, mouths agape, stifled laughter – the full range of upper-class British embarrassment was laid bare by this exposure to exuberant revivalist African-American culture. Camilla's shoulders were heaving – one understood why aristocratic ladies wore wide-brimmed hats to keep their facial expressions concealed.

Sitting beside Camilla, Kate Middleton gave her stepmother-in-law a sharp 'side-eye' in reproof. The newspapers and website commentators all caught it.

'We typically don't see such serious and stern behaviour from Kate,' reported Susan Constantine, the human behavioural expert, in *Good Housekeeping* magazine. It was 'a rather dignified way to reprimand Camilla'.

Prince Andrew's younger daughter Eugenie, due to be married that October, was wide-eyed with delight – 'Will she be booking Curry for *her* wedding?' asked one Internet observer.

But most comment was reserved for the unconcealed jaw-drop of Princess Anne's daughter Zara Tindall, captured by all the cameras and looking almost as if she was in pain. Later Tindall explained her uncomfortable expression in terms of the baby she was carrying in her eighth month of pregnancy. 'My bum sort of slid over either side,' she said to the *Telegraph*, 'and Lena kicked the hell out of me for an hour.'

Could any or all of these reactions to Bishop Curry's startling performance be described as 'racist'? The commentators – and they were numerous online – were divided. Many felt that every smirk and side-eye in the well-heeled congregation betrayed snotty white racial prejudice. But others argued that they would laugh and roll their eyes at any histrionic white sermoniser who preached over length – and this duality would characterise future criticisms of Meghan as the public's 'honeymoon' with her wore off in the months following her marriage.

In politically correct America, NBC's satirical *Saturday Night Live* ran a skit that parodied the bishop – without receiving any public complaint: 'I preached and I testified and I yelled,' declared actor Kenan Thompson playing the preacher with a remarkably similar set of sparkling dental work, 'while five hundred stuffy English people looked at me like I was a fart in an elevator.'

The great irony of Bishop Curry's rambling and extemporaneous style, of course, was that it had been developed in the slave settlements that British traders had established in America from the seventeenth century onwards. Here at Windsor, in the heart of the institution embodying Britain's imperial grandeur, financed historically by the revenues of the slave trade, was the descendant of a slave radiating the same defiant joy that slaves had first experienced in their churches every Sunday. This was their sole moment of 'revival' from a week of grinding labour when they could 'Steal away to Jesus' – and their music was echoed in Windsor by the Kingdom Choir of London gospel singers whose rendition of Ben E. King's Motown hit 'Stand by Me' was the musical highlight of the service. Zara Tindall rocked along to that one.

Bishop Curry was highly conscious of the historic connection. 'After I preached the sermon,' the sixty-seven-year-old wrote in his memoir *Love is the Way*, 'I just remember it was like I could feel slaves around the place … It was like their voice was somehow heard that day.'

Now the Reverend was talking about Martin Luther King and the practical hope of freedom that he had embodied. Queen Elizabeth II certainly 'got' this, for her own favourite form of preaching was the revivalist kind of Dr Billy Graham – white, but a good friend and supporter of Dr King, and the closest thing you could get to black preaching in a white church. The Queen would often invite Dr Graham to preach to her when he came to London – though in the early days those sermons were in private.

Later, in 2001, the Queen knighted Graham – quite a rare American knighthood – to make clear how committed she was personally to his evangelical message. And for Meghan sitting a few seats away, Bishop Curry's religious affirmation must have brought back memories of her teenage summer camps at which she had encountered and signed up for her own deity – 'Agape', the unconditional love of God for the world.

The entire cross-cultural experience of Bishop Michael Curry's sermon that May morning in 2018 in Windsor was a moving phenomenon – 'Raw God' was the approving verdict of Justin Welby, the Archbishop of Canterbury. Curry's words were loving in their purpose and content but they proved deeply complex in the contrasting range of reactions that they evoked.

'Making my beautiful mixed heritage family's shoulders stand a little taller,' tweeted the black British lawmaker David Lammy, former minister of state for universities, with enthusiasm. 'Against the odds a great new symbol of all that is still possible and hopeful in modern Britain.'

But Kehinde Andrews, professor of Black Studies at Birmingham City University, was less welcoming. 'The royal family is perhaps the most identifiable symbol of whiteness in the world,' he wrote for CNN Opinion on 21 May 2018. 'It is absurd to think that one black woman could transform an institution so rooted in colonialism and whiteness …

'We cannot ignore that Markle is not a dark-skinned, afro haired, flat nosed, black woman. She represents the image of blackness we have been sold as acceptable and marketable … Now the wedding frenzy is over, it will not be long until we all realise it was never a vehicle for racial progress, but just a pumpkin, masquerading as hope.'

Well, 'hope' was better than nothing. As Harry and Meghan stepped out of the chapel into the Windsor sunshine, they marched to the Kingdom Choir's rendition of the civil rights anthem, 'This Little Light of Mine, I'm Going to Let it Shine …'

24

Earrings to Die For

'Hello, I am the beach …
I literally don't give a fuck.'

(Matt Haig, *Notes on a Nervous Planet*, 2018)

Asked for a sample of poetry that she admired, Meghan Markle came up with these striking lines by the bestselling Sheffield author Matt Haig, their theme being the folly of body-consciousness and the beauty culture – the deadly sin of human vanity as viewed by one ancient stretch of seaside sand:

I am entirely indifferent to your body mass index.
I am not impressed that your abdominal muscles are visible to
  the naked eye.
I am oblivious.
You are one of 200,000 generations of human beings.
I have seen them all …
Why do you humans worry so much about a stranger's opinion?

It was a curious message to publish in British *Vogue*, the UK's bible of how to look good in the eyes of strangers. But that was the spiky nature of many of the contents that Meghan Markle – now Duchess of Sussex and about-to-be mother of Archie – contributed to *Vogue*'s upcoming September 2019 issue, the magazine's biggest edition of the year.

'Forces for CHANGE' would be the headline splashed across the glossy cover in luminous orange type, with the word 'CHANGE' standing out particularly strongly and not a photograph of Meghan in sight. That was another spikiness. Publishers Condé Nast had anticipated a sexy and commercial cover photo of their royal guest-editor that would help them to sell tens of thousands of copies, as they had frequently done in the past: Diana, Princess of Wales (four times), Princess Anne (three times), Lady Helen Taylor and Meghan's sister-in-law Catherine, Duchess of Cambridge – this last lady gracing *Vogue*'s cover in June 2016 wearing an elegant Burberry trench coat and £293 white jacquard shirt.

But Meghan had demurred. It would be 'boastful' to put her own face on the cover, she felt. Her concept was to display a gallery of the women activists she admired, from Jane Fonda to Greta Thunberg, with thirteen other multiracial campaigning women – by no means conventional beauties, some of them ('I want to see freckles!' said Meghan to cover photographer Peter Lindbergh). She also wanted an image of the reader – whoever and whenever they happened to be looking at the magazine.

'Can we have a mirror?' asked Meghan of *Vogue*'s British Ghanaian editor Edward Enninful.

'A mirror?' (Gulp, gulp) 'In the middle of fifteen other photographs?'

'Yes. So people can look in the mirror and see themselves among all those other forces for change.'

Somehow, a mini-mirror of reflective silver foil would be duly printed on the cover in the middle of *Vogue*'s feminist portrait gallery – and there were a few small, scarcely conspicuous working photographs of Meghan inside the magazine. As a rare male among the contributors, Harry conducted a campaigning ecological interview with conservationist and chimp expert Jane Goodall, eighty-five, who praised him for being so youthful.

'Am I?' he replied. 'Good. Phew! I hope to remain youthful for the rest of my life.'

Meghan rounded off her 350-page activist 'Markle Manifesto' by interviewing her heroine Michelle Obama and presenting an appeal for Smart Works, the latest charity she had adopted. Smart Works had been set up to provide clothes and coaching to help unemployed women in their job interviews, and the charity wasn't looking, Meghan explained, for just any old hand-me-down garments. A more appropriate donation might be the Gucci suit you had been wearing for that crucial interview on the day you secured the job of your dreams.

'This is the story of Wonder Woman,' wrote Meghan, 'ready to take on the world in her metaphorical and literal cape.'

Edward Enninful was overwhelmed by the onrushing energy of his guest-editor. 'I can't overstate,' he wrote, 'how much it meant to me to see HRH The Duke of Sussex marry this brilliant, bi-racial, American powerhouse. I simply never imagined that, in my lifetime, someone of my colour would – or could – enter the highest echelons of our Royal Family.'

Enninful described seven intensive months of meetings and phone calls and emoji-filled texts and emails from Meghan – 'always warm, purposeful and to the point ... Boy, was it an adventure!' And in the course of all this, his unpaid guest-editor gave birth to a baby!

In the same seven months, January to July 2019, the Court Circular showed the Duchess of Sussex carrying out just twenty-two royal engagements, less than one per week – though this period did include Meghan's maternity leave, along with a three-day tour to Morocco with Harry. But why had this 'powerhouse' recruit to the highest echelons of the House of Windsor spent seven months labouring so intensively on behalf of British *Vogue* – entirely unremunerated it must be emphasised again – while doing hardly any public work at all for the British royal family?

The answer lay in Buckingham Palace – or, rather, had been forcibly removed from the palace just four months before Meghan's official arrival on the royal roster on 27 November 2017, the date of her engagement to Harry. In July that year the Queen's most creative and senior courtier, her private secretary Sir Christopher Geidt, had been elbowed out of her employ in a backstairs coup inspired by Prince Charles and his brother Andrew – for once not at loggerheads, but working in cahoots.

Geidt, fifty-six in 2017, had run the royal show brilliantly and sensitively for the best part of ten years. Based in Buckingham

Palace, the Queen's private secretary could be described as the COO – chief operating officer – of 'the Firm', as the family themselves describe their monarchical business. A fiercely shrewd and reflective character who had previously worked in army intelligence, Geidt had played a key role in working out the mechanics of transitioning royal power to the next generation – from Queen Elizabeth II to King Charles III. First knighted in 2011 (in the Royal Victorian Order), he had been awarded a second knighthood in 2014 (in the Order of the Bath), for his 'new approach to constitutional matters … [and] the preparation for the transition to a change of reign'.

'He has been a great private secretary,' one close colleague told Valentine Low who broke the story of Geidt's deposition in *The Times*. 'He has really steered the Queen through a very successful ten years.'

But Geidt had infuriated Prince Charles with a speech that he had given in May 2017 to some five hundred royal staff – the assembled workforce of the Firm – announcing the retirement of Prince Philip from public life. This would call for more unified work than ever in support of the Queen, the private secretary had said, and the Prince of Wales's staff who heard him felt that this was both 'presumptuous' towards their boss and actually dangerous to his interests. They had envisioned Prince Charles enjoying *more* power in the aftermath of his father's departure, not less – and Prince Charles agreed.

Charles found an ally in his brother Andrew whom Geidt had forced to step down as UK trade ambassador in 2011 over his friendship with the convicted sex offender Jeffrey Epstein.

'Prince Andrew deeply dislikes him,' a source told Low. 'The feeling is mutual.'

As private secretary, Geidt had controlled Andrew's expenditure and he had blocked one too many helicopter and private jet excursions for the prince's fancy. Andrew wasted no time joining Charles in his complaints to the Queen – 'Geidt has got to go' was their combined message to their mother. The palace COO was doing far too much operating and interfering for their liking – and Elizabeth II, just ninety-one that April 2017, meekly surrendered.

At that age, commented one courtier, 'you don't want the hassle of having a big fight, do you? Isn't it better that everything calms down?'

'It was one of the most shameful and, frankly, shabby decisions that the Queen has made in her entire reign,' says one extremely senior and distinguished court correspondent. 'All Geidt wanted was to have everyone singing from the same hymn sheet. But that is not Charles's agenda any more.'

If Christopher Geidt had been private secretary when the question of Harry and Meghan's new role in the family had landed on the royal desk at the end of 2017, he would have applied his customary vision and analysis to a task that was actually weightier than the technicalities of how Charles should succeed his mother.

Here was the great step forward, to integrate a mixed-race recruit – the first ever – into the all-white royal family which needed to maintain its position in a society that was becoming more racially diverse by the day. It was a profound challenge, with massive implications for the long-term identity and relevance – and even perhaps the survival – of the crown in a changing world. But it was also an immense opportunity, since the interracial union of these two popular headliners, Harry and Meghan, 'the royal rock stars', represented a unique chance to knit the monarchy closer to the people – the bulk of the lowly and 'ordinary', less-than-privileged people.

'Geidt would have put on his thinking cap,' says one veteran royal analyst. 'He would have reflected on the big picture – what it meant to the monarchy and Britain as a whole. He would have talked to the couple themselves to ask them what *they* wanted to do, then come up with some defined strategy. He would have looked at our multiracial country and got them committed to some exciting new initiative, either local or possibly on a national basis. This would have got both of the couple personally invested in the project – Meghan as a newcomer and Harry as an already wavering team-member – so they felt pledged to the way ahead and could see how its success required them to stick at the job.'

But Geidt's successor, Sir Edward Young, did not do the vision thing. Young had been Geidt's deputy for many years and that was his character – to serve as sober clerk and pen-pusher to the visionary postmaster general. Until he became private secretary, Young's principal claim to fame had been helping to facilitate filmmaker Danny Boyle's memorable stunt by which the Queen and James Bond/Daniel Craig appeared to parachute together into the opening ceremony of London's 2012 Olympic Games.

In reality, it had been Angela Kelly, Elizabeth II's enterprising Liverpudlian dresser, who had persuaded the Queen to go along with the 007 parachute jape. Young was a jobsworth and a functionary, not a man to make waves or to stand up to the blood family – and that suited Charles and Andrew just beautifully. It was Young who sanctioned Andrew's use of Buckingham Palace for his disastrous *Newsnight* interview in November 2019 – though he had to clear up the mess that followed.

'He hasn't got the strength of character of Geidt,' one insider told Camilla Tominey of the *Telegraph*.

'Central authority weakened, the rest of the family increasingly doing their own thing' was how news anchor Tom Bradby described the palace post-Geidt. William and Harry's pal identified the crucial issue of character too.

'The atmosphere has been fractious within the family,' reported Bradby, 'ever since those close to Prince Charles pushed out the Queen's longstanding and well-regarded private secretary.'

Princess Anne and Prince Edward were said to share the widespread unhappiness with the new chief 'non'-operating officer and his subservience to their two wilful brothers. Young owed his job to Andrew and Charles, so even if he had the imagination and the willpower to 'do a Geidt', he lacked the centralised power and purpose that had previously gone with the private secretary's role in Buckingham Palace. Now it was the pen-pusher's function to step back and let things happen.

'There's no discipline,' complained one courtier to Tim Shipman of the *Sunday Times*. 'Everything leaks and then everyone engages in swearing and shouting and blames each other.'

Young failed particularly when it came to Meghan. 'As things started to go wrong,' says someone who watched the new duch-

Prince Andrew's ties to sex offender Jeffrey Epstein lead to calls for his
resignation as UK trade envoy. Peter Brookes, *The Times*, 8 March 2011

ess's relationship deteriorate with the private secretary, 'Meghan
came to perceive Young as the inflexible, bureaucratic figure who
summed up what was at fault with the BP mentality, and the
feeling was mutual. Young really came to dislike Meghan's style.'

Trooping the Colour; attending the opening of the Mersey
Gateway Bridge; Ascot races; the hundredth anniversary fly-past
of the RAF; a visit to Dublin; some tennis at Wimbledon; an
evening at *Hamilton*; an official visit to Sussex ... Meghan's
post-marriage schedule of engagements – sometimes with Harry
and sometimes on her own – was as safe, predictable and mildly
boring as Young himself.

* * *

The only dates in Meghan's calendar that gave a nod towards the imaginative crusade that might have been were a July visit to the Nelson Mandela Centenary Exhibition in London's Queen Elizabeth Hall, and the September 2018 celebration of *Together: Our Community Cookbook*, which was the product of Meghan's hands-on involvement with the survivors of the Grenfell Tower fire – and this had been a project entirely of her own devising.

Starting in January 2018, six months after the tragic fire that had claimed seventy-two lives in a rundown part of Notting Hill, fewer than three miles from Nottingham Cottage, the Sussexes' first married home in the grounds of Kensington Palace, Meghan had begun paying secret visits to the Hubb Community Kitchen ('Hubb' is a play on the Arabic word for 'love') in the cellar of a nearby mosque. Dressed in jeans and T-shirt, she learned how to cook curries and chapatis with the survivors of the fire – largely poor, non-white, non-English-speaking women. They were the dispossessed in every sense and they became her friends.

'She comes in natural, fits in, puts an apron on,' said Ghaswala, a mother of two from west London. 'It just feels very supportive, very real.'

That was the spontaneous and natural hands-on Diana-style of engagement that Meghan could bring to royal work. She and Harry launched the *Community Cookbook* in September 2018 at a casual garden party in the grounds of Nottingham Cottage, surrounded by her fellow Grenfell cooks in their national costumes displaying tasty samples of their produce. Meghan made an inspirational speech and Harry was caught on video trying to sneak out with some of the samosas.

'This is a tale of friendship,' she declared, 'and a story of togetherness. It is a homage to the power of cooking as a community, and the recipes that allow us to connect, share and look forward.'

It was a perfect example of the fresh human touch that the new Sussex couple could bring to the old royal routine – and a few weeks later they were bound for Australia to show the world how they could sprinkle their stardust beyond Britain.

On 15 October 2018 the journalists of the Royal Rota gathered for what they presumed would be a routine advance briefing on the sixteen-day tour of Australia, Fiji, Tonga and New Zealand on which Harry and Meghan were embarking next day – to be taken by surprise.

'The Duke and Duchess are expecting a baby,' announced Jason Knauf, still on the Sussex team as the spokesman they shared with William and Kate, via an iPhone 6 that had been laid across a tea cup to create a makeshift loudspeaker. 'We'll be sending out a statement in about fifteen minutes.'

Meghan was less than twelve weeks pregnant and the announcement would normally have been made at a later stage.

'But she was already "showing",' briefed an aide, 'and hiding it would not have been possible. The rumours would have dominated the coverage and taken away from the entire purpose of the tour.'

Pregnancy did not diminish the energy with which Meghan tackled fourteen flights and seventy-six engagements over the next sixteen days, starting in Sydney where Harry was hosting the fourth of his Invictus Games. Screaming crowds greeted the couple wherever they went.

They seemed specially blessed when they landed in the farming community of Dubbo in New South Wales which had been suffering its worst drought in half a century. As Harry and Meghan stepped off the plane, dark clouds appeared and the heavens opened – drenching Dubbo in more rain than it had received in the previous six months. Everyone got soaked to the skin at the picnic of welcome, including the royal guests, and everyone was thoroughly delighted.

Observers noted how positively local teenagers responded to these youthful British visitors. Indigenous Australians in particular were drawn to Meghan as a non-white face who represented them in a way that the formal and 'Pommie' royal family had never done before.

'It's cool to think there are young girls who look at the Duchess of Sussex and think, Hey, she kind of looks like me,' remarked Sherry-Rose Bih, an African-Australian social enterprise founder who had chatted for some time with Meghan in Melbourne at a reception for young community leaders.

But things went wrong a few days later in Fiji when Meghan arrived to visit a marketplace in Suva, the capital of the three-hundred-island archipelago, wearing a pretty pink dress and black-ribboned wedges. Not long into the twenty-minute engagement, with scores of smiling, largely female market vendors waiting to greet her, Meghan bristled suddenly and insisted on leaving.

'I was there at the time,' recalled the *Daily Mail*'s royal editor Rebecca English, 'and witnessed Meghan turn and "hiss" at a member of her entourage, clearly incandescent with rage about something, and demand to leave.'

The market vendors were shocked and disappointed by Meghan's premature departure. 'It is such a shame,' said one. 'We started preparing for the visit three weeks ago and had been meant to meet her, but she left without even saying hello.'

'She really didn't speak at all,' recalled Mrs Asenaca Salusalu, fifty, a farmer who had travelled more than a hundred kilometres and been lucky enough to be the first in line. 'Like she was a bit afraid … I want[ed] to ask her all about the baby too.'

One member of the royal party later suggested a reason for Meghan's premature departure. The duchess had taken offence, apparently, when she caught sight of promotional material advertising UN Women, an organisation for which she had once done volunteer work, but with which she had since severed relations.

In 2015 Meghan had given a rousing keynote address on gender equality to the group in New York, received with a standing ovation led by UN Secretary General Ban Ki-moon. She had rubbed shoulders with the likes of Hillary Clinton and actor Kiefer Sutherland, and might have hoped to join UN Women's distinguished roster of 'Goodwill Ambassadors' that included such top-drawer celebs as Nicole Kidman and *Harry Potter*'s Emma Watson. But in those pre-Harry days UN Women only assigned the cable actress the lesser role of 'Advocate'.

'Meghan does not cope well with what she perceives as "Rejection",' says a Los Angeles screenwriter close to those who were close to Meghan at the time of her first marriage. 'She's nice and smiley as can be until you step in her way or don't give her what she hopes for. Then she can be remorseless – heaven help you!'

Meghan had excised references to the UN Women organisation from her website and social media – and it, in turn, had removed her from its. She was not happy, it seemed, to discover that UN Women was involved in the Suva marketplace engagement, and she snapped when she saw the many posters and T-shirts advertising the organisation – apparently blaming her staff for having landed her in the middle of all this branding. CCTV cameras captured the duchess turning to speak to an aide in a way that made the younger woman's face blanch.

'I later saw that same – female – highly distressed member of staff sitting in an official car, with tears running down her face,' recalled Rebecca English. 'Our eyes met and she lowered hers, humiliation etched on her features.'

Other journalists have recalled to this author the same painful scene, but decline to give the name of the female aide in question out of respect for her privacy.

As before, the duchess's lawyers and PR staff have denied any suggestion of bullying on the part of Meghan in the Suva marketplace, explaining their client's abrupt departure in terms of heat, overcrowding and the effects of her pregnancy.

But Meghan's spokespeople found it harder to explain another Fiji mishap – her wearing of a pair of 'chandelier' diamond earrings valued at £500,000 ($695,000) that had been a wedding gift from Saudi Arabia's notorious Crown Prince Mohammed bin

Salman, commonly known as 'MBS'. Meghan wore the extravagant earrings to the tour's state dinner in Suva on 23 October 2018 – exactly three weeks after the murder and dismembering by Saudi agents of the dissident journalist Jamal Khashoggi inside the Saudi consulate in Turkey. This was three days after Saudi Arabia had publicly admitted that its own officials were responsible for the killing.

You can see Meghan wearing the earrings on page 5 of picture section 3 – spectacular triangular strings of coloured yellow diamonds set in white diamonds which palace sources erroneously attributed to Chopard, the Geneva watchmaker and jeweller. Meghan's online fans and followers, however, favour Butani, the glitzy Hong Kong jeweller whose Dubai outlet has been supplying bling to the oil sheikhs for decades.

'Vulgar either way!' says London antique jeweller Sandra Cronan. 'They're surely too flashy for the royal family. They're essentially a way of saying, "Look at all my money!"'

Taste aside, this author has personal skin in this painful and tragic game – since I had breakfast with my longtime friend and colleague Jamal Khashoggi in London just a few days before he flew to Istanbul to his death. We discussed an article we had recently written together for the *Washington Post* about what the Saudi dictator could learn from Queen Elizabeth II, from downsizing his family to earning respect through humility – not to mention the obvious virtues of encouraging free speech in his country. So, as a friend of thirty years' standing, I naturally remember every agonising aspect of Jamal's death as its details became public in the weeks that followed.

Meghan was probably not reading the newspapers in Fiji that October. She could be forgiven for not catching and understanding the sinister significance of her jewellery choice as she concentrated on her high-pressure tour of the Pacific.

But she too had a friendship stake in the game – or at least an acquaintanceship – not with Jamal Khashoggi but with another famous Saudi dissident, Loujain al-Hathloul, twenty-seven, with whom Meghan had been pictured in a shoot for *Vanity Fair* in October 2016. Meghan had posted the image on her Instagram page and there was more than one photograph of the two campaigners smiling together in Ottawa, along with such fellow female activists as Ireland's Mary Robinson, at the Global Summit for Young Leaders organised by One Young World.

Meghan was described as an 'Actor, Activist & Global Ambassador for World Vision', alongside Loujain al-Hathloul and other delegates, whom Meghan praised for 'speaking out against human rights violations, environmental crises, gender equality issues, discrimination and injustice. They are the change.'

So how was it possible for the soon-to-be Duchess of Sussex not to be aware that Loujain had been kidnapped in March 2018 by a Saudi hit squad just a week after the crown prince had had lunch with the Queen at Buckingham Palace? That was when MBS was said to have handed over the earrings ahead of the wedding two months later.

The March 2018 kidnapping of Loujain al-Hathloul was widely reported. Loujain was famous for campaigning for Saudi women's right to drive, which MBS had granted the previous year. Then he kidnapped the activist and detained her just the same for continuing her criticisms of his absolutism. It was inconceivable that Meghan did not know what had happened to her brave Saudi acquaintance, and in the months that followed disturbing reports emerged of Loujain being tortured in Saudi custody.

'She showed them her thighs,' her sister Alia said of her parents' visit to Loujain in prison. 'And it was not only bruises; it was burns … She thought she was going to die.'

Meghan's royal minders in Fiji were quite adamant they had made her aware of the embarrassing Saudi origin of the jewels. It is part of the job description of royal aides and private secretaries to keep their principals informed about 'topical' events and connections, and these earrings were so novel and spectacular that journalists were bound to ask where they came from.

Meghan's claim that the jewels were 'borrowed' was presumably designed to avoid admitting their awkward provenance – well, awkward for a professed human rights campaigner. When the story came out in February 2021 her legal apologists leapt forward to point out that the earrings were actually lodged as property in the name of the Queen, like all wedding gifts to members of the royal family. So the duchess had been technically correct in saying that she had only 'borrowed' them.

But Meghan had not borrowed the earrings in the same sense that she had been lent the Queen's tiara she wore on her wedding day. Despite the technicalities of ultimate royal ownership, it is established practice that royal ladies can treat their jewellery as their own property to do with as they wish in their lifetimes, so long as they do not sell or dispose of the item. When you see a female HRH wearing such a bauble it is quite definitely 'hers', until it eventually reverts to the crown upon her death.

As her spokespeople conceded, Meghan certainly knew the identity of the tyrant who had paid for the earrings when she wore them at the Fiji state dinner. At that time, she might not have known the macabre detail that MBS's hit squad had brought along a bone-saw and disposal bags to cut up Khashoggi's body while it was still warm. But that horrible truth soon emerged to widespread publicity, and it had certainly been published with other grisly details well before 14 November 2018 – when Meghan decided to wear the earrings for a second time at the dinner to celebrate Prince Charles's seventieth birthday in London.

A few months later Meghan would tell a gathering for International Women's Day that she had given up consulting Twitter. 'That is my personal preference, but I do read the *Economist*,' she explained, because she sought out 'journalism that's really covering things that are going to make an impact'.

Well, between 1 and 14 November 2018 the *Economist* ran at least two major articles examining the role of Mohammed bin Salman in the murder of Jamal Khashoggi and how the Saudis had used their diplomatic mission in Turkey 'as a torture chamber'.

In February 2021, after nearly three years behind bars, Loujain al-Hathloul was finally allowed to go home in a Saudi government gesture that was widely interpreted as an attempt to curry favour with America's new President Biden – 'We're not as barbaric as you think we are, Joe!'

Now thirty-one, the campaigner currently remains under supervision, unable to leave the kingdom – and at the time of writing, it is not known what contact, if any, Meghan has been able to establish with her 'friend' (*Express*), 'close friend' (*Sun*), or fellow 'activist and friend' (*Mail*).

'Loujain did not personally know Meghan,' wrote her sister Lina, in an email to this author on 30 March 2021. 'They were part of the same conference one day and took a picture – but that is it.'

One of the life goals attributed to Meghan Markle is an ambition to become US president, but that will require a more efficient separation between her taste in jewellery and her politics.

25

'Everyone Is Our Neighbour ...'

'... no matter what their race, creed or colour.'

(Queen Elizabeth II, Christmas Broadcast, 2004)

In November 1961 Queen Elizabeth II, then thirty-five, shocked the world by dancing the 'High Life', a popular West African reggae shuffle, in white gloves, tiara and sash in the arms of the controversial President Kwame Nkrumah of Ghana, fifty-two. The couple boogied and joked happily together for the best part of ten minutes in a striking image that challenged bigotry around the globe.

'This spectacle of the honoured head of the once-mighty British empire dancing with black natives of pagan Africa is extremely scandalous,' complained the apartheid newspaper *Die Oosterlig* in South Africa – 'a pitiful outrage of the dignity one associates with a white royalty.'

No one in America ventured openly to criticise the Queen, but the picture must have shocked more than a few. At that date interracial marriages were still prohibited by law in thirty-one of the fifty states. Just a few months earlier the black entertainer Sammy Davis Jr, who had campaigned tirelessly in black districts to help his friend Jack Kennedy win the presidency, found himself removed from the inauguration list of both guests and entertainers after he married a white woman, the Swedish actress May Britt – 'Stay in your lane, Sammy!'

In a racially prejudiced world, Elizabeth II stood for diversity before her time.

Elizabeth II dances with President Nkrumah of Ghana, 20 November 1961

'What a splendid girl she is!' exclaimed her prime minister Harold Macmillan.

'On racial matters she is absolutely colour-blind,' confirmed David Owen, her foreign secretary in the following decade.

'Everyone is our neighbour,' declared the Queen in her Christmas broadcast of 2004, 'no matter what their race, creed or colour' – going on to relate a story she had heard that year about a visitor to Britain who said the best part of his visit had been travelling from Heathrow Airport into central London on the Tube as the schools were coming out.

She repeated his words with relish: 'At each stop children were getting on and off ... of every ethnic and religious background, some with scarves or turbans, some talking quietly, others playing and occasionally misbehaving together – completely at ease and trusting one another. How lucky you are to live in a country where your children can grow up this way.'

The Queen glowed with pride as she recounted this description of 'her' country. Elizabeth II had been 'woke' on racial matters since before the word was invented. It went back to her childhood lessons with Sir Henry Marten who had first inspired her devotion to the ideals of the British Commonwealth of Nations – the free association of fifty-four countries, large and small, from Australia to India and Fiji to the Falklands. Human, social and racial equality were the animating principles of this family of former colonies transformed into friends – 2.4 billion people of every race and language.

Now one single person, Meghan Markle, had brought the same multiracial dimension into Elizabeth II's own blood family. This was one of the reasons why the Queen had welcomed Meghan so warmly into her grandson Harry's life early in 2017 – and why she was alarmed to hear two years later that her granddaughter-in-law was not settling into the family as smoothly as had been hoped.

The stories of people – well, women – being reduced to tears had gone round the palaces, along with balancing narratives. The new duchess would come into her office sometimes bearing bags of croissants at 11 a.m. – 'Break for breakfast, everybody!' On another occasion she had arranged for an ice cream and sorbet stand to indulge the palace staff.

These 'treats' came straight from Meghan's Hollywood play-book. Every week the 'Above the line' principals on any US or Canadian film/TV set confer to organise some such gesture at their own expense to compensate their 'Below the line' menials for the lowly scrambling around that is their daily lot.

'There is a real tradition of Hollywood assistants getting screamed at and humiliated,' says one distinguished British producer who has worked on both sides of the Atlantic. 'This culture of abuse is the next big issue that the US entertainment industry has to face, and in the meantime traces of it have drifted across to this side of the pond.'

It must be stressed that many of Meghan Markle's working colleagues have testified how she was not guilty of this 'culture of abuse'.

'From day one,' tweeted her *Suits* co-star Patrick J. Adams, 'she was an enthusiastic, kind, co-operative, giving, joyful and supportive member of our television family. She remained that person and colleague as fame, prestige and power accrued.'

The Queen had evidently noted the failure of Sir Edward Young and his staff to come up with a satisfactory role for the American newcomer's strongly defined talents – and Her Majesty was even ready to admit that she herself might have made a mistake in the casting aside of Sir Christopher Geidt.

Private Secretary Young remained in post but early in 2019, just eighteen months after his hustled departure, it was announced that Elizabeth II had invited Geidt to return to her side as her Permanent Lord-in-Waiting. This was a non-political appointment that would involve Geidt in ceremonial events but, more significantly, it would enable him to assume a new role as mentor to the Duchess of Sussex. Her Majesty valued Geidt's 'wise counsel', one courtier told Richard Eden of the *Daily Mail*.

The Queen had recently invited Meghan to team up with Harry as vice-president of the Queen's Commonwealth Trust which championed young people around the world who were 'driving positive social change'. The Queen had already made Harry the president, with Geidt the chairman of trustees. The idea was for Meghan to do special work 'supporting women and girls'.

'The support and encouragement which Her Royal Highness will bring to the young leaders with whom we work,' said Geidt, 'promises to have a profound effect.'

This was all part of a strategy to find new ways of integrating the young duchess more fully into royal life – 'Geidt will be Her Majesty's eyes and ears,' explained a courtier.

Geidt and the Queen had sat down to frame a plan with Sir David Manning, a former diplomat – ambassador to the United States from 2003–7 and since 2009 a part-time advisor to the joint household of William and Harry. The details of their discussions remain unknown, but we can guess the main drift from what we know about the Geidt–Manning strategy that emerged.

Not before time, in January 2019, Meghan took over from the Queen as royal patron of the National Theatre. It was a position that Elizabeth II had held for forty-five years with an almost total lack of engagement. Her Maj had little natural affection for the theatre and the feeling was mutual.

Over the years the largely anti-monarchist managements of the NT had been quite happy to let the Royal Opera and Royal Shakespeare companies enjoy their toffee-nosed titles. They had resisted branding themselves as the Royal National Theatre – though they were. Now director Rufus Norris welcomed Meghan not only as a fellow professional but as a social activist sharing 'our deeply held conviction that theatre has the power to bring together people from all communities'.

It was the obvious job to have given Meghan a year earlier in view of her ten years of acting experience. Still, better late than never …

Geidt-Manning's big idea was to get Harry and Meghan out of the country for a decent spell. It would give everyone a breather. The Queen wanted to offer both honour and responsibility to the couple by handing them their new youth role in her beloved Commonwealth – a highly personal token of trust, since it was arguably her greatest historic achievement.

Both Geidt and Manning would have seen two practical advantages to the plan. It would extract the activist Sussexes from the dangers of controversy in the increasingly fratchety British arena: Meghan could campaign in Africa to her heart's content to give teenage girls free access to sanitary products – she would be greeted with universal approval. And by handing the recently ennobled duke and duchess a semi-regal role visiting and being honoured ceremonially around the Commonwealth the plan also surely offered the best route yet devised to give a British 'spare' self-sufficient status that truly matched, but did not threaten, that of the heir.

The Queen added a personal touch. She had heard and read much of Harry and Meghan's wish to live an 'ordinary' existence. Well, she could recall such a period in her own life – her 'Malta Moments' between 1949 and 1951, when Philip was serving as a naval officer on the Mediterranean island and she would fly out to stay with him.

In Malta, Elizabeth had tasted 'normal' life as a young naval officer's wife, not a king's daughter – it was the first and last time that she was able to sunbathe and swim off a beach, to drive her own car unnoticed around the streets, to visit the markets if she wished to, and to do her own shopping with real money out of her handbag. It had set her up so well to come back home and do her duty.

Meghan and Harry were due to visit Southern Africa after the birth of their new baby, and to take the newborn child with them. Perhaps that would be a good time and place to start exploring the practicalities. Modern South Africa, with its black-majority rule, could be just the spot – and the couple themselves seemed interested by the notion.

'We can just take a step back,' Meghan would later say. 'We can do it in a Commonwealth country.'

'Take a breath,' added Harry.

The couple's relationship had taken flower in Africa after all, so maybe it, or somewhere else in the Commonwealth, might provide their next step. Cape Town could be their Malta.

In the meantime Meghan – seven months pregnant and right in the throes of her *Vogue* guest-editorship – began her new Queen's Commonwealth Trust duties on International Women's Day, 8 March 2019, with a panel discussion on how to support and empower women's lives around the world. The event was hosted by King's College London, of which the well-connected Geidt was chairman of the council, and he greeted Meghan warmly with a 'Mwah! Mwah!' brush of the cheeks.

'They clearly respected each other,' recalls one of the royal press pack at the occasion. 'You could tell Meghan looked up to him – although, in fact, once Geidt had greeted her, he stayed in the background, which was very much his style, of course.'

The panel included the pop star and activist Annie Lennox, as well as Julia Gillard, the former prime minister of Australia, with Anne McElvoy, senior editor of the *Economist*, in the chair. McElvoy introduced Meghan as 'a royal not afraid to embrace full-on feminism'.

Asked how her pregnancy was going, Meghan replied that she had been watching a Netflix documentary recently that referred to a pregnant mother feeling 'the embryonic kicking of feminism' inside her.

'I loved that. So boy or girl, whatever it is, we hope that's the case … I hope that men are part of the conversation. My husband certainly is.'

Not renowned as one of nature's monarchists, the liberal and sceptical Ms McElvoy later admitted that she was impressed by the way in which the young American held her own among the other formidable panel members. McElvoy got the feeling that Meghan might well become 'more frank in the future on the insidious effects of prejudice'.

'She is espousing a kind of pluralism and progress that crosses the political divide,' McElvoy wrote two days afterwards in the *Sunday Times* – though she did feel impelled to issue a warning against too much sermonising: 'If you preach about climate change,' she wrote, 'be careful with your use of helicopters.'

The best part of a year later, in January 2020, with the news of the departure of the Sussexes from Britain on the front page of every paper – the *Sun* coined the term 'Megxit' – McElvoy confessed that she had picked up no inkling of defection plans from anything Meghan had said on that International Women's Day panel the previous March, nor while chatting to her informally behind the scenes.

'I met a poised, warm, heavily pregnant woman,' she wrote. Meghan had presented herself as 'jovial and open' with a clear 'commitment to combining royal life with charitable work', and she had seemed to be in it 'for the long haul'.

Just ten months before Megxit, in other words, Anne McElvoy had not detected the slightest sign of disaffection or departure on the part of the Duchess of Sussex. But that was before Meghan and Harry were impacted by the arrival of their first baby and all that that entailed.

26

End of the Double Act

'It's not enough to just survive something, right?
That's not the point of life.
You've got to thrive – you've got to feel happy.'

(Meghan Markle, October 2019)

'S o, are you saying,' asked Oprah Winfrey, talking to Meghan and Harry in their interview of March 2021, 'that there were hints of *jealousy*?'

The grand inquisitor was enquiring about the Sussexes' wildly successful tour of Australia and the South Pacific of late October 2018, and the couple shifted uncomfortably in their plush wicker chairs.

'Look,' replied Harry, 'I just wish that we would all learn from the past.'

By bringing up 'the past', the prince was venturing into an area that was almost taboo. He was making a sensational comparison between his mother and his wife. Harry was suggesting that Meghan had demonstrated in Australia the same massive star quality as Diana – and was now having to face the family envy that went along with that.

'It really changed,' he said, 'after the Australia tour, after our South Pacific tour … It was … the first time that the family got to see how incredible she is at the job. And that brought back memories.'

Memories of what? Again Harry shied away from putting words to the almost unmentionable. But Oprah had prepared and polished this moment – like so many others – and she had a reference ready to prompt her prince's revelation. The latest, fourth season of TV's *The Crown* had depicted Charles and Diana's 1983 tour of Australia, showing how Diana had been 'bedazzling' in her ability 'to connect with people'. Episode Six had depicted how the crowds would groan when they realised that Charles, not Diana, was walking down their side of the street – hence the beginnings of the 'jealousy' on the family's part.

'So is that what you're talking about?' asked Oprah. 'It brought back memories of that?'

'Yeah,' Harry finally replied in a fashion that was both dismal and unmistakably aggressive.

What on earth had happened, viewers had to wonder, to the old and once-familiar happy side of Prince Harry?

When trying to define the moment that marked the real beginning of his rift with William, Harry would fix upon his triumphant return with Meghan from their Australian tour in the autumn of 2018 – and while William was significantly less inclined to address the subject, he would also have acknowledged a date around that time. It was the crucial turning point.

Both brothers agreed how bitterly they had clashed in the early days over William's attempt to slow Harry's courtship of Meghan – 'Don't feel like you need to rush this ...' But both of them had subsequently moved on. Harry's transparent contentment with Meghan had relaxed the tensions – give or take the odd row over bridesmaids' dresses. The 'no speaks' had eased by 19 May 2018 when the wedding rolled around, so the brotherly smiles were comparatively genuine as 'Best Man' William escorted his brother down the aisle.

But five months later came the true and decisive rift – the one that has lasted to the present day – though here the brothers' retelling of history diverged. As Harry explained it to Oprah, Meghan's Australian tour success sowed the jealousies that caused feelings to 'change'. According to this scenario, William and Kate resented the Diana-like popularity that was generated by Harry's wife. But William had a different recollection.

We now know that Princes William and Harry were no longer on speaking terms *before* the Sussexes set off for Australia on 16 October 2018. Feelings had already 'changed', as Harry put it – and drastically so. The brothers had parted on extremely poor terms, with the trouble centring on Meghan's stringent treatment and alleged bullying of her staff. The Sussex Survivors Club had finally hit back – and its organising agent had been Jason Knauf.

The joint communications secretary for Kensington Palace – who was still, at that date, working on behalf of both of the brothers and their wives – had become concerned by the numerous stories of mistreatment being brought to him by colleagues whom he knew well and trusted. Knauf was specifically worried by the early departure of Melissa Touabti and the likely resignations of other staff because of their problems with Meghan. Katrina McKeever, a senior communications secretary of whom Knauf thought highly, was already in the process of leaving.

Edward Lane Fox had departed that summer to be succeeded as Harry's private secretary by Samantha Cohen, a brisk and unstuffy Australian who had won high marks while working for the Queen for many years. A no-nonsense mother of three in her late forties, the well-liked 'Sam' Cohen had moved over to KP at the Queen's specific request to help Harry and Meghan on an interim basis, and she had appeared to be doing a good job. But Cohen too, in Knauf's opinion, had been coming under strange and unreasonable pressure from the American duchess.

'American' may be the key word in this saga, whose full details have yet to be uncovered. Texas-born and New Zealand-educated Knauf, thirty-four, was a popular character in Kensington Palace, widely noted for his friendliness and loyalty towards his colleagues. He had been considered a real 'catch' when the brothers snared him from the Royal Bank of Scotland in 2015, and one of his concerns was that professional management practices should be more effectively enforced inside the traditional British palace. Knauf's American sensibilities caused him to see the Meghan situation as raising principles of human resources management in the palace system that needed to be formally addressed.

'Meghan governed by fear,' claimed one courtier, '– so many people said it. Nothing was ever good enough for her. [She] humiliated staff in meetings, [would] shout at them, [would] cut them off email chains – and then demand to know why they hadn't done anything.'

To a degree this could be put down to a culture clash. As early as 2017, according to a report in *The Times* of 2 March 2021, a senior aide had spoken to the couple about the difficulties caused by their treatment of staff.

'It's not my job to coddle people,' Meghan was said to have replied.

'Americans can be much more direct,' wrote Omid Scobie and Carolyn Durand in defence of the duchess, 'and that often doesn't sit well in the much more refined institution of the monarchy.'

'She wasn't sleeping very well or very much,' explained a source in KP. Challenged herself, she challenged her staff. 'So she'd be firing off emails all through the night for people to wake up to a barrage in their inbox. Those stories of 5 a.m. emails were the tip of the iceberg. There was a big sense of injustice for the staffers, the way they'd been treated.'

These allegations were disputed, like all others, by Meghan's lawyers at Schillings, and in 2021 when *The Times* reported on them the duke and duchess's spokesman responded, 'The duchess is saddened by this latest attack on her character, particularly as someone who has been the target of bullying herself and is deeply committed to supporting those who have experienced pain and trauma.'

A Brit might have raised their eyebrows at Meghan's alleged behaviour, then looked the other way. The Yank decided to act. Knauf was actually one of Meghan's most senior advisors – her chief advisor, in fact, when it came to public relations. Earlier that year she had gone to Knauf for help when drafting the disputed letter of severance that she sent to her father. She valued his PR expertise.

Before that, Knauf had helped Harry word the fierce anti-media statements that he had framed to try to protect Meghan from press harassment, both as his girlfriend and then as fiancée. The PR man had taken considerable stick from some of his non-royal contacts who criticised him as being overprotective in fighting the newcomer's corner. Like so many people in all the palaces, Knauf had started off on Meghan's side.

But as the months went by the American's feelings became more ambiguous, as numerous colleagues – women whom he greatly respected – continued to bring him stories of what they said they had suffered at Meghan's hands.

'I can't stop shaking,' one aide had told a colleague in anticipation of an encounter with Meghan. Another reported that the prospect of confrontation with the duchess had made her 'feel sick'. 'Emotional cruelty and manipulation,' were the words of a third – 'which I guess could also be called bullying'.

The b-word featured prominently in the accounts of several, along with an even more sinister set of initials – PTSD. Post-traumatic stress disorder was a deeply serious condition to allege – flashbacks, nightmares and feelings of deep anxiety – but that was how one complainant said that they had felt.

Several people maintained they had been 'humiliated' by the duchess – and that criticism extended to Harry as well.

'I overheard a conversation between Harry and one of his top aides,' recalled one KP courtier. 'Harry was screaming and screaming down the phone. Team Sussex was a really toxic environment. People shouting and screaming in each other's faces.'

'Shouting and screaming? PTSD? Making people feel sick?' Prince William went ballistic when he heard the 'dossier of distress' that Knauf had gathered. We do not know whether the communications secretary brought his allegations directly to his boss or submitted them via William's private secretary Simon Case. What we do know is that the prince was astonished and horrified – he was instantly furious at what he heard.

'I remember Christian Jones [William's press secretary and later private secretary] explaining to me how the Cams are paternalistic with their staff,' recalls one royal correspondent. 'They copy the Queen in that respect with all her Christmas parties and Christmas presents to her people. They're proud to treat their staff like family. They recognise that they don't get paid loads of money, so they are just really nice to them. So this was a very deep clash of philosophies, with Meghan being used to a Hollywood service culture – getting exactly what she wanted whenever she wanted in that famous way that Harry said.'

William personally knew and liked all the individuals whom Knauf had named in his dossier. The prince regarded them as assets to his household – colleagues to be cherished and for whom he was responsible. Human beings. Like Knauf, the prince was appalled at the idea that his respected staff may have been put in this position.

For William, Knauf's allegations also clarified something that the prince had long suspected – that Meghan was fundamentally hostile towards the royal system, which she failed to understand as an outsider. William wondered if she had not wanted to leave from the very start – even dreaming, perhaps, that she could whisk Harry back with her to North America.

But Meghan's lawyers said this was quite the wrong interpretation of their client's thinking in a statement that they issued to *The Times* early in March 2021. The duchess wished to fit in and be accepted, they insisted. She had left her life in North America to commit herself to her new role.

This author does not know Jason Knauf. I have never met him. What you have just read is based upon the published accusations that Knauf set down on paper – refuted as 'defamatory', it must be stressed again, and 'based on misleading and harmful information' in the view of the Duchess of Sussex's lawyers. It also relies upon Prince William's personal account of these events to one of his friends who then spoke to this author.

The moment the prince heard the bullying allegations, he related to this friend, he got straight on the phone to talk to Harry – and when Harry flared up in furious defence of his wife, the elder brother persisted. Harry shut off his phone angrily, so William went straight round to find his brother on the Kensington campus. The prince was horrified by what he had just been told about Meghan's alleged behaviour, and he wanted to hear what Harry had to say.

The showdown between the two siblings was fierce and bitter. William's pre-engagement questioning of Meghan's suitability had been quite reasonable, in William's opinion. His fraternal doubts had been provisional – based upon how the new recruit appeared to be. The elder brother did not really know Meghan in those early days.

But now William had seen enough of his sister-in-law to feel sure that, sadly, he did know her and that many of his reservations linked unhappily with what Knauf's colleagues had alleged. William believed Meghan was following a plan – 'agenda' was the word he used to his friend – and the accusations he had just heard were alarming. Kate, he said, had been wary of her from the start.

Meghan was undermining some precious principles of the monarchy, if she really was treating her staff in this way, and William was upset that she seemed to be stealing his beloved brother away from him. Later courtiers would coin a hashtag – #freeHarry. It was only half a joke.

'Meghan portrayed herself as the victim,' recalled one KP staffer, 'but she was the bully. People felt run over by her. They didn't know how to handle this woman. They thought she was a complete narcissist and sociopath – basically unhinged. Which was why the pair of them were drawn to each other in the first place – both damaged goods.'

William felt deeply wounded. 'Hurt' and 'betrayed' were the two feelings that he described to his friend. The elder brother had always felt so protective. He had seen it as his job to look out for Harry – but this was the moment the protection had to stop. At the end of the day the British crown and all it stood for with its ancient traditions, styles and values – the mission of the monarchy – had to matter more to William than his brother did.

* * *

Harry, for his part, was equally furious that William should give credence to the accusations against Meghan, and he was fiercely combative in his wife's defence. Some sources maintain that in the heat of the argument Harry actually accused the family of concepts that were 'racist' in their treatment of Meghan. But it must be stressed that neither brother has ever confirmed that the hateful r-word was used face to face.

Only William and Harry can know what they said to each other and they have respectfully maintained their silence on that. But Harry made clear to the world in his interview with Oprah that he considered his family's response to Meghan to have been essentially racist – using the heavily freighted code words 'unconscious bias' to provide an intellectual framework for his analysis.

Where could the two brothers go after such painful and damning notions had been thrown into their debate?

We have reached the crux of the drama. What painfully unforgettable – and surely unforgivable – things have been said? These are not passing differences. They are two core sets of values in conflict, going to the very heart and deriving from the deepest beliefs and loyalties of each man – two opposing identities butting heads.

In the months following the tragic and not-obviously bridgeable rift of October 2018 between William and Harry, the younger brother solidified his belief that his family were suffering from 'unconscious bias'. We will be examining that devastating accusation in Chapter 38, following Harry's March 2021 conversation with Oprah Winfrey in which he revealed how radically life with Meghan had changed his own view of life.

William, for his part, felt just as strongly about Meghan and the need for her subversive 'agenda' to be removed from the operations of the British monarchy, which she did not appear to understand or respect. He certainly wanted Meghan removed, for a start, from the hitherto harmonious joint household that he and his brother had established together as far back as 2009. William simply did not want her or Harry around any more.

When accounts of the rift started seeping out through the winter months that followed, it was generally assumed that the volatile Harry must have set the pace in the splitting up of the joint KP household. He was the brother who visibly departed – stalking off to set up a new home in Windsor, with offices for himself and Meghan in Buckingham Palace.

But the reverse was the case. It was William who made the decisive move. Following his furious confrontation with his younger brother in the autumn of 2018, the prince instructed Simon Case to start the process of dividing their two households immediately. William wished to be separated from Meghan on a day-to-day basis – and that meant being separated from his brother as well.

'William,' says a friend, 'threw Harry out.'

William's expulsion order had preceded Harry and Meghan's departure on their tour of Australia and the South Pacific in October 2018 – so the knowledge they were now out on their own presumably strengthened the Sussexes' desire to shine even more brightly on their own account.

Jason Knauf had helped to set up the Sussexes' trip, but it was hardly surprising that he did not accompany the couple as their spokesperson. One dreads to imagine the atmosphere inside the aircraft cabin if the duke and duchess had been facing off across the aisle with the man responsible for compiling the 'dossier of distress' that had wrought so much havoc.

As it happened, Knauf had the perfect alibi for not travelling – a broken collarbone that he had sustained while setting up filming for William on his last Africa trip. So, confined to barracks and with half his charges on the other side of the world, the communications secretary set about cleaning up the debris from the great confrontation.

Knauf's first priority was to set down the facts, as he saw them, for the record: 'I'm very concerned,' he emailed to Private Secretary Simon Case, in a long and carefully drafted document dated 26 October 2018, 'that the duchess was able to bully two PAs out of the household in the past year.'

Knauf described Meghan's treatment of one aide as 'totally unacceptable … The duchess seems intent,' he wrote, 'on always having someone in her sights.' Specifying another staff member, Knauf alleged Meghan had been bullying her as well 'seeking to undermine her confidence'. His office had received 'report after report', he wrote, from people who had witnessed 'unacceptable behaviour' by Meghan towards this woman.

Knauf had already taken his personnel concerns for an airing with Samantha Carruthers, the head of human resources, who supervised the hundred-plus staff of Charles and Camilla in the Clarence House–St James's Palace complex, along with the so-far joint household of the two boys with their wives in Kensington Palace. Carruthers had agreed with Knauf that the situation was 'very serious', and had suggested that the communications secretary should write it all down. So Knauf concluded his document with the unresolved principle of HR practice that he had raised with Carruthers: 'I questioned if the Household policy on bullying and harassment applies to principals,' he wrote.

'Principals' was palace speak for members of the royal family – and here was Knauf's big question. Palace protocols set out regulations to protect staff from being bullied by each other – but they said nothing about what to do if staff felt themselves to be bullied by a member of the royal family itself. Carruthers could adjudicate between paid employees of the institution but she had no remit – she was not empowered – to deal with royal 'principals' in any way.

Having completed his foray into human resources work that had proved so momentous, Jason Knauf put his PR hat back on again. How was the outside world likely to react to the disclosure of this household split between the brothers when the news became public, he had to wonder? News management was his day job, after all. None of his four principal clients could possibly be keen for the underlying truth of their disharmony to emerge.

So on Saturday 27 October 2018 – the very day following Knauf's dispatch of his game-changing 26 October email to Private Secretary Simon Case – an article appeared in the *Sunday*

Times under the by-line of its royal correspondent Roya Nikkhah: 'Princes Harry and William to Call It a Day for Their Double Act,' ran the headline. 'Marriage, family life and changing royal roles are leading the brothers to set up separate courts after Meghan gives birth.'

Knauf had wasted no time – affording minimal opportunity for others to leak out their own versions of the unpleasant discord that had led to the separation of the royal households. According to Britain's highly respected Sunday paper, the setting up of 'separate courts' was simply logical – almost routine – with not a suggestion of personal anger or bad feeling on either side.

'The brothers have lent on each other and looked after each other since their mother died,' explained one 'source close to' William and Harry. 'But now they have their own families, they no longer rely on each other as before.'

For decades the *Sunday Times* has been a favoured channel for influential palace 'guidance' to the world. On a quiet weekend other British papers – and the international media – are very happy to pick up *Sunday Times* stories and reproduce them largely unaltered by queries or additional material.

'When William becomes Prince of Wales,' related another helpful source in the article, 'he will take on a lot of extra responsibility including the Duchy of Cornwall and all that entails. Harry and Meghan have none of that and seem ambitious about forging their own paths … If you have one private office trying to manage both, things get difficult.'

As published on that last Sunday in October 2018, the royal guidance neatly diverted attention from just what 'difficult' had meant in real life. With their baby arriving in the spring, it was obvious that Harry and Meghan would require a larger home than their two-bedroom cottage in the grounds of Kensington Palace – and *Sunday Times* readers were told how Charles would be helpfully funding the new separate households with income from his Duchy of Cornwall estates.

'Last year the amount [the Prince of Wales] spent on William, Harry and their wives rose by 40%,' explained the article, 'due mainly to the rising number of official engagements and costs associated with Meghan's arrival into the royal family.'

Another source 'close to the brothers' explained again how 'they have become different people with different outlooks on life. Splitting the household is the obvious thing to do.'

The six-hundred-word article, whose every significant message had clearly originated from inside Kensington Palace, concluded in the traditional way: 'Kensington Palace declined to comment.'

Filing from Sydney, where she was travelling with the Sussexes, Roya Nikkhah made no attribution to any specific palace and gave names to none of her sources. There was certainly no mention of Jason Knauf and the role that his damning charge sheet had played in the momentous rift that now separated the brothers for the foreseeable future, and the PR man doubtless hoped to keep it that way.

Good luck with that one, Jason!

27

Sussex Royal

'The Côte d'Azur with Elton, but no Balmoral
with Granny? They seem to be getting
their Queens mixed up!'

(Former attendant to Queen Elizabeth II,
August 2020)

A nd so, dear reader, these dramatic events take us back to the start of all this – to those first two chapters, you remember, with the mystery of the secret hospital birthplace of baby Archie on 6 May 2019 'somewhere in London' and all the haughty melodrama of those unnamed godparents? That was the beginning of our book – and now it has become the beginning of the end.

Now we can understand the strange background to Harry and Meghan's failing to pose for a picture with their newborn baby outside the hospital.

'We weren't *asked* to take a picture,' snapped Meghan aggrievedly to Oprah. It was all part of the downgrading of Archie in her eyes – no princely title, no 'protection' and no day-of-birth photograph.

Jason Knauf who might have arranged such a picture on the hospital steps had unsurprisingly skipped away from the Sussexes' service two months before Archie's birth, in the aftermath of his historic memo that had prompted the dramatic movement of the brothers in separate directions. As a clear indication of William's favour and support after the row, Knauf had been taken on to the Cambridges' staff and was now working exclusively for the older brother in the role of special advisor.

The Duke and Duchess of Sussex were clearly going their own way – as the picture editor of this book discovered when seeking to illustrate Archie's May 2019 birth in the glossy picture sections in the middle of the volume. Take a look at page 6 in section 3 – Harry and Meghan presenting their son Archie to the world in St George's Hall, Windsor.

It is a delightful image that is publicly available, but it is not the picture we wanted for the book. There is a still more warm and meaningful photograph of Meghan showing off her new baby to Archie's delighted great-grandmother and grandmother, one white, the other black, while Princes Harry and Philip, father and great-grandfather, smile approvingly from behind. This mixture of races beautifully captured the historic significance of the baby being welcomed into the royal family that May.

But when we approached the photographer Chris Allerton for reproduction rights, we discovered that he had been working on the day in a private capacity for Harry and Meghan. This particularly personal image was their own copyright, he explained, and they (or someone in their office) decided that they would not grant rights in the picture to a book called *Battle of Brothers*. Though, surprise surprise, the Sussexes did grant picture rights to the less stroppy and rather more authorised volume being prepared by their friends Omid Scobie and Carolyn Durand. That's *Finding Freedom* for you!

So what did this assertion of private control over what the world considered to be a public moment tell us about the Sussexes' changing frame of mind? The birth of Archie was clearly prompting Harry and Meghan to take their first steps outside the royal stockade – or, rather, to enter a new and more fiercely defended stockade of their own Sussex construction, right down to control of picture rights. The arrival of this baby, to both cherish and be fearful for, was pushing the couple's thinking in a new direction.

'I will always protect my family,' said Harry, following the birth of his son. 'And now I have a family to protect.'

'*Arche*', we have already heard, means 'source of action' in ancient Greek. Talk about a pretentious name for some poor unsuspecting little kid! But let us also acknowledge how precisely that meaningful name can be applied to Harry and Meghan's post-birth emotions in the summer of 2019, since all parents feel a renewed 'source of action' when they hold their fresh-born child in their arms. They sense its vulnerability and they worry about the survival, welfare and spirit of the new human being for which they are now responsible.

'Every single day,' Meghan declared when her son was eighteen months old, 'you go "how can I make this better for him, how can I make this world better for Archie?" And that is a shared belief between my husband and I.'

In the early summer of 2019 Meghan was still busily emailing and texting round the clock on her 'Forces for CHANGE' for British *Vogue*, and Harry was working on his own particular contribution to the magazine – his interview with Dr Jane Goodall, the chimp expert and campaigning anthropologist.

Goodall had come for the interview to Frogmore Cottage, the freshly renovated group of dwellings described in Chapter 1 that was the Sussexes' new family home in the grounds of Windsor Castle – and Meghan came into the room as the interview drew to a close. She was holding the newborn Archie tenderly in her arms and she offered the baby to the eighty-five-year-old Goodall for a cuddle.

'He was very tiny and very sleepy – not too pleased to be passed from his mummy,' recalled Goodall. 'I think I was one of the first to cuddle him outside the family. I made Archie do "the Queen's wave", saying "I suppose he'll have to learn this."

'Harry said, "No! He's not growing up like that."'

On 8 May, just two days after Archie's birth, BBC Radio 5 Live anchor Danny Baker, sixty-one, one of the corporation's most beloved and prolific award-winning presenters (Speech Radio Personality of the Year for 2011, 2012 and 2014), posted a vintage photograph on his massively popular Twitter account. The black and white image from 1925 showed a smartly dressed couple on some Tennessee courtroom steps holding the hand of a little chimpanzee dressed like them in overcoat, bowler hat, shiny shoes and spats.

It was an American propaganda shot that had been staged for the notorious Scopes Monkey Trial – subject of the movie *Inherit the Wind* – in which Fundamentalists and Modernists battled over Adam and Eve and the nature of creation. Had God literally moulded humans from dust in his own likeness, as per the Bible, or were we descended from apes as Charles Darwin said? This photograph, set up with actors and a well-known movie chimpanzee, had been meant to illustrate the Fundamentalist argument that you may dress a monkey in a bowler hat, but he is still a monkey.

However, this was not the message of the BBC's Danny Baker. 'Royal baby leaves hospital,' read his caption.

In the ensuing uproar Baker took down the image almost instantaneously, tweeting that he 'would have used the same stupid pic for any other Royal birth or Boris Johnson's kid or even one of my own. It's a funny image … Anyway, here's to ya Archie, Sorry mate.'

'Yes, OK, he took it down,' responded fellow 5 Live broadcaster Scarlette Douglas. 'But his apology for me wasn't really an apology. I don't think it's right.'

The BBC agreed, dismissing Baker immediately. 'This was a serious error of judgement,' said a Radio 5 spokesperson, 'and goes against the values we as a station aim to embody.'

Buckingham Palace maintained silence, as did Harry and Meghan – though we now know that the couple noted bitterly how 'non'-racist Britain quite failed to ignore Baker's tweet or to treat his attempt at 'humour' with the direct condemnation it deserved. On the contrary, the Monkey Trial image was lovingly reproduced by newspapers and social media across the country for several days, to be cluck-clucked over by millions.

The BBC had at least tried its best to do the right thing. But the corporation fared less creditably in a similar and rather sinister incident that had occurred a few months earlier, when Meghan was five months pregnant.

Early in December 2018 the BBC News website displayed a graphic image of a smiling Prince Harry splattered in bright red blood with a gun being held to his head. 'SEE YA LATER RACE TRAITOR!' The words were as shocking as the picture, which bore the credit of the Sonnenkrieg (Sun War) Division, a British neo-Nazi group that, said the BBC, was allegedly inspired by America's right-wing Atomwaffen Division. Atomwaffen (meaning 'atomic weapons' in German) celebrated both Adolf Hitler and the mass murderer Charles Manson, and had itself been linked to five murders of a racial and sexual character.

The BBC was rather proud of its revelations about the Sonnenkrieg Division, as a result of which Michal Szewczuk, nineteen, from Leeds, and Oskar Dunn-Koczorowski, eighteen, from Chiswick, west London, pleaded guilty to two counts of encouraging terrorism in June 2019, and were sentenced to quite lengthy periods of detention in a young offender institution.

Closer examination, however, revealed that these two young fanatics were the only named members of the so-called

Sonnenkrieg Division. The high-sounding BBC Investigations Unit had failed to come up with the names of any further 'members', let alone details of any gatherings that might have been expected in a genuine network of activists. The poster had been treated by the BBC as a news issue of major significance, broadcast nationally and lingered over for some minutes on the *News at Ten*, the BBC's main evening bulletin.

But did these two teenagers truly provide evidence of a 'group', much less a movement? Or were they just a couple of poisonous young nutcases whose proposition that 'Race Traitor' Prince Harry should be shot had been taken up for sensationalist reasons and had been given far more attention than it deserved?

This was the gist of the complaint that Prince Harry lodged with the BBC straight after the broadcast, on the grounds that publicising the invitation to kill him raised 'serious security concerns' and had 'caused his family great distress, specifically while his wife was nearly five months pregnant'.

The BBC rejected his complaint saying that it had been necessary to show the poster in order to illustrate 'the nature of the group' – and Ofcom, the national communications regulator, upheld the BBC's decision. There was 'clear public interest', it ruled, in conveying 'impactfully the offensive nature of the group's messages'.

It took a personal conversation between Harry and the BBC's director-general, Tony Hall, finally to secure a full apology nine months later, representing the reality that Harry, as the most prominent British ex-serviceman to have fought in Afghanistan, would be a Taliban target for the rest of his life – and that his father's 'Uncle Dickie' Mountbatten had been assassinated by Irish terrorists.

Every year the shadowy FTAC – the Home Office's Fixated Threat Assessment Centre – and the Metropolitan Police, working with MI5, have to monitor a thousand or more threats against the Queen and the royal family from stalkers and obsessives. Who knows which of these poor deluded souls is mad enough to carry a loaded gun?

Danny Baker's chimpanzee tweet, 'Here's to ya Archie', and the 'SEE YA LATER RACE TRAITOR' death threat – both deploying the racist-ly dismissive 'ya' in the same derogatory fashion – epitomised the way in which the great British public, for all their deference and respect and frequently expressed love towards their royal family, equally feel the right to kick it around for their amusement just whenever they wish. We love 'em when it suits, and we laugh at 'em when it doesn't. The nation finances the Windsors to the tune of £85 million or so per year in taxes, after all, so that makes them the nation's servants and playthings at the end of the day.

As two products of a loveless marriage arranged for the nation's benefit, William and Harry were living examples of the 'kick 'em around' syndrome. We saw in our Highgrove chapters how the young Harry was taught his dirty rascal role through his 'Drugs Shame' and Nazi armband incidents, and how William emerged with quite the contrary reputation.

Now it seemed that Harry's and his mixed-race wife had been selected for the same poisonous treatment from a prejudiced nation – and where was William the shining knight to come to their rescue when it mattered?

Nothing had been the same between the brothers since the fateful moment of William's intervention seeking to delay Harry's courtship of Meghan in the early days – followed by the still more decisive and catastrophic row over Knauf's bullying allegations that led to the division of households after October 2018.

'Really damaging things were said and done,' recalled their friend Tom Bradby, who would hear some of the details when he toured Southern Africa with the Sussexes a year later. 'The atmosphere soured hard and early … few meaningful attempts were made by anyone to heal the wounds.'

But few know the very innermost details of what those 'really damaging things' might have been. At the time of writing, no credible record exists of what William and Harry said to each other in these painful confrontations – and this must be stressed. The outside world knows the bare reality but not the innermost secrets of these moments of royal rupture.

This is rather to the credit of both brothers, since it shows that for all the disagreement that would drive them to opposite sides of the globe in March 2020, Diana's two sons have retained certain loyalties to each other and to their brotherhood. Born royal, the pair of them understand the royal rules. The details of their clashes have remained private to the two of them, with a minimum of recriminations getting shared with the outside world – at least until Harry and Meghan sat down with Oprah in 2021, and when Oprah's media friends joined in.

Let us not underestimate the anger. Harry has freely confessed to his own blazing temper from time to time – and as for his elder brother, well, he has proved no Sweet William when roused. In the years after her 2005 marriage to Prince Charles, Camilla recounted to her own family and close friends her surprise at discovering this unexpected side to Prince Charming – 'the boy's got a temper!' Charles's wife was horrified at the ranting and raving that William unleashed on occasion against her husband in her presence.

The rows were shattering, by Camilla's account in the early days, with William doing the shouting and Charles submitting meekly on the receiving end. As she described it, William held nothing back. The prince could summon up a wrath to match the importance he attached to his own role as the future king, and if his father failed to live up to William's view of the job, the young man released his fury.

In 2017, when marking the twentieth anniversary of Diana's death, William had proved fiercely uncompromising in his unwillingness to make some conciliatory remark about Charles's fathering of his motherless sons. Royal PR aides begged the young prince to give Charles some sort of nod when talking to journalists before the screening of the ITV documentary *Diana, Our Mother*, but he flatly refused. William was not prepared to pretend that the workaholic, ever-worrying Charles had made good on all the hands-on parenting that he had promised.

In the same way the elder brother had seen no reason to mince his words over Harry's haste in courting his future wife – nor, still more in October 2018, when William felt that Meghan had not been treating their loyal staff with sufficient respect. William had been speaking on these occasions less as a brother than as the chief personnel officer concerned with the defects apparently demonstrated by this newcomer to the Firm – which he, of course, would one day head.

So, here we have a couple of brothers who loved each other dearly but who could give as good as they got when it came to a clash over something that mattered intensely to them. For William it was the future state of his monarchy – his sacred trust; while for Harry it was the love of the complex and captivating woman who had finally made sense of his life.

Love versus duty – it was the dilemma at the heart of so many royal disagreements, not least the agonising conflict that had torn Edward VIII, and almost the monarchy itself, apart in the Abdication Crisis of 1936.

But even in the fierceness of their disharmony the two brothers could clearly see and agree on some of the things that they needed to do – extracting themselves from each other's pockets for a start, with relative discretion. It had clearly been impossible after their momentous row over the Knauf memo for the two of them to stay living in the confines of the same palace. In their fury the brothers could hardly stand the prospect of seeing each other on a daily basis.

The same went for their wives. Tales of a Meghan–Kate rift in the early months had had little basis in reality. But as the two loyal wives took their husbands' side, the rift had finally become all too authentic.

* * *

The saddest separation in many ways came from the need for the two brothers to split up their combined Royal Foundation, the thriving charitable enterprise that they had created together ten years earlier to promote their various good causes. Raising and paying out a good £7 million or £8 million per year for some twenty-six charities, the Royal Foundation seemed to embody both the legacy of Diana and the harmony of her sons in perpetuating her name.

When the short-lived 'Fab Four' had gathered in February 2018 to launch the first Royal Foundation Forum (see picture section 2, page 6) with the still unwed Meghan encouraging women to 'use their voices' to speak out against sexual harassment, it had looked as if the two couples could carry the Royal Foundation forward into a new dimension.

But that was not to be. On 20 June 2019, not long after Archie's birth, it was disclosed that the Royal Foundation's assets would be divided. William and Kate would take over the existing organisation – and that September the prestigious directorship of the Foundation, now under William's sole control, was handed to Jason Knauf.

Harry and Meghan for their part announced they would establish a new charity of their own that would be aiming at 'global outreach', and the following day, 21 June – which just happened to be William's thirty-seventh birthday – they filed trademark number UK00003408516 with the Intellectual Property Office of the UK government. Their new charity would be known as 'Sussex Royal – The Foundation Of The Duke And Duchess Of Sussex', and on 1 July 2019 Sussex Royal received its certificate of incorporation as a private limited company at London's Companies House.

Sussex Royal was the work of Harry, Meghan and her team of American advisors headed by the powerful Hollywood talent and PR agency Sunshine Sachs – the creation of the amiably named Ken Sunshine and the PR guru Shawn Sachs. Its clients included the likes of Jennifer Lopez, Barbra Streisand and Justin Timberlake – along with such left-ish US political figures as father and son Mario and Andrew Cuomo, and, on occasion, the National Convention of the Democratic Party.

When she got engaged to Harry in 2017, Meghan had announced a definitive end to her showbiz career. But she had retained her Hollywood 'three As' – her agent, her attorney and her accountant – to field calls relating to the professional side of her life, and she remained particularly close to Keleigh Thomas Morgan, the Sunshine Sachs representative with whom she had worked while she was acting in *Suits*.

Thomas Morgan had become a friend and in due course a fellow new mother – she had occupied a prime seat at the royal wedding – and as Meghan's relationship with Buckingham Palace went awry, Keleigh moved into the vacuum to give Meghan the benefit of her professional advice. Keleigh lent a hand with the recruitment of faces for the *Vogue* special issue and when the break-up of the Royal Foundation raised the question of how Meghan and Harry's new separate charity should be developed, she was part of the discussions that led to the clever brand name of Sussex Royal, with its elegant white 'HM' monogram on dark blue surmounted by a crown. She was also on hand at the end of July 2019 when the contents of Meghan's 'Forces for CHANGE' *Vogue* were previewed – and were met by stern and rather worrying disapproval from the British press.

'Meghan's "woke" *Vogue* is shallow and divisive,' wrote Melanie Phillips, leading the way in *The Times* with the African-American slang term that had recently won its place in the Merriam-Webster dictionary 'as a byword for social awareness ... "I was sleeping, but now I'm woke."'

'Meghan's virtue-signalling is all about boasting,' reported Phillips. 'It flaunts the signaller's credentials as a morally virtuous person. It screams, "Me! Me! Me!"' The new duchess clearly did not understand, said Phillips, that her royal status 'precludes political statements.'

The lack of political balance among the women activists Meghan had chosen for the *Vogue* cover, for example, was 100 per cent out of whack. All fifteen were quite aggressively left-wing – and some of them were famously subversive, like Jane Fonda.

'At the very top of the Duchess's list, moreover, should have been her own grandmother-in-law,' concluded Phillips. 'Probably, though, the Queen never entered her mind. After all, she stands for an overwhelming sense of duty, humility and self-effacement – unity rather than division.'

The *Sun* took up the same theme from the working-class point of view: 'A woman who genuinely wants to be a royal, championing society's poorest, shouldn't guest-edit a glossy mag stuffed with overpriced fashion for the world's richest people.'

Dresses at £12,000 and a pair of high heels at £600 were 'about as inaccessible to hard-working Brits as you can possibly get … And she should be non-political … OUR ROYALS SHOULD KEEP THEIR POLITICAL OPINIONS PRIVATE.'

It was a formidable chorus of disapproval – and not just from commentators who were paid to be controversial. Editors weighed in with serious constitutional concerns about the monarchy trespassing into politics. Meghan evidently did not know – or, maybe, did not want to know – what it meant to be a Windsor.

That feeling was coming to be shared among the Windsors themselves – and Prince William remained particularly disturbed. Many of the papers had identified Meghan's proclaimed refusal to be 'boastful' by appearing on the front of her issue as a not-so-sly put-down to Kate, whose face had featured on the cover of her own *Vogue* a few years earlier.

But William's concern went much deeper. Every paper had emphasised the need for royals to stay clear of controversy – as the *Sun* had put it: 'The fundamental reason that the monarchy still exists is because it sits above politics.' And the people's paper had added a scarcely veiled threat to Meghan: 'We fear she is heading for a fallout with the public which now funds her.'

'Forces for CHANGE' was an overt political statement by both Meghan and Harry – an act of rebellion. In terms of their royal duties it went along with splitting the joint household and moving down to Windsor. Suddenly it was announced that Harry, Meghan and Archie were no longer joining William, Kate and the other members of the royal family for their annual summer holiday that year with Grandma at Balmoral.

The official excuse, conveyed straight-faced by the palace, was that at three months Archie was still too young for the air travel involved. But that didn't stop the Sussexes somehow managing to travel to Minorca for a week that August, and then taking Archie with them for a few days in the South of France with Elton John and his partner David Furnish.

'The Côte d'Azur with Elton, but no Balmoral with Granny?' asked one former attendant to Elizabeth II. 'They seem to be getting their Queens mixed up.'

In the course of eleven days, Harry, Meghan and Archie travelled no fewer than four times on various excursions by private jet. Meghan might have wished she had heeded Anne McElvoy's caution about the use of helicopters.

'Prince Harry's Heir Miles,' ran one scornful heading in the *Sun* over a map showing an alarming number of private jet trips by Harry and Meghan. 'DUMBO JET,' proclaimed the same paper in the middle of August: 'Eco-Warriors Meghan Markle and Prince Harry Fly on Private Jet Again to France after Gas-Guzzling Ibiza Trip.'

Ex-royal protection officer Ken Wharfe weighed in: 'Frankly, it's hypocritical. Harry can't be preaching about the catastrophic effects of climate change while jetting around the world on a private plane.'

It was too good an opportunity for brother William to miss. On Thursday 22 August it was announced that he, Kate and their three children had flown from Norwich to Aberdeen – the nearest airport to Balmoral – on the routinely scheduled 8.40 a.m. flight operated by Loganair on behalf of the budget airline Flybe. They had sat in the same rows as the ordinary passengers, all paying like them a standard £73 per head.

'According to their fellow travellers,' reported the *Daily Mail*, 'the Cambridges slipped onto the plane discreetly, shortly before take-off and sat in the front few rows, exiting first.'

But the *Mail* also reported that the 8.40 Norwich–Aberdeen flight would normally have been operated in an aircraft bearing a Loganair logo, and Flybe wanted the full benefit of the publicity of having had five members of the royal family on board. The company had ordered an Embraer 145 passenger jet to be flown down empty to Norwich, so that William and his family could fly north in an aircraft that proclaimed the name Flybe on its side.

This was not William and Kate's fault, of course. But that extra trip of the Flybe jet meant that the environment-saving 'budget' flight with the royal party on board had actually generated an additional 4.5 tonnes of carbon emissions.

28

Different Paths

*'I lost my mother and now I watch my wife falling
victim to the same powerful forces.'*

(Prince Harry, 2 October 2019)

Prince William's non-ecological 'budget' flight to Scotland on 22 August 2019 proved something of an 'own goal', but there were many more goals to play for in the Cambridge–Sussex match – which, as summer waned, seemed to be heading towards a draw. The splitting apart of the two princes' homes, offices and charitable activities in the early months of the year had been reflected in a sprightly new Instagram account called @sussexroyal, controlled by Harry and Meghan and designed to signal their own philosophy and identity.

Indulge us for a moment, please, you younger readers, while this elderly author explains to his fellow members of the non-digital generation that an Instagram account is a platform or site on the Internet on which you post photographs or videos, usually of yourself and your family, with a few words of explanation, illustrating the latest incidents and people in your life. Babies and pets are especially popular in the genre – plus the occasional poem and reflection on the meaning of existence.

People who like what you have posted will sign up to be your 'followers', and since 2010 showbiz celebrities – and trendy royals – have used Instagram to grow their fan bases in a dynamic way that was not possible before the Internet. The older platform of Facebook also offers similar content-sharing, and if you are a politician or journalist you will probably have signed up to Twitter, because that is all about words and 'tweeting' out your arguments and opinions. But Instagram is definitely 2021's route to broadcast your beliefs and lifestyle to the world, and to demonstrate your popularity through the number of followers that you can attract.

So in 2019 social media, and Instagram in particular, became the arena in which the royal brothers, William and Harry, competed for influence. Established on 2 April, @sussexroyal set a Guinness World Record for reaching a million followers faster than any previous account in Instagram history – in five hours and forty-five minutes. This would take @sussexroyal close to, but not ahead of, the brothers' original @kensingtonroyal account, which they had hitherto shared, but which now became the vehicle of William and Kate. Through the spring and summer the two brothers' competing accounts each came to command similar allegiances in the region of 11.2 million to 11.3 million followers.

The dramatic and immediate success of @sussexroyal owed much to 'Digital Dave' – David Watkins, twenty-seven, a young

Irish social media whiz noted for his visionary video skills, who had been poached by the Sussex team from the fashion house Burberry. Watkins had made his reputation through his Internet role in the smoothing and sharpening of the old and fuddy-duddy image of the company into a successful, modern and even hipster-ish brand. As the summer months went by, Digital Dave brilliantly used events like the birth of Archie to draw in followers and take the new @sussexroyal site right up alongside the 11 million-plus level of @kensingtonroyal, securing the desirable draw.

Dave was a workaholic – like Meghan. He belonged to the same fellowship of early risers – some called it the '5 a.m. Club': 'Winning starts at your Beginning.' In his short life Watkins had already met the swimming-cycling-running endurance challenge of the Ironman in Thailand and he had completed marathons in both London and Paris. According to his personal website, he liked to 'recognise the positives in a situation' and he believed in 'constantly challenging the status quo with a "start with why" attitude'.

Does that remind you of anyone we have met recently? Dave was clearly the energetic digital ally that Meghan and Harry needed as the autumn of 2019 approached.

In September the Sunshine Sachs public relations agency was contemplating Meghan's 'Forces for CHANGE' PR disaster and the dramatic deterioration in its client's image that had occurred in recent months in the UK. There was no point in arguing that Meghan had edited her special issue of *Vogue* with the best of intentions – and there was even less point in maintaining that her messages of social activism and female empowerment were 'right'. The harsh reality was that the gospel according to Meghan was simply not royal nor in harmony with mainstream, 'un-woke' British opinion.

William and all the senior members of the royal family – not least Prince Charles and the Queen – had come to feel the same, and this growing disapproval at the top had started seeping downwards. The honeymoon was over. On the talk shows, Meghan and Harry had become topics of national controversy instead of celebration. Digital Dave might be doing a brilliant job 'challenging the status quo' with the younger generation on Sussex Royal's Instagram following, but that was not the mainstream. There was an urgent need for the image of the Harry– Meghan brand to be turned around in the eyes of Her Majesty's subjects.

Sunshine Sachs was an expert at this. Crisis management and image salvation were its trademarks – as it had demonstrated in 2013 with the notorious rearrangement of supermodel Naomi Campbell's Internet identity when mention of its client's 'several highly publicised convictions for assault' had been surreptitiously removed from her Wikipedia entry.

The agency had employed a 'Wiki wizard' who clicked the keys to delete the last three words of Wikipedia's sentence about Campbell's ghostwritten novel *Swan* – 'released in 1994 *to poor reviews*' – going on to remove the clause that described *Babywoman*, her attempt at a music album, as 'a critical and commercial failure'. The wizard had rounded off this re-editing of reality by removing the words 'ill-fated' from a sentence describing an unsuccessful restaurant chain in which Campbell had invested.

Sunshine Sachs proposed different tactics but similar cunning when it came to the ten-day tour of Southern Africa for which Meghan and Harry were preparing at the end of September 2019. Like all royal tours, the trip had been organised by the Foreign and Commonwealth Office in Whitehall to promote the British government's interests in the region. The tour's official purpose was to foster Britain's friendship with the countries they were to visit – South Africa, Botswana, Angola and Malawi – and to deliver a helpful boost on the side for local British-linked businesses and commercial interests.

From Buckingham Palace's point of view, there were the lingering elements of the Geidt–Manning strategy, to which Harry and Meghan were now signed up, intended to build on ambitions to develop the Commonwealth. And there was the 'Diana dimension' of the trip that Harry would make to Angola, where he was due to visit and be photographed walking through the very same minefield at Huambo that his mother had famously visited in 1997. Harry's speech for the occasion would deliver sentiments along the lines of finishing what had been started.

Within those limits Sunshine Sachs worked with the couple to develop their personal redemption tactics. There were to be a minimum of smart clothes or fashionable costumes and poses that suggested *Vogue*. Just some simple, ethically sourced dresses, please Meghan – 'cool brands that are doing things right'.

There must be no private jets – commercial flights only. And let's arrange some sessions of that community cooking that enjoyed such success among the Grenfell survivors. On the other hand, any talk of female empowerment must not be too strident. Sorry, Megs. Make some of the visits to girls' schools and centres private. And above all, let us see as much as possible of Archie. There was to be no more of this 'secret baby' nonsense.

Harry had experienced this sort of thing before, of course, in the days of Mark Bolland's campaign to rehabilitate Camilla's reputation. But when it came to the dark arts of public relations, Lord Blackadder had nothing on Mr Sunshine.

The early parts of the tour went largely to plan. The photography schedule was cleverly shifted away from the airport so that there were no shots of the couple coming down aircraft steps. The first pictures to go out in the newspapers – and on @sussexroyal – came from Nyanga, a poverty-stricken township in Cape Town, described by Tom Bradby, who was covering the trip for ITV, as 'the murder capital of South Africa and one of the most dangerous places on earth. Violence against women in Nyanga is endemic.'

Meghan and Harry visited Nyanga's Justice Desk, a charity supported by the Queen's Commonwealth Trust that they now jointly headed (with Christopher Geidt as their chairman of trustees), and they mingled informally with children who were learning about their rights and taking part in self-defence classes.

There were also some female empowerment lessons going on and it was impossible for Meghan not to give expression to what she felt in her heart. She just had to stand on a tree stump to speak to these young women with whom she identified, and for the first time since her marriage she referred to herself in public as a 'woman of colour'. As Harry watched her saying these words, the love and admiration shone out of his eyes.

Archie proved the star as planned. On Wednesday 25 September Meghan and Harry took their four-month-old son to meet Desmond Tutu, the Nobel Peace Prize-winning anti-apartheid campaigner, who, as Archbishop of Cape Town, was known as 'the Arch'.

'Arch meets Archie!' was Digital Dave's caption for the Instagram footage of the little boy giggling obligingly as Tutu held him in his arms. It was the first time that such a young royal baby had been featured on a royal tour and the happy pictures went around the world.

Leaving Meghan and Archie to enjoy some quiet time in Cape Town, along with some of Meghan's private and less-publicised engagements, Harry went north to Angola to do his stuff visiting Diana's still-not-totally de-mined minefield at Huambo.

'It has been quite emotional,' he said on Friday 27 September, 'retracing my mother's steps … to see the transformation that has taken place, from an unsafe and desolate place into a vibrant community.'

Harry said he knew what his mother would have done if she had still been alive. 'She would have seen it through … Let's finish what was started. Let us consign these weapons to the history books.'

Talking of finishing what was started, Harry had prepared a very private memorial to his mother for that last Friday in September. The prince had long been indignant that Rupert Murdoch's News International had not paid the full price for its phone-hacking activities against himself, William and Kate ten years earlier. The closed-down *News of the World* had been reopened within months as the *Sun on Sunday*, recycling the same diet of scandal and intrusion. For some time since his marriage, and with Meghan's encouragement, Harry had been consulting David Sherborne, the leading media and privacy barrister who had been winning cases for Murdoch's phone-hacking victims – and for Mirror Group victims as well.

The newspapers had settled with all of Sherborne's victorious clients for large sums of money at the court door – 'out of court' – to avoid the humiliation of their executives having to appear in the witness box and to confess in public to their personal knowledge of what the hacking entailed. But Harry was not inclined to settle. He did not appear in the mood for compromise. He wanted to go into court, it seemed, so that he and the rest of the world could see the Murdoch and Mirror men grovel – and maybe some women as well.

Harry's two lawsuits for the misuse of confidential information, filed in the High Court by Sherborne on 27 September 2019, would be his revenge for his mother – launched as they were on the day that he walked in Diana's footsteps through the mines of Huambo.

The climax of the trip, which would prove historic, were Harry and Meghan's interviews with Tom Bradby, whose cameras had been following them for his ITV documentary *Harry & Meghan: An African Journey*. Dramatically engulfed in the domed darkness of a southern hemisphere night, with the flames of a campfire flickering in the background, Harry admitted that he and William now found themselves moving through their lives and careers on 'different paths'. The prince finally acknowledged and revealed to the world the solid reality of the rift that was dividing him from his brother – but he tried to deliver the news with reflection and context.

'Inevitably stuff happens,' said Harry. 'But look, we are brothers. We will always be brothers. We are certainly on different paths at the moment but I will always be there for him and, as I know, he will always be there for me.'

Meghan did not fare so well. Bradby managed to catch the duchess with his cameras on the day before the couple were due to leave for home at the end of a tour that had proved a resounding success, thanks to the efforts of the FCO, Geidt–Manning, Sunshine Sachs – and, not least, the charm and positive energies of the couple themselves. But Meghan had gone into one of her negative 'victim' modes.

'How are you feeling, Meghan?' wondered Bradby.

'Thank you for asking,' she replied with a steely and defiant edge. 'Because not many people have asked if I'm OK.'

Bradby looked surprised, repeating the question, 'And the answer is? Would it be fair to say, not really OK? That it's really been a struggle?'

To which Meghan eventually replied, 'Yes.'

'I suppose I just told the story that was in front of me, really,' Bradby later recounted to ABC in a discussion of the interview. 'I knew that everything wasn't entirely rosy behind the scenes.'

Gently the interviewer, who was also a friend, tried to tease out some details from Meghan, getting her to explain how she had been trying hard to 'adopt this British sensibility of a stiff upper lip ... I tried, I really tried.'

But she had stopped trying, she said, because she was worried about the effect it might have upon her mental health – 'I think that what that does internally is probably really damaging ... I've said for a long time to H (that's what I call [Harry]), it's not enough to just survive something, right? Like that's not the point of life. You've got to thrive, you've got to feel happy.'

The problem with the interview was that Meghan's sense of persecution did not really need much teasing out.

'Look at any woman,' she said, going back before the birth of Archie, 'especially when they're pregnant, you're really vulnerable, you know. And especially as a woman, it's a lot. So you add this on top of just trying to be a new mom, or trying to be a newly-wed ...'

Her words tailed away as she tried to hold back the tears. Observers with long memories couldn't help recalling the self-destructive tone of Princess Diana in her 1995 interview with *Panorama* journalist Martin Bashir. There was no 'three of us in this marriage' moment in Meghan's contribution to *An African Journey*, but it ended the Sussexes' oh-so-promising tour of Southern Africa on a depressed and mournful note.

Writing in the *New York Times* the following year, Meghan would explain how she had been 'exhausted', breastfeeding Archie and 'trying to keep a brave face' when Bradby posed his question. Her honest off-the-cuff response, she said, 'seemed to give people permission to speak their [own] truth'.

One reason for Meghan's negative feelings as she flew 'home' to England at the beginning of October 2019 curiously provided some redemption from her distress. Both Harry and Meghan had shared with the world the ever-increasing fury that they felt about the unrelenting intrusion of the press. 'Every single time I see a camera,' Harry had said, in reference to his mother's death pursued and surrounded by photographers, 'every single time I hear a click, every single time I see a flash – it takes me back. So in that respect, it's the worst reminder of her life, as opposed to the best.'

For her part Meghan had recounted how her British friends had actually warned her against marrying Harry 'because the British tabloids will destroy your life'. The polished – and, she felt, quite hardened and experienced – TV star, had shrugged off their concerns. She never thought it would be easy, she said, 'but I thought it would be fair'.

Now Meghan admitted that she had been naïve.

'The first time I met Meghan, before her engagement to Harry, it was to talk about the press,' recalled Tom Bradby in the *Sunday Times* on the day that the Africa interview aired. 'She was already starting to find the attention difficult to cope with, with reporters trying to inveigle themselves close to her family … I sensed that Harry had introduced us so that I might reassure her it could be managed and would settle down. In retrospect, I did a lousy job.'

Sunshine Sachs reckoned that it could do better, and the agency had simple advice for its two beleaguered royal clients – the same considered, professional advice that it was now giving to many of its top clients in the States: SUE THE FUCKERS TO HELL!!

This was a recently developed tactic of American PR agencies. If you could get your client into the law courts in the age of mass media and social media, ran the rationale, you had secured them a very effective platform as well as a hearing in the court of public opinion – and it did not matter greatly if you should win or lose. With clients who could comfortably afford retainers to their PR agents in the region of $10,000 to $20,000 per month, legal fees and even legal penalties were small change.

This was a ploy pursued in the British courts in July 2020 by the American actor Johnny Depp. The alleged wife-beater lost his libel case against the *Sun*, but flooded every variety of media on both sides of the Atlantic with his own point of view – eloquently presented by barrister David Sherborne. The loss hardly harmed Depp's DVD sales and Dior actually signed up the not-so-alleged wife-beater for another season promoting its fragrance Sauvage.

Sunshine Sachs reckoned that Harry and Meghan were sitting on a much stronger grievance that they could lay out in a court of law – and the agency also knew that its two royal clients were ardent to fight it.

Early in February 2019, when Meghan had been six months pregnant, the American celebrity magazine *People* had splashed a cover story – 'Exclusive! The Truth About Meghan: Her Best

Friends Break Their Silence.' Upset by the 'heart-breaking' lies and 'bullying' aimed at Meghan by the British press, 'her real friends' had opened up 'about the woman they know and love' – presumably with Meghan's knowledge, since 'real friends' would scarcely have spoken to America's bestselling weekly without at least consulting her.

Over seven lavishly illustrated pages – and speaking anonymously – five of her very best buddies extolled her virtues, from her ability to rustle up 'a five-star meal out of the garbage in your refrigerator' to her 'very close relationship with God'. Her nameless pals defended Meghan against the widespread media hostility that had now solidified in Britain, as well as the alleged behaviour of her father before the wedding – and these remarks about Thomas Markle opened the possibility of legal action.

The friends recounted the troubled history of Tom Markle's pre-wedding mishaps and misadventures the previous May – as narrated in our own Chapter 23 – all set out from Meghan's point of view. They also revealed that after the wedding she had written her father a letter that they had not read themselves but which, on the basis of what Meghan had told them, they characterised as being friendly and conciliatory: 'She's like "Dad, I'm so heart-broken. I love you. I have one father. Please stop victimising me through the media so we can repair our relationship."'

Reading the friends' account of this apparently fence-building message, the *Mail on Sunday*'s Los Angeles bureau chief Caroline Graham decided to travel to Mexico to visit Thomas Markle to see if he would show her the letter – which he did. In his eyes,

Markle argued to Graham, the letter was anything but conciliatory. It had made no attempt to heal the rift with his daughter, in his opinion, and had left him feeling 'devastated'.

'I thought it would be an olive branch,' he said to Graham. 'Instead, it was a dagger to the heart.'

Markle handed over the five pages of his daughter's elegantly handwritten text to Graham to publish, neither asking for, nor receiving, any payment – as the *Mail on Sunday* was at pains to make clear when it printed much of the letter's contents in its edition of 10 February 2019.

Olive branch or dagger? Public or private? Those questions lay at the heart of the civil prosecution in the British High Court that Meghan Markle instituted against Associated Newspapers, publishers of the *Mail on Sunday*, on 1 October 2019, through Schillings, her London libel lawyers, shortly before she left Africa with Harry and Archie.

The central issue on which Meghan based her case was that she retained personal copyright in the five pages she penned and sent to her father. She complained that the *Mail on Sunday* had breached her copyright by publishing them – though some experts in publishing law said that the power of personal copyright is significantly modified once a letter has been received, opened and read by its intended recipient.

Following this argument, Thomas Markle – and hence the *Mail on Sunday* – was entitled to cite the letter's contents as evidence that Meghan had not been as conciliatory towards him as her friends told the readers of *People* magazine. What rights do you possess as a letter recipient if someone informs the world that they wrote to you saying (a), when you interpret their letter as saying (b) – which you feel to be conveying precisely the opposite meaning?

On Thursday 11 February 2021, Mr Justice Warby set this argument aside to consider a simpler issue. Meghan's privacy had been invaded, he ruled in the High Court in London, by the large quantities of her letter that had been quoted by the newspaper without her permission. The extent of the *Mail on Sunday*'s publication of her letter was 'manifestly excessive and hence unlawful … The claimant had a reasonable expectation that the contents of the letter would remain private.'

The judge did not adjudicate on the question of (a) versus (b). Privacy was the issue. The newspaper had made a serious mistake in quoting large sections of Meghan's letter verbatim, he declared, and even reproducing numerous pages of her handwritten script. The report would have been quite in order if it had simply condensed and summarised the gist of what she said to her father. But by displaying so much of the actual letter to the world, the paper had invaded Meghan's privacy – and on that issue Mr Justice Warby came down solidly on her side.

One of the ironies of this highly significant privacy judgment was that it was originally provoked by a breach of privacy on Meghan's part. The world would never have heard about the private letter to her father if her friends had not revealed its existence to *People* magazine. Another irony was that Mr Justice Warby disclosed in his judgment considerably more of her poignant and painful thoughts – some 1100 words – than the *Mail on Sunday* had revealed.

'I ... urged you day after day to stop reading the tabloids,' wrote Meghan in one lengthy section of the letter never published before. 'But you couldn't – and your fascination grew into para- noia (and then rage) of how you were being portrayed. You know how much anguish [the] tabloid press has caused – lies simply for click bait.'

'What a weird thing to say to your dad,' commented Camilla Long in the *Sunday Times*.

During the Sussexes' momentous tour of Southern Africa in September 2019, Tom Bradby had noticed how 'incredibly tired, even burnt-out' Harry had appeared at times as the trip progressed – and Meghan later testified to the same fatigue. But then on 1 October, while still in Johannesburg, the couple released their press statement announcing Meghan's defiant legal action against the *Mail on Sunday* and Associated Newspapers – 'alongside a more general attack on the tabloid press' – and that seemed to lift the mood.

It 'was a shock,' wrote Bradby, 'but made sense.'

In conjunction with Harry's two cases launched in previous days against the Mirror and Murdoch groups, the young royal couple were lined up directly against Britain's three largest media conglomerates – a formidable prospect as they headed back to London at the beginning of October 2019.

Let battle commence!

29

Christmas Message

'Prince Philip and I have been delighted
to welcome our eighth great-grandchild
into our family.'

(Queen Elizabeth II, 25 December 2019)

Windsors do not do campaigns of social upheaval. They do not do headline-grabbing lawsuits in pursuit of personal crusades. And, most of all, they do not air their grievances like any other Johnny Depp. To be royal, sometimes, is to ride the punches, to take it on the chin – and to just shut up.

At the end of a foreign tour it is not unknown for the member(s) of the family who have carried out the mission to pay a courtesy visit to Windsor Castle or Buckingham Palace to report back to the Queen. Her Majesty is 99 per cent certain to have visited those territories herself and to have personal knowledge of some of the presidents and places involved. These sessions tend to be informal get-togethers over tea or a gin and tonic – and occasionally the gist of the gathering gets leaked to the press to convey the Queen's gratitude to those who have carried the flag in her name. But there was no such leaking in October 2019 to tell the world the Queen was happy with what Harry and Meghan had achieved in Africa.

As she sat in front of her TV watching *An African Journey*, Elizabeth II must have been delighted by the uplift and hope that her grandson and his wife had brought to the township of Nyanga in the name of her Queen's Commonwealth Trust. Meghan's leap onto the tree stump to speak out as a 'woman of colour' was brave and visionary.

But then to start emoting against the backdrop of one of the most blighted corners of the planet to complain about the personal problems you are experiencing in your adjustment to life inside a palace – Meghan's litany of grievance had suggested indifference bordering on contempt for the true concerns of the human beings among whom she had been smiling. It also demonstrated a bizarre tone-deafness as to how miserably self-indulgent her self-pity must appear.

This was unquestionably the view of a powerful constituency inside Buckingham Palace, headed by Sir Edward Young. When it came to any Sussex matter, the royal private secretary's authority was now being disputed by the Sunshine Sachs channels through which both Harry and Meghan had insisted on running their outreach activities since early September. If Sir Edward judged 'no comment' the best answer to some tricky question about Harry, Sunshine Sachs would propose to give out an answer – and Sunshine Sachs often won.

The three major law cases against the British media establishment launched by Harry and Meghan while they were in Africa were the supreme examples of this – plain insubordination, not just to Young and his staff, who would have to process the implications as they affected the crown, but ultimately to the Queen. It was absolutely unknown for one, let alone three, such major conflicts with the outside world to be initiated by any member of the family without the Queen's blessing – which Harry and Meghan had neither asked for nor received.

So, somehow, somewhere, in some royal setting or other in the autumn of 2019, there must have been the most godawful explosion over what Harry had done – and let his wife do – without the courtesy of consulting the boss. Was the whole issue delegated to Prince Charles to try to talk some sense into his rebellious son? William could hardly help – he had walked away from his younger brother. So perhaps it was just handed over to Sir Edward Young …

These are some of the possible developments – but sorry, folks, once again we are confronted by that challenge of credible evidence. It is not easy to establish the key ingredients in the Windsor winter of discontent that followed the Sussex tour of Africa and would culminate in the spring of 2020 with Meghan and Harry kicking the dust of Britain – along with their entire royal status – from their shoes.

The couple themselves have already let slip a few details via the semi-authorised pages of *Finding Freedom*. But the rest of the family – whom we must now define as 'the other side' – have stayed resolutely 'mum'. The Queen, Prince Charles and brother William have all strictly observed the precautionary practice that we have already noted between the two brothers – 'the less said, the safer'. Yet silence can only hide so much of the truth.

A month after Archie's birth in May 2019, just at the time that their new separate identity from 'Kensington Royal' was getting started, Harry and Meghan decided to trademark a range of items that they would like to sell under the name of Sussex Royal – from bookmarks to pyjamas, from bandanas to hoodies. The Duke and Duchess of Sussex were planning to set up shop.

When the Queen, Charles and William got a glimpse of this selection of a hundred or more products, registered for all to see on 21 June with the UK Intellectual Property Office at 10 Victoria Street, just round the corner from Buckingham Palace, the extent of royal fury at Sussex impertinence rose to even higher levels. 'Hopping' was a mild description of how mad the family was – and you should have seen Sir Edward Young! Once again Harry had totally failed to consult the Queen about a major initiative affecting his royal work and image – and the image of the crown as a whole.

There was nothing intrinsically taboo about royals selling something in order to generate funds – it was one of the royal steps forward that had been introduced by Queen Elizabeth II. For decades there had been a highly successful souvenir shop at Buckingham Palace which over the years had opened regional branches in sites like Sandringham and Balmoral, and had developed an Internet business offering a wide range of items from

Buckingham Palace Green Tea with Lemon and Elderflower to a Windsor Castle Wooden Spoon. Only that summer of 2020, the Queen's own, personal favourite Buckingham Palace Gin, priced at £40, and flavoured with twelve botanicals including mulberry leaves handpicked from the palace gardens, sold out in eight hours after it was advertised via Instagram.

Prince Charles had taken this 'nation of shopkeepers' tradition into the next generation with his Duchy Originals line of products, derived but separate from his private Duchy of Cornwall estate. Set up in 1990 to sell largely organic food products, Duchy Originals had eventually gone into business with Waitrose – thus becoming part of the John Lewis Partnership – and

The royal family discuss the terms of Harry and Meghan's departure.
Morten Morland, *The Times*, 14 January 2020

currently generated some £3 million or so a year from a whole range of items headed by its beloved Duchy Originals oaten digestive biscuits.

One might have expected Harry to have consulted his father when it came to going into business himself. Duchy Originals had been bailed out by Waitrose when the company got into difficulties after the 2008 financial crash – with Charles making regular appearances to boost Duchy sales at Waitrose ever since. Like the initiation of court cases, the starting of any commercial activities by a member of the royal family required liaison with Buckingham Palace – depending, again, upon the ultimate approval of the Queen herself.

But as 2019 wore on, family consultation was ceasing to be Harry's style. The prince was sensitive to the coldness that his father and brother had displayed during such controversies as Meghan's 'Forces for CHANGE', and he was even more suspicious of the palace aides who handled the family's emails – their contents seemed to get leaked so frequently to the press. The young couple became more and more determined to find some new way ahead for themselves, and that simply increased family indignation when their activities on the blind-side were discovered.

Listed under Class 45 in Sussex Royal's June 2019 trademark applications, for example, were 'social care services, namely organising and conducting emotional support groups; counselling services; emotional support services; provision of personal support services to help, care for and support persons in need … Mentoring and personal care services.'

Duchy Digestives were one thing – but Sussex Royal personal therapy sessions? It was beyond parody.

The family finally hit back. As the Christmas holidays approached, Harry and Meghan appeared to cold-shoulder the Queen for a second time. They had not gone to stay at Balmoral with her in the summer, and they decided that they couldn't join her at Sandringham for the New Year break either.

'Having spent the last two Christmases at Sandringham,' explained a Sussex spokesperson, 'Their Royal Highnesses will spend the holiday this year, as a new family, with the Duchess' mother Doria Ragland. This decision is in line with precedent set previously by other members of the royal family.'

These last words were a pointed reference from Harry to 2012 and 2016 when William had made the same decision to drop Sandringham and spend Christmas with his wife's family. Then the press approvingly described William as wanting 'to spend quality time' with the Middletons. Now, as could have been predicted, Harry and Meghan were criticised by the tabloids for administering 'a snub' to the Queen.

Her Majesty let it be known that she understood and supported the Sussexes' decision to spend time with their other grandmother. As we approach the climax of this family crisis, we must imagine a matriarch who was deeply torn by the bitter divisions she could see developing in her clan. Elizabeth II had always had a soft spot for Harry, and she had been delighted by the arrival of Meghan whose personal energies seemed to complement her grandson's so well.

As Head of the Commonwealth and reigning over an ever more multicultural society in Britain, the Queen had especially welcomed the exciting new dimension that a mixed-race recruit brought to the Windsor identity – and we have seen how Elizabeth herself had spotted when things were going wrong. At the beginning of 2019 she had brought back Christopher Geidt to work with David Manning on devising the fresh Sussex strategy that followed her own Malta model.

But there were some matters on which Elizabeth II would not compromise – and chief among them was the authority of the crown. By failing to seek permission for their anti-media lawsuits, Harry and Meghan had trespassed dangerously on that authority, and now their undisclosed plans to market merchandise under their own royal trademark took their rebellion one step too far. To commercialise the crown required the crown's consent – and the Sussexes had not sought that.

It has become normal in the Queen's Christmas broadcast for the sovereign to deliver her annual message of goodwill from behind a desk on which recent photos of her family have been placed looking outwards so that they can be studied by her audience. Harry and Meghan had featured smiling in a silver frame in 2018. But there would be no sign of them in 2019, nor any mention of the name of Sussex – since that name was, apparently, now to be used to sell merchandise for which permission had not been asked from the Queen.

Who does and who does not feature on the royal Christmas desk has always been like the changing panorama of faces on the historic balcony of Moscow's Kremlin. It showed who was in favour and who was not – and at Windsor in December 2019 this even extended to babies.

It was unheard of for the royal Christmas desk not to feature a cosy image of the latest royal grandchild or great-grandchild. But in 2019 there was no sight of Archie. A brief video clip flashed onscreen during the broadcast showing the Queen and Doria cluck-clucking over the little boy, but there was no name check. The Queen simply acknowledged the arrival of her great-grandchild in passing, without mentioning his name or his parents, then moved straight on to the baby who really mattered – the Christ child and his entrance into Bethlehem.

Take a second look at the epigraph at the head of this chapter. No, I will save you the trouble, here it is again: *'Prince Philip and I have been delighted to welcome our eighth great-grandchild into our family.'* Study it closely – do you detect any trace of the word 'S-U-S-S-E-X' in this? Any H-A-R-R-Y or M-E-G-H-A-N, let alone the name of the little boy himself? This is the Queen's only reference to the new arrival and his parents in her 2019 address to the world – an anonymous 'eighth great-grandchild'. The Sussex family had been 'non-personed' as effectively as the Soviets non-personed Trotsky and Khrushchev – another charming custom, of course, that had been developed by the Kremlin.

Elizabeth's beloved father King George VI; her husband Prince Philip, recently retired from royal duties; the smiling William, Kate and their three little Cambridges; plus Prince Charles with

Camilla beaming beside him – all in different frames. That was the limit of the images to the right of the Queen's shoulder in front of the Christmas tree in December 2019. Look at the picture for yourself on page 7 of picture section 2.

There are those who maintain that the pictures on the Queen's Christmas desk are really the choice of that year's TV producer. If so, he or she would surely have requested an image of the hottest set of British royal personalities of the moment – Harry, Meghan and their new baby Archie, who were a matter of avid fascination to TV audiences around the world. Who cares about King George VI in Timbuktu? The absence of a single Sussex from the 2019 assemblage of significant royal faces reflected a deliberate decision on the part of Queen Elizabeth II. She would be providing no brand endorsement opportunities this year for Sussex Royal.

The new royal picture that the Queen did release in the middle of December 2019 and as a new decade approached showed Queen Elizabeth II herself, the future King Charles III, the future King William V – and, going even further, King George VII in the shape of little Prince George, just coming up to seven years old. The prince had been placed on a red-carpeted step in order to bring him up closer to the level of his great-grandmother. What a fascinating and historic image to remind us of the essence of the royal system! The current monarch with three future monarchs. All the living heirs – and not a suggestion of a 'spare'.

According to insiders, this formal photograph, taken in the Buckingham Palace Throne Room a week before Christmas 2019, was the idea of Prince Charles, anxious to promote his cause of the 'slimmed-down monarchy'. Palace sources have also let it be known that the plan of depicting the direct line of royal succession was enthusiastically supported by Prince William, who was not saying anything for the record – but who wanted to send his younger brother an unmistakable message.

The message was received and it was taken to heart. 'For Harry and Meghan,' wrote Sussex scribes Scobie and Durand, the Queen's Christmas choice of pictures 'had been yet another sign that they needed to consider their own path'.

The couple had taken refuge with Archie for the Christmas break – and for several weeks of rest and reflection before that – on a wooded, four-acre Vancouver Island estate off the west coast of Canada.

'Away from the courtiers and all things royal,' wrote Scobie and Durand, 'they could think for themselves.' It was a sort of sabbatical.

Meghan had located the secluded haven through Canadian contacts she had made during her seven Rachel Zane years in Canada filming *Suits* – and all of a sudden it looked as if the Sussexes might have found their 'Malta'.

Canada was very much British Commonwealth – an ideal base that met the Geidt–Manning requirements – while the pleasant urban area of Vancouver, just three hours on the plane in a single shuttle-hop from Los Angeles, had effectively become a northern suburb of Hollywood in recent years. Numerous American film-makers lived and worked there. Lifetime TV's two successful romantic drama movies about Meghan and Harry had even been shot there. At Thanksgiving the previous November, Grandma Doria had been able to fly up easily from LA to spend time with the family.

Whether or not Harry and Meghan chose to remain on this particular island property that was currently for sale for US$14 million–$18 million, they might well be able to make this corner of Canada their base for the next few years, both as family home and as the international headquarters of Sussex Royal. Vancouver could provide a marvellous launching pad for their Commonwealth work – particularly the sometimes-neglected Pacific side of things – and they could fly back to Britain at regular intervals to carry out some of their royal duties on the basis of their own chosen itinerary, free from the tyranny of the palace.

Before leaving London Harry had spoken to his father and grandmother with a few of his ideas about how things might change for himself and his wife within the royal structure. It was a pity that William was now so angry that he was not speaking to him any more. It was as if Harry had become un-brothered. But Charles and the Queen sounded reasonably sympathetic – although Harry had not really given them any specifics. He and Meghan 'didn't want to walk away from the monarchy,' the couple later explained via Scobie and Durand. 'Rather they wanted to find a happy place within it.'

Yet as the weeks went by and the two of them discussed the tumultuous sequence of events since the wedding – what had gone right and what had gone wrong – they came to realise that they simply could not just go back to the old way of things in Britain. It was a tough decision to make, but they would have to

step back from their roles as senior royals. They could become
some sort of semi-royals, they thought, and cut themselves off
from access to royal money. Their three Hollywood As – attorney
Rick Genow, accountant Andrew Meyer and agent Nick Collins
– all flew up from Los Angeles with Keleigh Thomas Morgan,
now the head of Sunshine Sachs in Hollywood, to hash out the
practicalities, particularly when it came to income.

Money, both Harry and Meghan had come to realise, was at
the root of the problem. The British newspapers were forever

Departure of the Duke and Duchess of Sussex to North America.
Private Eye, 24 January–6 February 2020

beating them round the heads about the cost of refurbishing their home at Frogmore Cottage. It was crucial that they should pay off – and should clearly be seen to pay off – the £2.4 million that had become a persecutory refrain in almost every story about their base in Windsor. Prince Charles had actually been quite sympathetic when Harry had discussed this particular issue with him, saying that he would help contribute – though why a couple whose combined net worth was then reliably estimated at £30 million–£40 million should need help from Dad to pay off their 'mortgage' was not immediately obvious.

And there was a deeper reason why the couple should pay off the Frogmore debt and live henceforward on an independent basis, as they would later explain via sussexroyal.com, the website that they developed during their Vancouver sabbatical. If the couple were able to finance themselves sufficiently to come off the Sovereign Grant – the royal payroll financed by the British taxpayer – their financial self-sufficiency would 'remove the tabloids' justification in having access to their lives'.

There were other practical problems to sort out, not least the question of family security and who would pay for it. Would the Ottawa government be happy for them to pursue projects that were close to their hearts in Canada? But after discussions with their Los Angeles advisors, the couple felt so confident that Harry emailed both his father and grandmother shortly before Christmas to say that he and Meghan thought that they had worked out a new way in which they could carry out their work.

They proposed to step back and spend more time abroad, while still visiting Britain sufficiently to carry out their basic royal and military duties – essentially the one-foot-in one-foot-out strategy that Geidt and Manning had first suggested. By being in Canada more and also travelling round the Commonwealth, Harry and Meghan would be able to maintain their work for the Queen, while stepping away from the pressures of the royal maelstrom in Britain.

The new website that they planned to debut when they got back to London set out their ideas as a manifesto with headings like 'Supporting Community', 'Serving the Monarchy', 'Strengthening the Commonwealth' and, most important, their personal hope to 'carve out a progressive new role within [the institution of the royal family]'.

Sussexroyal.com was the work of Ryan Sax, the Canadian website designer who had previously helped Meghan devise her lifestyle blog 'The Tig', named after her favourite Italian red wine Tignanello. The Tig had broadcast Meghan's thoughts on fashion, food and beauty, as well as highlighting her humanitarian work and the activist women who inspired her. She had closed The Tig in the spring of 2017 as her relationship with Harry intensified. Now she worked again with Sax on the navy blue and grey design that expounded the new Sussex strategy almost as a fait accompli.

Worried that the news of their plans might leak if he put too much in writing, Harry emailed his father to say that he was looking forward to discussing the practicalities in detail when he and Meghan flew back to London early in the new year. They were due to arrive on Monday 6 January, and Harry suggested that he and Meghan could head straight off the plane for Norfolk that morning. They could meet up personally to discuss the whole scheme with Charles and with William, if he was happy to join them – and most of all, of course, with Granny herself at Sandringham.

Finally, it seemed, the Sussexes did have some plans for which they were willing to seek the permission of Her Majesty.

30

Sandringham Showdown

*'The monarchy is something that needs to be there
… It's a form of stability and I hope to be
able to continue that.'*

(Prince William, 21 June 2003,
his twenty-first birthday)

When Prince Harry had outlined his adventurous new plans for his half-in half-out future with Meghan, speaking to his father and grandmother on the phone in the lead-up to Christmas 2019, the Prince of Wales and the Queen had both seemed open to the prospect of talking further – though Harry would complain to Oprah in 2021 that his father had stopped taking his calls after their second conversation. The suggestion came later from Charles's side that he had got tired of his son continually asking for money.

Still, it was agreed Harry should come up to Sandringham to speak to the family when he and Meghan got home early in the new year.

When Harry phoned the palace, however, from Vancouver in order to fix a definite date in the diary, it seemed that he was not so welcome. Her Majesty would not be available for another month, he was told by her staff. How about 29 January?

Harry and Meghan were seething as their Air Canada flight made its dawn touchdown in London on Monday 6 January. Was this strange scheduling delay to month's end the work of 'the men in suits' – the stick-in-the-mud private secretaries and courtiers at Buckingham Palace? Or did it reflect some real push-back from the Queen herself that may also have involved Charles and William?

It was only on 3 January that the Sussexes had actually been confronted online and in the media by the message-laden 'Four Monarchs' image of the main line of heirs, shot at the palace before Christmas but not released until the new year. The 'spare' had received and understood the clear message that he and Meghan were being 'marginalised', and the excuses from 'royal sources' only confirmed the obvious.

'The Duchess of Cambridge [Kate] was not in the picture, neither was Camilla,' leaked one such royal source to the *Sun*. 'So it is ludicrous to interpret the picture as some form of snub.'

The couple toyed with the idea of driving straight from Heathrow to Sandringham – which would certainly have provided a new year surprise for the Queen. But an unannounced arrival could also have put important noses out of joint, and the pair opted for prudence, for the moment, driving instead to Windsor where they summoned a meeting at Frogmore Cottage with their top aides.

Heading the team was a young diplomat, their recently recruited private secretary Fiona Mcilwham, who had joined the Sussexes from the Foreign Office just before their trip to Africa – she had travelled with them for three days to get some flavour of how a tour worked. A 'wannabe supermum', according to her Twitter account, the stylish Mcilwham had become one of the youngest British ambassadors in UK history when she was appointed head of mission to Albania in 2009 at the age of thirty-five.

Since the defection of Jason Knauf to William, Sussex communications had been in the hands of a red-haired American, Sara Latham, who had served her apprenticeship in Bill Clinton's White House, then gone on to become senior campaign advisor to Hillary Clinton in her presidential campaign. A dual US-UK citizen, Latham had also done time with the Blair administration as special advisor to culture secretary Tessa Jowell.

But the key negotiator and spiritual head of the whole team, to whom Harry himself would defer was, of course, Rachel Zane. Meghan had not spent seven years playing that hotshot lawyer in *Suits* without developing the confidence that she could handle the cut and thrust of a high-stakes duel like this – nor without some of the prized techniques of her screen character rubbing off.

'Don't sign anything unless you can get something in return' was the key commandment drilled into Rachel by her father Robert Zane, the high-powered black attorney who was both her nemesis and her inspiration in the series – along with 'Stand Your Ground' and, most frightening of all, 'Never Underestimate the

Power of a Good Slap – or Two!' These were some of the choice Zane negotiating tactics featured by her TV network in an April 2018 article, 'What Rachel Zane Has Taught Us About Getting What We Want'.

Meghan was only staying in Britain for a few days before flying back to join Archie in Canada on Thursday 9 January. But the plan was for her and Harry to keep closely in touch by phone and Internet as events unrolled. They were now very much a team – on their own against the world – and they briefed their British squad about the details of the plan that they had worked out in Vancouver with their three Hollywood As and with Keleigh Thomas Morgan.

The cost of security was clearly going to be a tricky issue given the complication and expense of so much travel. 'Protection' was a major factor for the couple, as they would make clear in their interview with Oprah the following year – and then there was the wider question of money.

How could they support themselves if they went off the royal payroll and could no longer rely on the Bank of Dad – who was clearly losing patience already? Their US managers had been confident that both of the couple could command substantial fees from talking engagements in the States and Canada. Agent Nick Collins was even then negotiating contracts worth hundreds of thousands of dollars per appearance and was in discussions with Oprah Winfrey and Disney over some charity deals.

'What about streamers?' a friend would suggest, referring to the wealth of Netflix and the other new TV streaming channels.

It was also central to the whole project that the Canadian government should sign on for their long-term residence requirements and should be happy with the character of the local projects that they were hoping to pursue in Canada. They had a meeting arranged for the following day, Tuesday 7 January, in London, to discuss the details with the Canadian High Commission, and when they arrived in Trafalgar Square a crowd of fans was waiting, waving Canadian flags.

There were lots of jokes about their wet weeks on the Pacific coast – 'It had rained throughout,' Harry told one Canada House employee – and the high commissioner, Janice Charette, seemed fully on board for the couple's social reform agenda.

'Today's visit provided an opportunity to discuss some of the common priorities and values shared by Canada and Their Royal Highnesses,' Charette told *Vanity Fair*, specifying 'a commitment to conservation and fighting the challenges of climate change; supporting the economic and democratic empowerment of women and girls; and encouraging young people and youth leaders in Canada and across the Commonwealth to actively engage in the social, economic and environmental challenges of their generation.'

How wordy, worthy and thoroughly Canadian! It was as if Harry and Meghan had dictated to the high commissioner precisely what to say. But that cleared the residence hurdle neatly, and the couple were keen to keep moving forward. Meghan was planning to return to Archie in Vancouver shortly and Harry wanted to follow her quite quickly with the essence of their new royal deal agreed.

'At this point,' a source told Scobie and Durand, 'they felt like they had brought up the subject enough times with family members ... and they were fed up with not being taken seriously.'

Harry and Meghan were also worried about press leaks if they delayed announcing their plan much longer. They had known since Christmas that the *Sun* had got hold of the story and their fears were borne out the next day, Wednesday 8 January, when the tabloid broke the news of their intention to leave.

'We're Orf Again!' revealed a front-page splash from the *Sun*'s well-connected executive editor Dan Wootton, who had discovered their departure plans some two weeks previously and had been checking the details of his scoop with the couple's own communications staff, giving them ten days for a chance to comment and reply to his story.

The Sussexes were not planning to stay in Britain, revealed Wootton. They were intending to fly 'back to Canada', and Harry was hoping to hold talks with the Queen and the family in the next few days before he left about some substantial changes to his 'royal role'.

Wootton, thirty-six, had been on holiday staying with his parents in New Zealand when he received this remarkably accurate tip-off – whose source he naturally declined to reveal. Had the leak possibly come from someone in Charles's office – as Harry had feared and predicted when explaining his unwillingness to 'put things down on paper' as his father had requested? The information could equally have come from Canada, where quite a chain of individuals were now aware of the Sussex plans to settle in North America for a time.

All that Wootton would disclose was that he had *not* been fed the story by the Sussexes themselves – as some conspiracy theorists later suggested. This was on the grounds that the result of the explosive 8 January leak was to give more rapid effect to the family rupture.

Nor, Wootton insisted, did his story come from either Prince Charles or Prince William – as many close to the Sussexes later tried to imply.

'It was clear,' wrote Scobie and Durand in *Finding Freedom*, 'that someone within the palace had briefed the tabloid.'

'It astonishes me,' responded Wootton, 'when I hear allies of Harry and Meghan trying to claim that they were somehow "blind-sided" by my 8 January story revealing their intention to move to Canada and begin talks about their future royal role. I first went to their communications secretary straight after Christmas. There was then over ten days before publication – when there was much coming-and-going back and forth between myself and the Sussex staff.'

The couple might express hatred of the tabloids, but they were evidently prepared to work with Rupert Murdoch's tabloid-of-tabloids if it helped in their battle with the family for whom they were coming to feel such hostility.

'Harry and Meghan,' says Wootton, 'must have been fully aware that I had the story and was intending to publish. I even included quite a few words of "briefing" from the couple themselves in the final article as published, giving them the space to express the annoyance they felt when they discovered they had been left out of the Queen's Christmas pictures.

'So not only were they NOT blind-sided by me, they had ample opportunity to contribute to the story – and they actually did so via their official staff.'

'Blind-siding' is a reference to the tactic in American or Canadian football whereby the quarterback is caught unawares when his opponents attack him from the 'blind' or unexpected side. By choosing to react to Wootton's story so rapidly on the false excuse that its publication had taken them by surprise – and by then revealing the details of their departure to Canada that very same Wednesday – the Sussexes executed a massive blind-siding of the Queen and the palace.

They only gave the royal family ten minutes' notice of what they had in mind.

Wednesday 8 January 2020 is one of those dates that is engraved on the hearts of royal correspondents. Gently recovering from Christmas and New Year, and wondering if the Queen's visit to church would have to be their strongest story for the weekend, journalists were abruptly confronted with an *embarras du choix*.

The bombshell news that Harry and Meghan were planning to leave Britain, and to sever their links with the royal family in some fashion, confirmed all the suspicions of palace unhappiness and family discord. Suddenly history was happening. This was the moment to clear the front page so that the long-nursed 'royal rift' stories could go live.

'I was just going home on the Tube at the end of the day,' recalls Valentine Low of the *The Times*, 'when suddenly something flashed up on my iPad about Harry and Meghan and "a personal statement". The reception was bad and I couldn't make out all the details, but I immediately knew what I had to do. I got straight off at the next station … walked across to the opposite platform and got back onto the next train to the office.'

The Sussexes had pressed the button to activate their website with its array of claims and promises at 6.30 p.m. that Wednesday and the journalists scrabbled to decide which of the myriad issues to pursue first. Where would Archie go to school – in both the UK and in Canada? What exactly did it mean 'to carve out a progressive new role within this institution'? Exactly how would the couple become 'financially independent'? And what did this splitting of their lifestyle across the Atlantic mean for the carbon footprint of these valiant eco-warriors?

'Figures show,' wrote the *Daily Mail* accusingly, 'that one person flying first class on a return commercial flight from London to Toronto contributes 6.77 tonnes of CO_2 to the Earth's atmosphere. This would mean, even if Harry, Meghan and Archie were to go on just one trip … their total carbon footprint would be 20.31 tonnes.'

But media shock was nothing to the dismay and anger felt inside the palaces – to whom Harry had given so little notice of the detailed news.

'Harry has been talking to his family for some weeks about all this,' explained Tom Bradby to *People* magazine. 'And certainly as I understand it, what happened is he was asked by members of his family – or at least their officials – to put some of these ideas in writing. He said, "I really don't want to do that because it normally leaks."

'They were very insistent in order to go forward and discuss it properly it had to be put in writing. He did put it in writing, and it did leak. So yes, I don't think [the royal family] got much heads-up as to the actual announcement, but they certainly knew what was going on. I think [Harry] felt once it had been leaked, all bets were off.'

Prince Charles was only just getting himself organised after returning from an official trip to the Middle East – and out at Sandringham both the Queen and Prince Philip were said to be 'devastated'. Once again their grandson had acted unilaterally. Instead of consulting the family when the *Sun* broke the story, Harry had gone out alone with his defiant and incendiary news of their departure.

'Discussions with the Duke and Duchess of Sussex are at an early stage,' said Buckingham Palace tersely in a statement that it managed to rush out in just fifteen minutes. 'We understand their desire to take a different approach, but these are complicated issues that will take time to work through.'

Still, Harry had finally got his family to respond. Next day he kissed Meghan goodbye then settled down for a conference call with William, Charles and the Queen, who had all suddenly found time in their diaries to talk. We do not know the details, but in the first emotions of the moment no real progress could be made. The Queen concluded that the four of them – Harry, William, Charles and herself – should sit down with their respective private secretaries at Sandringham the following Monday to hash things out, though William apparently felt that he would much rather leave all the haggling to the staff.

'I put my arm around my brother all our lives,' he said in a statement that the *Sunday Times* sourced to 'a friend', 'and I can't do it any more. We're separate entities.'

The inference of this apparently kindly remark was that William could not deal with his brother as a separate entity – or did not choose to. The new Meghan-fired Harry clearly flummoxed and infuriated him. William's 'arm around my brother' – his lifelong care for Harry dating back to when he liked to display the newborn as his favourite toy – had always been based on some element of control, and that had now surely vanished.

William maintained his distance for the Sandringham Summit. The Queen had suggested that the family should gather for lunch before their big pow-wow in the library that afternoon, but one of the two brothers was so incandescent with rage that he refused his grandmother's invitation. That was William. He would obviously turn up at 2 p.m. for the meeting, he said, according to one source, but he only wanted to talk business.

Everything William had feared and predicted in the October 2018 row over Meghan's alleged bullying and the Jason Knauf email had now come to pass. William told a friend he was so furious with Harry's latest set of tricks that he would not be able to endure the hypocrisy of smiling at his younger brother over lunch.

When a story broke in that morning's *Times*, however, that Harry regarded himself 'as having been pushed away from the royal family by the "bullying" attitude of his brother, the Duke of Cambridge', the two princes were still able to react in concert. In a matter of hours – before lunchtime that Monday, in fact – their two press offices had got together to put out a joint statement angrily refuting the allegation and making it clear that, on this issue, the brothers stood side by side.

'Despite clear denials,' ran the palace rebuttal as early as 12.09 p.m., 'a false story ran in a UK newspaper today speculating about the relationship between the Duke of Sussex and the Duke of Cambridge. For brothers who care so deeply about the issues surrounding mental health, the use of inflammatory language in this way is offensive and potentially harmful.'

William did not want to be seen as a bully, and Harry did not want to appear to be the bullied one – with the b-word also carrying all the connotations of the brothers' row over Meghan fourteen months earlier.

For all their animosity, it was still Diana's two sons against the world. They might be only on the barest of speaking terms, but this current disagreement would eventually get sorted out someday, somehow – and that proved to be the conclusion reached in the family meeting in the Long Library in Sandringham that afternoon.

According to Scobie and Durand's account, which could only have come from Harry, the four members of the royal family, headed by the Queen, adopted a 'practical workmanlike approach' when they sat down together. They agreed that it was in everyone's interest to work out a deal as soon as possible, and that Harry should marshal his aides to confer with their aides in the next few days back at Buckingham Palace in order to hammer out the details of a compromise.

Hammer, sadly, was the operative word. The Sussexes' tough tactics in giving the palace so little notice when they activated their provocative website the previous Wednesday had come straight from Rachel Zane's maxim, 'Never Underestimate the Power of a Good Slap – or Two'. And having administered one good slap, Meghan had prepared another.

'Prince Harry and Meghan Markle May Threaten Queen With Tell-All Oprah Interview to Get Their Way at Today's Royal

Harry and Meghan agree not to use their styles as 'HRH'.
Peter Brookes, *The Times*, 22 January 2020

Summit,' Emily Andrews had revealed in the *Sun* that Monday morning.

'Perhaps Harry and Meghan will use this as a negotiating tactic,' speculated Andrews, 'as there is no way the royals want their dirty laundry out in the open. It is believed Meghan's team has been in contact with ABC, NBC and CBS and celebrity chat show hosts such as Oprah.'

Andrews was only a year early in her prediction. A 'Tell-All Oprah Interview' was precisely the tactic the couple would employ in March 2021 in pursuit of their ongoing battle with the palace.

'It was like dealing with a hard-nosed Hollywood lawyer,' says a senior palace source familiar with the Sandringham and immediately post-Sandringham negotiations of January 2020. 'The Sussexes wanted guarantees on every single point as if it were a contractual negotiation.' It was Robert Zane again – 'Don't sign anything unless you can get something in return.' Meghan may not have been physically present in England from Tuesday to Saturday, 14–18 January 2020, but her spirit reigned – while Harry, square-jawed and bubbling with anger, played her loyal proxy.

Even the normally sympathetic Scobie and Durand admitted that the fast and aggressive Sussex approach 'created a complete headache for everyone,' and generated 'a lot of ill will in the household and especially in the family'.

'They totally misplayed the negotiations,' says the palace insider. 'But then so did the palace.'

Directing the palace strategy was private secretary Sir Edward Young.

'The trouble with Edward,' says the source, who worked with Young for many years, 'is that he is not very good at doing humans. He is incredibly difficult to read – impossible to fathom. And he has these nervous tics. He has a funny high-pitched "tee-hee" laugh that makes him sound insincere. He is also deeply cautious and non-creative. He's a letter-of-the-law kind of man.'

Rachel Zane had been confronted by the post-office clerk. It was a transatlantic cross-cultural conflict that pitted the stereo-typical all-American superwoman against a Monty Python parody of a toffee-nosed royal sucker-up – and it left little room for outside intervention.

Serving as Prince Charles's representative, and trying to mediate between the two sides, was his private secretary Clive Alderton, an experienced diplomat who had been ambassador to Morocco. Charles had originally felt some sympathy with his younger son and he gave Alderton the brief of trying to bring the two sides together.

But over the years Harry had come to distrust the man who organised so much of his father's life – and hence aspects of his own life too.

William was represented in the room by his private secretary Simon Case, who as a high-flying Downing Street official had previously worked with both David Cameron and Theresa May and was developing close links to Boris Johnson. But Case was not able to bring his political gifts into play – his boss the Duke of Cambridge was as confrontational as anyone.

'The tragedy,' says the palace insider, 'was that the Queen's broader objective was actually to bring everyone back together, not to split them apart. There were obviously points of principle to defend, but Edward got stuck in the detail. He could not see the bigger picture. This sort of family negotiation requires trust, along with the accepting of uncertainties and ambiguities. There can be no absolute guarantees for either side. Christopher Geidt would have handled it so differently – he had the skills. Geidt might even have landed that classic royal compromise in which nobody loses.'

That man Geidt again. When the Queen had brought back her dismissed private secretary the previous year to try to help Meghan and Harry, Christopher Geidt had, with David Manning, picked up her suggestion that the couple could benefit from some time abroad, as she had done in Malta. The Sussexes' entire in-out project of settling in Vancouver had developed from that original suggestion – from the Queen herself – after Cape Town had proved to be unfeasible as a home or HQ.

Presumably the next stage would have been to tackle the thorny question of how the Sussexes could support themselves financially in the New World while staying royal. Windsors from Edward and Sophie Wessex to Princess Anne's children had successfully managed the trick of mixing commerce and royal connections. It was by no means unprecedented or impossible. But somehow the potential sources of the Sussexes' income became the issue on which the whole project foundered.

Meghan and Harry had rushed in so impetuously – and they had over-prepared. Edward Young had dug in his heels so fiercely. Both sides were to blame and now this week of ill-natured, on-the-brink negotiations had turned the Queen's positive suggestion of a foreign base for the couple's Commonwealth work into a querulous and rather grubby 'exile'.

It was too late for a Geidt-style intervention. The settlement that was wearily announced by telephone to royal correspondents on Saturday 18 January proved a succession of negatives. The deal was dressed up with talk of it being 'a constructive and supportive way forward', but it involved Meghan and Harry being 'required to step back from royal duties'. Harry would lose his beloved military appointments and his role as Commonwealth youth ambassador too. The Sussexes could no longer represent the Queen and 'will not use their HRH titles as they are no longer working members of the Royal Family'.

Harry and Meghan say they wish 'to step back' from royal duties.
Morten Morland, *Sunday Times*, 12 January 2020

The fact that the Sussexes themselves had volunteered to forgo all access to the Sovereign Grant and public funds as their own proposed price for freedom – along with paying off the costs of Frogmore Cottage's renovation – was presented as a punishment: 'They will no longer receive public funds for royal duties.' And when it came to their plans for earning their own money using the name of Sussex Royal, that decision was delayed 'pending further palace deliberations'.

On the face of it, Rachel Zane's tough tactics had backfired disastrously. The Sussexes could still call themselves 'Duke and Duchess' if they chose and they had the right to go on living in Canada as they were at that date – but not much more. Small wonder that when Harry was offered the possibility of a review of the whole arrangement after twelve months, his first impulse was to refuse. He wanted no more to do with the royal family.

As for Sir Edward Young, his dismissal of the Sussex demands had won his Queen a short-term victory. 'You're either in or you're out' – and in interpreting Her Majesty's wishes so stringently Sir Edward had made sure that the Duke and Duchess of Sussex were now most certainly 'out'.

But Young's critics complained that he had fatally holed the monarchy below the water in racial terms for generations to come. Sussex Royal may have represented a commercial and reputational risk. Harry and Meghan may have been nightmares to deal with but the British crown has risked worse in the past – and in terms of modern inclusivity the exclusion of the mixed-race Meghan and her descendants from the official face of the royal family was to prove a priceless opportunity spurned. A catastrophe, in fact.

And so Prince Harry came to my neck of the woods – St John's Wood to be precise, a leafy neighbourhood in north London just round the corner from the Abbey Road Studios where in 1969 the Beatles had recorded their famous LP of that name, then walked out across the white-striped zebra crossing to pose for the picture on the cover that became even more famous.

Here in the summer – in non-pandemic times – residents can scarcely leave home in the morning for tourists parading in smiling, waving foursomes across that famous pedestrian crossing. The locals wait politely in their cars and taxis and buses for all these visitors from around the world as they take their John-Paul-George-and-Ringo-style photographs of each other – and today, Friday 28 February 2020, it was Harry's turn. He was appearing with Jon Bon Jovi and a wheelchair-bound ex-serviceman to raise funds and create publicity for his Invictus Games for disabled veterans.

Things had not looked up greatly for the prince since those dour January days of haggling with Sir Edward Young & Company in Buckingham Palace. As predicted, the Queen deliberated for several weeks, then ruled that Harry and Meghan could not use Sussex Royal as the brand name to market their merchandise and various activities in North America.

It was reliably reported that Her Majesty remained well-disposed towards her grandson and granddaughter-in-law. She wished them well in their new life in Canada – and her 'eighth great-grandchild' as well, of course. But it was also said by those in the know that the couple's erratic and impulsive behaviour for the past year had not inclined Queen Elizabeth II to entrust the Sussexes with the use of the word 'royal' any time soon.

For several weeks that January of 2020 Harry returned to Vancouver to spend time with Meghan and Archie. Now he was back in London living up to his commitments and fulfilling his pre-arranged schedule of engagements – his final 'royal' engagements – before 31 March, the exit day that he refused to call Megxit Day, since he insisted that he had made the decision to leave himself.

Here in Abbey Road the crowd was buzzing. Thirty minutes before the prince was due to arrive, the pavements were already packed. Half of north London seemed to have heard that Prince Harry was due in NW8 this morning and was eager to wish him well. That has always been the thing about Harry – when they get to meet him people really LIKE the guy.

'He's so warm and human. He's natural, not like the rest of them.'

'I reckon that she was always scheming to get him back to America – people say she's planning to run for president one day.'

'Just as well William is the sensible one – I wonder what went wrong between those brothers? They started off so close.'

Then cheers and applause broke out. A Range Rover came into sight from the south and out got that familiar red-haired, lanky-looking fellow wearing black jeans and a denim shirt. It

Peter Brookes, *The Times*, 11 March 2021

seemed like Harry was planning to play George Harrison when he got out on the crossing. In 1969 the other three Beatles dressed up in smart, almost formal suits for their LP cover shot, but not George the Hippy, the cool and unpretentious one – Meghan's favourite.

'Is that why they gave "Harrison" to Archie as his second name?'

There was suddenly an electricity among us all – a palpable sense of emotion: lumps in throats and tears starting. That is how it always is with our royal family, stirring the irrational depths of us gullible Brits – 'our finest hour' etc. There were no public address speakers outside the studio to share whatever Harry and Bon Jovi were singing inside, so people tried a few choruses of their own.

A firestorm of camera flashes greeted the smiling prince as he emerged from the studio and headed up the road to the zebra crossing – and well, turn to page 7 in picture section 3 to see how it all turned out that chilly February morning on Abbey Road with Harry and Bon Jovi and two members of the Invictus Games' choir.

So you have deprived us of all this happy craziness, have you, Sir Edward? You and the other characters in grey suits who have so cleverly negotiated Harry and Meghan out of our lives and across to the other side of the world?

Well, thank you very much. Of course, Harry and Meghan represented a bizarre exercise in self-indulgence. I am sure you found them a nightmare. They were – and they remain – a deeply flawed fairy tale. But could you not say exactly the same of the monarchy that you serve?

31
Abbey Farewell

*'I can assure you, marrying a prince or
princess is not all it's made up to be.'*

(Prince Harry, March 2020)

I t would have been an imaginative gesture for Prince William
and his wife to walk down the aisle of Westminster Abbey in
the company of Harry and Meghan on Monday 9 March 2020
to celebrate Commonwealth Day, since that afternoon would be
the couple's final 2020 appearance as working royals in Britain.
Anyway you looked at it, the service was a historic occasion that
the newspapers had billed loudly as the brothers' farewell – and
unbeknown to the media, Meghan was already booked to fly
back to Vancouver to rejoin Archie that very evening.

This was the hallowed site, after all, where for centuries British
monarchs have walked in procession to be crowned – we are
talking Edward the Confessor here, nearly a thousand years ago.
And this was the aisle down which the two young princes had
stepped it out together so bravely and poignantly, side by side,

twenty-three years earlier, following in the wake of their mother's coffin.

Now they had the chance to step it out again side by side as brothers, supporting their grandmother in celebrating the seventy-first anniversary of her beloved Commonwealth of Nations – though in a confusing, almost contradictory way. Working with the Queen's Commonwealth Trust was one of the few post-Megxit roles that Harry and Meghan had been allowed to keep – but at the same time Harry had been deprived of his status as Commonwealth youth ambassador.

The distinction seemed mean-spirited. Harry was allowed to stay president of the Queen's Commonwealth Trust (with Meghan as his vice-president), Buckingham Palace explained, because he had been appointed by the trustees and not by the Queen. But he was barred from being youth ambassador because that was a job 'in the Queen's gift' – the honour having been stripped from him as so many others had been in the palace negotiations of the previous month.

It was difficult not to agree with the verdict of Meghan's friends Scobie and Durand. 'Harry and Meghan would have reached a more beneficial agreement to allow them to live the life they wanted,' reported the joint authors, 'if they had handled things in a [more] private, dignified way.'

The couple had been so hustling and aggressive, in other words, that they had shot themselves in the foot. Putting it another way – they had been punished.

* * *

When it came to the procession that day, protocol also interfered. The Queen, it was decreed by custom and precedence, should walk down the aisle behind the Commonwealth flag and mace accompanied by Prince Charles and Camilla, with William and Catherine also processing in their company, since they were classed as 'senior' royals – plus a gaggle of dignitaries including Prime Minister Boris Johnson.

Harry and Meghan were *not* included in this senior royal group. As 'junior' royals they would have to shuffle their way to their seats that afternoon like any other member of the congregation and take their places on the sidelines alongside their fellow 'juniors', Edward and Sophie Wessex.

The curious thing was that Harry and Meghan had been classed as 'seniors' in the previous two years. In 2018, when Meghan was still only engaged to Harry, and then again in 2019, when she was visibly pregnant with Archie, the couple had walked proudly and oh-so-promisingly with William and Catherine in the main procession. The House of Windsor had been proud and happy to display their new starring couple.

Now, in 2020, the Sussexes' abrupt demotion was cruelly apparent. It would have cost nothing to include them. It would have been quite a generous gesture, in fact – and the couple were not due officially to relinquish their working royal status until the end of the month, in any case.

When Harry heard that he and Meghan had been so graphically shunted aside on this final appearance, he was furious. The subservience of a 'spare' – one of the basic reasons for this very sad parting of the ways – could not have been more strikingly illustrated. The phone lines had hummed over the preceding weekend (the service was on a Monday afternoon) – and fortunately Prince William had more sense than his underlings. He and Kate would be quite happy, he declared, to skip the procession and to take their places without ceremony in the congregation alongside Harry and Uncle Edward.

It was a small, but sensitive outreach of peace. Within minutes of each other, the two princes and their wives slipped quietly into their seats, and both couples then sat waiting with everyone else for the Queen and Prince Charles to process in senior splendour down the aisle to open the ceremony.

The only problem was that two thousand orders of service had already been printed and distributed round the abbey, explaining to the congregation that the Duke and Duchess of Cambridge would enter and process down the aisle with the main royal party – making no mention at all of William's younger brother and his wife. So there was the snub in black and white – plainly set out for all to see.

Nor could it be said that the two royal brothers made any great personal efforts to 'chum it up' together once they found themselves seated close. The longest coherent sentence that TV-viewing lipreaders could work out was a coronavirus comment from William to Kate as he sat down, after his meeting and greeting of the clergy, evidently worried about the risk of infection – 'This whole handshaking thing is weird. We're going to have to put a load of hand gel on after this.' It was still two weeks to Monday 23 March – the fateful date of Britain's oh-so-tardy lockdown.

The boys' father, Prince Charles, had already worked out his own approach to the developing COVID-19 dilemma – no rugby club elbow-bumpings for the prince, as then were being recommended by the medical authorities. Instead, Charles had devised himself an elegant hands-together greeting, palms touching and fingers pointing upwards, with a nod of the head and the Hindu greeting '*Namaste!*' 'I bow to the divine in you.'

By 2020, every TV commentary team worth its salt featured a specialist in 'body language', and as the two brothers ostentatiously failed to talk to each other in the minutes before the service, these experts swung into action.

'It wasn't exactly the warm reunion we were hoping for,' said Judi James to the Press Association. 'The tension in Harry's body language especially was palpable.'

Ms James noted how the moment Harry and Meghan took their seats and stopped holding hands, 'he immediately reached for his wedding ring – which is a self-comfort'. Harry's face was 'quite tense and unsmiling' – and when William arrived with Kate, the elder brother could hardly have been more formal.

'He literally said: "Hello, Harry", and that was it,' Harry reported to Meghan of William's response. 'And he didn't say anything more than that!'

The character of the service itself had a remarkably African-Caribbean flavour, with *X Factor* singer Alexandra Burke belting out the Motown hit 'Ain't No Mountain High Enough'.

'My name is Anthony Oluwafemi Olaseni Joshua,' declared the towering 108-kilo world heavyweight boxing champion,

Anthony Joshua, thirty, as he stood in the abbey pulpit to deliver his address.

'Like many of you here, I'm a child of the Commonwealth. I was born in Watford and my heritage is Nigerian … Like me, so many children of the Commonwealth have two homes, two identities, two cultures and two ways of viewing the world … So here's to fish and chips, egusi soup and pounded yams,' he concluded to a torrent of delighted applause across the abbey. 'To the UK and Nigeria and the children of the Commonwealth!'

Throughout the service, Meghan had been megawatting away in her best *Suits* TV-style smile – truly, her sparkling teeth and lips exuded a mesmeric quality! 'Big smiles!' had been her whispered instruction to her husband as he took his seat, but as

Lockdown in LA – 'They were a gift from the Queen. Do you think she's trying to send us a message?' Paul Thomas, *Daily Mail*, 28 July 2020

the ceremony progressed, Harry actually appeared to grow gloomier.

'His facial expression looked distant,' reported Judi James, 'and his accelerated blinking even suggested he might have been fighting back tears.'

It was not until the service was over, with the other royals out of the church ahead of him and on their respective ways home, that Harry became Harry again, throwing a cheeky thumbs-up signal to Anthony Joshua and congratulating the boxer on his speech that had brought the house down.

Outside, the prince laughed and joked with the crowds, lifting his eyes to the heavens and raising his hands as a symbol of what – thanksgiving or farewell? There was definitely some sense of relief and release from an ordeal accomplished. Meghan gave her husband a kiss, then headed straight for the airport.

In the days that followed came another explanation of why Harry might have seemed especially preoccupied in the abbey on that afternoon of 9 March. In the previous weeks he had been the victim of hoax phone calls that had coaxed him into some embarrassingly frank disclosures that he knew were on their way into the public realm – and they duly appeared in the papers the next day. Would the media ever leave him alone?

The deception had been the work of 'Vovan' and 'Lexus', a pair of Russian pranksters who a few years earlier had managed to persuade Elton John that he was speaking on the phone with Vladimir Putin about how to promote gay rights in Russia. For Harry, the hoaxers had adopted a ruse that would also fool US presidential hopeful Bernie Sanders – enlisting a female accomplice to mimic the Swedish accent of teenage climate activist Greta Thunberg, along with her 'father' Svante.

'Greta', of course, had been one of the faces featured on the cover of Meghan's 'Forces for CHANGE' issue for *Vogue*, and she quickly got Harry to condemn President Trump as a man who had 'blood on his hands', and even to give his opinion – a real 'no-no' for a member of the British royal family – on the character of Prime Minister Boris Johnson. The prince described Boris as 'a good man', but in need of some personal help from Greta.

'You are one of the few people who can reach into his soul,' Harry told her, 'and get him to feel and believe in you.'

The prince was prudent enough not to be drawn by 'Greta's' probing on the subject of his Uncle Andrew and his relationship with the convicted sex offender Jeffrey Epstein.

'I have very little to say on that,' replied the prince. 'Whatever he has done or hasn't done is completely separate from me and my wife.'

That was canny. But as more details of the conversation emerged in the coming days it became clear that Harry and his new non-royal minders – most of them connected with Sunshine Sachs – had been appallingly lax. There had been phone calls from the practical jokers to the Sussexes' landline in Vancouver. According to one source, it was even Harry who had called 'Greta' on the number that the Russians had helpfully provided, believing that the activist was in Davos attending the World Economic Forum.

The hoaxers would never have been able to get through the safeguards built into the Buckingham Palace switchboard. 'They're pretty vigilant,' explained the Queen's former press secretary Dickie Arbiter, adding: 'If you're outside the system, you're open to anything … For all its faults, the system does, and is there to, protect.'

Soon after Arbiter spoke, the entire conversation between Harry and 'Greta' was going up on the Internet for everyone to relish. 'Greta' even asked the prince if he could help her arrange a marriage into the royal family, confiding that she was rather attracted to the six-year-old Prince George – the ten-year age gap between them being no problem, apparently. She wondered if such a dynastic marriage 'will help me in fighting for climate change'?

'I can assure you,' responded Harry, 'marrying a prince or princess is not all it's made up to be.'

From the point of view of Harry's ecological credentials that lay at the heart of the conversation, the prince's most appalling mistake came when 'Greta' and 'Svante' requested his help with the fate of fifty penguins which, they told him, were stuck in customs in Belarus.

'We are searching,' explained 'Greta', 'for some ship, maybe, to transport the poor penguins to their native place.'

'[The] North Pole,' prompted her 'father' with well-crafted mischief. 'Maybe you have any contacts who can help us to find a catamaran or something like that?'

'I do have a man who deals with the North Pole,' responded Harry helpfully.

Morten Morland, *The Times*, 21 April 2020

The problem, of course, was that there are no penguins at all in the Arctic. The aquatic flightless birds are native to Antarctica – the *South* Pole …

The paradox of all this relentless trickery was that Prince Harry Duke of Sussex would eventually emerge from his poisonous encounter with 'Greta' and 'Svante' with a certain amount of credit. The Russian pranksters had succeeded in coaxing him into speaking from the heart. 'You forget,' said Harry, 'I was in the military for ten years, so I'm more normal than my family would like to believe.'

Normality! Normality! This was what Harry and his wife had been searching for. 'Being in a different position,' he said, 'now gives us the ability to say things and do things that we might not have been able to do … Seeing as everyone under the age of thirty-five or thirty-six seems to be carrying out an activist's role … we are just taking a little bit more time to think about how we can use our voice to try and encourage real change.'

'To try and encourage real change …' Here was Reason One for Harry and Meghan having surrendered their not-so-treasured royal status – to enjoy the freedom to speak out and to agitate for change more easily, without royal constitutional constraints. The couple wanted the chance 'to try and make more of a difference without being criticised'.

And Reason Two for their leaving was no surprise – the hated British tabloid media, 'because they have so much power and influence and no morals … From the moment that I found a wife that was strong enough to be able to stand up for what we believe in together,' said Harry, '[that] has basically scared them so much that they've now come out incredibly angry. They've come out fighting, and all they will try and do now is try and destroy our reputation and try and, you know, sink us.'

The media onslaught had been 'a dreadful ordeal' for him and Meghan, confided Harry, as he opened his heart to 'Greta'. 'It hasn't been very nice. It's been horrible. But we will come out of it stronger people.'

And Reason Three for leaving Britain was Baby Archie: 'Sometimes the right decision isn't always the easy one,' said Harry. 'And this decision certainly wasn't the easy one. But it was the right decision for our family – the right decision to be able to protect my son.'

The fatal rift with brother William was not mentioned. That was too private a topic to be shared, even with a Swedish heroine who was saving the world. But normality, freedom, the British press and the safety of Archie …

And then the couple got an unexpected break. In the March 2020 days and weeks following Commonwealth Day, the coronavirus flooded out of China, through Italy and Spain into Britain and across the rest of the world in panic-striking proportions. Abruptly the tabloids shifted their focus. Here was a threat to civilised existence that was even greater than Meghan and her rebellious prince.

32

Social Distancing

*'We don't see each other as much as we used to …
As brothers, you know, you have good days,
you have bad days.'*

(Prince Harry, 1 October 2019)

S ussex Royal was the first Windsor website or Instagram account to respond to the threat of COVID-19. 'This moment is as true a testament [as] there is to the human spirit,' proclaimed Harry and Meghan at 3.17 p.m. on their Instagram page for Wednesday 18 March 2020 – nine days after the Commonwealth Day Service in Westminster Abbey and five days before Boris Johnson's government finally imposed lockdown upon Britain. 'These are uncertain times. And now, more than ever, we need each other.'

The Sussexes promised their followers that they would share updates and help in the troubled times ahead, 'from posting accurate information and facts … to learning about measures we can take to keep ourselves and our families healthy … We are all in this together.'

The speed and emotion of the Sussex response reflected their hands-on management of their social media outlets – many observers suspected that Meghan herself had tapped out the eloquent words. But @kensingtonroyal was also online before the day was out: 'Whenever and wherever adversity strikes,' ran William's Instagram post at 5.40 p.m., a little over two and a quarter hours later that same Wednesday, 'the people of the UK have a unique ability to pull together … The public's desire to help in the wake of tragedy needs to be managed and channelled in the best possible way – which is why the establishment of the National Emergencies Trust was so important.'

The wording of William's post was less emotional than the message from @sussexroyal, but it was more practical and it was also British-centred. The National Emergencies Trust (NET) was an organisation that had been established in the wake of the Grenfell fire to shortcut the bureaucracy between fundraising and practical assistance to the victims. The NET had launched its '#coronavirus outbreak' appeal that day and William was using his 11.361 million followers to spread the news.

At this date Harry's @sussexroyal was showing 24,000 fewer followers than William's site, at 11.337 million – the same sort of differential we saw in Chapter 28 when @kensingtonroyal led @sussexroyal by some 11.3 million to some 11.2 million in the spring/summer of 2019. This pattern had held good throughout the family upheavals of the months between. Whatever the head-lines and controversy, William had maintained his narrow lead over Harry in the digital popularity stakes – and he was set to gain a further advantage.

On 13 February, the Sussexes had let go fifteen British-based members of their staff to whom they could offer no further employment now they were leaving for North America. Among these was 'Digital Dave' Watkins – and Prince William moved swiftly. Within weeks Digital Dave had been offered the chance to cast his magic over @kensingtonroyal, where he took up his duties on 1 April 2020, the day after Meghan and Harry officially laid down their working royal roles.

'*Corona*' is the Latin word for 'crown' – hence 'coronation'. So it was, perhaps, appropriate that the future King Charles III should succumb to the virus in the spring of 2020. The prince went into self-isolation on the national day of lockdown on 23 March, retiring to his Birkhall home on the Balmoral estate for seven days of quarantine from which he emerged on 30 March.

Somehow Charles's involvement with the virus did not catch the national imagination like that of the Queen, whose speech to the country on Sunday 5 April attracted 23.97 million peak viewers. Sitting alone in a spacious Windsor Castle state room, Elizabeth II spoke to a single, masked and socially distanced cameraman who was dressed in personal protective equipment – with all other technical staff operating from another room.

It was only the fifth time she had addressed her people directly in this way, and as she looked squarely at the camera her broadcast had something of the spirit of the Second World War about it. She praised the workers of the NHS – the current deities of the crisis – for 'helping to protect the vulnerable' and she concluded with the immortal wartime words of Vera Lynn, 'We'll Meet Again.'

With her bright green dress and towering barnet of silver hair, the Queen provided a reassuring image that was promptly elevated to a place of honour on the huge digital screen in Piccadilly Circus. The fact that her prime minister, Boris Johnson, was admitted to St Thomas's Hospital on the day of her broadcast, moving on to some dangerous days in the ICU, emphasised the seriousness of the crisis she addressed.

Later that summer at Windsor Elizabeth II received and knighted the heroic centenarian Captain Tom Moore who had raised millions for the NHS by completing laps of his Bedfordshire garden using his walking frame. Captain Tom had hoped to reach £1,000, but Internet publicity had expanded that target dramatically to £32.7 million – $45.3 million – a world record sum for a single fundraiser.

Harry and Meghan crept away from Vancouver on Saturday 14 March, two days before corona lockdown was imposed on both sides of the Canada–United States border. The island had always been a penance for them – neither one thing nor the other. Now that the Queen had struck them off the payroll there was no further need of Commonwealth residence and Meghan wanted to quarantine close to her mother.

Oprah Winfrey's friend and business partner, movie producer Tyler Perry, sent his 124-seater Embraer-E190 private jet to pick up the Sussexes. He also threw open his £15 million hilltop mansion sitting on twenty-two acres of land inside the Beverly Ridge Estates – the very comfortable temporary Los Angeles home where Harry, Meghan and Archie lived before acquiring their own home in Santa Barbara.

'The borders were closing and this was always the ultimate destination,' says one insider. 'Los Angeles is where Meghan's agents and advisors are based – and now they are Harry's team as well.'

Santa Barbara – or more precisely Montecito, the upscale neighbourhood where the couple bought their $14.65 million (£11.09 million) mansion on 18 June 2020 – is, in fact, a ninety-minute drive north of Los Angeles. It is home to celebrities like Oprah Winfrey and Gwyneth Paltrow who enjoy – and can afford – the French Riviera atmosphere of estates beside the sea. And the Sussexes had certainly bought themselves an estate, extending over 5.4 acres and featuring a swimming pool, tennis court, cinema room and a two-bedroomed guest house for Doria.

Official deeds appeared to show Harry and Meghan trying to finance the purchase themselves the traditional way with a mortgage – albeit at the eye-watering level of £7.25 million, suggesting repayments in the region of £30,000 per month. For this the young family could enjoy nine bedrooms and no fewer than sixteen 'bathrooms' – what the British would call 'loos' – even more than the twelve bathrooms that had been on offer at the Tyler Perry estate.

'Could it be,' commented Camilla Long sardonically in the *Sunday Times*, 'that 12 bogs were simply no longer enough for all the crap this couple spouts?'

Notwithstanding, Harry and Meghan stepped out promptly on some local COVID-19 errands of mercy – though their major plans were COVID-cornered like everybody else's. In the absence of Sussex Royal they had registered 'Archewell' as the name for their new foundation, having to delay the full-scale start of their activities until the world's return to health.

Yet coronavirus did not stop Meghan delivering a 'virtual' commencement address to the graduation class of her Immaculate Heart High School on 3 June. The recent killing of George Floyd and the Black Lives Matter demonstrations provided her theme.

'As we've all seen over the last week,' she declared, 'what is happening in our country … has been absolutely devastating. And I wasn't sure what I could say to you. I wanted to say the right thing and I was really nervous that I wouldn't or that it would get picked apart, and I realise the only wrong thing to say is to say nothing. Because George Floyd's life mattered …'

Meghan reflected on her own memories of the 1992 Los Angeles riots following another 'senseless act of racism' – the beating of Rodney King.

'I remember my teacher at the time,' she continued, 'one of my teachers Miss Pollia, said to me before I was leaving for a day of volunteering, "Always remember to put others' needs above your own fears." And that has stuck with me through my entire life and I've thought about it more in the last week than ever before.'

Meghan called on the students to 'channel' their education and all the skills that they had acquired over the past four years.

'Now all of that work gets activated,' she said. 'Now you get to be part of rebuilding and I know sometimes people say, "How many times do we need to rebuild?" Well, you know, we're going to rebuild and rebuild and rebuild until it is rebuilt. Because when the foundation is broken, so are we …

Soon after on 30 July, Prince Harry spoke of his latest enthusiasm – sustainable travel and his new company Travalyst – to an online gathering of Third World travel providers, setting out the 'responsibility we cannot avoid or dismiss, for us to reshape this industry in a way that benefits everyone and everything for decades to come'.

'Businesses are hurting significantly,' he said, 'and I've heard from some of you who are currently struggling to put food on

Meghan Markle signs a voiceover deal with the Walt Disney Company.
Peter Brookes, *The Times*, 10 January 2020

your families' tables and make ends meet because there are no tourists and therefore no income. We need to build back – but we need to build back better.'

Anti-monarchist Graham Smith of the campaign group Republic criticised Harry for getting involved with the commercial side of the travel business, but the prince's representatives rejected the charge with a blistering response: 'This is his life's focus and his devotion to charity is at the very core of the principles he lives by.'

Prince William has always been a fan of English football. Many of the royal family – including Prince Harry and, it is said, the Queen – are discreet and private supporters of north London club Arsenal. But William, defying the trends, has long supported the claret-and-blue of the unfashionable Midlands team Aston Villa, buried in the suburbs of Birmingham.

As president of the Football Association, the prince nursed hopes that Villa might make it to the 2020 FA Cup Final. As fate turned out, Fulham dispatched Villa in the third round and Arsenal made it to the final against Chelsea. But that did not stop the Duke of Cambridge focusing on the match for his favoured cause of mental health.

'We're going to really use the final as a moment to promote good, positive mental health for everyone,' he declared in June. 'It's quite timely bearing in mind what we've all been through with this pandemic. I think there's going to be, sadly, a lot of repercussions from this in society, not just in football, in terms of people's mental health.'

The duke got the final renamed the Heads Up FA Cup Final in honour of his mental health partnership between the FA and his Heads Together campaign.

'It's not a weakness to talk about mental health,' said William. His aim with Heads Up was to 'harness the influence and popularity of football to help show the nation that we all have mental health, and it is just as important as physical health.'

'Wonderful initiative,' declared one fan, 'helping people talk about their feelings … Great work! Your mother would be so proud.'

'Future best king,' enthused another. 'Very intelligent man, well-deserved to be king … Using sport is a great idea because of the amount of people that watch and take part.'

As it turned out there was nobody to watch on Saturday 1 August 2020. COVID rules had taken their toll. The Heads Up FA Cup Final was played in a deserted Wembley Stadium – without even William being present.

The prince was 108 miles away in Norfolk hosting a socially distanced outdoor screening on the lawn at Sandringham. He watched the match relaxing in a blue-and-white-striped deck-chair with other supporters of Heads Up.

'I'm thinking 2–1 Arsenal,' said the prince, correctly predicting the result.

The victorious captain Pierre-Emerick Aubameyang had to pick up the FA Cup trophy unassisted from a little stand on the pitch and promptly dropped it in front of his teammates, to general hilarity.

'That's why you need the president there!' shouted William from his deckchair.

Three days later on 4 August 2020, Meghan celebrated her thirty-ninth birthday in Los Angeles. Harry cooked her a three-course dinner while Doria babysat Archie.

'Harry has become a better cook since marrying Meghan,' confided a friend. '[But] he still has a way to go.'

William and Catherine sent birthday wishes by Instagram – 'Wishing a very happy birthday to The Duchess of Sussex today!' And the Queen sent the same with a photograph of her trip to Chester with Meghan in 2018, their first official engagement together for the opening of the Mersey Gateway bridge.

The Queen and Prince Philip had just completed four months of COVID-19 lockdown in Windsor, which they ended by flying north to Balmoral. But before she started her holiday the Queen found time to finalise legal action against Prince Charles's former butler Grant Harrold who, while publicising the etiquette classes offered by his company The Royal Butler, had revealed that Elizabeth II preferred her milk added to her tea *after* the hot water.

That may possibly have been indiscreet, but it was not the reason for Her Majesty's displeasure. The basis of the Queen's complaint was that nobody could trademark the term 'Royal' without her express permission.

33
'Tungsten'

*'I found a wife that was strong enough to be able
to stand up for what we believe in together.'*

(Prince Harry, March 2020)

Tungsten is a hard, steel-grey metal that is noted for its extraordinary strength. At 3,422°C, it has the highest melting point of any element on earth – over 6,000°F! Tungsten's toughness is why you'll find it in the high-temperature filaments of incandescent light bulbs, high-velocity missiles and armour-penetrating bullets. Weapons manufacturers can't get enough of it – twice the tensile strength of titanium!

Soon after Prince Charles met Meghan he came to feel that 'Tungsten' was the perfect nickname for his dynamic American daughter-in-law. He rather admired what others were coming to doubt. Meghan was so robust and unbending, and after seventy years as a royal, Charles reckoned he knew all about the toughness – and sometimes the unpopularity – that the job entailed.

'Prince Charles admires Meghan for her strength,' explained one of his friends in the early days of the Sussex revolution, 'and [for] the backbone she gives Harry who needs a Tungsten-type figure in his life … He can be a bit of a softy.'

The metallic nickname developed further when Charles met Meghan's mother. Doria Ragland came to tea at Clarence House shortly before the May 2018 wedding, and Charles warmed instantly to the social worker–yoga teacher. Then the prince's offer to walk Meghan down the aisle – well, half the aisle – in the absence of Thomas Markle increased the connection still more.

'Thank God he was there,' said Markle himself afterwards, 'and [I] thank him for that. It might have been a treat for him as he never had a daughter.'

Visitors to Clarence House in the months after the wedding noted the appearance of a new silver-framed black-and-white photograph in pride of place – the future king escorting Meghan on her way to becoming his new daughter-in-law.

The bond strengthened in the following months when Harry and Meghan went to spend the best part of a week with Charles at the Castle of Mey, the Queen Mother's sixteenth-century getaway near John O'Groats in the far north corner of Scotland. They walked the dogs in the parkland, strolled around the beautiful walled garden and spent hours together talking.

'Charles has been very supportive of Meghan and everything she is going through with her own father,' a source told Katie Nicholl. 'He's got a real soft spot for her and thinks she's the best thing to have happened to Harry.'

William, of course, had developed other opinions ...

Meghan enjoyed learning about her new family and its arcane heritage through these long chats with her father-in-law. 'They have a shared love of history, art and culture,' said one insider, 'and that's the common ground between them.'

At that stage Charles thought he had finally found someone in the family with whom he could share his enthusiasm for the paintings in the Royal Collection, as well as his fondness for traditional architecture. Meghan welcomed his input into the renovations she was supervising at Frogmore Cottage, built in 1801 – and, in more contemporary terms, she was totally signed on for her father-in-law's ecological concerns and his anxieties for the fate of the planet.

This understanding with Charles appeared to stand Harry and Meghan in good stead as the brothers went their separate ways following the Knauf memorandum of October 2018. Charles declined to stake the Sussexes to the full-scale 'court' they had hoped to create down in Windsor in the spring of 2019, but he did finance their new office set-up in Buckingham Palace, and he remained supportive as family relations deteriorated over the Sussex plan to move across the Atlantic.

Charles had some sympathy with the intentions behind Meghan and Harry's ambition to fund an independent future through their Sussex Royal project – which was essentially Duchy Originals on a transatlantic basis. The possibility of internationalising the monarchy tempted the visionary in the fatally visionary Prince of Wales. 'Highgrove Thinking' had long argued quietly that the House of Windsor could surely bend its ways a little more to the twenty-first century – and Charles had pushed for his own adaptations. His cherished drive for a slimmed-down monarchy had been built on the twin pillars of his two sons sharing the load in their different ways.

But now Harry was proposing a *very* different way and at the Sandringham showdown of January 2020 Charles aligned himself with the Queen and William. Relations were foundering between father and younger son – though Charles noted how Meghan had in the end deferred to her husband in the arguments over Sussex Royal. The actress's Rachel Zane persona may have egged on Harry's negotiating battles with the courtiers, but she became the loyal wife when her spouse told her that ultimately he would bow to the will of the Queen – 'What Granny wants, Granny gets.' When the Queen finally said no to Sussex Royal in February 2020, both the Sussexes had meekly accepted the verdict.

Either you are in or you are out, they had come to see and grudgingly acknowledge as the Queen's bottom line. So, let's get on with Archewell.

Duchess Tungsten demonstrated her metal in July 2020. Make that mettle.

'It was a July morning that began as ordinarily as any other day,' Meghan later wrote. 'Make breakfast. Feed the dogs. Take vitamins … Throw my hair in a ponytail before getting my son from his crib.'

Suddenly Meghan was struck by a sharp cramp, dropping to the floor with the fourteen-month-old Archie in her arms and 'humming a lullaby to keep us both calm, the cheerful tune a stark contrast to my sense that something was not right. I knew, as I clutched my firstborn child that I was losing my second.'

Meghan was rushed to hospital, where Harry took his place beside her bed.

'Holding my husband's hand,' she later wrote, 'I felt the clamminess of his palm and kissed his knuckles, wet from both our tears. Staring at the cold white walls, my eyes glazed over. I tried to imagine how we'd heal.'

Four months later Meghan described her miscarriage in a moving op-ed piece for the *New York Times*, 'The Losses We Share', seeking to relate her own rending experience to that of other women – and still more broadly to the pandemic pain being suffered by all.

'Loss and pain have plagued every one of us in 2020,' she wrote, 'in moments both fraught and debilitating … This year has brought so many of us to our breaking points.'

She then extended her theme still further, marshalling her thoughts for the great American family festival of Thanksgiving that was coming up the following day. She deployed her words with power.

'Losing a child means carrying an almost unbearable grief,' she wrote, 'experienced by many but talked about by few. In the pain of our loss, my husband and I discovered that in a room of 100 women, 10 to 20 of them will have suffered from miscarriage.'

Meghan's words struck a special chord with Camilla Tominey, the respected associate editor of London's ultra-loyal *Telegraph*.

'I am among the estimated one in five women in Britain to have lost a baby,' Tominey wrote in her royal newsletter that day, describing how she had been 'completely devastated' by the experience. 'So believe me ... when I tell you I both sympathise and empathise with what the Sussexes have been going through. My only question is why reveal this extraordinarily painful and personal trauma now?'

Tominey struck a rare note of dissent from the chorus applauding Meghan for disclosing her membership of the 'secret club that no one wants to join', as Dr Zeynep Gurtin, lecturer in Women's Health at University College London, approvingly put it in the *Guardian*.

Three years after Meghan's appearance on Britain's royal scene the 'Duchess of Woke' had become catnip to Fleet Street's midweek mavens, the largely female regiment of columnists who delighted in feasting on the House of Windsor's latest and unfailing source of amusement – often with great humour themselves. You will have read some examples in the previous pages.

Now the mavens fell carefully silent, with only the broadcaster Carole Malone venturing to speak out in the *Express*. 'There are legions of women who don't actually want to talk about losing their baby,' Malone wrote, going on to point out how Meghan 'has repeatedly said she wants privacy and won't engage with the press ... Yet here she is now serving up her devastating miscarriage experience on a platter for the world to dissect and discuss.'

Tominey, for her part, stressed how she absolutely respected Meghan's 'right to share her agony in such a public way', but joined Malone in accusing the duchess of invading her own privacy yet again. For months Meghan had denied speaking to the authors of *Finding Freedom*, but it had recently emerged that she had authorised the passing of information to them.

In describing Harry's weeping beside her hospital bed, Meghan had 'disclosed one of the most intimate moments in her own marriage' – making her 'more of an open book than a closed one'.

'I'm questioning,' wrote Tominey, 'whether to press "Send" on the paragraphs above as I write this.'

Tominey's honest caution was understandable, still finding the subject painful to share after eight years – though Meghan did have an alibi for her own self-exposure. There had been several reports from miscarriage charities of significant spikes in people seeking help following her article – 'precisely how taboos are broken', in the approving words of psychotherapist Jody Day.

'Meghan has no regrets whatsoever about sharing her grief,' revealed an 'exclusive source' in *US Weekly* a few days later. Prince Charles, Prince William, the Queen and other royal family members had privately 'reached out', said the same 'insider', when Harry had informed the family of the miscarriage that summer.

Private or public, did the sharing ever end? With Meghan there was always a good reason for her extraordinary self-exposure – but always a question mark as well. You could see why this passionate, reveal-all, oh-so-American crusader-for-the-good could not possibly survive comfortably alongside the 'Never complain, never explain!' protocols of the British royal family.

What were the words of that gospel song to which Meghan chose to leave St George's Chapel with Harry after their wedding?

This little light of mine
I'm going to let it shine …
All around the neighbourhood
I'm going to let it shine …
Hide it under a bushel? No!
I'm going to let it shine …
Let it shine, all the time, let it shine.

So, how to bankroll the great adventure? Harry and Meghan's life and work to this point had been financed by several sources including the British taxpayer through government payment of the Sovereign Grant – a total of £85.9 million in 2020 handed over to the Queen to administer as she saw fit: nearly £3 per taxpayer or £1.30 per head of the UK population. Pro-monarchists always quote these figures as a bargain, especially since the government also benefits from the revenues of the ancient Crown Estate (£345 million for the financial year 2019/20).

As the media noted frequently, the Queen had allocated £2.4 million of the Sovereign Grant to the upgrading of Frogmore Cottage, previously used as Windsor estate offices, to create that single and 'simple' ten-bedroom family home. The Sussexes' intention was to retain Frogmore as their British base whenever they returned to the UK, and now they also had to finance their fuller-time American residence, not to mention their domestic and work arrangements in North America. Finding funds was a top priority.

Meghan's lawyer and agent had been looking for backers since early 2020 and there was no lack of interest. Disney, Netflix, Apple,

NBCUniversal – many of the biggest TV streaming channels put in bids, and it was Netflix who made the largest offer. It was a matter of principle for Ted Sarandos, the innovative joint CEO of the 'on-demand' channel, never to be outbid by a rival if he could help it. The multi-year deal was said to be worth some $100 million–$150 million (£70 million–£105 million) per year for Harry and Meghan to produce a range of shows and films centred on the social messages that the couple held dear – racial justice, gender equity, mental health and environmental stewardship.

'Our focus will be on creating content that informs but also gives hope,' said Harry and Meghan. 'As new parents, making inspirational family programming is also important to us.'

Buckingham Palace was immediately sniffy. Such commercial deals, pronounced one 'royal insider' standoffishly, would be

Harry and Meghan sign a production deal with Netflix, Inc.
Paul Thomas, *Daily Mail*, 9 September 2020

'subject to discussion'. The palace would cast a 'critical eye' over the megabucks deal, reported the *Mirror*. 'It goes without saying any deals they are making will be scrutinised by the royal household.' The suggestion was that Harry and Meghan's moneymaking activities would lower the royal tone.

It was unfortunate, therefore, that two days later royal sources proudly announced that the Queen was opening the grounds of her Sandringham home to the public as a drive-in cinema with showings of *Toy Story* and other movies. Tickets would cost £32.50 per car – plus £7.50 for a deckchair and popcorn. Talk about tasteful! It was of a piece with the Buckingham Palace Gin and the shower caps on sale in the royal shops, along with the Luxury Tea Caddy, Charm Keyring and Guardsman Teddy Bear. Take a look for yourself – here's a link to the online palace store displaying worldwide delivery rates: https://www.royalcollection-shop.co.uk/children-s-pink-corgi-socks.html

So how was this £32.50 screening of *Toy Story* (popcorn extra) more tasteful than a contract to produce inspirational TV family programming – with content that was intended to 'inform but also to give hope'?

On 22 September 2020, Harry and Meghan were videoed together in the lush garden of their new Montecito home urging US viewers to go out and vote in the upcoming presidential election of 3 November that pitted Democrat Joe Biden against the Republican incumbent Donald Trump. It was so important, exhorted the couple, for people to exercise their precious right to vote.

'Many of you may not know,' said Harry, 'that I haven't been able to vote in the UK my entire life' – referring to the tradition (though it is not the UK law of the land) that members of the royal family should demonstrate their impartiality by not voting or standing for election. This had made the prince especially conscious of what a privilege it was to be able to vote, so 'as we approach this November,' he said, 'it is vital that we reject hate speech, misinformation and online negativity'.

'Every four years we are told the same thing,' added Meghan, 'that this is the most important election of our lifetime. But this one is. When we vote, our values are put into action and our voices are heard. Your voice is a reminder that you matter, because you do and you deserve to be heard.'

The words 'Democrat', 'Republican', 'Trump' and 'Biden' never crossed their lips, but critics in Britain felt it obvious that the Sussexes were making a political statement. How could such a famously 'woke' couple not be taking sides where Donald Trump was involved?

According to the *Sunday Times*, Roya Nikkhah's impeccable royal sources felt that the comments had crossed a dangerous line. 'If Trump is re-elected and makes another visit here,' explained one, 'what is the Queen supposed to say when her grandson and his wife have effectively campaigned against him? They know the political arena is meant to be absolutely off limits to members of the royal family.'

But Professor Vernon Bogdanor, Britain's leading constitutional scholar, begged to differ. 'The Duke and Duchess of Sussex … are not required to speak and act on the advice of ministers,' he explained. 'Their only constraint is that they must not do or say anything that could embarrass the sovereign ... The injunction to vote is not a partisan comment but an encouragement to civic participation. In my view the comments of the duke and duchess do not raise any constitutional issue.'

Dickie Arbiter, the former press secretary to the Queen, agreed. 'Harry seems to be being very careful with what he says. He is edging towards the line, but he has not crossed it. Telling people to vote is not crossing the line.' Arbiter pointed out how before the Scottish independence referendum of 2014 the Queen herself had urged voters to 'think very carefully' about how they voted.

The trouble was that in her pre-Harry days Meghan had made some disparaging remarks about Donald Trump, describing him in 2016 as 'misogynistic' and 'divisive'. Now Trump saw the chance to get his revenge.

'I'm not a fan of hers,' the president said next day in a White House press conference with gleeful malice. 'I would say this – and she has probably heard – that I wish a lot of luck to Harry because he's going to need it.'

The couple had tried to stay away from controversy but the crafty pol had dragged them in, and a week later they became further enmeshed through their comments on Britain's Black History Month that started on 1 October.

'You know,' Harry remarked in an interview with the *Evening Standard*, 'when you go into a shop with your children and you only see white dolls do you even think: That's weird there is not a black doll there?'

His question echoed Meghan's touching story of how her father had given her a mixed set of black and white Barbie dolls as a child, and Harry paid tribute to how his wife had changed his perspective on race. He described how he had had 'a sort of awakening' as he credited his switch of outlook to 'living a day or a week in my wife's shoes'. It had made him aware of the world's 'unconscious bias' on race.

The couple's remarks were largely upbeat. 'Being a dad myself,' said Harry to the activist Patrick Hutchinson, 'the whole point in life, I guess, for me, is to try to leave the world in a better place than when you found it.' But in the course of their interview they made a glancing reference to 'structural racism' and the *Standard* made this its headline – 'Harry and Meghan's Call to End Structural Racism in Britain'.

'Nice to catch up – but Harry's not OUR problem any more'

Paul Thomas, *Daily Mail*, 25 September 2020

It was all the mavens needed. So the privileged, California-dwelling Sussexes were criticising the diverse and relatively harmonious United Kingdom, were they, as per usual, accusing Great Britain of structural racism? What about the vexed and endemic racial conflicts closer to their North American home? It seemed strange that this couple who were so hostile to the mass media and so opposed to racism should choose the United States, of all countries, to escape from both.

Talking to *Fortune* magazine two weeks later Meghan ruefully admitted the dangers she had encountered in speaking her mind on almost anything. 'For my own self-preservation,' she revealed, 'I have not been on social media for a very long time … I try to be very clear with what I say, and not make it contro-versial.'

But somehow controversy had pursued her just the same and she was now trying to limit her words. When it came to saying 'certain things', she explained, 'I am cautious of putting my family at risk.'

On 8 November 2020, the royal family gathered at the Cenotaph in Whitehall for the solemn ceremony of Remembrance Sunday. The COVID-19 pandemic had modified the ritual drastically in some respects. There was no grand march-past by medal-wearing veterans and no gathering of the ten thousand or so crowd who normally flooded into central London for the wreath-laying and the two-minute silence that took place at 11 a.m.

But the essence of the rite was carried out. Watched from a nearby balcony by the Queen dressed in black, alongside Kate,

Camilla and other members of the royal family all wearing poppies, floral wreaths were laid by the socially distanced prime minister, Prince Charles, Prince William and others – but no Prince Harry.

Both Harry and his Uncle Andrew had proudly laid wreaths in previous years as the two members of the family who had seen active service. While Andrew's disgrace had rendered his presence out of the question, Harry had planned to attend the ceremony until COVID-19's unexpected autumn spike-back – so he asked Buckingham Palace if a wreath could be laid on his behalf.

When the news of his enquiry became public it seemed quite reasonable to most people. But when Harry's request reached his grandmother, it took her 'all of two seconds' to issue a refusal, according to a strongly sourced article by *Daily Mail* royal editor Rebecca English the following year.

The Remembrance Sunday ceremony was absolutely 'sacrosanct' to the Queen, explained English, and 'nothing' happened without her knowledge. She wanted it known that she had 'enormous admiration' for her grandson's achievements both inside and outside the military, but she saw his wreath-laying request 'as an example of his lack of understanding at what it means for him to be a non-working royal'.

It was greatly to Harry's credit that he had created his militarily linked projects like the Invictus Games and the expeditions of the charity Walking with the Wounded. But to stand at the Cenotaph and lay a wreath – or have a wreath laid on his behalf – was to represent the Queen in the most solemn capacity, and Harry's somewhat casual request simply showed how he still had not grasped the consequences of his momentous choice to sign off from royal duties. 'The Queen is very firmly of the opinion,' confirmed English, 'that you can't pick and choose what you do when it comes to the institution.'

And here came that expression again – 'Either you are in, or you are out.'

The Queen's firm rejection cut Harry to the quick and he tried to keep it secret. When the story of his declined request was made public at the time of the Cenotaph ceremony on 8 November, Sussex spokespeople were at pains to stress that the prince had not put the appeal directly to his grandmother. The suggestion was that the rejection had come from those ever-convenient culprits in grey suits, the courtiers, who had failed to pass the request on to Her Majesty.

Harry's ten years in the British Army, including two tours on active service in Afghanistan, had occupied the most richly fulfilling period in his life to date. The military had given the young man meaning like no other vocation he had encountered, and his exclusion from the Whitehall Remembrance ceremony stung.

Talking with Meghan they came up with an alternative – that they should find his own cenotaph in Harry's own newly discovered corner of the world. On Sunday 8 November 2020, the same day as the royal wreath-laying in London, the Duke and Duchess of Sussex drove the 83 miles from Montecito to the National Cemetery in Los Angeles, where they laid their own wreath at an obelisk 'In Memory of the Men Who Offered Their Lives in Defense of Their Country'.

Previous page: Prince Harry, 23, on patrol in Garmsir, Helmand Province, Southern Afghanistan, 28 February 2008.

Top: Prince Harry greets the press shortly before his fourth birthday, August 1988.

Below: In Botswana with the Tusk Trust charity, Prince Harry taunts his brother with a snake, June 2010.

Above: Meghan Markle with her parents Doria Ragland and Thomas Markle.

Right: Woman in a Man's World. A production still of Meghan Markle playing the role of top lawyer Rachel Zane in the successful US TV drama series *Suits*.

Top: Meghan Markle with her mother Doria on their way to St George's Chapel, Windsor, on her wedding day, 19 May 2018.

Below: Prince Charles escorts Doria Ragland (left) and Camilla (right) from St George's Chapel after the wedding of Meghan and Harry, 19 May 2018.

Fiji, 23 October 2018

London, 14 November 2018

Top: Meghan's first engagement with the Queen, opening the Mersey Gateway Bridge, 14 June 2018, supported by aides Amy Pickerill (rear left) and Samantha Cohen (centre).

Below: Meghan in Butani earrings, a wedding gift from Saudi Crown Prince Mohammed bin Salman (centre), in Fiji and to celebrate Prince Charles's seventieth birthday.

Facing page: Harry and Meghan present their son Archie to the world in St George's Hall, Windsor Castle, 8 May 2019.

Top: Meghan introduces Archie to Archbishop Desmond Tutu during their royal tour of South Africa, Cape Town, September 2019.

Below: Harry joins with Jon Bon Jovi and members of the Invictus Games Choir to recreate the Beatles' Abbey Road zebra crossing image, 28 February 2020.

Above: Parting of the Ways. William and Harry follow the family out of Westminster Abbey at the end of their last public appearance together prior to the Sussexes' departure for North America – at the Commonwealth Day Service of 9 March 2020.

Left: United in Sorrow. Princes William and Harry enter St George's Chapel, Windsor, following the coffin of their grandfather Prince Philip, the Duke of Edinburgh, at his funeral on 17 April 2021. Between them – but a step behind, so not depicted in this picture – was their elder cousin, Peter Phillips. Harry wore his Knight Commander of the Royal Victorian Order Breast Star with his Jubilee and Service medals. William wore his Jubilee medals and his Order of the Garter Star.

The 90,000-grave cemetery was virtually deserted. The UK's November Remembrance Day marks the armistice that ended the First World War for Britain in 1918 on the 11th day of the 11th month (at 11 a.m.), while America's Memorial Day is a Civil War-connected commemoration observed at the end of May. The couple were dressed formally and sombrely wearing poppies, while Harry sported on his chest his Afghanistan Operational Service medal for 2008, alongside Golden and Diamond Jubilee medals presented to him by his grandmother.

Husband and wife solemnly laid flowers that Meghan had picked from their garden on the grave sites of two Commonwealth soldiers – one Australian, one Canadian – and Harry signed a personal message on his wreath: 'To all of those who have served and are serving. Thank you.'

It was a moving private ceremony, carefully considered. But just how private was it – and did it, perhaps, reflect too much careful consideration? Within a few hours of the wreath-laying, images of the mourning couple, heads bowed in the California cemetery, were flashing their way to news agencies around the world. The stylish photographs of the pair strolling in the sunshine through the endless rows of white war graves were to be credited, said the press release, to Lee Morgan, a Hollywood celebrity photographer noted for his work with Kanye West and *Vogue*.

'My God,' tweeted *Good Morning Britain* host Piers Morgan. 'They've even turned Remembrance Sunday into another self-publicity stunt! Have they no shame?'

Morgan was a proudly proclaimed Meghan-sceptic, and that would subsequently lead to his abrupt exit from the morning show on 9 March 2021 when his assertion that he didn't 'believe a word' Meghan told Oprah about her mental health issues elicited 57,121 complaints to Ofcom, the UK's communications regulatory authority. 'I wouldn't believe her if she read me a weather report,' he said.

But in November 2020 the audience largely backed Morgan in his critique of the Sussexes' Remembrance Day gesture – and the British media concurred. Go and pay your private respects by all means, Harry, was their general consensus, but why take along a photographer to stalk you through the headstones with his telephoto lens? And why was Meghan wearing three-inch stilettos to pick her way across the rough and hilly turf?

'Can't someone save them from themselves?' asked Jan Moir in the *Daily Mail*. 'Here lie the ruins of their reputation.'

At best, the couple's 160-mile round trip with entourage and photographer was tasteless publicity. At worst, it was a calculated and angry riposte to a decision that Harry and Meghan resented from Buckingham Palace.

It would not be their last.

34

All About Rose

'Everyone knows about the affair, darling!'

(Tweet by Giles Coren of *The Times*, April 2019)

Catherine, Duchess of Cambridge, thirty-six, gave birth to Louis, her third child, on 23 April 2018, just one month before the 19 May wedding in Windsor of Prince Harry and Meghan Markle. But some 'insiders' – whoever they were – maintained that Kate was less excited than she might have been by these joyous events. Twelve months later stories emerged claiming that, during her pregnancy, the future queen had become concerned over her husband William's friendship with their Norfolk neighbour the beautiful Rose Hanbury, thirty-four, Marchioness of Cholmondeley.

Cholmondeley is pronounced 'Chumley' – but you knew that already, didn't you?

Former model Rose is certainly a sight to behold. Take a look at her photograph in full colour on page 6 of our glossy picture section 2. The marchioness seems properly wistful and intriguing. Goodness, she's almost as beautiful as Kate!

There is not the slightest evidence to suggest that Prince William's friendship with Rose Hanbury was improper in any sense. But that did not stop the newspapers speculating about it – and the foreign newspapers made a great deal more of the story than did their British counterparts.

'It was extraordinary to be travelling on the Eurostar that spring,' recalls documentary filmmaker Sue Summers. 'There were photos of Rose and William splashed together over all the papers and gossip magazines in Paris. Then you would arrive in London and there was virtually nothing.'

The loyal British press remained tight-lipped. But they did venture to touch gingerly on the question of what was described as Rose and Kate's 'rural rivalry'. So that's what they call it these days? Trying to work out what was going on via the terminology of Britain's side-of-the-mouth Rose Hanbury coverage, reflected Tom Sykes in the US-based *Daily Beast*, required 'a PhD in Cryptography'.

The Times's restaurant critic, Giles Coren, forty-eight, tweeted, 'Everyone knows about the affair, darling!' Then swiftly deleted the tweet.

Coren might have heard about the sharp-worded letter that William's lawyers Harbottle & Lewis had sent that April to at least one British publication which had indulged in a few speculations too many. On this matter, the elder brother had clearly taken a leaf from the hit-back-hard legal tactics of Harry and Meghan.

'In addition to being false and highly damaging,' wrote William's lawyers, 'the publication of false speculation in respect of our clients' [*sic*] private life also constitutes a breach of his privacy pursuant to Article 8 of the European Convention on Human Rights.'

The special closeness between William and Rose and their respective spouses went back to 2014 when William and Kate moved to take up full-time residence in Anmer Hall, their magnificent Georgian country house dating from the eighteenth century near the village of Anmer beside the Queen's horse-racing stud and on the very edge of her Sandringham Estate just over a hundred miles north-east of London.

Acquired in 1898 for some £25,000 by the future King Edward VII, Anmer had been leased out over the decades to various tenants including the Queen's cousins, the Duke and Duchess of Kent, until the Queen called in the lease to bestow the wide, greyish ten-bedroom mansion upon William and Kate as a gift to mark their 2011 wedding. Along with the house went £1.5 million of refurbishments at the Queen's private expense – a new roof, a new kitchen, a conservatory designed by Prince Charles's architect Charles Morris, and an extensive tree-planting programme 'to afford the Duke and Duchess greater privacy'.

Anmer Hall became the couple's principal home when William started work as a pilot for the East Anglian Air Ambulance, shortly before the birth of their second child, Princess Charlotte. It was the perfect country home in which to raise a young family, with the Queen's Sandringham residence just two miles to the east.

Two miles to the west across the fields lay Houghton Hall, the home of Rose Hanbury and her husband. Surrounded by a thousand acres of parkland, Houghton was the Palladian creation of Sir Robert Walpole, known to history as Britain's first prime minister. Walpole essentially invented the top job – and he enjoyed the perks that went with it. In 1797 Houghton Hall passed by marriage and inheritance into the possession of the Cholmondeley family and in 1990 Rose's husband David (the couple would meet in 2003 and marry in 2009) became the 7th marquess of that name and owner of the fine-grained silver-white stone palace.

With his new title (marquess is the second-highest rank in the British peerage after a duke), David Cholmondeley took over the hereditary position of Lord Great Chamberlain of the United Kingdom – one of the Great Officers of State, ranking beneath the Lord Privy Seal and above the Lord High Constable, with special responsibility for the royal apartments and Westminster Hall inside the Palace of Westminster. This entitled him to a distinctive scarlet and gold court uniform – plus a long white stave of office that he would carry at the Opening of Parliament rituals, when Cholmondeley was required to walk backwards in front of the Queen as a sign of respect. On coronation day it was the job of the Lord Great Chamberlain to dress the monarch (which meant, in practice, nothing more intimate than placing a robe around their shoulders) and also to serve them water before and after the coronation banquet.

These colourful duties passed to a man who had no little sense of style himself. Prior to inheriting the title, the 7th marquess had borne the less senior dignity Earl of Rocksavage, working as an actor and filmmaker under the professional name of David Rocksavage. In 1987, he had played a small role in Eric Rohmer's film *4 Aventures de Reinette et Mirabelle*, a 'tale of artists, beggars, thieves and swindlers'. Then in 1995, he would direct the film adaptation of Truman Capote's novel *Other Voices, Other Rooms*.

David Rocksavage was far from being an average member of the Norfolk landowning fraternity – generally dismissed as the 'Turnip Toffs' on account of the historic root vegetable they had cultivated beneath their rolling acres for generations. The mildly spicy turnip was a staple on British dining tables for a millennium and a half until the arrival of that bland American interloper, the potato, popularised by Sir Walter Ralegh in the sixteenth century. In 2008 the *Sunday Times* Rich List estimated the marquess's largely inherited net worth, which included a second Cholmondeley stately home – a castle, in fact – in Cheshire, at around £70 million, or some $100 million.

Cholmondeley was already forty-three in 2003 when he met the still-teenage Rose Hanbury, nineteen, on an Italian holiday. Rose was the daughter of landed gentry herself and she had her own royal connections – her maternal grandmother, Lady Elizabeth Lambart, had been one of the bridesmaids to Princess Elizabeth on her 1947 marriage to Philip Mountbatten.

After a reasonably successful education as a student in the originally all-boys' school of Stowe in Buckinghamshire, Rose undertook the plucky challenge of aiming for a degree via the Open

University, before trying her hand at modelling, and she enjoyed some success with Storm, the agency notable for discovering Kate Moss. She also worked for a period in the mid-noughties as a researcher for Michael Gove, then a freshly elected Tory MP in opposition to the still powerful Blair–Brown government.

Hanbury and Cholmondeley announced their engagement on 23 June 2009 and got married the very next day in a civil ceremony at Chelsea Town Hall. They were rapidly blessed with twin sons, setting up a cosy family unit whom they raised largely in Norfolk – and it was in these years that the couple were first reported to be friends of the still-unmarried William and Kate. The foursome were observed together on double dates.

Cholmondeley's duties as Lord Great Chamberlain already brought him and Rose to London and the palaces quite frequently, where they mingled on easy terms with senior royals at garden parties and official events.

'David is very colourful and entertaining,' says one of his local friends, a 'Suffolk Swede'. 'He certainly proves how wrong Noël Coward was – "very flat, Norfolk". And he's one of the Queen's most favourite men. She had great fun helping him to rehearse the walking backwards!'

His pretty wife the marchioness was judged by those who keep a beady eye on such matters to perform rather well on these occasions – and Rose would, in later years, be entrusted with such weighty state banquet responsibilities as being seated close to President Donald Trump when he came to London in June 2019.

*   *   *

It was William and Kate's move to Norfolk after their 2011 marriage, however, and their setting up in full-time family existence that really brought the neighbouring Cholmondeleys and Cambridges close together. Rose and David had been among the personal guests of the couple at the wedding in Westminster Abbey.

As William carried out his ambulance helicopter duties, Kate raised young George and Charlotte at Anmer – while also finding time to get thoroughly stuck into the texture of local life. East Anglia was one of the original kingdoms of Anglo-Saxon England, and Kate identified with projects that celebrated their local roots, chief among these being EACH – East Anglia's Children's Hospices, whose royal patron she became as early as January 2012, within months of her marriage.

'She felt an empathy with EACH as a child-centred charity,' says one friend. 'And she was particularly attracted to the focus that the hospices made upon children who were severely ill or disabled. She loved meeting their families.'

Just thirty, Kate made her first ever public speech in March 2012 when she opened the Treehouse hospice for EACH near Ipswich.

'I remember how nervous she was,' recalled Graham Butland, the chief executive, talking to Simon Perry of *People* magazine in 2019. 'It wasn't just the two hundred people in front of her, but the world's press and TV and everything there.'

As Kate travelled with William in their early foreign tours she networked on behalf of EACH, forming links with Hospis Malaysia on their September 2012 Diamond Jubilee visit to

Singapore, then linking up with Queensland's Hummingbird House during their visit to Australia in April 2014. In August that year, Kate helped EACH join an International Children's Palliative Care Network twinning agreement with Queensland Kids.

'I feel as though we have grown up with her,' said Butland. Kate helped EACH, while EACH – as one of the twenty or so charities she came to work with after her marriage to William – definitely helped the new princess to get started in public life.

'I've noticed how comfortably she has grown into her new position,' said EACH's former CEO. 'In the very early days, I remember her coming into a room and her head would be slightly down and the long hair would be across. Now she comes in with her head held high.'

According to Butland, Kate would make private visits to her local hospices in order to spend quality time with the young residents and their parents away from the gaze of the press.

'The feedback we get from families is tremendous,' he said. 'She is so natural when I see her with children and families. This is not someone struggling to stay in character. That IS her character.'

Hospices, let us remember, are usually for people who are dying, seeking to reduce pain and suffering in their final days of life. EACH offers 'respite' care by taking severely ill children into residence, thus offering 'time out' to parents under stress. But the direction of travel is, usually, one way. You don't stay for ever in a hospice, and when you finally leave it is seldom to go back home again. Physical care and emotional care – then spiritual consolation. After nineteenth-century beginnings in France and the US, the modern hospice movement started in Great Britain.

EACH was a successful charity before the Duchess of Cambridge joined it, but her involvement provided a magic touch. Recent figures show the charity's assets increasing from £10 million to more than £23 million in recent years, and when in 2014 Kate launched a specific appeal to build the Nook, a new facility near Norwich for severely ill children, EACH was able to raise nearly £10 million ($13 million) with her help. When, in November 2019, Kate finally opened the Nook, with its hydro-therapy pool, state-of-the-art sensory room and music studio, the building was hailed as 'the best equipped hospice for kids in the UK'.

What a credit this represented to Kate's years of support for this local EACH project so close to her heart – and what, you may ask, has all this to do with the rumours of the alleged split from her friend and neighbour Rose Hanbury in May 2018?

Well, it just so happens that May 2018 was the month when Rose Hanbury joined EACH as a patron to work alongside her friend Kate.

'I feel honoured to become a patron of EACH,' declared the Marchioness of Cholmondeley on 24 May 2018 on the charity's website.

Influenced by her friend and neighbour, Rose had already been helping EACH for several years – hosting, for example, a 2016 fundraiser for the Nook at Houghton Hall with her husband, alongside Kate and William. You can see the couples greeting each other outside Houghton in page 6 of picture section 2. Now Rose was officially joining EACH at the very moment when rumour would later claim she was falling out with her friend.

This author has made quite an effort to track down the solid evidence behind the miasma of the Rose Hanbury scandal, to be met with embarrassed looks from those who asserted and published the slander so strongly – and who do not even appear to have visited Norfolk to check on the alleged 'facts'.

'It was London dinner party conversation,' confessed one journalist who put out one of the larger articles on the subject – 'pulling together what all the other papers said.'

'Blah! Blah! Blah!' confessed another, when invited to provide or indicate his sources.

The truth was as elusive as Giles Coren had observed in his ironically intended tweet: 'Everyone knows about the affair, darling, even us Jews – although admittedly I'm quite a posh Jew – if such a thing exists …'

Two years later Coren confessed both amazement and remorse that his quickly withdrawn message of March 2019 should have provoked such error and embarrassment.

'With hindsight, I genuinely felt sorry for William,' says the restaurant critic and columnist. 'There was Giles, appearing to confirm something about which he knew absolutely nothing – and cared about still less.'

Coren had tapped out his words satirically on his cell-phone from a taxi in the aftermath of a gossipy liquid lunch – and he took the tweet straight down again the moment he realised his mistake.

'The Jew stuff,' he says, 'was classic me when pissed' ['Pissed' meaning 'tipsy' in the British connotation – not 'angry' in the American sense].

As the proud – and emphatically non-religious – descendant of a north London Jewish family, Coren was trying to emphasise 'how unlikely I am as a candidate for inside knowledge of royal shenanigans'.

But the world drew the opposite conclusion – as Coren would discover to his chagrin. 'I found myself getting quoted as some sort of major expert for months afterwards all over the United States and goodness knows where!'

This particular urban – or rather, rural – myth had gone berserk, in other words, although no one could produce a scintilla of proof. When examined closely, all the apparently compromising pictures published in the foreign media turn out to be photographs taken on separate occasions then spliced together to create a misleading impression. And the only vaguely solid allegation – that Kate and Rose went through some sort of spat or falling out as friends around May 2018 – was dated to the very month when the record showed Rose joining Kate's cherished charity as patron.

Some 'rural rivalry'! The two women have continued working with EACH in the three years since – despite the challenges of lockdown after March 2020.

'*Honi soit qui mal y pense!*'

It is impossible to prove a negative, but Prince William and his wife might well feel like citing the famous slogan attributed to an earlier prince – King Edward III, after the Battle of Crécy in

1346. The motto was later adopted by the Order of the Garter to which Prince William belongs, as well as by the Blues and Royals Cavalry Regiment in which both he and Harry served. The old Norman French tag is even inscribed, for reasons that remain obscure, on the gates of singer Michael Jackson's Neverland Estate in Santa Barbara. The '*Honi soit*' challenge centres on concepts of shame, and medieval scholars have offered varying translations. But William could not be blamed for choosing the toughest:

'Evil be to him who evil thinks!'

35

'New Firm'

'What animal do you think will become extinct next?'

(Prince George talking to David Attenborough,
August 2020)

After Harry and Meghan's departure to North America at the
end of March 2020, the challenge for William and Kate was
how to occupy the public space that the exiles had left behind.
William felt no more kindly towards his brother – and still less
towards his sister-in-law – than he had since the bullying showdown of October 2018. Reconciliation was not on the cards, and
William totally agreed with the family line laid down by his
grandmother – you are either 'In' or you are 'Out'.

For those who stayed 'In' there was a pandemic health emergency to confront, and William was reminded of this forcibly
when he himself succumbed to COVID-19 in April 2020. His
father had already gone down with coronavirus in March –
retreating to Birkhall at Balmoral, where the Prince of Wales and
his wife self-isolated in separate parts of the house. Then Boris

Johnson succumbed as well, almost dying in early April by some accounts, rushed into intensive care where his portly frame was pumped up with 'litres and litres' of oxygen.

When William discovered that he had also tested positive he decided to keep the news secret, on the grounds that the virtually simultaneous collapse of the prime minister and two heirs to the throne might imperil national morale.

'There were important things going on,' he later told a well-wisher, 'and I didn't want to worry anyone.' A few days earlier a social media panic that the Queen's husband had died had led Buckingham Palace to prompt the headline 'Prince Philip's Still Alive.'

William was hit hard by the virus. 'It really knocked him for six,' said a source. 'At one stage he was struggling to breathe.' The prince vanished to self-isolate at Anmer, suspending his emails and telephone calls for a week, from 9 April to 16 April, when he got back on to Zoom to celebrate the opening of a new Nightingale Hospital on a video call. A week later he appeared on the BBC's Comic Relief telethon with Kate and the children George, Charlotte and Louis. That evening the whole family helped lead the nation in that night's 'Clap for Carers'.

When the story of William's illness leaked out seven months later several critics declared that the prince had given himself too much importance by going to ground. But William offered no apology. He certainly had his well-developed open and 'modest' persona that he could deploy as charmingly as Harry in interviews and encounters – 'I'm just a bloke like the rest of you.'

But William also had his regal side about which he felt no reservations whatsoever. It ran right through him. William never forgot that he was a future king.

Talking of future kings – what next for George? When the six-year-old had posed for that message-laden image of the 'Four Monarchs' the previous December 2019, the little prince had not known, by several accounts, that he was standing on the Throne Room steps as a future king. The boy was just told, says a source, that they were all taking a few minutes out from the Christmas party to gather round and show their love and respect for 'Gan-Gan' – and George had no reason to question why he had been included in that very select group.

From George's earliest days, William had made no secret of his wish to spare his firstborn the casual initiation – or non-initiation – that he felt he had suffered as a child.

'There'll be a time and place to bring George up and understand how he fits in, in the world,' William told the BBC's Nicholas Witchell in 2016, when his son was coming up to three years old. 'Right now it's just a case of keeping a secure, stable environment around him and showing as much love as I can as a father … I want to bring my children up as good people, with the idea of service and duty to others.'

Delaying the moment of realisation gave George the precious gift of normality – for a few more years, at least. Out at Anmer the boy had started attending the local Montessori school before moving to Thomas's in Battersea, a progressive fee-paying academy in south London whose number-one rule, as noted on its website, was to 'be kind'.

William has not revealed to the world how and when he broke the big news to his son. Maybe one day George will tell us the story himself. But sometime around the boy's seventh birthday in the summer of 2020 it is thought that his parents went into more detail about what the little prince's life of future royal 'service and duty' would particularly involve.

William's aim as a father, the prince stressed, was to give his son 'a normal family upbringing', enabling the monarchy 'to stay relevant and keep up with modern times'.

'Normal', 'relevant' – 'modern'? Those adjectives hardly sprang to mind a few months later when the news emerged that the seven-year-old George had been spotted watching his father shooting grouse near Balmoral.

'Like father, like gun!' declared the *Daily Mail* at reports of George joining William and other senior royals as they shot down birds on the moors near Corgarff Castle, a dozen miles to the north of the royal family's Scottish estate.

'It's extremely disappointing' was one of the more moderate reactions in the resulting Twitter storm of disapproval. 'There is nothing educational or entertaining about killing animals.'

Mimi Bekhechi, director of PETA – People for the Ethical Treatment of Animals – complained that to help George grow into a responsible and compassionate leader, his parents should surely 'teach him respect for all living beings … Very few people these days view shooting for "sport" as anything other than a violent perversion that hurts and kills beautiful birds that are minding their own business.'

'Killer Wales' was wearing thin as a joke. The general public reaction to this country pursuit of the otherwise admired William and Kate was more a matter of sorrow than anger. But if the British monarchy survives to the end of the twenty-first century it seems unlikely that blasting innocent creatures out of the sky will be listed as one of their favourite pastimes.

'Shameful,' commented social media user Carmen Driver on William's introduction of his children to blood sports. 'I thought by 2020 the royals would have progressed.'

Fortunately public attention was captured in a more positive fashion that autumn when George made his screen debut along with his younger siblings Charlotte and Louis, talking to the venerable and beloved TV naturalist Sir David Attenborough, ninety-four, about the future of the planet and how to save it.

'What animal do you think will become extinct next?' asked George.

'Let's hope there won't be any,' replied Sir David, relating the tale of how he had worked with some success over the years to preserve the endangered mountain gorillas of Central Africa. 'There are lots of things we can do when animals are in danger of extinction. We can protect them.'

Princess Charlotte, five, was up next. 'I like spiders,' she declared, talking on the video filmed by her parents in the garden of Kensington Palace. 'Do you like spiders too?'

'I love spiders,' replied Sir David. 'I'm so glad you like them. I think they're wonderful things. Why is it that people are so frightened of them?'

Sir David hazarded a guess that the eight hairy legs of the spider and its ability to move unpredictably in any direction was unnerving to people, and he suggested that Charlotte should study how a spider weaves its web – 'That is extraordinary.'

The star of the show was little Louis, just two, who piped up to ask, 'What animal do you like?' – charmingly mixing up the consonants as 'aminal'.

'I think I like monkeys best,' replied Sir David, 'because they're such fun! They can jump all over the place and they don't bite. Some do – but if you're careful, they don't!'

The endearing interviews, released early in October 2020, were met with a chorus of delight and approval across the media and social media. What a fresh and wonderful young contrast to the jaded moaning that always seemed to be emanating these days from a certain couple in California!

But reflective observers wondered whether the precocious young royals would ever have been exposed so candidly on camera by their parents at such a tender age if William and Kate had not felt the need to make some sort of riposte to their in-laws across the Atlantic. The articulate young trio of George, Charlotte and Louis proved themselves a wonderful surprise weapon in the publicity war against the Sussexes, but how often could they be used again – and what was the effect upon the children?

* * *

The entire UK-based royal family reacted creatively to the joint challenge of rebellious relatives and the perils of COVID-19 – with the virtual encounters on Zoom and Skype providing a fresh and unexpected dimension to royal work. The ninety-four-year-old Queen led the way with her beloved iPad in which she linked up digitally in screened encounters that combined her family with members of the public.

'Can you see everybody?' Princess Anne asked her mother in a joint video session to mark National Carers' Week in early June 2021, when the royals hooked up with four carers across the UK who had distinguished themselves looking after their families

Nick Newman, *Sunday Times*, 14 March 2021

during the pandemic. 'You should have six people on your screen.'

'Yes, well,' replied the Queen, peering at her screenshots of the carers who were staring back anxiously at her – 'I can see four anyway.'

'Actually,' responded the princess, 'you don't need me. You *know* what I look like!'

Social media loved the clip: 'One is amused,' responded one viewer. 'Awesome!'

'Puts a smile to my face!' said another.

'Brilliant!' chipped in a third. 'Princess Anne is great, and it's been lovely watching the Queen during lockdown!'

Certain members of the family even proved to be 'virtual' virtuosos, with Camilla taking fondly to a video app known as Houseparty on which she appeared with her dogs Beth and Bluebell sitting on her lap. Charles's wife recorded messages of support for nurses from the Royal Naval Medical Service, as well as Roald Dahl's Marvellous Children's Charity – 'Extraordinary times call for extraordinary people,' she told them.

Kate and her aunt-in-law Sophie, the Countess of Wessex, developed an amusing double act when they spoke that June to nurses in seven Commonwealth countries around the world.

'I hope you're feeling some of the love as well,' said Sophie, talking to Army Nurse David Thomas, who reported that his children were doing better than expected with the challenge of home schooling thanks to his ex-wife, who had stepped in to perform sterling work as a teacher.

With two teenagers of her own at home, Sophie gave Kate a knowing look before joking, 'Be careful! She's about to be recruited!'

'I'd quite like her to come and help me out with home schooling,' agreed Kate, appreciatively.

The previously obscure Sophie was hailed as an especially natural and unaffected performer in these computer screen calls.

'The Countess of Wessex has really come into her own spotlight during this quarantine,' remarked Roberta Fiorito, host of the Podcast *Royally Obsessed*. 'I love Sophie. I want more of her … She's so comfortable with speaking to people.'

'She's really shone in the spotlight that she's been given,' agreed Roberta's co-host Rachel Bowie. 'I think that they're noticing that and are including her more in these big royal family updates.'

Half a century after the failed experiment of the *Royal Family* documentary, the House of Windsor had stumbled on a strikingly direct way to communicate their ordinariness to 'ordinary' people. Royal fans loved playing the 'peek-over-the-shoulder' game that COVID provided in its profusion of virtual video encounters, sneaking a look into the nooks and crannies in the backgrounds of the famous figures on the screen – 'Look at those papers stacked so untidily on that chair!'

In Prince Charles's case, scrutiny revealed an embarrassing antique lamp fitting in the shape of a 'Blackamoor' on the wall behind him in Birkhall. In the case of the Queen, it was the chunky old white 1970s telephone receiver on which she could be seen conducting her weekly prime ministerial audience with Boris Johnson – another first. Never before had the public been admitted in picture, if not in words, to this momentous weekly encounter between the head of state and head of government. In the middle of one podcast on mental health from Kensington Palace, Prince William shared pictures of himself serving up a curry.

The statistics of the Court Circular demonstrated how the royals had adapted over the months to the pandemic. In the course of 2020 the most senior members of the family – the Harry-and-Meghan-less team that insiders were starting to call the 'New Firm' – had carried out a total of 638 engagements.

Of these, 245 were 'virtual'.

William and Kate's share of this royal workload was 249 engagements from January to December 2020, of which 90 were 'virtual'. But the most historic of them was carried out in traditional style, standing in the Throne Room of Buckingham Palace on 7 October 2020, when the Duke and Duchess of Cambridge received Ukraine President Volodymyr Zelensky and his wife Olena on their state visit to London. Here was a major diplomatic occasion – with one head of state formally meeting and greeting another.

It was not the first time that the Cambridges had performed such an audience in the absence of the Queen. But the encounter was significant because the Queen had just returned to work following her Scottish vacation – so this was no substitution.

'It is very interesting that William and Kate were chosen to greet a head of state at Buckingham Palace,' declared ITV's royal correspondent Chris Ship. 'This reflects their growing importance in the seniority of the royal family. The Queen is back at

Windsor Castle and we understand is prepared to commute to Buckingham Palace. So technically she could have done this morning's engagement – but the Cambridges were chosen.'

It was also significant that the younger and junior couple were chosen to fulfil this full state engagement in preference to the Queen's senior heir and his consort, the Prince of Wales and Camilla, Duchess of Cornwall. Celebrating fifteen years of marriage and respectability in the spring of 2020, Charles and Camilla had worked hard to put their controversial past behind them – but the opinion polls showed they still had a way to go. In late 2020 one YouGov tracker assigned Charles and Camilla 'favourability' ratings of 24 and +1, as compared to 65 and 62 for William and Kate – and 71 for the Queen.

Buckingham Palace professed indifference to the polls. Still, it was William and Kate who got the nod early in December when the exotic and extravagant Royal Train – the Windsors' answer to the Orient Express, with multiple bedrooms and bathrooms and a twelve-place dining room – was rolled out for an unusual tour of the UK mainland for several days, making stops in England, Scotland and Wales.

The idea was for the crown to take smiles and thank yous to a nationwide selection of inspiring organisations and individuals who had gone 'above and beyond' – as the official royal website put it – in fighting the good fight against COVID in the previous year. On behalf of the Queen, William and Kate would be passing on 'the nation's sincere thanks and gratitude' to health workers and volunteers in all corners of the kingdom who had been sacrificing so much 'to keep people safe and keep the country going'.

Shakin' Stevens – Britain's ancient and wobbly answer to Elvis Presley – gave a rousing performance of 'Merry Christmas Everyone' at Euston Station while a socially distanced crowd (can there be such a thing?) cheered a festive farewell to the couple as they set off northwards on Sunday 6 December.

The nationalist leaders of Wales and Scotland did not share the festive spirit. Welsh Health Minister Vaughan Gething flatly told the BBC he'd prefer it if 'no one was having unnecessary visits'.

'I'm not particularly that bothered or interested,' the Welshman added, with a zinger that made clear his republican sympathies – 'People have *views* about the monarchy.'

In this, Minister Gething was echoing the barbed comments of Scottish National Party leader Nicola Sturgeon, bristling with Celtic fringe disapproval of Miss Jean Brodie proportions. Scotland's first minister declined to express the slightest welcome to the royal couple, emphasising that her office had 'made plain the restrictions in place' before the Cambridges arrived in Edinburgh. Loyalists viewed her jibe as 'rude' and 'petty'.

The Cambridges' welcome was all the more comforting, therefore, when they returned home to London on 8 December after their three-day 1250-mile expedition.

'The Prime Minister,' announced No. 10 Downing Street, at daggers drawn with Sturgeon, 'is delighted to see the warm reception the Duke and Duchess of Cambridge have received on their hugely valuable train tour.'

The glamour of Prince William and his wife had provided much-needed uplift to Boris Johnson's attempts to stem the momentum for a Scottish independence referendum, and the premier praised the Cambridges' 'welcome morale boost to front-line workers who have done so much during the pandemic'.

The couple's warmest reception came in Windsor, where the Queen, dressed in a festive red hat and coat designed by Angela Kelly, was singing along to a Salvation Army band playing carols as Christmas lights twinkled. The entire festive scenario of welcome on the castle steps, briefed the courtiers, had been the personal idea of Her Majesty.

On either side of the Queen were the senior members of the family in a first formalised parading of the New Firm – Charles and Camilla, Princess Anne (no Prince Andrew, of course), with Prince Edward and Sophie, whose emergence from the shadows marked the Wessexes as major beneficiaries of the Sussexes' departure.

With the addition of William and Kate, this New Firm added up to what some were hopefully describing as Elizabeth II's 'Magnificent Seven'.

The New Firm featured prominently in the Queen's Christmas TV and radio address seventeen days later – though the royal scene-setters were careful to avoid the 'political' selection of family photographs that had delivered such a powerful non-Sussex message the previous year. This December Elizabeth II had just one image beside her in a simple oval frame – a touching shot of her still-feisty husband of seventy-three years, Prince Philip, ninety-nine.

But the film footage that was played during the broadcast made very clear who had been doing the real royal work in recent months in Her Majesty's opinion – Charles and Camilla, Princess Anne, Edward and Sophie, William and Kate – her Magnificent Seven again.

Harry and Meghan, for their part, let it be known they regarded Christmas as time for a 'truce'. The couple had gone on a shopping expedition to some of the finest boutiques near their Santa Barbara home, and Meghan used her now-famous calligraphy skills to send personalised messages to Archie's cousins George, Charlotte and Louis. The Sussex PR team, operating under the name of Archewell, went to work as usual to spread around the stories of the shopping trip that had produced these charmingly personalised Christmas presents.

The PR team did *not* reveal that Harry and Meghan had been working for some time with their friend Oprah Winfrey to prepare an equally personalised but rather different type of New Year's present for their family in Britain.

36

Service Is Universal

'We can all live a life of service.'

(Harry and Meghan, Duke and Duchess of Sussex,
19 February 2021)

Diana never had much time for Oprah Winfrey. In the mid-1990s the American interviewer had been fussing around the princess so much, actually flying to London to try to persuade her to do a primetime interview, that Diana decided she would have to deal with the problem over lunch.

She invited Oprah to Kensington Palace and issued special instructions to her chef, Darren McGrady. At that time America's grand inquisitor was embarking on another of her much-publicised diets, trying to get down from the weight of 237 lbs that she had disclosed in 1992 – nearly 17 stone – to a level on the right side of 200. So Diana asked McGrady to prepare his famous tomato mousse.

After a few mouthfuls Oprah put down her spoon to ask, 'Diana, how do you stay so slim eating rich food like this?'

'I just eat small portions,' replied Diana demurely, 'and I work out.'

But that was not quite the full story. Diana had instructed McGrady – formerly chef to the Queen – to prepare and serve her with a fat-free version of the mousse, while Oprah was served with the full-fat dish, loaded with mayonnaise, sour cream and a dollop of heavy cream as well.

'Diana never did tell her the truth,' McGrady liked to relate with delight.

'Diana felt very uncomfortable with Oprah,' recalls her friend and confidante, Simone Simmons. 'She thought that Oprah was only after sensationalism – like when she interviewed Fergie about her book, and all she wanted to talk about was Diana. That laid bare for Diana the basic lack of respect that she felt Oprah had towards her subjects and how she was just manipulating her to garner higher ratings.'

Meghan took a more positive view of Oprah, having grown up as part of an American generation for whom the stars of daytime TV were gods circling the galaxy – with Oprah's ground-breaking brand of black empathy providing a charismatic role model for a mixed-race actress seeking the limelight. Until Meghan met Harry, she had been a mid-league cable drama star who could only have dreamed of featuring on Oprah Winfrey's primetime show – let alone be classed as Oprah's 'friend'. But her link to British royalty transformed all that.

Meghan and Oprah did not meet in America. Their first encounter was in London in March 2018, when Oprah, sixty-seven, approached Meghan on behalf of the US broadcaster CBS. Meghan invited Oprah to Kensington Palace – she did not offer her any tomato mousse, so far as is known – and suddenly the two women were the very best of friends. There was Oprah at the royal wedding in May that year sitting at the very top of the guest list.

Celebrities had become Meghan's new family – the allies to whom she could turn as her royal relationships turned toxic. In the jostling before the Sandringham Summit of January 2020, Los Angeles sources told the *Sun*'s Emily Andrews that Meghan's US team were sounding out the potential for a 'dirty laundry' interview 'as a negotiating tactic' of last resort with the royal family. An eye-opening encounter with Oprah could put a nuclear bomb under Buckingham Palace.

'I don't think it would be pretty,' revealed the couple's confidant Tom Bradby.

The Sandringham Summit had progressed so rapidly and had led to exile in Canada that there had been no time for the nuclear option to be deployed. But through the course of 2020 the possibility of a 'Tell-All' chat to Oprah remained in the Sussex armoury – intensified by the growing personal closeness between the two women, especially when Oprah's friend, the multi-millionaire tycoon-entertainer Tyler Perry stepped forward at the outbreak of the COVID-19 pandemic to provide not only a temporary US home for the royal fugitives, but bodyguards as well.

Perry's eight-bedroom bolt-hole in the gated Beverly Ridge Estates got Harry and Meghan firmly settled in the United States. Now they wanted to launch themselves properly from their new base, and the idea of a 'dirty laundry' session loomed ever larger with the approach of the end-of-March-2021 deadline proposed by the Queen for the final resolution of the Sussex Split.

When, early in 2020, Harry's grandmother had first suggested the twelve-month review period, some sort of reconciliation between Harry and the family had not seemed entirely out of the question. But all the squabbles through the subsequent spring and summer – worsened by COVID's barriers to resolving matters face to face – made reconciliation between William and Harry an ever more distant prospect. Well before Christmas 2020, both camps were briefing that 'status quo' was now the best outcome that could be hoped for by the March deadline. There would be no reconciliation, in other words – no coming back to Britain. Matters were heading towards a permanent split, without significant change or compromise on either side.

But as the Sussexes' strategists contemplated this final period of waiting for Granny's verdict, the three-month delay came to seem less and less attractive. Were the couple supposed to sit meekly twiddling their thumbs until the end of March, when the Queen's command would be issued to chop off their heads? Meghan was feeling like an outcast, but she did not wish to be seen as one. In this developing scenario, the Oprah interview resumed its potential as a weapon – the chance for Harry and Meghan to go public on their own terms and, effectively, to jump before they were pushed.

PR agency Sunshine Sachs wanted to launch its two clients' new American lives with a flourish, and an idea emerged that would supplement the plan for a 'Tell-All' session with Oprah. Harry's bright and smiley actor friend James Corden, already a star in Britain with his critically acclaimed sitcom *Gavin and Stacey*, had encountered still more success in America. In 2015 Corden had taken the ratings of CBS's *The Late Late Show* to new heights – and he had become an internet star in his own right with his 'Carpool Karaoke' sessions. These twenty- to thirty-minute sketches showed Corden driving around the streets with celebrities, from singer Adele to ex-Beatle Paul McCartney while the actor-comedian sang along to their songs in a jokey fashion. In 2016 Corden's karaoke with Adele had been YouTube's biggest viral video of the year – scoring 221 million hits.

Brash and mischievous like Harry, Corden could provide the ideal foil for the prince in some similar drive-around exercise in Los Angeles. So over New Year 2021 Archewell's strategists came to mix Oprah and Corden together as the ingredients of a two-pronged push to get Harry and Meghan started with a splash

Paul Thomas, *Daily Mail*, 20 February 2021

in the United States – hopefully provoking still more high-ticket contracts for their services. Harry already had his Netflix documentaries and had started work with Oprah on her programmes examining mental health. As Helen Lewis remarked in *The Atlantic*, the prince's skill set of flying helicopters and shaking hands with mayors needed amplifying in his new life of podcasts.

Harry and his wife could only commit seriously to these money-making projects, however, after they had cut their remaining ties with Buckingham Palace. So early in January 2021 courtiers began noticing a new haste developing on the Sussex side. Though the arguments over the Remembrance Day wreath-laying had ended badly for Harry, the conversations had paradoxically confirmed the importance of his personal 'hotline' to the Queen. One positive from the difficult year of separation had been the direct line of communication that had developed between grandmother and grandson, who would talk to each other with some regularity and genuine affection – often resolving quite confrontational issues in principle, then handing them over to their respective staffs to formalise as words on paper.

These conversations intensified with the start of the new year when courtiers were struck by the 'puzzling sense of urgency' with which Harry was now seeking to confront his grandmother over the unresolved issues of his ex-working-royal status. One of these talks was said to have lasted as long as an hour.

There was the question of the cherished regimental titles that Harry had hoped to keep, along with the Commonwealth jobs that he and Meghan had been allowed to retain after their departure. Most important of all, could the couple retain their 'HRH'

Royal Highness status which they were not actually deploying, but which it would be humiliating to see removed? The prince did not wish to delay another two months to settle these issues, which represented the essence of the final break.

Five weeks into 2021 the reason for all the haste became clear. On Friday February 5, Harry was spotted travelling around Los Angeles on an open-top bus chatting happily with James Corden, who appeared to be conducting quite an ambitious televised interview, complete with multiple cameras, a police escort, Harry's personal security team – and an English cream tea being served to the prince on a silver trolley.

What on earth was going on? The celebrity interviewer and royal guest had visited the location of the NBC sitcom *The Fresh Prince of Bel-Air*, with Harry, dressed casually in his blue jeans, playing the role of a new 'fresh' prince arriving in Hollywood – even testing out the mansion's guest loo.

Press and internet reactions next day speculated that some new royal 'Carpool Karaoke' session must be in the works, promising another YouTube hit for Corden. (At the time of writing, the James Corden–Prince Harry cream tea bus trip around Los Angeles, finally broadcast on February 25, 2021, had generated 24,057,729 views: https://www.youtube.com/watch?v=7oxlCKMlpZw).

The secret was out! Sometime in the subsequent week, February 8–12 – according to tweets from Emily Andrews – the Queen emailed Harry the personal letter that laid out her final terms for what would become the official separation, and the following Monday 15 February the full picture became clear. An over-eager producer working for Oprah's production company Harpo

(Oprah backwards) had approached ITV in London requesting permission to use footage from Harry's famous October 2019 interview with Tom Bradby in Africa revealing that the brothers were on 'different paths'.

Broadcaster CBS had to confess shamefacedly that a major 'Tell-All' Oprah Winfrey interview with the Duke and Duchess of Sussex was indeed in the works – and was due to be broadcast in the forthcoming weeks. Once again, it seemed, Harry and Meghan had done their best to blind-side the Queen.

In Harry and Meghan's interview with Oprah, which would finally be broadcast by CBS in America on Sunday 7 March 2021, and on the following evening by ITV in Britain, Harry described how the terms of his final separation from the working royal family had been hashed out in a series of personal phone calls with his grandmother. Buckingham Palace confirmed this, with notes to newspaper editors clarifying that there had actually been conversations between Harry and 'Members of The Royal Family' in the plural – suggesting that Prince Charles had also been involved.

Six weeks ahead of deadline – on Friday 19 February 2021 – the House of Windsor's most drastic royal rift since the abdication of King Edward VIII in 1936 was duly finalised in a comparatively brief statement from Buckingham Palace. The Queen was 'saddened' to see the couple go, it declared, but the duke and duchess 'remain much loved members of the family'.

This blending of kindness with confrontation was in line with every official statement that the Queen had issued from the very beginning of the crisis – even at the height of her surprise and anger at Sandringham the previous January. Harry's grandmother was insistent on putting her personal sympathy for her grandson on the record.

But as Queen, Elizabeth II was equally insistent on laying down the royal law that it was her job to defend. So she made clear on 19 February 2021 that 'the honorary military appointments and Royal patronages held by The Duke and Duchess will … be returned to Her Majesty, before being redistributed among working members of The Royal Family'.

'Working' members – it was as if Elizabeth II had underlined the word. The two sides of her response to Harry as loving grandmother and as unrelenting Queen were almost schizophrenic. But the clarity of the Queen's vision in both respects reflects the subtlety with which she has always fulfilled her dual role as monarch and head of her family.

There was a stumble, however, at this final hurdle. 'Following conversations with The Duke,' her statement ran, 'The Queen has written confirming that in stepping away from the work of The Royal Family it is not possible to continue with the responsibilities and duties that come with a life of public service.'

Public service? Harry and Meghan took offence at this. In their view, the long-drawn battle they had pursued for the last year with Queen and palace had been all about the technicalities of *royal* service. They wanted to pursue their idea of *public* service without royal constraints, and they snapped their response back in a rapidly released riposte.

'As evidenced by their work over the past year,' they replied at 12.27 p.m., just seventeen minutes after the palace statement, 'the Duke and Duchess of Sussex remain committed to their duty and service to the UK and around the world, and have offered their continued support to the organisations they have represented, regardless of official role. We can all live a life of service. Service is universal.'

Most neutral observers took their point. The dictionary distinction between the words 'royal' and 'public' is quite clear, and the palace statement almost seemed to be claiming that when it came to good works, the royal way was the only way. But loyalists rallied round, with sources close to Prince William claiming he considered the Sussex push-back 'insulting and disrespectful' to the Queen, while royal aides described the response as 'downright rude'.

'Don't disrespect your granny, Harry!' declared one source quoted by the *Sunday Times* on 21 February, with another issuing the warning: 'You don't answer the Queen back – it's just not done.'

Harry and Meghan, however, had already 'done' precisely that. On 16 February, three days before the Queen issued her statement, they had sat down in California with Oprah Winfrey to record their 'Tell-All' interview. What *they* had to say was already in the can.

Recollections May Vary …

'Hold up! Hold up! Stop right now …
There's a conversation about how <u>dark</u> your
baby is going to be?'

(Oprah Winfrey to Meghan, Duchess of Sussex,
March 2021)

Love it or loathe it, the mass-audience confessional TV inter-view is a modern art form – and Oprah Winfrey has made herself the ultimate Grand Master of the genre. Edward R. Murrow, John Freeman, Phil Donahue, David Frost – Oprah has outlasted them all. Starting in the 1990s, her mixture of personal empathy with forensic analysis made her interviews with Michael Jackson, Whitney Houston and doping scandal cyclist Lance Armstrong landmarks in the popular culture of their times – and her Meghan and Harry interview of 7 March 2021 (taped on 16 February) would surpass them all.

'Tell me what your intention is,' she had texted to the couple before the show, 'so that we can be aligned in our goal.' It was not surprising, therefore, that it should be a co-ordinated theatrical production from the get-go.

'Do you know,' asked Oprah, in the first of her many clearly well-rehearsed questions, 'if you're having a boy or a girl?'

The interviewer was responding to the news that Meghan and Harry had chosen to release two days prior to the taping – on 14 February, Valentine's Day (Diana had announced her pregnancy with Harry on Valentine's Day 1984) – that they were expecting a second child.

'I'll wait for my husband to join us,' responded Meghan coyly, 'and we can share that with you' – thus guaranteeing viewer attention for the next sixty-seven minutes until Harry bounced in to announce, 'It's a girl!' to squeals of female delight.

Oprah: 'You're going to have a daughter! Wow!'

Cynics later wondered whether it might not have been sexist to so clearly prefer the arrival of a girl to a boy. And if it was acceptable to get so excited about the sex of the second child that this interracial couple would produce, how about speculating on the likely colour of the baby's eyes or hair – or even skin?

We will get to that delicate issue later …

The first major revelation of the sit-down – conducted on the luxurious veranda of a friend and neighbour of Oprah – was that Harry and Meghan had got married not once, but twice!

'Three days before our wedding,' said Meghan brightly, 'we got married … No one knows that! But we called the archbishop and we just said, "Look, this thing, this spectacle is for the world. But we want *our* union between *us*".'

After three weeks of embarrassed silence the Archbishop of Canterbury, the Most Reverend Justin Welby, broke cover flatly to deny the truth of this. The prelate had presided, he agreed, over a touching private exchange of vows in the couple's small garden at Nottingham Cottage in the grounds of Kensington Palace – but this was not in any way a licensed wedding ceremony or venue.

'The legal wedding was on the Saturday,' the archbishop told the Italian newspaper *la Repubblica* at the end of March. 'I signed the wedding certificate, which is a legal document, and I would have committed a serious criminal offence if I signed it knowing it was false.'

This dose of reality set the tone for so many of the 'truths' revealed in the 'Tell-All' interview that followed. Many of them were not 100 per cent true – in fact, nothing was quite what it seemed when it came to Meghan's memories. She and Harry had *not* got married three days before they got married, her comms team subsequently conceded – though they had chosen to pledge their love to each other in a touching private ceremony that demonstrated thoughtfulness and commitment.

So why not say that in the first place? Why talk to the world in misleading headlines – or rather, perhaps, in soundbites? And why did Oprah, their fearless interviewer so renowned in usual circumstances for her forensic analysis, accept at face value just about everything the pair of them claimed, without digging deeper to get at the real and objective truth? There was no examination, for example, of the disastrous state of relations between Meghan and her father. Was Oprah 'pulling her punches' –

suspending her normally rigorous standards of enquiry to do favours for her friends?

Much of the interview was dedicated, for instance, to Harry and Meghan's by-now ritual denunciations of the British tabloid press, and Oprah's Harpo production team had done extensive research to back up their claims with pictures of racist and sexist headlines – all taken, apparently, from the UK media. But when Britain's Society of Editors took the trouble to examine these lurid headlines and front pages as displayed on the screen, it discovered that more than a third of them (11 out of 30) were not British at all. They actually came from foreign and US celebrity magazines, notably America's tabloid king the *National Enquirer*.

At the heart of the interview's credibility lay the variable nature of 'Meghan's Truth' – abetted by the failure of her interrogator to probe the factual basis of the succession of explosive stories being produced. The duchess complained at one stage that she had had to surrender 'my passport, my driver's licence, my keys' – giving the impression she had been confined in some sort of Kensington purdah or even prison cell.

So how come, Oprah might have asked, did you undertake at least three personal and family plane trips between February and August 2019 – including a solo private jet excursion to New York for a two-day baby shower, attended by, among others, mutual friend TV host Gayle King, editor-at-large of Oprah's own *O* magazine – then fly off to four Southern African countries in September?

Had Meghan, indeed, ever previously travelled so far, so frequently and so luxuriously in any seven-month period of her

'A shy woman famous for hating publicity told the entire world last night: "I'm having another nipper …"' *Daily Star*, 15 February 2021

life? That might have seemed an obvious question to pose in response. But Oprah failed to ask it. Her story this evening was of how her dear friend from quite a simple American background had fallen in love with a prince and gained admission to the fairy-tale setting of a palace.

So Oprah's concern was not to recount banal details of what did or did not happen. Her objective was to lay out the fairy tale of what her friend Meghan *felt* – and felt very intensely – about what had happened in that exotic setting.

* * *

'Recollections may vary,' the Queen would later comment dryly on the accuracy of her granddaughter-in-law's memories, and this caveat applied particularly to the lack of emotional support and 'protection' Meghan felt she had received from what she frequently described in the interview as the 'institution' – her portmanteau term for the palace structure of courtiers and conventions that made up the monarchy. Diana had dismissed them scornfully as 'the men in grey' – and Harry, Meghan and Oprah had prepared one particular story to illustrate this enduring and pernicious influence, complete with back-up newsreel footage.

'We had to go to this event at the Royal Albert Hall,' Meghan recalled, describing how 'right before we had to leave for that' she had had a dramatic conversation with Harry. Her interviewer had clearly heard this story before and she wanted to make the most of it.

OPRAH: 'You had the conversation you don't want to be alive any more?'

MEGHAN: 'Yeah.'

OPRAH: 'Whoo …'

MEGHAN: 'But we had to go to this event, and I remember him saying, "I don't think you can go". And I said, "I can't be left alone".'

OPRAH: 'Because you were afraid of what you might do to yourself?'

MEGHAN: 'I just didn't want to be alive any more. And that was a very clear and real and frightening constant thought.'

All through this disturbing dialogue – which this author, like the majority of viewers, found deeply alarming and authentic at the time – Oprah's production team were running onscreen footage that showed the couple attending the premiere of a Cirque du Soleil concert on Wednesday 16 January 2019 at London's Royal Albert Hall.

'And every time that those lights went down in that Royal Box,' related Meghan, 'I was just weeping, and he was gripping my hand.'

The emotional sequence, complete with the graphic footage, led up to Meghan's devastating accusation that she had gone to 'the institution' the very next day – she spoke to some senior courtier, she later explained – to say that she needed 'to go somewhere to get help ... And I was told that I couldn't, that it wouldn't be "good" for the institution.'

If precisely true as described, this was a shocking indictment of Buckingham Palace. But here are some questions ...

Why didn't Meghan, at this extreme moment of crisis and distress, first raise the question of getting help by turning to her husband who had been gripping her hand so hard as she wept? Harry's response to the shocking revelation that Wednesday evening that his wife didn't want to be alive any more was, in one sense, a typically Windsor solution – 'Put on your jewels and glad rags, wear a smile on your face, and go out and meet the public!' And that had actually worked well for the moment, it appeared. Meghan had somehow survived the evening.

But what did Harry do next? The prince himself had been in therapy in recent years – as had brother William. Therapy was no shame at all for this new generation of royals, both of whom had commendably chosen to make mental health their focus of special concern. The brothers' cherished royal charity Heads Together – still jointly operated at that date – offered an array of some of Britain's most skilled and sympathetic therapists and treatments. So why did Harry not offer to call one of these that very night – or maybe his own shrink – to arrange immediate support for his wife?

Meghan was five months pregnant. Surely the very first thing to do was to ring her trusted obstetrician Penelope Law at the Portland Hospital?

Elsewhere in the interview Meghan talked warmly of Diana's old friend and counsellor Julia Samuel – 'one of my husband's mom's best friends … who's continued to be a friend and confidant'. So why, at this moment of crisis, did Meghan not turn to this tried and tested pillar of strength? Why venture off alone to talk to some palace functionary? And on the basis of the evidence and dates given by Meghan herself we can take a good guess at who that palace functionary might have been …

On Thursday 17 January 2019 Harry and Meghan were still living in 'NottCott' – Nottingham Cottage, Kensington, in whose garden they had exchanged their private vows – and they were still sharing palace staff inside the joint household headed by William with his private secretary, Simon Case. The cataclysmic row between the brothers over Jason Knauf's bullying allegations had occurred just three months earlier, and the separation of their offices was under way. But both brothers were still trying to keep the truth of their split hidden from the world.

In January 2019, the record shows, Meghan's private secretary was still the cheery Australian Samantha 'Sam' Cohen, the down-to-earth mother of three whom we met earlier – the 'special gift' and item of wise personal support provided at the Queen's specific suggestion to help and sustain Meghan in her royal life. (You can see Sam Cohen in picture section 3 page 5, sitting with a smile on her face right behind and between Meghan and the Queen.)

Sam Cohen was the senior officer of 'the institution' who ran Meghan's calendar, travel arrangements and every detail of her official life. If any royal, including the Queen, wants to 'go some-where' to see a friend, go out for lunch, carry out some official engagement – or 'get help' – they broach the subject with their private secretary who will then take charge of all the details, from transport to security and press coverage, if any.

No one who knows the very human Sam Cohen could imagine her greeting Meghan's request for emotional help with indiffer-ence or the snootiness described by the duchess. Quite the contrary, in fact, unless ...

Let us go back to Meghan's actual words as spoken to Oprah in March 2021 – 'I needed *to go somewhere* to get help.' She was not simply asking for emotional support. She was saying that she wanted to *go* somewhere to find it. Travel was the essence of her request.

But why did Meghan need to go anywhere if there were shrinks, therapists and support counsellors aplenty in London –

including Julia Samuel – who could come rushing to the palace at the click of a finger? Could it possibly be that Meghan had fixed on the idea of going 'somewhere' to get help in a comforting and non-British environment where she could take refuge away from all the trials and tribulations of Kensington Palace? In North America, perhaps? In Arizona even, where Oprah's friend Dr Deepak Chopra offered his 'Whole Health Retreat' in the aptly named city of Carefree? Take a look for yourself: https://chopra.com/retreats/whole-health-retreat

Meghan's wish to escape was perfectly understandable. But if some form of travel was the proposal that she presented to Samantha Cohen, or to any other courtier in 'the institution' on that dark and chilly day in the depths of a British winter, it was surely understandable that *their* first response should be to ask how this would look – not just for the institution, but for the sake of Meghan herself? Why attract massive press attention and curiosity to her personal plight by 'going somewhere', they would reasonably ask, when the obvious therapeutic resort was right at hand with a loving husband and family and the most sympathetic possible expertise and support in London? Why not try some of that first?

And let us consider one additional possibility – drawn again from Meghan's own words to Oprah – since there was one other senior courtier in 'the institution' to whom Meghan might plausibly have turned on 17 January 2021, if she did not speak to Samantha Cohen.

This was another Samantha, as it happened – Samantha Carruthers, the head of human resources based across town in

Clarence House and St James's Palace – and Meghan's words in her interview would seem to confirm this: 'I went to Human Resources,' she told Oprah, 'and I said, "I just really – I need help". Because in my old job there was a union and they would protect me.'

A couple of days after the interview Meghan's actress friend Janina Gavankar backed up the idea that Meghan went to Carruthers by revealing that Meghan had 'emails and text messages' in her possession to support her version of events. 'The truth will come out,' said Gavankar. 'There are plenty of emails and texts about that.'

This certainly fits with the evidence on the ground. In order to speak to Samantha Cohen, Meghan would have simply needed to walk into Cohen's office on the Kensington campus and sit down for a chat. To contact Samantha Carruthers in the St James's Palace compound some three miles across town, Meghan would first have made contact by texts and emails – and alert readers will have spotted that we have already heard of someone else going from KP to Samantha Carruthers just three months earlier, in October 2018, asking for help with a human resources problem: Jason Knauf, when he filed his complaints about the bullying that his female colleagues had allegedly received at the hands of Meghan.

So are we looking at some sort of stand-off here? That could well be the case. Meghan told Oprah in minute 53 of her interview (transcript page 16) that she got a response from this human resources person as follows: 'My heart goes out to you because I see how bad it is. But there's nothing we can do to protect you, because you are not a paid employee of the institution.'

Where have we heard this before? Turn back to page 336 in Chapter 26, 'End of the Double Act', and you will read of Samantha Carruthers delivering almost exactly the same message to Jason Knauf – namely that the rules of her human resources protocol were designed to support and protect the paid employees of the palace, one against another. The regulations said nothing about what should happen when 'principals' – that is, members of the royal family – got involved.

So Samantha Carruthers was not empowered – she had no remit – to intervene and help protect Amy Pickerill and the other members of Meghan's staff from her alleged bullying. And if Meghan herself now came to human resources asking for help, that was equally outside HR's jurisdiction.

The desirable resort at this stage of our enquiry would obviously be to go and ask Samantha Carruthers what happened – if anything did. But Samantha left Clarence House and St James's Palace as human resources director in August 2019 after more than six years in post, and she is now working at the children's charity Winston's Wish. You can read some tantalising snippets about her on her LinkedIn/Facebook pages, where you can also see her photograph.

Samantha looks very approachable, as an HR director should. But you will not get any information out of her on the subject of Jason Knauf, Meghan Markle or the happenings inside Kensington Palace. On leaving royal employment Samantha Carruthers signed a legally binding non-disclosure agreement to prevent her talking to the likes of this author – rather as the several hundred employees of Harpo have to sign a similar hush agreement on the day they start working for Oprah.

So that leaves us with just one more thought. It is standard procedure in corporate America if someone goes to the HR department to lodge a complaint against you that you should go to the HR department and retaliate by placing some complaint of your own. It is the first thing that Meghan's union would have advised her to do to protect herself – it creates that stand-off we were wondering about. And it also gives a new and mildly menacing meaning to those words of Meghan's friend Gavankar – 'The truth will come out. There are plenty of emails and texts about that.'

So did the Duchess of Sussex text and email human resources because she really needed and wanted to 'go somewhere' in January 2019 – or because she wanted to hit back at the hated institution and lodge a complaint of her own?

And here's just one more question that Oprah could have asked her friend. Jason Knauf and his colleagues had one specific 'principal' inside the palace – HRH the Duchess of Sussex – against whom, rightly or wrongly, they felt that human resources protection was needed. But who or what specifically was there inside the British royal system against which Meghan felt she should be protected in January 2019?

At that date, the American newcomer was under scarcely imaginable stress from the British and overseas press. She was under still more stress from the vicious and racist abuse being directed against her via social media from all over the world. She was five months pregnant. She was missing her friends like Oprah, who were all on the other side of the world – along with her mother, the only relative with whom she remained on speaking terms. She was alienated from her father. We can all understand and sympathise with how she must have felt at that moment.

But what exactly did Meghan expect the Kensington/St James's Palace human resources department to do about all this? When it came to protection, Samantha Carruthers and her HR department had, in fact, done the best they could to make sure that whatever damaging charges Meghan's staff had made against her, their accusations were kept in total confidence and did not find their way to the outside world. Meghan's good name was shielded for two years and five months until March 2021, when Meghan and Harry had announced their intention of 'Telling-All' to Oprah.

At that date the bullying claims were leaked to *The Times* by one or more of the individuals who knew the story and who felt personally aggrieved. They wanted to counteract the impression of injured saintliness that they felt sure that Meghan would project on the screen – and Meghan's PR people were, in this sense, quite correct to describe the leaks as a 'smear campaign' against her.

But the smears had come from aggrieved individuals, not from 'the Palace'. *Times* journalist Valentine Low naturally declined to reveal his sources. The most he would confirm is that the leak was not an officially sanctioned palace briefing. In other words, 'the institution' had done everything in its legal power to extend to Meghan whatever protection it could.

*   *   *

And on that delicate question about Archie's skin colour – well, on that subject, Oprah did do her job quite forensically.

No one who watched that moment in the interview – viewed by some 64 million people around the world – could forget it. Meghan was telling her truth again, after Oprah had asked her 'why they didn't want to make Archie a prince' – thus depriving the baby of both status and security protection, as Meghan and Harry saw it.

'I can give you an honest answer,' replied Meghan. 'In those months when I was pregnant, all around this same time ... We have in tandem the conversation of "He won't be given security. He's not going to be given a title" – and also concerns and conversations about how dark his skin might be when he is born.'

'What?' responded Oprah, in what many viewers considered to be the night's ultimate moment of drama – as Oprah surrendered, apparently, to melodrama, then miraculously recaptured her analytic sense.

'There is a conversation?' Oprah asked. 'Hold on. Hold up. Hold up. Stop right now ... There's a *conversation* with you?'

'With Harry,' admitted Meghan.

Here was the first moment of truth-truth – so let's go over to Oprah now. While sympathising with Meghan's feelings at that particular moment, the interviewer also established quite clearly that what Meghan was saying was not actually true. Meghan had certainly been in the advanced stages of pregnancy sometime early in 2019, and she was apparently scared at that time about the safety of her baby for complicated reasons of royal precedence that we will be examining later. But when questioned by Oprah, Meghan admitted that no one in the royal family had ever asked her personally about the colour of Archie's skin – neither then, when she was pregnant, nor at any time.

This delicate question had not been put to Meghan but to Harry, Oprah established, and when the prince turned up the best part of an hour later and Oprah had the chance to put the question directly to him, he almost shrugged his shoulders.

OPRAH: 'Meghan shared with us that there was a
   conversation with you about Archie's skin tone.'
HARRY: 'Mm-hmm.'
OPRAH: 'What was that conversation?'
HARRY: 'That conversation I'm never going to share. But at
   the time ...'

Oprah pushed him further – 'Can you tell us what the question was?'

Once again Harry prevaricated, but finally he admitted: 'That was right at the beginning ... Right at the beginning.'

The skin colour conversation, as Harry described it, had actually taken place before the couple had even got engaged, at quite an early stage of their relationship – and it had been in general terms. The question had not been asked specifically about Archie, but about any babies that Harry and Meghan might possibly produce.

'Yeah,' said Harry, repeating the question that some unnamed person had put to him – 'What will the kids look like?'

'What will the *kids* look like?' repeated Oprah, emphasising the plural, and the striking difference between Meghan's reporting of an Archie-based conversation and what Harry was now telling her.

'That was right at the beginning,' repeated Harry, 'when she wasn't going to get security, when members of my family were suggesting that she carries on acting.'

Meghan announced that she would be giving up acting at the time of her engagement to Harry on 27 November 2017. So the conversation about the possible darkness of her children's skin had happened before she ever got married – and a full year before she was pregnant.

Once again, the controversial Duchess of Sussex had told the world *her* truth, and on this occasion, Oprah had quite clearly demonstrated – with Harry's help – that what Meghan said had somehow emerged from her imagination. Nobody had had 'conversations' with Meghan while she was pregnant about Archie, nor asked her 'how dark his skin might be when he is born'.

She made that up – though that is not to say that it did not matter.

In the days following the screening of this sensational sequence in Britain, some interracial couples insisted it was not a matter of racism but simple curiosity to ponder the possible features of a mixed-race baby – the 'quality of hair, shape of the nose, hue of skin,' wrote black politician and broadcaster Trevor Phillips. 'In mixed families the range of possibilities can be gloriously infinite.'

Phillips got passionate about the non-racist essence of such discussions. 'I am a black divorcé in a mixed-race marriage,' he wrote. 'Like Harry, I have fathered two mixed-race children. Their mother is herself of mixed heritage. One daughter has recently given birth to my first grandson, a gorgeous melange of genes from four different continents, whose skin colouring may not be a million shades off Archie's.'

On the evidence presented so far, declared Phillips, a committed and thoroughly 'woke' campaigner for diversity of every sort, 'the royal family looks no more or less prejudiced than any other family in multi-racial Britain'.

In other conversations, one interracial parent reported how black grandmothers would frequently ask the skin-colour question in order to work out what shade of baby clothes they should knit for their mixed-race grandchild. It would be 'weird', they said, if this perfectly natural question was not asked and addressed.

The problem lay in Meghan's having linked the question of her son's skin tone to the question of his royal status. Had racism played a role in whether Archie was or was not a royal prince?

At the time of Archie's birth in May 2019 both Harry and Meghan had been refreshingly dismissive about royal status. They had decided, explained author Omid Scobie, 'to forego a title for their son, because they wanted him to be a private citizen until he was at an age where he could decide which path he would like to take'.

But by the time the couple were talking to Oprah in 2021, their thinking appeared to have changed. 'There's a convention,'

Meghan explained to Oprah. 'I forget if it was the George V or George VI convention – that when you're the grandchild of the monarch ... automatically Archie and our next baby would become prince or princess.'

Archie was not a prince at present, in other words. But he would become a prince – a full HRH – the moment that his grandfather Charles became king. The convention went back to 1917 when King George V (reigned 1910–36), the founder of the House of Windsor, was formalising the rules for his newly created 'representative' monarchy. The old king (grandson of Queen Victoria and grandfather of Queen Elizabeth II) was trying to limit the hitherto traditional profusion of princes and princesses.

Meghan insisted that 'all the grandeur surrounding this stuff' did not matter a jot to her. 'I've been a waitress, an actress, a princess, a duchess,' she told Oprah. 'I've always just still been Meghan, right?'

But the American duchess seemed to have acquired quite a concern about the grandeur 'stuff'. In pursuing his own cause of the slimmed-down monarchy, Prince Charles had been making noises about limiting the number of HRHs created by George V's 1917 convention still further, thus cutting out Archie from his future prince-ship – and Meghan took that personally. Declining to accept that this might be for reasons of modernisation or to save money, she came to believe it was because of the colour of Archie's skin – and she explained to Oprah why this worried her. It was partly a matter of Archie's title and status, but it was also because of 'the safety and [physical] protection' that went with Archie being called a prince.

It seems likely that Meghan's thinking had been affected by her early months living in the Kensington Palace compound in a veritable rookery of the Queen's cousins and their spouses – the Dukes and Duchesses of Gloucester and Kent and Princess Alexandra of Kent – who were all royal highnesses under the 1917 convention by virtue of being children of King George V's sons. These 'junior royals', as they were sometimes called, enjoyed such royal perks as KP's prestigious, if sometimes cramped, historic palace apartments, along with enjoyment of the communal courtyards and gardens.

Going to visit Kensington Palace today is rather like trying to gain admission to a high-security country club, where the guards at the gate will not admit you without an appointment, then check your credentials very thoroughly. Inside there is a cosy communal atmosphere in the shared royal facilities – most of the people you will see strolling round are royals or their flunkies – along with all the neighbourly rivalries that one might expect in such a high-status confraternity. Princess Diana, for example, liked to enjoy temporarily 'kidnapping' Princess Michael of Kent's microchipped Burmese cats.

Those Kents and Gloucesters in the palace complex who choose to carry out royal work also receive a financial subsidy from the Queen – in return for which some of them choose to work quite hard. In 2018 the little-known HRH Prince Richard of Gloucester, seventy-six and a cousin of the Queen, was rated the tenth-hardest-working royal in the whole of Europe on the basis of his 193 charitable engagements – more than were carried out in that year by Sophie Wessex (166), Prince William (150), or Camilla (149). To be a low-profile working Windsor prince of this sort is a worthy and not disagreeable way of life – with police-protected palace accommodation thrown in.

Harry and Meghan seem to have viewed this profusion of HRH-titled relatives as an option that Archie might choose to go for at some time in the future if he was so inclined. It was certainly the model of what they thought they might negotiate for themselves when they had first thought of stepping back – but were not, in the early stages, planning to go abroad or remove themselves entirely from the full-time grind of working royal life.

'It's not reinventing the wheel,' Meghan said to Oprah, clearly aggrieved that it had not proved possible to modify and extend this relatively pleasant KP pattern of public service to their own decision to live abroad. She and Harry were particularly focused on the question of security and 'protection' – a word that, with 'protect', came up no fewer than nineteen times in the course of their conversation with Oprah.

The problem is that royal protection – the twenty-four-hour attendance of London's Metropolitan Police – is paid for by the British taxpayer, and it is not related to royal inheritance or title. It is strictly a matter of royal *work*. If you are carrying out royal duties at the Queen's request, the British taxpayers will pay for your protection. If you are not carrying out such duties, they will not – and they will certainly not pay to protect you or your children if you choose to go and live in Canada or California, whether your son Archie is a prince or not.

Harry appeared to have some difficulty grasping this. 'I never thought that I would have my security removed,' he confessed to Oprah, 'because I was born into this position. I inherited the risk.'

It was a fair point. HRH Prince Harry Mountbatten-Windsor was just as much a target for intrusive paparazzi and potentially dangerous cranks or even terrorists on the day after he stopped work as he had been on the day before. But that payroll choice, as his grandmother had spent his first year of exile trying to make clear to him, was the very essence of the option he had chosen – the difference between being 'In' and being 'Out'.

Meghan seemed to suffer from the same confusion when it came to Archie – no title, no security – and in this context, of course, it seemed to her particularly unfair, and even life-threatening, that Archie's title and status should apparently be a matter of his skin colour.

Oprah's precise questioning – and Harry's evasive answering – about when and how the poisonous issue of race entered this complicated equation made clear that while somebody's query about the possible skin colour of any Sussex offspring might have been offensive, it had not affected Archie's princely status.

Prince Charles's decision that he might alter the 1917 convention about his HRH grandchildren, however, did have a bearing on the situation.

In *Finding Freedom*, authors Omid Scobie and Carolyn Durand described the concerns that Harry and Meghan raised with Prince Charles at the time of Archie's birth as to whether their children 'could inherit the titles of prince or princess' – and Charles seems to have shared with them the plans he was nursing for changing the rules. For Archie to be saddled with an elevated HRH title could be 'just a burden', explained one senior aide who was close to the couple. Princess Anne's children did not carry the 'handle', and Prince Edward had decided that his children would be better off without it.

This proposed abolition of Archie's HRH was all part of Charles's mildly obsessive desire to create a slimmed-down monarchy. The prince had been pursuing the cause since the Way Ahead group meetings of the 1990s, and perhaps he took it so seriously because it was the disaster of his own marriage that had made the Way Ahead group necessary.

Charles's moment of triumph had come in 2012 when, in the absence, owing to illness, of his father Prince Philip who enjoyed the company of his royal relatives, the Prince of Wales had managed to clear all the Kents and Gloucesters, along with Princess Alexandra, off that Diamond Jubilee balcony.

But to what effect? Many royal fans said they rather enjoyed seeing all those uncles and cousins and aunts – and especially the children – lined up and waving cheerily along the balcony. It was such fun to work out who was who. And who wanted to look at no one but Charles and Camilla? The Duchess of Cornwall should be kept hidden away among the cousins!

Charles had opposed his nieces Beatrice and Eugenie becoming prominent figures in the working royal family – to the considerable annoyance of their father Prince Andrew, though it was now obvious that these two lively and intelligent young women (great friends of both William and Harry) could have played quite useful public roles in the post-split, Sussex-deprived, royal family. And now the future King Charles III was, apparently, set on eliminating Harry and Meghan's two children from full HRH prince and princess status for reasons of what – economy and modernisation?

It was surely a false economy. And how 'modern' was it to deny full HRH status to the only members of the British royal family who, with their mother Meghan, were of mixed race? By the time King Charles III ascends to the throne it seems likely that he will have just five grandchildren – George, Charlotte, Louis, Archie and the eagerly awaited female baby Sussex. In 2012 the Queen changed the rules of the 1917 convention by new Letters Patent extending HRH status to all William's children – and not just to George, who received his HRH automatically since he was in direct line of succession.

So at the time of the Oprah interview in March 2021, Charles already had three HRH grandchildren, but seemed ready to change the rules himself in order to deny HRH status to his two mixed-race grandchildren by Harry and Meghan.

No wonder Meghan cried foul, and Oprah cried 'What?' The failure of imagination and empathy was staggering. And if most of the world chose to call that decision 'racist', you really could not blame them.

38

Living In Her Shoes

'It doesn't take very long to suddenly
become aware of it.'

(Prince Harry, March 2021)

The most hurtful in the roster of sharply honed accusations that Meghan and Harry levelled against his family to Oprah Winfrey in their interview of 7 March 2021 came when Oprah asked Harry – 'Your relationship with your father? Is he taking your calls now?'

Harry had earlier revealed that he had had no fewer than three direct conversations with his grandmother the Queen during the lead-up to the Sandringham Summit confrontation of January 2020, but had spoken just twice with his father – 'before he stopped taking my calls'.

Prince Charles had asked him, Harry explained, 'Can you put this all in writing?'

OPRAH: 'Your father asked you to put it *in writing*? ... Why did he stop taking your calls?'

Through the course of the interview, Harry had often mumbled when confronted by Oprah's direct questioning, but on this occasion he shot his answer back straight away: 'Because I took matters ... into my own hands,' he explained. 'It was like "I need to do this for my family ... It's really sad that it's gotten to this point, but I've got to do something for my own mental health, my wife's and for Archie's as well".'

When Oprah asked him later, towards the end of the interview, how things were now going with brother William, Harry answered again without hesitation. He had clearly prepared his conciliatory response – a polished and shortened version of what he had said to Tom Bradby in Africa.

'You know,' he replied, 'as I've said before, I love William to bits. He's my brother. We've been through hell together. I mean, we have a shared experience. But ... we're on different paths.'

When it came to father Charles, however, Harry was definitely *not* extending the hand of friendship.

'There's a lot to work through there,' he said to Oprah – then he paused.

At this point, Harry could quite easily have slipped sideways into compromise or conciliation, as he had on the subject of William. But this was a different Harry. The younger son's jaw seemed to stiffen, and he spat out his critique quite deliberately

– 'I feel really let down,' he said. 'Because he's been through something similar.'

What was the 'something similar' that Charles had suffered? Having to endure the slings and arrows of family disapproval for staying true to a woman he loved but who did not fit neatly into the royal system?

'He knows what pain feels like,' Harry continued – and then he reverted to his grievance over the possible removal of Archie's future HRH status.

'Archie's his grandson!' he complained – still bemused, evidently, that Charles could even contemplate depriving the boy of his royal birthright.

The media explanation of why Charles had stopped taking Harry's calls was all about money – the long-suffering father was apparently tired of being 'treated like a cash dispenser', as one royal source put it. But there were more profound issues at stake.

'There's a lot of hurt that's happened,' said Harry, before turning to talk about his family as a whole. 'They only know what they know …' he said sadly – and a tad patronisingly. 'I've tried to educate them through the process that I have been educated.'

Harry's 'process' of education had been his new life with Meghan, and with all the zeal of a convert he was referring to the concept of 'unconscious bias'. This was a transformational idea that had come to consume him since he had started trying to experience life through the eyes of his mixed-race girlfriend.

'If you go up to someone,' he had explained to the anthropologist Jane Goodall in May 2019, 'and say, "What you've just said,

'If it's Harry … I'm in a meeting.'
Kipper Williams, *Spectator*, 11 March 2021

or the way that you've behaved, is racist" – they'll turn around and say, "I'm not a racist".'

Harry had clearly encountered this sort of reaction from his family – and from his father in particular.

'Your unconscious bias,' he explained to Goodall, is 'because of the way that you've been brought up, the environment you've been brought up in … That you have this point of view – unconscious point of view – when naturally you will look at someone in a different way.'

Harry was talking about racism.

'My God,' he said to Oprah, 'it doesn't take very long to suddenly become aware of it.'

OPRAH: 'Until you met Meghan?'

HARRY: 'Yeah. You know, as sad as it is to say, it takes living in her shoes …'

'Living in her shoes' was an expression that Harry had taken to using quite often since his wedding to explain how the racism directed at his wife had profoundly changed his own view of the world. It had also changed his view of his family, since they had treated Meghan, in his opinion, with the 'unconscious bias' that he had come to see everywhere.

When his family judged his wife to be 'pushy', 'attention-seeking' or forever concerned with her PR image, they might feel they were delivering a verdict they would pass on any Hollywood-cultivated celebrity, irrespective of their sex or colour. But Harry was convinced that their critique of Meghan was influenced by her race. The concepts of 'racism' and 'unconscious bias' had infected the brothers' bitter argument and decisive rift of October 2018 that had led to the division of their households – and those poisonous concepts had hung in the air ever since.

Here was the crux of the matter – the reason why the Oprah interview of March 2021 raised far deeper and more painful issues than run-of-the-mill family grievance. But if Harry and Meghan chose to accuse his family of such weighty prejudice, they in turn could charge Harry, and Meghan in particular, with what William had described as Meghan's 'agenda' – leading to William's separation from his brother.

Meghan saw slights being aimed at her from every direction. She had a propensity to feel victimised that was perplexing in a personality that in some ways was so strong. Worst of all, there was the way in which her tendency to self-pity seemed to have distorted Harry's hitherto cheery world view.

In the couple's Southern Africa interviews with Tom Bradby in October 2019, Meghan had been the only 'Poor Me' – 'Thanks for asking … Not many people have!' Sixteen months later with Oprah, the couple were 'Poor-Me'-ing together in their jointly proclaimed victimhood. With their timely glances and nods and hand-pattings, it was extraordinary to see the personal dynamic – the happy captivity – displayed so vividly onscreen.

William could no longer recognise this chip-on-the-shoulder, always-seeking-a-grievance Harry. The process of walking in his wife's shoes had somehow caged his younger brother in a subversive ideology. Harry told Oprah he considered his father and brother to be 'trapped'. Well, what about Harry himself?

The only sequence in the Oprah interview that was filmed in the Sussexes' own home had been in their chicken coop, where they 'cluck-clucked' among the hens they had rescued from a factory farm.

'Well, you know,' said Meghan, 'I just love rescuing.'

Harry had clearly become his wife's own rescue chicken. He talked about walking in her shoes, but the problem lay at the other end of his lanky frame – he had become brainwashed.

'Harry had a heart bigger than a house, God bless him, but he was always a bit of a slow learner,' recalls his mother's close friend Simone Simmons. 'The army gave him the structure he so desperately needed in his life after the death of his mother. They

Ben Coppin, March 2021

gave him the orders that he could follow and obey without thought – and now Meghan is giving him the orders.'

'Rejection sensitivity' was the term a psychologist might apply to Harry and Meghan's shared readiness to seek and take offence. The syndrome's more positive side often includes highly developed people-pleasing skills, coupled with a paradoxical tendency, when thwarted, to resort to aggressive, and even bullying, behaviour.

These were the personal issues raised by the interview. And then there was the wider dimension – how did the outside world view the confrontation? Oprah's magnificently staged TV production had engrossed huge audiences in both Britain and America, but to judge from the differing reactions on opposite sides of the Atlantic, those audiences had been tuned into two totally different shows.

Popular British reaction was virtually unanimous. UK tabloids branded Harry and Meghan as 'selfish' and 'nauseating' in their litany of complaints, deploring the harm and pain that they had caused the Queen by reducing the thousand-year-old institution of monarchy to 'celebrity talk show fodder'.

Disapproval centred particularly on Harry's 'shocking yet woolly claim', as Michael Deacon described it in the *Telegraph*, that someone in the royal family had said 'something that might be construed as racist'. By only exempting the Queen and Prince Philip, Harry had brought suspicion on every single member of the family.

'The whole world,' wrote Deacon, 'will [now] be playing a game of "Who's the Royal Racist?" like some hideous twenty-first-century version of Cluedo.'

'I was disgusted with them,' said Pauline Farren, fifty, an interviewee on NBC News. 'It was extremely classless to air their dirty linen in public after all the royal family has done for them … I dislike Meghan intensely and I feel sorry for Harry.'

This view was reflected in the UK opinion polls. Meghan was already deep in negative territory so far as most Britons were concerned – with a YouGov rating of minus 14. The interview took her down to minus 27 – with Harry going negative for the first time ever. 48 per cent of Britons now took an adverse view of the prince – a massive drop of fifteen points in his popularity since the start of the month.

America could hardly have reacted more differently.

'The first thought I had, watching Meghan Markle, was that she was so genuine,' said Chris Pluto, forty-four, a Pittsburgh line cook, to NBC. 'I was immediately struck by her clarity, and that she was telling the absolute truth about her experiences.'

Pluto praised Meghan for the 'courage' with which she spoke about her mental health. 'That made me cry,' he said. 'I felt that experience.'

This reaction was echoed by US celebrities. Former First Lady Michelle Obama and singer Beyoncé both applauded Meghan for speaking so openly about race and mental health – and White House press secretary Jen Psaki made clear that President Joe Biden felt the same.

'For anyone to come forward and speak about their own struggles with mental health and tell their own personal story – that takes courage,' Psaki told reporters. 'That's certainly something the president believes.'

Feelings went further for some Americans. There were calls on social media to 'finish what the American Revolution started' and to 'burn down' Buckingham Palace and the monarchy. The United States had been built on rebellion against the British crown in 1776 – though you might not guess it from the lines of modern American shoppers gazing at the images of British royals smiling out at them from the celebrity magazines adorning every supermarket checkout.

In the spring of 2018 a mixed-race American woman had stepped forward to enter this fantasy world that appeared to offer such glamour and comfort, and twenty-nine million Americans had got up at dawn that 19 May to share Meghan's dream – only to discover, via Oprah, that it was all, apparently, a poisonous nightmare of stuck-in-the-past elitism shot through with racist condescension.

This was bad for the image of the hitherto sainted monarchy, and it was bad, in an international sense, for Brand Britain as a whole – with the hostility still worse in the Commonwealth. The royal family's rejection of Meghan was 'part of the whole legacy of colonialism,' declared Jamaican professor Carolyn Cooper, in disdainful reference to her country's bond to the British crown. 'It's a disreputable institution. It's responsible for the enslavement of millions of us who came here to work on plantations … We need to get rid of it.'

Barbados had recently jettisoned Elizabeth II as its head of state – if not its membership of the Commonwealth. It was due to become a republic in November 2021, and now other Commonwealth monarchies seemed set to follow. In a TV interview shown across North America Malcolm Turnbull, the former prime minister of Australia, cited the Oprah interview as another reason for Australia to sever its constitutional ties to the British monarchy. There should be no place for an Australian King Charles III.

'After the end of the Queen's reign,' Turnbull told the Australian Broadcasting Corporation, 'that is time for us to say, "OK, we've passed that watershed". Do we really want to have whoever happens to be the head of state – the king or queen of the UK – automatically *our* head of state?'

Canadians took up the same refrain. A poll taken shortly after the interview showed 48 per cent viewing the monarchy as a 'racist institution', with more than half saying they believed the time had come for the royal link to be abandoned.

Jagmeet Singh, leader of the New Democratic Party, said that the British royal family appeared to be systemically racist and 'is in no way beneficial to Canadians in terms of their everyday life'.

In the past Justin Trudeau, forty-nine, the Canadian prime minister, would have fought back stoutly against such criticism. But post-Oprah and Meghan his defence of the monarchy was strangely half-hearted. Many institutions in Canada had been built around colonialism and systemic racism, he agreed, 'but my focus is getting through this pandemic. If people want to talk later about constitutional change and shifting our system of government that's fine, and they can have those conversations.'

Harry and Meghan had gone out to the world on a Sunday night. On Monday morning, 8 March, Buckingham Palace went into crisis mode. The three royal households representing the Queen (BP), Prince Charles (Clarence House/SJP) and Prince William (KP) were locked in discussions that lasted all day. For more than a century, commented royal author Sarah Gristwood, the point of the monarchy had been to represent the best of Britain. Now Meghan and Harry had 'left them looking as though they represent the worst'.

By the end of Monday the combined efforts of the three households had hashed out a statement – a very short statement – and the press was panting at the gates. The media wanted and expected some reaction in time for the evening TV news.

But Elizabeth II – in touch with all the family and palace discussions that day via telephone and video conference from Windsor – decided they could wait. The Queen wanted 'to sleep on it'. And the interview had not yet been seen by most people in Britain, since it was not scheduled to go out on ITV until 9 p.m. that night.

When the four-sentence statement of just sixty-one words was finally released the following afternoon at 5.26 p.m. – nearly forty hours after the Sussexes had first gone on air in the United States – it started in the now traditional way, with an expression of the Queen's personal concern for the feelings of her grandson and his wife: 'The whole family is saddened to learn the full extent of how challenging the last few years have been for Harry and Meghan,' ran sentence one. Sentence four concluded on a similar note: 'Harry, Meghan and Archie will always be much loved family members.'

The meat – sentences two and three – lay in the middle of the sandwich: 'The issues raised, particularly that of race, are concerning. While some recollections may vary, they are taken very seriously and will be addressed by the family privately.'

In the days that followed it became clear that the word 'privately' referred only to the resolution of the specifically family-based disagreements. On 14 March, palace guidance to Roya Nikkhah revealed in the *Sunday Times* that 'independent external investigators' from 'a third-party law firm' were now being brought in to conduct a review of the human resources issues – specifically the bullying allegations lodged by Jason Knauf.

'The actual worst incidences haven't come out,' one source claimed to Nikkhah. 'There are some harrowing stories to tell.'

A week later a leak to Kate Mansey of the *Mail on Sunday* revealed the planned appointment of a 'Palace Diversity Tsar' to handle the racial matters.

'We haven't seen the progress we would like,' admitted a senior royal source, 'and [we] accept more needs to be done. We can always improve.'

Diversity! Diversity! Meghan and Harry had delivered some low blows in talking to Oprah in a thoroughly non-familial fashion, but it was impossible to swat away their essential truth. When Meghan had arrived in Buckingham Palace some three years earlier and had walked down any corridor – or the corridor of any other palace – to enter any office, the face of virtually every senior official whom she encountered had been white.

Across St James's Park the stuffy old Tory government had a non-white chancellor of the exchequer (Rishi Sunak) handling the wealth of the nation, with a non-white home secretary (Priti Patel) handling many other vital aspects of national life – including the police. But Elizabeth II, head of the multiracial Commonwealth, was still running her show with a virtually all-white team.

What had happened to the brave diversity principles established and championed so boldly more than half a century ago by the colour-blind young monarch who had danced in the arms of President Nkrumah of Ghana? In 1961 Elizabeth II's diversity principles had shocked, challenged and inspired the world. Now her palace was the object of worldwide scorn – and even horror.

The monarch who 'never put a foot wrong' had taken a misstep. Elizabeth II might feel she had nothing to prove when it came to accusations of racism, but while she had included Ghanaian-born Lieutenant Colonel Nana Kofi Twumasi-Ankrah as military equerry for a period in her public circle, it was different when it came to her private tribe. She had entrusted the essentials of her reign to the custody of those clubby white father figures who comforted her as her private secretaries over the years – from the grave and grey-suited Tommy Lascelles and Michael Adeane to the giggling and grey-minded Edward Young. None of them have had the vision to shake up the white Anglo-Saxon system inside the palace to reflect the diverse modern world outside. Sir Edward and his blinkered, male upper-class ilk cannot long survive the coming changes in the identity of a modern courtier.

Prince Charles employed black women in senior positions – British-Guyanese Colleen Harris ably advised him, William and Harry on press matters for the best part of twenty years, with British-Nigerian Eva Omaghomi-Williams serving in communications from 2008 until recently. But the prince's mother and her advisers had failed to follow his example, and here were the sad consequences – which she now had to deal with at the very moment she had lost the support of the man on whom she had always relied in moments of difficulty like this.

39

Between Brothers

'Now bid its angry tumult cease,
And give, for wild confusion, peace;
O hear us when we cry to Thee,
For those in peril on the sea.'

('The Sailors' Hymn' – words by William Whiting,
1860. Sung at Prince Philip's funeral, 17 April 2021)

Prince Philip started feeling below par early in February 2021 – though he was not that unwell to judge from outward appearances. The duke might have been ninety-nine years old – with his hundredth birthday only four months away – but he was reported to be in reasonable shape when he headed off on the evening of Tuesday 16 February to King Edward VII's Hospital in central London for a few days of 'observation and rest'. His visit was described as 'a precautionary measure' by a palace source, who reported that the duke had stepped out of the car in Marylebone strong enough to enter the clinic unaided.

'He's OK,' reported his grandson William, a few days later. 'They're keeping an eye on him.'

All that the palace would disclose in the days that followed was that Philip's condition was not related to coronavirus. But after two weeks at King Edward VII's the duke was transferred to St Bartholomew's – 'Barts', the historic specialist and teaching hospital in Smithfield (founded 1123) where William Harvey carried out his pioneering research into the human heart and circulation of the blood in the seventeenth century.

Here Philip spent some time recuperating following what the palace described as 'a successful heart procedure' on 3 March – but matters were starting to look more serious. Harry and Meghan's Oprah interview was scheduled for broadcast on 7 March in the US and 8 March in the UK, and commentators were urging CBS and ITV to postpone their screenings. The broadcasters and the Sussexes ignored the appeals and the programmes went ahead anyway.

Philip was unconcerned, according to his friend and biographer Gyles Brandreth. What did worry him, said Brandreth, was 'the couple's preoccupation with their own problems'.

'I know from someone close to him,' revealed the bestselling author and broadcaster, 'that he thought Meghan and Harry's interview with Oprah Winfrey was "madness" and "no good would come of it".'

Brandreth recalled the prince saying exactly the same to him about the interviews that Charles and Diana had given back in the 1990s.

'Give TV interviews by all means' was the rule the duke shared with all his children – it was part of the royal job in the modern world. But they should never forget that discretion and modesty were integral to being a member of the British royal family – 'Don't talk about yourself.'

Prince Philip died in his sleep at Windsor Castle three weeks and three days after leaving hospital, unable to play any part in his family's response to grandson Harry and his wife's wounding accusations of racism and indifference that had, by Meghan's account, driven her to the brink of suicide.

The Queen had said all that she wished to in her four-sentence reply. Prince Charles could only manage a feeble chuckle in response to a reporter's shouted question: 'What did you think of the interview, Sir?' But Prince William had his own response ready and waiting. 'We are very much *not* a racist family,' William declared – speaking out clearly and firmly to a group of reporters through his face mask, with all the anger of a man whose brother had linked him to those lethal code words 'unconscious bias'. It was very obvious who was going to be the family's next Prince Philip.

When it came to the funeral the following weekend, William and his grandmother worked out together how, in all the circumstances, he could not possibly walk in harmony with Harry behind his grandfather's coffin in the way that he might have done in the past. Aged ninety-four, Elizabeth II was coping with her bereavement by personally supervising every detail of her husband's farewell – complicated as it was by the COVID requirement that there be no more than thirty mourners in the chapel.

The device of recruiting cousin Peter Phillips, Princess Anne's beefy son, to serve as a diplomatic buffer between the two brothers had been deployed before – two years earlier at the Easter Sunday service at Windsor in April 2019. William and Harry had just gone public with the news that they were splitting their combined households, and that very month the Sussexes were in the process of moving from Kensington to Frogmore Cottage. These were all perfectly normal developments, according to Jason Knauf and the other palace spin doctors at the time – the routine consequence of Harry and Meghan expanding their family and their official interests. It was nothing to get excited about.

But sharp-eyed observers suspected otherwise as they studied the family dynamic that Easter Sunday in 2019 – six months, as we now know, after the cataclysmic confrontation of October 2018. Harry had turned up at St George's Chapel on his own, leaving Meghan heavily pregnant in Frogmore – Archie would be arriving only three weeks later – and as the prince selected his place in the line of grandchildren greeting the Queen on her way into the chapel, it was noted how he had not taken his normal spot at the head of the line beside William and Kate. Harry had opted for a more lowly position of precedence, insulated from the Cambridges by Princess Anne's children and their spouses.

'They almost look like strangers,' reported body language expert Judi James to the *Mail Online* – noting this previously unseen physical distance between William and Harry and the mysterious failure of the brothers to look at each other or even to exchange a word of greeting. Harry, she said, actually seemed 'desperate to avoid' his brother William.

Judi James had been a pioneer in the interpretation of the royal family's private emotions through their public gestures, facial tics and body movements. But two years later, at the 2021 funeral of Prince Philip, she was jostled by an entire new crew of binocular-wielding competitors. The rift between William and Harry had stimulated a veritable cottage industry of lip-readers and body language analysts.

Prominent among these was 'Believing Bruce', a guru who delivered his thoughts via the *Daily Mirror* and who noted how both William and Harry had faced up to each other displaying what he called the 'regal stance'.

'This is where our front (ventral area) is actually exposed,' explained Bruce. 'But the arms are clasped behind our back as opposed to hanging loosely. This is a display that screams "I am here – but please keep your distance!"'

Looking at Kate as she stared across at Harry during the course of the service, Bruce was sure she was radiating 'a mother's need to care for him'. Catching her gaze, Harry looked away and upwards. This 'relieves pressure in the thoracic region,' explained Bruce, 'and opens up the airways to oxygenate the system'.

Buckingham Palace was dismissive of reading messages into anything – and certainly not the question of who was marching beside whom. Some pointed out how Peter Phillips (born 1977) was by far the duke's eldest grandson, so it was only correct for him to be right in the centre with his cousins on either side. The processional order, said Buckingham Palace, was 'a practical change rather than sending a signal … This is a funeral and we are not going to be drawn into perceptions of drama.'

No one needed to be a body language expert to read the way in which the Queen, hunched and sitting on her own beside the altar at the end of a very long wooden pew, presented the most poignant sight of all.

Philip had been Elizabeth II's 'strength and stay' – her 'rock', as she had put it on one of the rare occasions he had allowed her to get soppy in public about their seventy-three years of love and mutual reinforcement. Philip had also been her ideas man – the source of the surprising amount of original thinking that had brought distinctive character to the second Elizabethan age.

Right in the early years, even as he was battling the formidable combination of Tommy Lascelles and Winston Churchill to secure due credit for his Mountbatten surname, Philip had come up with the concept of the Duke of Edinburgh's 'Award Scheme'.

Marian Kamensky, 16 April 2021

In the tradition of the Duke of York's camps founded by his father-in-law George VI, the programme extended to disadvantaged and working-class youth the fortifying experience of hearty expeditions and challenges in the great outdoors – climbing mountains, pitching tents, braving thunderstorms – from which Philip felt he had learned so much among his privileged companions at Gordonstoun.

By 2021 some eight million young people in 140 countries around the world had profited from the DofE programme which, apart from its inherent achievements, said two important things about its founder. The scheme was actually the agent of quite dramatic empowerment and social change – just the sort of thing that a government should have come up with. It was a remarkable example of what an old-fashioned institution like the monarchy could achieve in modern times. And, while it did carry the duke's name, it had never served as a vehicle for his personal glory.

Modesty had come to be a paradoxical characteristic of this often brash and extrovert man's man who, when the time came, had surrendered his naval career to devote his life to coaxing his shy wife into directions she would not otherwise have dreamed of going. And while Philip had not achieved great success administering the Gordonstoun medicine to his eldest son – his parenting of the future monarch was significantly less than a triumph – he had played a more redemptive role in the lives of William and Harry.

It was Philip who had persuaded the boys to walk behind their mother's coffin in 1997, with that touching gesture while marching under the Horse Guards Arch, where he thought there were no cameras and had placed a reassuring hand on William's shoulder. He had taught the young 'Killer Wales' their country crafts, from pheasant slaughter to how to flip a steak on the open grill.

And then again it was Grandpa who came up with the notion of those Windsor Sunday lunches that had coached William so brilliantly for his future royal role, while also connecting Harry more closely to his grandmother – the crucial personal link, as it proved, that had prevented this latest year of rift becoming a disaster of total alienation.

Philip's particular role in his wife's lunches with William had been to vanish quietly when the conversation moved to constitutional matters. This was to make the point that the duke, as consort, left that sacred and central element strictly to those who were consecrated for it, and that he would concentrate on his multitude of other responsibilities. One of the problems provoked by Philip's death was that no single successor or even group of successors could possibly take over the 837 military, social and charitable positions that he had held in the course of his life.

At the start of the reign, for example, the duke had taken over the chairmanship of the local Windsor Rugby Club from King George VI, finding time most years, amid all his other commitments, to visit the club to attend its annual dinner – or, at the least, to share a few beers and hand out the trophies to that year's award winners.

'He would arrive on time without fail and without any publicity,' recalled longstanding club stalwart James Noakes. 'There were no press releases – and he was always wearing the club tie and the club cufflinks.' One year another member asked if, as a favour, he could be introduced to the duke so that he could shake his hand – and after Prince Philip had safely left the clubhouse, this member proudly and loudly proclaimed his own scabrous rugby club version of royalism.

He'd handled the hand that had handled the Queen, he exclaimed to general cheering – though his actual words were more physically graphic than that. As obituary tributes went, it could never have been published in the average family newspaper – but it did, perhaps, provide a subconscious explanation of why so many of the paper's readers might find the duke an object of fascination.

It was a moving service that Saturday 17 April 2021, rendered the more mournful and tender by the pandemic restrictions – the spare and spaced congregation, the black masks that so conveniently kept private emotions private, the lack of fancy military uniforms (a matter of COVID tone, not family politics), and the purity and simplicity of the sound from the four-person choir echoing in the empty chancel where on normal occasions some eight hundred would be assembled. The duke had personally chosen every detail of his farewell, the commentators kept repeating. So it was difficult not to well up at the sound of the bugle trumpeting out the Last Post, and the mourners praying 'for those in peril on the sea'.

'Throw my coffin in the back of a Land Rover,' the duke had said, apparently. So that is what they did – in a Land Rover that he had, of course, modified to his own specifications. And he had insisted that he wanted no personal tributes or address during the service – no eulogy of lifetime achievements. That modesty again.

As Prince Charles emerged afterwards into the bright afternoon sunlight he stripped his face mask from his ears. The prince had clearly been crying, but he had the presence of mind to dismiss the waiting funeral cars with a wave of his hand – leading to a finale that no one had expected. Instead of driving up the hill to the castle in the wake of the Queen who left first in her limousine, the rest of the family blinked and straggled out into the fresh air, talking to each other mask-less – and once again the lip-readers came into their element.

'Yes, it was great, wasn't it?' remarked William to Harry as if the pair of them had been talking quite naturally and had not been at no-speaks, daggers-drawn for the past year.

'It was as he wanted,' Harry apparently replied in the same spirit.

'Absolutely beautiful service, ah, the music!' said William, according to yet another body language analyst, Adrianne Carter – who described how the brothers seemed to be moving together as naturally as they used to in the days before Meghan.

'Kate seemed to take the lead in chatting,' said Carter, remarking on how 'at ease' the trio seemed as they moved off informally up the hill. 'When the brothers started to walk together it was entirely natural with no sign of stress or discord in their companionship. There was no forced show and no sign of avoiding each other.'

Every TV viewer around the world noted what seemed to be a touching reunion between the two brothers after the funeral. The sight of their brief but relaxed conversation raised the spirits, and many noted how discreetly Kate, having got the pair of them talking, moved off sideways to leave them together – 'Perfect Queen material!' remarked one royal correspondent approvingly.

The apparent reunion inspired one British newspaper to claim hopefully that the brotherly encounter had led to a two-hour family conference or 'mini-summit' of reconciliation – but this was firmly denied by both sides. William and Kate told friends they could see no point in talking to Harry, since any discussion of substance would go straight back to Meghan to be leaked out via Oprah, Gayle King or some other tentacle of the Sussex network that had not stopped spreading stories in the weeks since the interview that they had sworn would be their final word. So William and Kate said goodbye to Charles, who headed to Wales where he had been mourning at his Llandovery estate, then went back to KP together to put the children to bed.

Harry, for his part, proudly showed around snaps of Archie on his mobile phone, then let it be known via the ever helpful Omid Scobie that he had seen the Queen twice before he got back on the plane to California on Monday. His grandmother liked to walk her dogs in the grounds of Frogmore House, so it seemed likely that he had joined her there. Oh, to be a corgi and listen in to what the Mistress had to say to the Young Master!

Family anger ran deep. It was not by accident that neither Anne nor Sophie had exchanged a word with Harry in the course of the afternoon. People felt incensed by what they saw as the calculated and focused cruelty of the TV interview and by the hypocrisy of Meghan – relating so brightly to Oprah how she had phoned the

Queen to show her concern about Philip's condition without even considering, apparently, the impact that their televised catalogue of grievance might have upon the invalid's morale and health.

And then came the episode of the wreath.

'Go forth upon thy journey from this world, O Christian soul, in the name of God the Father Almighty who created thee ...'

The Dean of Windsor was just addressing the final commendation to the congregation in the chapel when journalists' phones started to 'ping'. Timed at 15.39 BST (British Summer Time), just before the end of the funeral service, it was another tweet from Omid Scobie passing on *Harper's Bazaar*'s 15.35 report on the 'sentimental tribute' from the Duke and Duchess of Sussex 'to the late Prince Philip at his funeral today'.

'BAZAAR.com can confirm that Prince Harry and Duchess Meghan [*sic*] contributed a custom wreath that was laid in honor of the Duke of Edinburgh at his funeral service at Windsor Castle today. A card, handwritten by Meghan herself, also accompanied the wreath.'

The Sussexes' wreath could be seen at that moment leaning among the other eight simple white and green family tributes in St George's Chapel propped against the stalls on either side of the duke's coffin, and it had already attracted some attention on account of its unconventional and rather autumnal pink-ish-brown flowers.

'It looks like the sort of party wreath you might put on your front door around Thanksgiving time,' commented one American observer. 'It's not really a funeral wreath at all.'

The detailed Sussex press release explained why this was so. Harry and Meghan had, apparently, invited their favourite Cotswold florist to handpick locally sourced flowers – *Acanthus mollis* (bear's breeches), the national flower of Greece, to represent the prince's birthplace, together with *Eryngium* (sea holly) recognising his connection with the Royal Marines. 'The wreath also features campanula for gratitude and everlasting love, rosemary to signify remembrance, lavender for devotion and roses in honour of June being Philip's birth month.'

There had been no press release about any of the other family tributes. They were all 'private', explained Buckingham Palace aides, declining to provide any details. Only the Queen's funeral wreath had been a matter of some restrained disclosure – 'white blooms including lilies, roses, freesia and sweet peas'. These had all been chosen personally by the Queen to be placed on top of her husband's coffin, together with a concealed handwritten card that was thought to bear the childhood name by which he fondly called her – 'Lilibet'.

But when it came to Meghan and Harry's wreath there was still more data to absorb. In case you might want to commission a wreath like this for yourself, the details were provided of Willow Crossley, the florist 'that the Sussexes had turned to time and time again for special occasions,' enthused *Harper's Bazaar*, including the couple's May 2018 wedding reception and Archie's christening the following year. The talented Willow had her own website, www.willowcrossley.com, where you could view her rural designs, and you could discover still more about her through IP Publicity – 'Rooted in our DNA is a deep understanding of reputation management to ensure our clients are always at the top of their respective fields.'

So even Meghan's flower arranger had her own PR agency! Social media could hardly believe it. 'Do you feel you got enough recognition for your wreath now, Meghan?' asked one Twitter user sarcastically. 'Did your PR work how you wanted?'

'Just when I didn't think she could get lower,' tweeted another. 'The flowers are private, between you and the deceased.'

There were a few diehard Meghan supporters who came to her defence. 'If it had transpired that Meghan had NOT sent a wreath,' asked one, 'what would you say then?' But most fell silent.

'She just can't help herself' was a response that seemed to speak for many. 'Me. Me. Me. It's quite sickening.'

Wreaths aside, there were two powerful memories that most viewers took away from the funeral of Prince Philip, Duke of Edinburgh, at Windsor Castle on 17 April 2021.

The first was of that final commendation farewell, when the duke's coffin, draped in his personal standard and bearing his naval sword and cap, started its slow and oh-so-mortal descent into the vault beneath the chapel. Television was allowed only a brief glimpse of this solemn moment, just a second or so, and commentators did not dwell on the sad reason why – because this would *not* be the duke's final resting place.

The prince's coffin was due to stay lying there in the Windsor crypt until the Queen herself passed away, when her husband's remains would be transferred to share her own resting place in

Westminster Abbey, at Balmoral – or most likely, in the opinion of insiders, alongside her father and the Queen Mother and the ashes of Princess Margaret in the King George VI Memorial Chapel, inside St George's Chapel itself. With the family – for eternity.

The final destination remains Queen Elizabeth II's own decision – and in the meantime, her husband, ever dutiful, lies there in Windsor awaiting the summons to join her. RIP, oh Master of the Royal Barbecue …

The second more joyful memory was that sight of the two brothers walking together across the courtyard after their grandfather's funeral chatting to each other with apparent animation – and even smiling, were they? – as if their now open and processionally proclaimed rift had never been.

'It's often said that funerals are a time for reconciliation,' remarked Tom Bradby, who was running the ITN commentary that afternoon – 'and that is a scene that a lot of people wanted to see.'

But can we realistically hope to see any more of those chats, and even smiles between the brothers? Will the bitter rift end? Will reconciliation – *can* reconciliation – truly come to pass?

Let's take just one more chapter to consider the chances of all that.

40
The Deal

'It is always inspiring to be reminded of the diversity of people and countries that make up our worldwide family.'

(Queen Elizabeth II, Commonwealth Day Message, March 2020)

As this book went to press in May 2021, Britain's royal watchers were looking towards Thursday 1 July, eight weeks hence. That was the date when the Princes William and Harry had promised to join together, if they could, in front of the statue that they had jointly commissioned in honour of their mother Diana who made them swear, when they were boys, that they would always stick together.

'You must promise me that you will *always* be each other's best friends,' Diana told them, according to Simone Simmons. 'And *never* let anyone come between you.'

Both boys promised they would keep to that, Simmons remembers. They high-fived each other and gave their mother a big cuddle.

'Anybody would have melted at the sight,' recalls Simmons. 'Then they went out to play soccer.'

The first of July was chosen since it was the sixtieth anniversary of Diana's birth.

We had known the name of the statue's sculptor, Ian Rank-Broadley, for some time and the world was expecting a fairly safe and representational piece of work – even old-fashioned, perhaps. Nothing to frighten the horses. Ian crafted the effigy of Queen Elizabeth II that has been appearing on UK coins since 1998 – a stirring image, but definitely conventional.

Maybe Ian had a surprise in store? At the time of writing both boys had given their thumbs up to the design for what would clearly become an object of pilgrimage for visitors from around the world – and certainly a positive boost to Brand Britain. Reconciliation or rift? Either way, it would do no harm to the UK's post-COVID tourist figures.

The location of the statue was perfect – inside the White Garden, formerly known as the Sunken Garden, in the grounds of Kensington Palace where William, Kate, Meghan and Harry were all living in relative harmony until the brothers' disastrous confrontation over those bullying accusations of October 2018.

So that raised the question of who was likely to be attending the unveiling ceremony? The scheduled birth of Archie's sister, Baby Sussex 2, was due sometime in those summer months. So once again maternal responsibilities would provide Meghan with an alibi for non-attendance – as she had at the time of Prince Philip's funeral.

Sighs of relief all round! Not that physical absence was likely to prevent the dynamic duchess from being 'virtually' present at the occasion in one way or another. Harry loves comparing his wife to Diana, and that 'Little Light' of Meghan's would be certain to find some way to make itself shine on 1 July.

We could imagine that Kate would almost certainly be there at William's side, hopefully building the bridge between the brothers that she started to construct so cleverly while crossing the courtyard after the Duke of Edinburgh's funeral in Windsor. Would George and the other little Cambridges also be there to pay tribute to the glamorous granny they never knew but whose genes bubble around inside them in ways that we have still to witness?

Might Prince Charles be invited to join this homage to the wife that he treated with such disdain? And what about his current wife and Princess Consort-to-be, Camilla – the Cruella de Vil of *The Crown*'s Season 4? An early July trip abroad for the sunshine seemed called for.

All this is totally im-pure speculation, of course – and from a departed and vanishing point in time. As you, dear reader, are scanning these pages sometime after 1 July 2021, you are doubtless laughing your head off at these fruitless imaginings.

'Get on with it!' you will say – knowing, as you do, all about who was there, what the statue looks like in the beautiful White Garden with its meadow of billowy grasses, as well as who was supposed to have said what to whom at the ceremony – according, at least, to the binocular observations of Judi James and her fellow lip-readers. Perhaps by then the British royals will have adopted the precautions of British football managers who, when the cameras are around, now hold a hand to their mouths when discussing tactics with their players.

So let us focus our speculation more fruitfully on a more distant but also absolutely decisive point in the future – 2 and 3 June 2022 when, God willing, Queen Elizabeth II will celebrate the seventieth anniversary of her accession to the throne in February 1952. Already the plans are in motion to honour Her Majesty's 'Platinum' Jubilee that will be marked with not just one but two successive bank holidays off work, creating a four-day-long week-end for Britain – Thursday to Sunday – with grandiose processions aplenty. The intention is for all of us to pour out on to the streets to cheer the Queen and her family in our millions – with many more millions watching on television and online around the world.

The $64,000 question is exactly who will be the objects of our cheers? What names and faces will be occupying that famous balcony as the visual embodiment of Britain's post-Oprah royal family?

Buckingham Palace might not put it that way, but we have to face facts. Loathsome and showbizzy though it might have seemed to the Queen, to the royal family and to many staunch royalists, the Oprah Winfrey TV interview of March 2021 created a historic divide in the road ahead for the British monarchy. It raised the question of race and the royal family in a way that cannot be shelved …

Will the House of Windsor now continue to move forward in its current disunited state? Or will the family be jolted by the event to reunite as a clan and institution that can face the world with a truthfully multiracial identity? Will we see Meghan and Harry and their two children, in other words, up there on that balcony waving in June 2022? Or is the House of Windsor planning to proceed, Harry and Meghan-less, into a Sussex-free – and hence all-white – future?

There can surely be only one answer, which is why, sooner or later, the future King William V and his brother have no choice

Ben Coppin, March 2021

but to sit down together in some fashion – practically, metaphorically, Zooming or Skyping 'virtually', on the telephone, or maybe through some intermediaries – and start talking to each other again seriously. Somehow the two brothers must hash out between themselves the substance of a deal in which they will have to make some very raw decisions and some even more painful concessions – on both sides.

The Duke and Duchess of Sussex will have to get a grip on themselves, for a start, to stop passing on the inside scoop of these discussions to the media. There can be no serious negotiations over what really matters if Charles, William or the Queen herself suspect that whatever they say when they open up their hearts will find its way back to the Sussexes' twin Os – Omid and Oprah – not to mention the gossipy Gayle, the supportive cast of *Suits*, the anonymous friends who spoke, so unprompted, to *People* magazine … The outlets seem endless.

Do you remember, Harry, how angry you got at the start of 2020, when you suspected that your private communications with your father and brother were getting spilled to the media by somebody? Serious personal discussions are impossible on that basis.

So please, dear Meghan, could you shut down your PR machine for just a month or so while these important matters get sorted out? Sunshine Sachs, Sussex spokespeople, Archewell – give them all a holiday. They are a remorseless mechanism generating material to fill a space that does not have to be filled. Create a 'comms team' and what else can they do but keep putting out the 'comms' – demonstrating their 'reputation management', as your florist's PR team put it, 'to ensure our clients are always at the top of their respective fields'.

Well, for better or for worse, the British monarchy is an institution where there can only be one person at the top – which can never be Harry or Meghan.

The consequences of the Sussexes' self-promotion have been self-defeating. That Sandringham confrontation of January 2020 might have been mitigated, for example, if there had not been such a swathe of Sussex Royal website material all prepped up and ready to go, with every picture and paragraph so meticulously polished – but all so presumptuous in its final effect. That photographer lurking in the Los Angeles war cemetery; those floral details of 'bear's breeches' and 'sea holly' at Philip's funeral, all assembled and put out so devotedly by the hardworking research team – it was just too much.

That is not the way that people do things in Britain. And if, at the end of the day, Meghan wishes to be a genuine and respected part of this British royal family whose fame and history, let's face it, have transformed her from a talented US cable actress with worthy ambitions into a global figure who can really make a difference, then she will have to surrender just a few aspects of her eager American style to the stuffy old British way of doing things.

That 'Little Light' of hers in the duchess's wedding day theme song does not refer to the singer of the song but to Jesus and the Holy Spirit – a greater truth than 'my truth'. There are certain objective realities to which everyone must bend the knee.

*   *   *

Then too, angry King-to-be William V will have to make some difficult compromises if he wants his monarchy to move ahead in a clearly inclusive and visibly diverse fashion. Diversity must begin with his own brother and his family.

It is a very good thing – essential, in fact – for a king to have backbone and to exercise an aggressive, and even nasty, side. Britain's greatest monarchs all carved out their places in history with aggression and by sticking to their principles. William is the undoubted future of the House of Windsor, alongside his immaculate future Queen Catherine – but when it comes to Harry and Meghan he will have to find some way to bend. The quality of Mercy is not strained … How William finds it in his heart to resolve this rift between love and duty will define his historic stature as a king.

It is certainly Kate who can help William accomplish this. They are already a magnificent royal partnership and she clearly has the steel to match her Hollywood-hardened sister-in-law. So Kate was not the victim in that argument over the bridesmaids' dresses? She was actually the one, we now learn, who made Meghan cry?

'Well, good for her!' shout out her partisan future British subjects! When she joined the royal family Kate ignored her way calmly through the cruel and belittling insults – 'Waity Katie', 'Middleclass Middleton' – with which Britain traditionally 'hazes' and initiates royal recruits. She was a swan gliding serenely over the waters through which Meghan would splash in such a thin-skinned fashion. The feeling is all one way in the UK these days when it comes to taking sides between the two brothers' British and American spouses. Kate is the queen whose style and purpose Britain cannot wait to embrace – a middle-class girl from origins that were no more royal than Meghan's.

What was Kate's message when she was seen to walk quietly, with no bodyguards or photographers in evidence, to lay her flowers in memory of the murdered Sarah Everard on Clapham Common last March? It was a reminder of how Kate started her adulthood as a single woman walking the streets of London in fear after dark without adequate police presence or protection. She shared the anger of Britain's women as a whole and she wanted to show it.

'She is one of us' so far as her future subjects are concerned. The day of Queen Catherine's accession cannot come soon enough.

So that raises the question of Prince Charles, so harshly attacked by his younger son in Harry's interview with US podcast host Dax Shepard in early May 2021. Complaining of 'genetic pain and suffering', Harry added the charge of poor parenting to Meghan's accusation in the Oprah interview that the Prince of Wales had been planning to deny royal status to his two mixed-race Sussex grandchildren.

As this book went to press, we were eagerly awaiting the birth of Harry and Meghan's promised daughter, and that will surely be the time when Queen Elizabeth II intervenes to sort out the confusion over that dratted protocol of 1917 – 'I forget,' Meghan said, 'if it was the George V or George VI convention' – and exactly which of Charles III's grandchildren will become Royal Highnesses and which will not. The Queen intervened in 2012 to change the rules so that HRH would apply not just to her first-in-line grandson George, but to his siblings Charlotte and Louis as well.

Now Her Majesty can greet Baby Sussex 2 with the news that the existing rules will *not* be changed for her or for her brother Archie. As matters now stand under the George V convention, Archie and his sister should automatically become a prince and princess when their grandfather becomes King Charles III.

So let things stay that way – and if, at the time of Grandpa's accession, Archie and sister are students in some California elementary school, there is no need for them instantly to take up their new royal dignities. They can remain children in the playground with the other kids in their sneakers and baseball caps – and they can decide for themselves on matters of royal status when they come of age. That was Harry and Meghan's original plan for Archie, they said, at the time he was born.

At the age of eighteen, Archie and his sister will be able to make their own choice as to whether they see their futures as going in a British or American direction. Thanks to their dual parentage, both children have dual nationality. And at that time – or later, as they wish – they can decide whether or not and how they want to fit their HRH entitlement into the mix. There is no need for anyone to feel 'trapped'.

This is the current situation of their two second cousins Louise (seventeen) and James (thirteen), the children of the Queen's youngest son Edward and his wife Sophie Wessex who is proving such an asset to the New Firm. As grandchildren in the male line of the reigning monarch, both Louise and James carry an HRH status that is not currently in use. That will become an option, according to Sophie, when they reach the age of eighteen – and then only if they want to take up the title.

Edward and Sophie have brought up their children, she explained to the *Sunday Times* in 2020, 'with the understanding they are very likely to have to work for a living'.

Well, there's a refreshing idea!

'Hence we made the decision,' Sophie continued, 'not to use HRH titles. They have them and can decide to use them from eighteen, but it's highly unlikely.'

So that surely is the model to apply to the children of Harry and Meghan and their royal status, which has nothing – and everything – to do with the speculative brownness of their skins.

Please let the Windsors get on with being Britain's very own Kardashians – never more popular than when arguing but who will always find a way to make up. Tune in next week to discover what the clan will get up to – who knows what scandal will come next?

I will certainly be watching – and so, I am sure, will you. It is over now to those two battling brothers to find some way to embrace and to seek the way ahead. We know how Meghan likes the last word on everything – but let us hand the microphone, on this occasion, to one of her friends.

'My hope is that, when I think about what they're going through,' said Michelle Obama in March 2021, 'I think about the importance of family … I just pray that there is forgiveness, and there is clarity and love.'

SOURCE NOTES

Chapter 1 – Brothers at War

The story of the 'warming pan' baby and its significance for the British Constitution is related by Dr Charles Littleton in the journal *The History of Parliament* for July 2013. This account of Archie's birth is based upon the media coverage of May 2019. For Prince William's interview about his time at St Andrews University see: https://news.bbc.co.uk/1/hi/uk/4026131.stm

Chapter 2 – Family Matters

The first-hand insights of Angela Levin's book *Harry: Conversations with the Prince* (London: John Blake, 2019) have been invaluable. Caroline Davies published some well-informed speculation on the origin of Archie's name in the *Guardian* for 8 May 2019. See *People* magazine for 20 September 2017 by Simon Perry, 'How Prince William Trained to be King as a Teen', and Ingrid Seward, *My Husband and I: The Inside Story of 70 Years of the Royal Marriage* (London: Simon and Schuster, 2017).

Chapter 3 – Dynastic Marriage

I am grateful to the late Lord Patrick Beresford for his insights into both Prince Charles and Camilla, and to Jonathan Dimbleby's excellent authorised biography *The Prince of Wales: A Biography* (London: Little Brown, 1994). See also, Sally Bedell Smith, *Prince Charles: The Passions and Paradoxes of an Improbable Life* (New York: Random House, 2017).

Chapter 4 – Agape

Caroline Graham has been assiduous in her California coast research into Meghan's origins and the beginnings of her complicated relationship with her father. The 'Welcome' prospectus of Immaculate Heart High School is helpful: https://www. immaculateheart.org/about-ih/welcome. See also Joy Resmovits, 'At L.A.'s Immaculate Heart School, the Mission Is to Tell the World About "the Real Meghan Markle"', *Los Angeles Times*, 18 May 2018, retrieved from: https://www.latimes.com/local/education/la-me-markle-school-experience-20180518-story.html

Chapter 5 – 'Whatever "in love" Means'

Andrew Morton's *Diana: Her True Story* (New York: Simon and Schuster, 1997) was a classic when it appeared and has remained a classic ever since. I am grateful for the numerous insights from my friendship and conversations with the late James Whitaker. As editor of the *Sunday Times* Harold Evans was one of the first to focus seriously on the wider significance of Diana. See Harold Evans, *Good Times, Bad Times* (New York: Atheneum, 1984).

Chapter 6 – Party Pieces

Carole Middleton has spoken only rarely to the press so her interview of 30 November 2018 with Lisa Armstrong of the *Telegraph* is especially helpful. Thanks too to Katie Nicholl for her comprehensive study *Kate: The Future Queen* (New York: Weinstein Books, 2013). It was Matthew Bell who first suggested that it was no accident that Kate Middleton found herself at the same university as Prince William. See Matthew Bell, 'Just the Ticket', *Spectator*, 6 August 2005. Michael E. Reed has published his fascinating research into the aristocratic ancestry of the Middleton family in the *Telegraph* and the *Guardian* and kindly supplied me with photographs of Baroness Airedale in her costume for the coronation of 1911.

Chapter 7 – An Heir and a 'Spare'

The early sections of this chapter rely heavily on Diana's interview with Martin Bashir for *Panorama* shortly before her death in 1997: https://www.bbc.co.uk/news/special/politics97/diana/panorama.html. Tina Brown's *The Diana Chronicles* (New York: Doubleday, 2007) has greatly enriched our understanding of the princess. See also Ralph G. Martin, *Charles and Diana* (New York: Putnam, 1995), and Rosalind Coward, *Diana: The Portrait* (London: HarperCollins, 2004).

Chapter 8 – Bringing Up Babies

I am very grateful for the help of Anne, Lady Glenconner and her first-hand contacts with Nanny Barbara Barnes. Ingrid Seward's *William and Harry* (London: Carlton, 2008) is packed with inside information. Robert Jobson gives unparalleled insights into Harry's military service. See Robert Jobson, *Harry's War: The True Story of the Soldier Prince* (London: John Blake, 2008).

Chapter 9 – Entitlement

The well-connected Penny Junor has written a masterful biography of the young *Prince William: Born to Be King* (London: Hodder and Stoughton, 2012). Wendy Berry's *The Housekeeper's Diary* (New York: Barricade Books, 1995) contains original material on life below stairs. Fred Bernstein's striking profile of Prince William made waves when it was published. See Fred Bernstein, 'William the Terrible', *People*, 7 July 1986, retrieved from: https://people.com/archive/cover-story-william-the-terrible-vol-26-no-1/

Chapter 10 – Exposure

This is the moment when James Whitaker's first-hand contacts with Diana add hugely to the picture – together with the revelations of Andrew Morton. This chapter owes much to Rebecca English's *Daily Mail* article of 22 August 2017, 'Moment Our Father Told Us Our Mother Was Dead', retrieved from: https://www.dailymail.co.uk/news/article-4814266/Prince-William-Harry-reveal-reaction-Diana-s-death.html

Chapter 11 – Camillagate

Having anatomised American leading ladies Jackie Onassis, Elizabeth Taylor and Nancy Reagan, Kitty Kelley brought her focus to bear on the Windsors in 1997 in *The Royals* (New York:

Warner Books, 1998). Tim Clayton and Phil Craig added to her work in their study, *Diana: Story of a Princess* (London: Hodder and Stoughton, 2001).

Chapter 12 – 'Uncle' James

I am grateful for the personal insights of Diana's friend and healer Simone Simmons – and also for the help of Ingrid Seward who collaborated with her for their joint study, *Diana: The Last Word* (New York: St Martin's Press, 2007). Thank you too to Diana's bodyguard Ken Wharfe for his perspective included here, along with the details set out in his book: *Diana: Closely Guarded Secret* (London: John Blake, 2016). Doesn't Stuart Higgins provide a graceful flourish to end the chapter? Thank you for that.

Chapter 13 – People's Princess

The *Daily Mail* is an unfailing source of insights into the young royals, thanks to its outstanding team of royal and investigative journalists: Rebecca English, Robert Hardman, Richard Kay, Geoffrey Levy and Jonathan Mayo. See, for example, Jonathan Mayo, 'Minute by Minute, How Preparations Were Made for Diana's Funeral', *Daily Mail*, 23 August 2017, retrieved from: https://www.dailymail.co.uk/news/article-4817944/How-preparations-Diana-s-funeral.html

Chapter 14 – Scallywag

This is one of several chapters that relies heavily on the memories and insights of royal private secretaries who have retired or who, in some cases, are now working in various government depart-ments. See also Stephen Bates, 'Prince Andrew's Fall from Grace Brings Uncertain Times for the Monarchy', *Guardian*, 22 November 2019.

Chapter 15 – Forget-me-not
'Lord Blackadder' – Mark Bolland – provided Ian Katz of the *Guardian* with a rare insight into the background of these difficult years in his profile, 'It Was Me What Spun It' in the *Media Guardian* for 27 October 2003: https://www.theguardian.com/media/2003/oct/27/mondaymediasection.themonarchy. See also 'Prince Harry Sent to Drugs Clinic', *BBC News*, 13 January 2002, retrieved from: http://news.bbc.co.uk/2/hi/uk_news/1757448.stm. Thanks too to Geoffrey Kent for his inside story of Harry's secret safari in Botswana.

Chapter 16 – Killer Wales
Several off-the-record sources contributed to this chapter and I am grateful to Simone Simmons for her personal testimony and for providing its title. As so often, the digging of Katie Nicholl supplied a wonderful story – how the princes furnished the corgis with juicy midnight feasts. Ingrid Seward's biography of Harry added an extra dimension.

Chapter 17 – Wobble
Simon Perry of *People* magazine was a regular visitor to St Andrews during Prince William's time in Scotland: 'The Student Prince – William Goes to College', *People Weekly*, 5 November 2001. Prince William's own interview on his time at St Andrews

can be viewed on https://news.bbc.co.uk/1/hi/uk/4026131.stm. See also Christopher Andersen, *Diana's Boys: William and Harry and the Mother They Loved* (New York: William Morrow, 2001).

Chapter 18 – Kate's Hot!

The full text of Tom Bradby's royal wedding interview with Prince William and Kate Middleton can be retrieved from: https://www.telegraph.co.uk/news/uknews/royal-wedding/8138904/Royal-Wedding-Prince-William-and-Kate-Middleton-interview-in-full.html. See also Richard Kay, 'How the Court Jester Had the Last Laugh: Tearaway Guy Pelly – Who Took the Blame for Harry's Teenage Drug-taking and Has Two Drink Drive Convictions – Is Made a Royal Godfather', *Daily Mail*, 9 July 2018, retrieved from: https://www.dailymail.co.uk/news/article-5935483/Guy-Pelly-took-blame-Harrys-teenage-drug-taking-royal-godfather.html

Chapter 19 – Kate's Not!

Katie Nicholl is a tireless and reliable source on the relationship between William and Kate. See, for example, 'World Exclusive: Wills and Kate Are Dating Again', *Mail on Sunday*, 24 June 2007. See also Matthew Bell, 'By Royal Appointment: How an ITV Hack Won the Prince's Trust', *Independent*, 21 November 2010. The Canadian opinion poll data at the end of the chapter derives from Eric Grenier's article for the *Huffington Post* Canada of 28 June 2011 – 'Prince William for King: Poll Finds Canadians Prefer Will Over Charles'.

Chapter 20 – Line of Duty

Stephen Bates has brilliantly combined coverage of those two very similar subjects – religion and royalty – for the *Guardian* for many years. His book *Royalty Inc.: Britain's Best-Known Brand* (London: Aurum Press, 2015) is an insightful study of the modern monarchy. See also Carmen Nobel, 'Prince Harry in Afghanistan: Miguel Head Shares the Story of a Historic Media Blackout', *Journalist's Resource*, 18 April 2019. This version of Harry's moving experience on his 2008 flight back from Afghanistan comes from ITV royal correspondent Chris Ship (report of 26 October 2017). My thanks to Miguel Head for the equally moving story that rounds off the chapter.

Chapter 21 – Fantasy of Salvation

Visit https://sentebale.org/who-we-are/ for details of Prince Harry's Sentebale charity which helps vulnerable children in Lesotho, Botswana and Malawi. See also Cecilia Rodriguez, 'Prince Harry Opens Up', *Forbes*, 18 April 2017. I am grateful to Simon Perry for his notes on General Dannatt's press briefing of 2007 on the 'virtuous circle' linking the royals and the military.

Chapter 22 – White Knight

With the arrival of Meghan Markle, I must express my gratitude to the research of Emily Andrews and her insightful profiles in both the *Sun* and the *Mail on Sunday*. See also Morgan Evans and Eileen Reslen, 'A Definitive History of Prince Harry and Meghan Markle's Royal Relationship', *Town & Country*, 8 May 2019. Thanks too for the first-hand reporting that makes Omid Scobie and Carolyn Durand's *Finding Freedom* such an invaluable resource. Further first-hand testimony was provided by Meghan herself in her Oprah interview of 7 March 2021. Roya Nikkhah provided further insights into Meghan's relations with her staff in her *Sunday Times* article of 7 March 2021, 'Unmerry Wife of Windsor'.

Chapter 23 – This Little Light

Meghan's account to Oprah of her notorious dispute with Kate over the bridesmaids' dresses and who made who cry has been modified in the light of confidential sources. Similarly, Meghan's account of her wedding tiara selection, as conveyed in *Finding Freedom*, has also been modified by independent input. The publication of Bishop Curry's memoir *Love is the Way* has helped amplify the description of the wedding ceremony of May 2018.

Chapter 24 – Earrings to Die For

I am grateful to Matt Haig for permission to reproduce lines from his *Notes on a Nervous Planet* (Edinburgh: Canongate, 2018) and to Valentine Low for his insights into the ousting of Sir Christopher Geidt in 2017. The descriptions of the Sussex visits to Australia and Fiji are based on the first-hand accounts of journalists who were present and who covered the trip – notably the events in the Suva marketplace. The account of the earrings gifted by the Saudi crown prince is based on confidential Saudi sources. I am especially grateful to Elana DeLozier and to Lina al-Hathloul.

Chapter 25 – 'Everyone Is Our Neighbour …'
I am grateful to a Buckingham Palace source for insight into Elizabeth II's racial and Commonwealth attitudes – as well as for perspectives on the shortcomings of both Meghan Markle and Sir Edward Young. Thanks too to Anne McElvoy for confirming the details of her meeting with Meghan Markle described at the end of the chapter and for her two articles: 'Meghan: The Polite Revolutionary in the Palace', *Sunday Times*, 19 March 2019, and 'The Meghan I Met', *Evening Standard*, 9 January 2020.

Chapter 26 – End of the Double Act
As described in the chapter, the key material concerning the October 2018 rift between the brothers derives from Prince William's account to a friend. This has been supplemented by a source with particular insight into the relations between Meghan and Harry and their staff while they were still based in Kensington Palace. The fundamental data on the alleged behaviour of the Duchess of Sussex towards her staff is derived from Valentine Low's meticulously documented articles in *The Times* of 2 March 2021. These were twice reviewed in draft by the duchess's London lawyers Schillings and amended to take account of their comments. Roya Nikkhah's article 'Princes Harry and William to Call It a Day' can be found in the *Sunday Times* for 27 October 2018.

Chapter 27 – Sussex Royal
My thanks to Suzanne Hodgart for her insights into Sussex Royal's control of the May 2019 picture rights granted to Omid

Scobie and Carolyn Durand, but withheld from others. I am also grateful to Tom Bradby for confirming his account of the 'really damaging things [that] were said and done'. The account of William's anger and temper tantrums towards his father comes from sources who have heard these described by Camilla.

Chapter 28 – Different Paths

Again Caroline Graham proves an invaluable source on the relationship between Meghan Markle and her father Thomas, in which Ms Graham was personally involved. See also Megan Hills, 'Harry and Meghan Documentary: The Most Powerful Quotes', *Evening Standard*, 21 October 2019. I am grateful to Tom Bradby for confirming the details of his important interviews both with Prince Harry and with Meghan in Africa. See also Camilla Tominey, 'How Prince Charles and William Became Closer Than Ever', *Telegraph*, 23 June 2020, and Sarah Vine, 'My Memo to Meghan Markle', *Daily Mail*, 29 July 2019.

Chapter 29 – Christmas Message

I am grateful for the work and insights of my longstanding friend Carolyn Durand and her research with Omid Scobie in their book *Finding Freedom* (New York: Dey Street Books, 2020). Thanks too to Katie Nicholl who provided an uncanny prediction of events in her *Vanity Fair* article of 13 November 2019 – 'A Particularly Frosty Christmas'. The Queen's Christmas Broadcast for 2019 can be found at: https://www.royal.uk/queen%E2%80%99s-christmas-broadcast-2019

Chapter 30 – Sandringham Showdown

I am grateful to the sources who have shed light on their experiences with Sir Edward Young and the inside workings of Buckingham Palace. Dan Wootton's scoops for the *Sun* are essential for understanding the events of these months, and he has been kind enough to provide crucial timetabling details which challenge the claims of the Sussexes that they did not 'blind-side' the Queen. See also Valentine Low, 'Princes Fell Out', *The Times*, 13 January 2020.

Chapter 31 – Abbey Farewell

The Commonwealth Day Service of 9 March 2020 can be viewed at: https://www.westminster-abbey.org/abbey-news/commonwealth-service-2020. For the details of the Russian prank call see Matt Wilkinson, 'Hoodwinked: Prince Harry's Russian Pranksters', *Sun*, 10 March 2020.

Chapter 32 – Social Distancing

Important sections of this and other earlier chapters relied upon the Duke and Duchess of Sussex's @sussexroyal website and Instagram account, both now closed. See also Caroline Hallemann, 'Meghan Markle Speaks Out About George Floyd's Death', *Town & Country*, 4 June 2020, and 'FA Cup Final Renamed', *Royal Foundation UK*, 11 June 2020.

Chapter 33 – 'Tungsten'

Charlotte Griffiths and Stephanie Linning revealed Prince Charles's unusual nickname for his daughter-in-law in the *Mail on Sunday* for 18 June 2018. The detail of the Clarence House photograph showing the prince escorting Meghan down the aisle comes to us via *Finding Freedom*, page 201. 'The Losses We Share', Meghan's article on her miscarriage, can be found in the *New York Times* for 25 November 2020, with Camilla Tominey's commentary in the *Telegraph* on the same date. For details of the Crown Estate revenues see www.thecrownestate.co.uk

Chapter 34 – All About Rose

Various 'Turnip Toff' and 'Suffolk Swede' sources who wish to remain anonymous have been very helpful in this controversial area – heavy with innuendo but light on reliable fact. Thanks too to Simon Hempsall at EACH – East Anglia's Children's Hospices – as well as to Simon Perry who wrote the original article on Kate's work for the charity in *People*, 13 November 2019. Giles Coren was both exemplary and professional in explaining the background to his notorious 'Everyone knows … darling!' tweet.

Chapter 35 – 'New Firm'

The *Sun* revealed Prince William's bout with COVID in an exclusive by Matt Wilkinson and Clemmie Moodie of 2 November 2020. The suggestion that Prince George did not know he was a future king when he posed in the 'Four Monarchs' photograph of December 2019 comes from someone who has discussed the subject with Kensington Palace sources who decline to confirm or deny its truth. Emily Nash of *Hello!* magazine set out the fullest account of the encounter between Sir David Attenborough and George, Charlotte and Louis in her illustrated article of 3 October 2020. For details of the growth in 'virtual' royal engagements, see the Court Circular for 1 January 2021.

Chapter 36 – Service Is Univeral

Diana's healer and confidante Simone Simmons has provided key insights into her friend at several stages in the book, not least here in her thoughts about Oprah – whose mysteriously brief previous acquaintance with Meghan was thoroughly investigated for *The Times* by Valentine Low on 16 February 2021. I am grateful to Emily Andrews for confirming the details of her US research into the plans for a major 'Tell-All' Oprah interview as early as January 2020. Thank you too to sources for explaining the Sussex view on the conflict between 'royal' and 'public' service.

Chapter 37 – Recollections May Vary . . .

My thanks to Sean Langton for setting up the links that made it possible for me to view the original Oprah interview of 7 March 2021 – the first of several viewings. A confidential source inside one of the royal mental health charities briefed me on the wide range of therapeutic support available for Meghan to call upon in the years 2018 and 2019. The descriptions here of such palace staff as Samantha Cohen and Jason Knauf are based on interviews with royal correspondents who have worked closely with them over the years. The fascinating league table of Europe's hardest-working royals can be found in *The Times* for 26 September 2020.

Chapter 38 – Living in Her Shoes

I am grateful to several close sources for helping to unravel the 'racist' element in the dispute between William and Harry – and for particular analysis of the confidence that Harry came to place in the theory of 'unconscious bias'. I turned to several medical contacts to dig deeper into the syndrome of 'rejection sensitivity'. My thanks to Susan Link Camp for illuminating America's very different reaction to the complaints of Harry and Meghan. A friend who worked at Buckingham Palace for nearly a decade tried to defend the palace record on diversity, but I was not convinced.

Chapter 39 – Between Brothers

I am grateful to the BBC for providing special access to people, events and emotions in Windsor on the day following the death of Prince Philip and on the day of his funeral. There is nothing like being there. Thank you to Gyles Brandreth for confirming the views of his old friend on the Harry and Meghan TV interview. I am sorry that considerations of taste made it impossible to reproduce verbatim the comments of James Noakes's Windsor Rugby Club friend after shaking the hand of the duke. But James's account of the prince's regular visits to the club said a lot about the man.

Chapter 40 – The Deal

My thanks to the well-placed sources who explained the complications surrounding the King George V Convention of 1917.

ACKNOWLEDGEMENTS

It was my friend Peter Morgan who inspired me to embark on this book – so thank you, Peter, for the inspiration. As if *The Crown* was not inspiring enough! Then Arabella Pike leapt on the idea and made everything possible with the help of her team at HarperCollins. A thousand thanks to my family and dear ones who tolerated the disruptions of routine needed to get the writing completed in time. Coronavirus was actually rather helpful in that respect.

I am grateful to numerous professional colleagues and friends who have helped me complete the project by the deadline: Emily Andrews, Barbara Barnes, Tom Bower, Tom Bradby, Gyles Brandreth, Humphrey and Christina Burton, Michael Cole, Giles Coren, Sandra Cronan, Peter Davies, Elana DeLozier, Benjamin Dyal and 'Mrs Norris', Edward Enninful, Harvey Frankel, Jonathan Frankel, Anne Glenconner, Matt Haig, Robert Hardman, Lina al-Hathloul, Miguel Head, Simon Hempsall, John Jones, Richard Kay, Geoffrey Kent, Gregorio Kohon, Angela Levin, Valentine Low, Anne McElvoy, Lorraine McKechnie, Andrew Morton, Katie Nicholl, Simon Perry, Michael E. Reed, Jack

Royston, Ingrid Seward, Simone Simmons, Sue Summers, Tom Sykes, Camilla Tominey, Dr Yvonne Ward, Ken Wharfe, Nicholas Witchell and Dan Wootton.

Thank you to Donal McCabe for explaining why he did not feel that Buckingham Palace could help with this project. Thank you too to Iain Hunt and Jo Thompson at HarperCollins UK who helped Arabella move mountains to get the book published on time – as well as to Lisa Sharkey at HarperCollins US and to publicists Katherine Patrick and Kate D'Esmond.

My thanks to Claire Collins and Sibilla Vaccarin at Effra Digital for their advice with the design side of the book, and to Suzanne Hodgart for the marvellous picture research. My thanks to Peter Brookes and to Ben Coppin for their help with the cartoons – and my special gratitude to Katie Boxer for providing her father's superb drawing of the Queen in 1976.

From America Susan Link Camp has provided such a firm and constant research foundation. My daily discussions with my daughter Scarlett have been inspirational – and my thanks to my sons Sasha and Bruno for their thoughts on cycling and pizza. Here in Britain 'JC', Jane Corrin, has been a source of strength every day. Thank you to the steadiest of agents, Jonathan Pegg. And my warmest thanks of all to my darling Jane, who has inspired me from start to finish – and, as I say on the dedication page, also contributed the best joke in the book.

Robert Lacey
May 2021

BIBLIOGRAPHY

Andersen, Christopher. *The Day Diana Died*. New York: William Morrow and Company, 1998.

Andersen, Christopher. *Diana's Boys: William and Harry and the Mother They Loved*. New York: William Morrow and Company, 2001.

Andersen, Christopher. *William and Kate: A Royal Love Story*. New York: Gallery Books, 2011.

Andersen, Christopher. *Game of Crowns: Elizabeth, Camilla, Kate, and the Throne*. New York: Gallery Books, 2016.

Bates, Stephen. *Royalty Inc.: Britain's Best-Known Brand*. London: Aurum Press, 2015.

Bedell Smith, Sally. *Diana in Search of Herself: Portrait of a Troubled Princess*. New York: Signet, 2000.

Bedell Smith, Sally. *Elizabeth the Queen: The Life of a Modern Monarch*. London: Random House Trade Paperbacks, 2012.

Bedell Smith, Sally. *Charles: The Misunderstood Prince*. London: Penguin, 2017.

Bedell Smith, Sally. *Prince Charles: The Passions and Paradoxes of an Improbable Life*. New York: Random House, 2017.

Berry, Wendy. *The Housekeeper's Diary: Charles and Diana Before the Breakup*. New York: Barricade Books, Inc., 1995.

Bower, Tom. *Rebel Prince*. London: HarperCollins, 2018.

Bradford, Sarah. *Elizabeth: A Biography of Her Majesty the Queen*. London: Mandarin, 1997.

Bradford, Sarah. *Diana*. New York: Viking, 2006.

Brandreth, Gyles. *Philip and Elizabeth: Portrait of a Royal Marriage*. New York: W. W. Norton & Company, 2004.

Brandreth, Gyles. *Charles & Camilla: Portrait of a Love Affair*. London: Century, 2005.

Brett, Samantha and Steph Adams. *The Game Changers*. North Sydney, Australia: Penguin Random House, 2017.

Brown, Tina. *The Diana Chronicles*. New York: Doubleday, 2007.

Burnet, Alistair. *In Private – In Public: The Prince and Princess of Wales*. New York: Summit Books, 1986.

Butler, Mollie. *August & Rab: A Memoir*. London: Weidenfeld & Nicolson, 1987.

Clayton, Tim and Phil Craig. *Diana: Story of a Princess*. London: Hodder and Stoughton, 2001.

Coward, Rosalind. *Diana: The Portrait*. London: HarperCollins, 2004.

Crawford, Marion. *Queen Elizabeth II*. London: George Newnes Limited, 1952.

Curry, Bishop Michael. *Love is the Way: Holding onto Hope in Troubled Times*. London: Hodder & Stoughton, 2020.

Dimbleby, Jonathan. *The Prince of Wales: A Biography*. London: Little, Brown, 1994.

Evans, Harold. *Good Times, Bad Times*. New York: Atheneum, 1984.

Glenconner, Anne. *Lady in Waiting: My Extraordinary Life in the Shadow of the Crown*. London: Hodder and Stoughton, 2019.

Graham, Billy. *Just As I Am: The Autobiography of Billy Graham*, revised edn. New York: HarperCollins, 2007.

Graham, Caroline. *Camilla and Charles: The Love Story*. London: John Blake Publishing, 2005.

Greene, Mark and Catherine Butcher. *The Servant Queen and the King She Serves*. UK: Bible Society, HOPE & LICC, 2016.

Haig, Matt. *Notes on a Nervous Planet*. Edinburgh: Canongate Books, 2018.

Hardman, Robert. *Our Queen*. London: Arrow Books, 2012.

Harris, Carolyn. *Raising Royalty: 1000 Years of Royal Parenting*. Toronto: Dundurn, 2017.

Heald, Tim and Mayo Mohs. *H.R.H.: The Man Who Will Be King*. Westminster, Maryland: Arbor House, 1979.

Holden, Anthony. *Diana: Her Life & Her Legacy*. New York: Random House, 1997.

Holden, Anthony. *Charles at Fifty*. New York: Random House, 1998.

Hubb Community Kitchen. *Together: Our Community Cookbook*. London: Ebury Press, 2018.

Hutchins, Chris. *Harry: The People's Prince*. London: Neville Ness House, 2014.

Irving, Clive. *The Last Queen: Elizabeth II's Seventy-Year Battle to Save the House of Windsor*. London: Biteback Publishing, 2020.

Jobson, Robert. *Harry's War: The True Story of the Soldier Prince*. London: John Blake Publishing, 2008.

Jobson, Robert. *King Charles: The Man, the Monarch and the Future of Britain*. New York: Diversion Books, 2019.

Jobson, Robert. *William & Kate: The Love Story – A Celebration of the Wedding of the Century*. London: John Blake Publishing, 2010.

Jobson, Robert. *Diana's Legacy: William and Harry – From Boys to Men*. Essex: Rex Publications Ltd, 2019.

Junor, Penny. *Charles: Victim or Villain*. New York: HarperCollins, 1998.

Junor, Penny. *The Firm: The Troubled Life of the House of Windsor*. London: HarperCollins, 2005.

Junor, Penny. *Prince William: Born to be King*. London: Hodder and Stoughton, 2012.

Junor, Penny. *Prince Harry: Brother | Soldier | Son*. New York: Grand Central Publishing, 2014.

Junor, Penny. *The Duchess: Camilla Parker Bowles and the Love Affair that Rocked the Crown*. New York: HarperCollins, 2018.

Kelley, Kitty. *The Royals*. New York: Warner Books, 1998.

Kelly, Angela. *Dressing the Queen: The Jubilee Wardrobe*. Royal Collection Trust, 2012.

Kelly, Angela. *The Other Side of the Coin: The Queen, the Dresser and the Wardrobe*. London: HarperCollins, 2019.

Kent, Geoffrey. *Safari: A Memoir of a Worldwide Travel Pioneer*. New York: HarperCollins, 2015.

Lacey, Robert. *Majesty: Elizabeth II and the House of Windsor*. New York: Harcourt Brace Jovanovich, 1977.

Lacey, Robert. *Princess*. London: Times Books, 1982.

Lacey, Robert. *Monarch: The Life and Reign of Elizabeth II*. New York: Free Press, 2003.

Leete-Hodge, Lornie. *Royal Family Library: Prince Andrew & Prince Edward*. New York: Crescent Books, 1980.

Levin, Angela. *Harry: Conversations with the Prince*. London: John Blake Publishing, 2019.

Lewis, Brenda Ralph. *Diana: An Extraordinary Life*. London: Weidenfeld & Nicolson, 1998.

Martin, Ralph G. *Charles and Diana*. New York: Putnam, 1985.

Morton, Andrew. *Diana: Her True Story – In Her Own Words*. New York: Simon and Schuster, 1997.

Morton, Andrew. *William & Catherine: Their Story*. New York: St Martin's Press, 2011.

Morton, Andrew. *Diana: In Pursuit of Love*. London: Michael O'Mara Books, 2013.

Morton, Andrew. *Meghan: A Hollywood Princess*. New York: Grand Central Publishing, 2018.

Morton, Andrew and Mick Seamark. *Andrew: The Playboy Prince*. London: Severn House Publishers Ltd, 1983.

Nicholl, Katie. *William and Harry: Behind the Palace Walls*. New York: Weinstein Books, 2010.

Nicholl, Katie. *Kate: The Future Queen*. New York: Weinstein Books, 2013.

Nicholl, Katie. *Harry and Meghan: Life, Loss and Love*. New York: Hachette Books, 2019.

O'Meara, Barry Edward. *Napoleon in Exile, Volume II*. London: H. C. Carey and I. Lee, 1822.

Palmer, Dean. *The Queen and Mrs Thatcher: An Inconvenient Relationship*. Stroud: The History Press, 2016.

Pasternak, Anna. *Princess in Love*. London: Bloomsbury Publishing, 1994.

Pimlott, Ben. *The Queen: Elizabeth II and the Monarchy*. London: HarperPress, 2012.

Scobie, Omid and Carolyn Durand. *Finding Freedom: Harry and Meghan and the Making of a Modern Royal Family*. New York: Dey Street Books, 2020.

Seward, Ingrid. *The Queen and Di: The Untold Story*. New York: Arcade Publishing, Inc., 2001.

Seward, Ingrid. *William and Harry*. London: Carlton, 2008.

Seward, Ingrid. *My Husband and I: The Inside Story of 70 Years of the Royal Marriage*. London: Simon and Schuster, 2017.

Seward, Ingrid. *Prince Philip Revealed*. New York: Atria Books, 2020.

Simmons, Simone and Ingrid Seward. *Diana: The Last Word*. New York: St Martin's Press, 2007.

Simmons, Simone and Susan Hill. *Diana: The Secret Years*. London: Michael O'Mara Books, 1998.

Spock, Dr Benjamin and Dr Michael Rothenberg. *The Common Sense Book of Baby and Child Care*. New York: E. P. Dutton, Inc., 1985.

Wharfe, Ken. *Diana: Closely Guarded Secret*. London: John Blake Publishing, 2016.

Whitaker, James. *Diana vs. Charles: Royal Blood Feud*. New York: Dutton, 1993.

Wilson, Christopher. *A Greater Love: Prince Charles's Twenty-Year Affair with Camilla Parker Bowles*. New York: William Morrow and Company, 1994.

INDEX

by Mark Wells